MW01259058

# THE MacARTHUR
# NEW TESTAMENT
# COMMENTARY
# LUKE 18-24

*John MacArthur*

MOODY PUBLISHERS/CHICAGO

Cover Design: Smartt Guys design

Library of Congress Cataloging-in-Publication Data

MacArthur, John
    Luke 18-24 / John MacArthur.
        p. cm. — (The MacArthur New Testament commentary)
    Includes bibliographical references and indexes.
    ISBN 978-0-8024-0969-0
    1. Bible. N. T. Luke XVIII-XXIV—Commentaries. I. Title. II. Title: Luke eighteen-twenty-four.

BS2595.53.M33 2013
226.4`077—dc22

                                                                2013021035

We hope you enjoy this book from Moody Publishers. Our goal is to provide high-quality, thought-provoking books and products that connect truth to your real needs and challenges. For more information on other books and products written and produced from a biblical perspective, go to www.moodypublishers.com or write to:

Moody Publishers
820 N. LaSalle Boulevard
Chicago, IL 60610

3 5 7 9 10 8 6 4

*Printed in the United States of America*

*To Iain Murray*

*Whose noble efforts to bring to life Spirit-blessed men of God from the past have given life to men of God in the present. I am one such indebted man. Iain has brought many saints to seem like personal friends and in the process become a friend himself.*

# Contents

# Preface

It continues to be a rewarding, divine communion for me to preach expositionally through the New Testament. My goal is always to have deep fellowship with the Lord in the understanding of His Word and out of that experience to explain to His people what a passage means. In the words of Nehemiah 8:8, I strive "to give the sense" of it so they may truly hear God speak and, in so doing, may respond to Him.

Obviously, God's people need to understand Him, which demands knowing His Word of Truth (2 Tim. 2:15) and allowing that Word to dwell in them richly (Col. 3:16). The dominant thrust of my ministry, therefore, is to help make God's living Word alive to His people. It is a refreshing adventure.

This New Testament commentary series reflects this objective of explaining and applying Scripture. Some commentaries are primarily linguistic, others are mostly theological, and some are mainly homiletical. This one is basically explanatory, or expository. It is not linguistically technical but deals with linguistics when that seems helpful to proper interpretation. It is not theologically expansive but focuses on the major doctrines in each text and how they relate to the whole of Scripture. It is not primarily homiletical, although each unit of thought is generally treated as one chapter, with a clear outline and logical flow of thought. Most truths are illustrated and applied with other Scripture. After establishing the context of a passage, I have tried to follow closely the writer's development and reasoning.

My prayer is that each reader will fully understand what the Holy Spirit is saying through this part of His Word, so that His revelation may lodge in the mind of believers and bring greater obedience and faithfulness—to the glory of our great God.

# Persistent Prayer for the Lord's Return (Luke 18:1–8)

**1**

Now He was telling them a parable to show that at all times they ought to pray and not to lose heart, saying, "In a certain city there was a judge who did not fear God and did not respect man. There was a widow in that city, and she kept coming to him, saying, 'Give me legal protection from my opponent.' For a while he was unwilling; but afterward he said to himself, 'Even though I do not fear God nor respect man, yet because this widow bothers me, I will give her legal protection, otherwise by continually coming she will wear me out.'" And the Lord said, "Hear what the unrighteous judge said; now, will not God bring about justice for His elect who cry to Him day and night, and will He delay long over them? I tell you that He will bring about justice for them quickly. However, when the Son of Man comes, will He find faith on the earth?" (18:1–8)

The Bible teaches both by precept and example that prayer encompasses many different matters. For example, the Old Testament records numerous prayers for people and their needs. Abraham prayed that God would make Ishmael his heir (Gen. 17:18), for God to spare Sodom and Gomorrah (Gen. 18:23–32), and for Him to heal Abimelech and his household (Gen. 20:7, 17). David prayed for the recovery of his infant son (2 Sam. 12:16), and for Solomon as he assumed the throne (1 Chron. 29:19). Elijah prayed that the Lord would raise a widow's son from the dead (1 Kings 17:20–21), and Elisha did the same for the Shunammite woman's son (2 Kings 4:33). Job prayed for God to forgive his friends (Job 42:8–10). Moses prayed that God would spare Aaron (Deut. 9:20), heal Miriam (Num. 12:13), and lift the plagues from the Egyptians (Ex. 8:12–13, 30–31; 9:33; 10:18–19).

The Old Testament also records prayer offered for the nation of Israel as a whole, by David (2 Sam. 24:17; Ps. 25:22), Daniel (Dan. 9:3–19), Ezekiel (Ezek. 9:8), Ezra (Ezra 9:5–15), Hezekiah (2 Kings 19:14–19), Joshua (Josh. 7:6–9), Moses (Ex. 32:11–13, 31–32; 34:9; Num. 11:1–2; 14:13–19; 21:7; Deut. 9:26–29), Nehemiah (Neh. 1:4–11), Samuel (1 Sam. 7:5–9; 12:23), Solomon (1 Kings 8:22–54), and the people of Israel (Ex. 2:23; 14:10; Judg. 3:9; 1 Sam. 12:10; Neh. 9:27).

People in the Old Testament also brought their personal requests to God. Abraham prayed for God to give him a son as his heir (Gen. 15:2–3); his servant prayed that God would make his mission to find a wife for Isaac a success (Gen. 24:12); Jacob prayed that God would deliver him from Esau (Gen. 32:9–12); Moses prayed that he would find favor in God's sight (Ex. 33:12–13) and that God would reveal His glory to him (v. 18); Hannah prayed for a son (1 Sam. 1:10–11, 27); David prayed for help and deliverance from affliction (Pss. 18:6; 22:19; 69:1, 13, 29), as did the sons of Korah (Ps. 88:1–2); Hezekiah prayed that God would spare his life (2 Kings 20:2–3); and Jonah prayed that God would deliver him from drowning (Jonah 2:2–10). David (Pss. 25:18; 32:5; 51), Daniel (Dan. 9:20), and Manasseh (2 Chron. 33:11–13) prayed for God to forgive their sins.

The New Testament also records prayers for the needs of individuals. Jesus prayed for His disciples (John 17), for Peter's faith (Luke 22:32), for God to forgive those who crucified Him for what they had done (Luke 23:34), and for children who were brought to Him (Matt. 19:13); Paul prayed for Philemon (Philem. 4–6), Timothy (2 Tim. 1:3), Publius's father (Acts 28:8), and the salvation of Israel (Rom. 10:1); Philemon prayed for Paul's release from imprisonment (Philem. 22); the early church prayed for Peter's release from prison (Acts 12:5); Peter prayed that God would raise Dorcas from the dead (Acts 9:40); John prayed for Gaius's health (3 John 1–2); the various churches that Paul ministered to prayed for him (Acts 13:3; Rom. 15:30–32; 2 Cor. 1:11; Eph. 6:19; Phil. 1:19; Col. 4:3; 1 Thess. 5:25; 2 Thess. 3:1), and he prayed for them (Rom. 1:9–10; 2 Cor. 13:7, 9; Eph. 1:16–21; 3:14–21; Phil. 1:3–4, 9; Col. 1:3, 9; 1 Thess. 1:2; 3:10; 2 Thess. 1:11–12). Epaphras prayed for the Colossian church; Peter and John prayed that the Samaritans would be filled with the Holy Spirit (Acts 8:14–15).

In addition, Scripture commands prayer for civil rulers (1 Tim. 2:2), all believers (Eph. 6:18), and lost sinners in general (1 Tim. 2:1)—even those who persecute believers (Matt. 5:44).

But an often overlooked element of prayer is prayer for the return of the Lord Jesus Christ, which the apostle John pled for in Revelation 22:20 and a prayer all believers should pray (v. 17). It is such prayer that is the theme of our Lord's parable, which may be examined under four headings: the illustration, the intention, the interpretation, and the inquisition.

## THE ILLUSTRATION

**"In a certain city there was a judge who did not fear God and did not respect man. There was a widow in that city, and she kept coming to him, saying, 'Give me legal protection from my opponent.' For a while he was unwilling; but afterward he said to himself, 'Even though I do not fear God nor respect man, yet because this widow bothers me, I will give her legal protection, otherwise by continually coming she will wear me out.'"** (18:2–5)

The setting for the Lord's illustration is a **certain** fictitious **city**. Though the story is invented, the situation Jesus described was an all too familiar one to those listening, who had much experience with needy widows (Luke took a particular interest in widows [Luke 2:37; 4:25–26; 7:12; 20:47; 21:2–4; Acts 6:1; 9:39, 41]) and with unjust judges.

The Lord characterized this **judge** as one **who did not fear**

**God and did not respect man.** That description was used in ancient literature to describe the most wicked and rebellious people, who had no regard for what God commanded or people expected. This man was ultimately and consummately immoral. He was not moved by reverence or worship, or by compassion or sympathy. He had no interest in the first commandment, to love God, or the second commandment, to love his neighbor. Not only was he wicked, but he was also comfortable with his corruption, as his boast in verse 4, **"I do not fear God nor respect man,"** reveals. His confession is consistent with his reputation. Here was the most immoral kind of man in the most important position of moral responsibility; a judge whose disregard for God and man had far-reaching implications for all who came before his bench.

The court over which he presided was not a religious court, but a civil one. He did not rule on the significant matters of the Old Testament law and the religious traditions, but on the application of the law to the affairs of everyday life (cf. Matt. 5:25; Luke 12:14). Nonetheless, he had a very serious duty before God to uphold the law with justice and demonstrate sympathy and compassion with wisdom. After appointing judges in the cities of Judah, King Jehoshaphat charged them,

> "Consider what you are doing, for you do not judge for man but for the Lord who is with you when you render judgment. Now then let the fear of the Lord be upon you; be very careful what you do, for the Lord our God will have no part in unrighteousness or partiality or the taking of a bribe." (2 Chron. 19:6–7)

But despite their sobering responsibility before God, judges were often corrupt. Through the prophet Amos, God indicted Israel's judges:

> They hate him who reproves in the gate, and they abhor him who speaks with integrity. Therefore because you impose heavy rent on the poor and exact a tribute of grain from them, though you have built houses of well-hewn stone, yet you will not live in them; you have planted pleasant vineyards, yet you will not drink their wine. For I know your transgressions are many and your sins are great, you who distress the righteous and accept bribes and turn aside the poor in the gate. Therefore at such a time the prudent person keeps silent, for it is an evil time. Seek good and not evil, that you may live; and thus may the Lord God of hosts be with you, just as you have said! Hate evil, love good, and establish

justice in the gate! Perhaps the Lord God of hosts may be gracious to the remnant of Joseph. (Amos 5:10–15)

Alfred Edersheim wrote concerning Israel's corrupt judges, "Jewish wit designated them, by a play on words, as *Dayyaney Gezeloth*—Robber Judges, instead of their real title of *Dayyaney Gezeroth* (Judges of Prohibitions, or else of Punishments).... The Talmud ... accuses them of ignorance, arbitrariness, and covetousness, so that for a dish of meat they would pervert justice" (*The Life and Times of Jesus the Messiah* [Grand Rapids: Eerdmans, 1974], 2:287).

*Entrepō* (**respect**) means "to be put to shame." Middle Eastern culture then as now was a shame and honor based culture. People sought to do what would bring them public honor, and avoid at all costs doing anything that would bring them public shame. Good social behavior was encouraged by appealing to a person's shame, much as the contemporary expression, "Shame on you!" does. Thus, the point of the expression **did not respect man** is that this judge was not ashamed before people. He had no shame; he could not be put to shame. Because he had no reverence for God and could never do anything that would cause him to feel shame in his behavior toward people, he was impervious to any appeal to justice or righteousness. No one could move him to do what was right.

Into his court came a **widow** from **that city.** She had been seriously defrauded by someone and as a result she was destitute. Because of that **she kept coming to him, saying, "Give me legal protection from my opponent."** Her persistence indicates that her financial situation was desperate and she needed what was rightfully hers. Further, her destitution extended beyond financial matters. She was not only bereft of material resources, but evidently there was no man in her life to look after her in the absence of her husband. Courts were the province of men, and women came there only when there was no man available to plead their case. This widow represents those who are alone, destitute, powerless, helpless, unloved, uncared for, and desperate.

The Old Testament taught that widows were to be treated with justice and mercy. Exodus 22:22 prohibited afflicting a widow (cf. Isa. 1:23; Jer. 7:6; 22:3), while Deuteronomy 24:17 commanded that they be treated fairly. In Isaiah 1:17 God instructed His people to "plead for [lit., "contend for," or "fight for"] the widow," while Deuteronomy 10:18 says that God "executes justice for . . . the widow" (cf. Pss. 68:5; 146:9; Prov. 15:25) and Deuteronomy 27:19 warns, "Cursed is he who distorts the justice due an alien, orphan, and widow." Eliphaz, one of Job's would-be counselors, insulted Job by falsely accusing him of having "sent widows away empty" (Job 22:9), while Job denounced the wicked as those who "take the widow's ox for a pledge" (Job 24:3; cf. 24:21). Based on the teaching of the Old Testament, the fictitious judge was obligated to do something to help this widow, if not on a legal basis (though she apparently had the law on her side, since she requested **legal protection from** her **opponent**), then purely on the basis of mercy. He, however, was utterly indifferent, unsympathetic, and without compassion toward her.

Her desperate need made the widow relentless and determined in her pursuit of the justice due her, so **she kept coming to** the judge, probably on an almost daily basis, demanding that he **give** her **legal protection from** her **opponent.** She insisted that he recognize the validity of her complaint and render a just verdict in her favor. Initially, **he was unwilling** to help her, but eventually her persistence wore down his resistance. Exasperated by her constant requests **he said to himself, "Even though I do not fear God nor respect man, yet because this widow bothers me, I will give her legal protection, otherwise by continually coming she will wear me out."** He affirmed, as noted above, his utter disdain for both God and men, thus disclaiming any noble motive for what he was about to do. He decided to give **this widow** the **legal protection** that she requested solely because she bothered him. Her **continually coming** to him was more than he could handle and threatened to **wear** him **out.** *Hupopiazō* (**wear out**) literally means "to strike in the face," "to treat roughly," or "to beat black and blue." Paul used it in 1 Corinthians 9:27 to speak of the severe self-discipline he imposed on himself. The widow was figuratively beating up the judge. Though women were powerless in that male-dominated culture, they were respected and honored. Because of that, they could get away with behavior that would not be tolerated in a man. The trouble and annoyance she caused him was relentless, and it was not going to stop until he acquiesced. In the end, the powerful and seemingly impervious judge was worn down by the persistence of the weak, helpless widow. He decided to give her the **legal protection** (from the verb *ekdikeō*;"to vindicate," or "execute justice") that she asked for.

THE INTENTION

**Now He was telling them a parable to show that at all times they ought to pray and not to lose heart,** (18:1)

Before He related this **parable,** Luke gave its point. The Lord **was telling** His followers (17:22) **that at all times they ought to pray and not to lose heart.** This fictional story continues His discourse on the second coming that began in 17:22. Jesus' point is that believers are to continually **pray and not to lose heart** as they wait for His return.

The Lord knew that there would be a long (by human reckoning, not God's; cf. 2 Peter 3:8) interval between His first and second comings, so far lasting for two millennia. During that time Christ has been continually dishonored and denied His rightful place. The Word of God has been unappreciated, assaulted, and denied. Christians have faced rejection, hostility, persecution, and martyrdom at the hands of Satan and the evil world system. It is only natural that they should long for the Lord Jesus Christ to return and judge the ungodly, destroy sin, end the reign of Satan, and set up His earthly kingdom. But until the second coming, Christians must not **lose heart** (give up, become weary, or lose courage) and stop praying (cf. 21:36). This verse is not a call to unceasing prayer in general (cf. Eph. 6:18; 1 Thess. 5:17). As noted above, the context (see also v. 8) indicates that the prayer in view is specifically for Christ's return (cf. 11:2; Matt. 6:10; Rev. 6:9–10). In fact, such prayer is part of the means of bringing about the second coming, since prayer is a means God uses to accomplish His work.

The doctrine of the second coming brings comfort, promotes holy living, and spurs evangelism. It has implications on how believers view everything they own, how they live their lives, and how they pray. Prevailing, persistent prayer for the Lord's return drives the heart to leave the things of this passing world and to love Christ's appearing (2 Tim. 4:8; cf.

7

Titus 2:13). That should be a defining characteristic of every Christian's life.

## THE INTERPRETATION

**the Lord said, "Hear what the unrighteous judge said; now, will not God bring about justice for His elect who cry to Him day and night, and will He delay long over them? I tell you that He will bring about justice for them quickly.** (18:6–8*a*)

The phrase **the Lord said** introduces Christ's explanation of this story in the context of His return. He began by contrasting the **unrighteous** (dishonest, corrupt, unjust) fictional **judge** with the true God, who is holy, just, and righteous. The judge was cruelly indifferent to the widow's plight. Yet in the end, worn down by her persistent determination to force the justice due her, he finally gave in and did the right thing, albeit for purely selfish motives.

In an argument contrasting the lesser with the greater, Jesus asked, **"Will not God bring about justice for His elect who cry to Him day and night, and will He delay long over them?"** The elect, like the widow, are helpless, and at the mercy of God as their judge. But the corrupt, wicked judge was not at all like God. Yet even though he was indifferent to the demands of justice and mercy he finally, reluctantly, and for his own selfish interest, did what was right for a person for whom he had no feelings. How much more will God, who loves His own perfectly, do what is right for them, whom He chose from "before the foundation of the world" (Eph. 1:4), when they **cry to Him day and night** because they "long to see one of the days of the Son of Man" (17:22; cf. 1 Thess. 1:10; Rev. 6:10)? He is the one, in contrast to the unrighteous judge, "who judges righteously" (1 Peter 2:23); who has said, "Vengeance is mine, I will repay" (Rom. 12:19); and whose "judgments are true and righteous" (Rev. 19:2). Unlike the uncaring, merciless judge, God is "compassionate and gracious, slow to anger and abounding in lovingkindness" toward His people (Ps. 103:8).

The phrase **delay long over them** might better be translated "be patient over them." The long interval between the first and second comings of Christ is a period in which God is exercising patience on be-half of His own. **Delay long** translates a form of the verb *makrothumeō* from *makros*, which in terms of time means "far distant," or "remote," and *thumos*, which refers to anger or wrath. *Makrothumeō* here indicates that God has delayed for a long time His eschatological wrath in order to extend His mercy in gathering the elect. "The Lord is not slow about His promise, as some count slowness," wrote Peter, "but is patient toward you, not wishing for any to perish but for all to come to repentance" (2 Peter 3:9; cf. Rom. 2:4; 9:22; 1 Tim. 1:16; 1 Peter 3:20). God is bringing salvation to His elect; His patience is for their redemption (2 Peter 3:15). Once all the elect have been gathered, He will both satisfy His justice and glorify them. When God does vindicate His elect He will do so suddenly and quickly, as the Lord's rhetorical question, **Will He delay long over them?** indicates.

## THE INQUISITION

**However, when the Son of Man comes, will He find faith on the earth?** (18:8*b*)

Jesus concluded this section by asking this pensive question. When He returns, will He find anyone faithfully praying in eagerness for the second coming? Any who have loved His appearing? Who cry out, "Maranatha" ("come Lord") (1 Cor. 16:22)?

Some think that eschatology, the doctrine of the last things, is mere sensationalistic speculation with little practical value. But as the Lord's teaching in this passage indicates, nothing could be further from the truth. Paul's dealings with the infant church at Thessalonica further emphasizes the importance and practical value of teaching on the end times. The apostle's two epistles to them reveal that in the brief time he spent with them (cf. Acts 17:1–2), he taught them an amazingly compre-hensive eschatology (2 Thess. 2:5).

In the salutation to his first epistle Paul praised the Thessalonians for their "steadfastness of hope in our Lord Jesus Christ" (1:3), which is "to wait for His Son from heaven" (v. 10). In 2:12 he exhorted them to "walk in a manner worthy of the God who calls you into His own kingdom and glory," while in verse 19 he referred to "the presence of our Lord Jesus at His coming." Paul prayed that God would "establish [their] hearts without blame in holiness before our God and Father at the coming of our Lord Jesus with all His saints" (3:13). In chapter 4 Paul gave them a detailed description of the rapture (vv. 13–18), while in chapter 5 the apostle reminded them of what he had taught them regarding the Day of the Lord and the second coming of the Lord Jesus Christ (vv. 1–11, 23).

In his second epistle to that Thessalonian congregation, Paul continued his detailed instruction regarding eschatology. In chapter 1 he described God's judgment and the coming of the kingdom (vv. 5–10), and the eternal punishment of the wicked (v. 9). In the second chapter he gave them detailed teaching on the rise of Antichrist, the return of Christ, and the coming of the Day of the Lord.

The extensive eschatological teaching Paul gave this young church reveals that such doctrine is critical, foundational, and highly useful to living a godly life (2 Peter 3:11, 14; 1 John 3:1–3). Knowing the end of the story encourages Christians to "be steadfast, immovable, always abounding in the work of the Lord, knowing that [their] toil is not in vain in the Lord" (1 Cor. 15:58).

True Christians live in hope, waiting expectantly for the promise of Christ's return to be fulfilled. To that end they pray for His glory and honor to be revealed. Such prayer is life changing.

# Who Can Be Right with God?
## (Luke 18:9–14)

**2**

**And He also told this parable to some people who trusted in themselves that they were righteous, and viewed others with contempt: "Two men went up into the temple to pray, one a Pharisee and the other a tax collector. The Pharisee stood and was praying this to himself: 'God, I thank You that I am not like other people: swindlers, unjust, adulterers, or even like this tax collector. I fast twice a week; I pay tithes of all that I get.' But the tax collector, standing some distance away, was even unwilling to lift up his eyes to heaven, but was beating his breast, saying, 'God, be merciful to me, the sinner!' I tell you, this man went to his house justified rather than the other; for everyone who exalts himself will be humbled, but he who humbles himself will be exalted." (18:9–14)**

The most crucial question facing every person is how he or she can be reconciled to God. Countless manmade religions, philosophies, and worldviews attempt to answer that question, but in the end there are only two possibilities: people can either make themselves right before

God, or they cannot. Every religion that has ever existed, except for the religion of divine accomplishment revealed in Scripture, has been based on human achievement—being morally good (by human standards), along with performing rituals and ceremonies. The popular notion is the vain and damning hope that people's salvation is based on the illusion of their good deeds outweighing their bad ones. As I wrote in an earlier volume in this commentary series,

> There have always been but two systems of religion in the world. One is God's system of divine accomplishment, and the other is man's system of human achievement. One is the religion of God's grace, the other the religion of men's works. One is the religion of faith, the other the religion of the flesh. One is the religion of the sincere heart and the internal, the other the religion of hypocrisy and the external. Within man's system are thousands of religious forms and names, but they are all built on the achievements of man and the inspiration of Satan. Christianity, on the other hand, is the religion of divine accomplishment, and it stands alone....
>
> Jesus repeatedly pointed out two things: the necessity of choosing whether to follow God or not, and the fact that the choices are two and only two. There are two gates, the narrow and the wide; two ways, the narrow and the broad; two destinations, life and destruction; two groups, the few and the many; two kinds of trees, the good and the bad, which produce two kinds of fruit, the good and the bad; two kinds of people who profess faith in Jesus Christ, the sincere and false; two kinds of builders, the wise and the foolish; two foundations, the rock and the sand, and two houses, the secure and the insecure. (*Matthew 1–7*, The MacArthur New Testament Commentary [Chicago: Moody, 1985], 451, 452)

The standard that God demands is absolute perfection through perfect obedience to His law. In Matthew 5:48 Jesus commanded, "You are to be perfect, as your heavenly Father is perfect." The Lord was reiterating God's command in the Old Testament, "You shall be holy, for I am holy" (Lev. 11:45; cf. 19:2; 1 Peter 1:16). Making the divine standard even more unattainable is the reality that it applies not only to external obedience, but also to internal obedience from the heart (Matt. 5:21–47). That obedience must be complete. James wrote, "Whoever keeps the whole law and yet stumbles in one point, he has become guilty of all" (James 2:10). Obviously, the divine standard is impossible for people to meet. In response to the disciples' question, "Who can be saved?" (Matt. 19:25), Jesus replied, "With people this is impossible, but with God all things are possible" (v. 26).

The previous sections of Luke's gospel have focused on the coming of the Lord Jesus Christ and His kingdom (17:20–18:8). That kingdom in its present form is a spiritual kingdom, in which Christ reigns in the hearts of those justified believers who have put their trust in Him. He will return one day to establish His literal, earthly millennial kingdom. After that thousand-year kingdom, He will establish the eternal kingdom, the new heavens and the new earth. Only those who are in the spiritual kingdom will be in the earthly and eternal kingdoms.

The discussion of the kingdom raises the basic, fundamental, and crucial question of how one enters the spiritual kingdom. How can one be reconciled to God? How can a sinner be acceptable to the infinitely holy God? That is the issue that Jesus addressed in this story.

The question is not an easy one to answer. As noted above, the Old Testament clearly teaches that God is absolutely holy, and calls people to be holy. Yet it is impossible for sinners to become holy and righteous on their own. Jeremiah 13:23 asks, "Can the Ethiopian change his skin or the leopard his spots? Then you also can do good who are accustomed to doing evil." A few chapters later God declared, "The heart is more deceitful than all else and is desperately sick; who can understand it?" (Jer. 17:9). Job asked, "How can a man be in the right before God?" (Job 9:2), and one of his would-be counselors echoed his question: "How then can a man be just with God? Or how can he be clean who is born of woman?" (25:4). Self-righteousness will never result in a person being justified before God; "All our righteous deeds are like a filthy garment" (Isa. 64:6), therefore "in [His] sight no man living is righteous" (Ps. 143:2; cf. 1 Kings 8:46; Prov. 20:9; Eccl. 7:20).

Because people are utterly incapable of justifying themselves before God, the Old Testament, like the New, teaches that justification is solely by faith (Gen. 15:6; Hab. 2:4) in the righteousness of God imputed to the sinner. That reality, pictured by the sacrificial system, was made possible by the sacrificial death of the Messiah, the Lord Jesus Christ, who would "justify the many, as He [would] bear their iniquities" (Isa. 53:11; cf. Ps. 32:1).

But the Jews of Jesus' day had lost sight of the Old Testament's teaching. In its place they had concocted a false, legalistic system of salvation by self-righteousness, based on good works, rituals, and outward keeping of the Old Testament law and the rabbinic additions to and embellishments of it.

In this section of Luke's gospel Jesus presented the correct answer to the question of how people can be justified before God. Like many of His stories, this one was counterintuitive; the reverse of everything the Jews believed regarding salvation. It is the story of two men. One was a self-righteous, outwardly religious Pharisee and the other an outcast sinner, a tax collector, a despised traitor to his people. That it was the irreligious tax collector in Jesus' story who was justified, not the religious Pharisee, would have seemed outrageous, shocking, incomprehensible, and shameful to His hearers. It expressed truth that had no place in their theology.

This powerful story of two men, two postures, two prayers, and two results may be discussed under four headings: the comprehensive audience, the contrasting analogy, the confounding answer, and the central axiom.

### THE COMPREHENSIVE AUDIENCE

**And He also told this parable to some people who trusted in themselves that they were righteous, and viewed others with contempt:** (18:9)

There is no time indicator or transitional statement to indicate whether Jesus told this **parable** on the same occasion as the preceding one (vv. 1–8). As noted above, however, it fits here well because it logically follows the previous discussion of the kingdom by describing how one enters it.

The Lord addressed this parable **to some people who trusted in themselves that they were righteous, and viewed others with contempt.** The Greek phrase translated **some people** (lit., "whoever the ones") encompasses all those outside the true faith—all those who trust that their own righteousness will gain them entrance to the kingdom.

In particular, the parable was aimed at the Pharisees, who were the architects of the legalistic system of self-righteousness that dominated life in Israel. Their theology, which was taught in the synagogues, greatly influenced the populace. As a result, the people believed that their self-righteousness would gain them entrance to God's kingdom. In their sinful pride, they conveniently set aside the clear teaching of the Old Testament that they were evil and incapable of meritorious human works, and that salvation was by grace through faith.

But the Pharisees and their followers also represent all those who seek salvation through self-effort and self-righteousness; all who believe that they have the power to live a life that pleases God sufficiently to gain them eternal life in His kingdom. That has always been and still is the dominant, commonly believed, and damning lie that Satan has used to lure people to their eternal doom.

Before his conversion the apostle Paul believed that lie. He detailed his outwardly impressive credentials in Philippians 3:4–6:

> If anyone else has a mind to put confidence in the flesh, I far more: circumcised the eighth day, of the nation of Israel, of the tribe of Benjamin, a Hebrew of Hebrews; as to the Law, a Pharisee; as to zeal, a persecutor of the church; as to the righteousness which is in the Law, found blameless.

Because of those credentials, Paul "was advancing in Judaism beyond many of [his] contemporaries among [his] countrymen, being more extremely zealous for [his] ancestral traditions" (Gal. 1:14). But after his salvation Paul's perspective changed radically, as he wrote to the Philippians:

> But whatever things were gain to me, those things I have counted as loss for the sake of Christ. More than that, I count all things to be loss in view of the surpassing value of knowing Christ Jesus my Lord, for whom I have suffered the loss of all things, and count them but rubbish so that I may gain Christ. (Phil. 3:7–8)

Fifteen hundred years later another leading figure in church history also came to realize the futility of trying to obtain righteousness by his own efforts:

In the sixteenth century, a German monk named Martin Luther sat in the tower of the Black Cloister in Wittenberg, meditating on the perfect righteousness of God. Although he was the most scrupulous of monks, attending confession for hours each day, seeking forgiveness for the minutest of sins, he realized that the standard of perfect righteousness was absolutely unattainable. He thought of divine righteousness as an unrelenting, unforgiving, avenging wrath and believed his state was hopeless. Recounting the experience that transformed his life, he later said:

> That expression "righteousness of God" was like a thunderbolt in my heart.... I hated Paul with all my heart when I read that the righteousness of God is revealed in the gospel [Rom. 1:16–17]. Only afterward, when I saw the words that follow—namely, that it's written that the righteous shall live through faith [1:17]—and in addition consulted Augustine, I was cheered. When I learned that the righteousness of God is his mercy, and that he makes us righteous through it, a remedy was offered to me in my affliction.

The remedy Luther found was the doctrine of justification by faith. His discovery launched the Reformation and put an end to the Dark Ages. What Luther came to realize is that God's righteousness, revealed in the gospel, is reckoned in full to the account of everyone who turns to Christ in repentant faith. God's own righteousness thus becomes the ground on which believers stand before him. (John MacArthur, *The Gospel According to Jesus*, Revised and Expanded Edition [Grand Rapids: Zondervan, 1994], 196)

No matter how zealous they may be for God (Rom. 10:2), none who trust in their own righteousness will be justified. "For I say to you," Jesus warned, "that unless your righteousness surpasses that of the scribes and Pharisees, you will not enter the kingdom of heaven" (Matt. 5:20).

Tragically, most of the Pharisees, unlike Paul and Luther, never made the discovery that entrance to God's kingdom cannot be gained by human achievement. They remained sickeningly, obnoxiously self-righteous—so much so that they **viewed others,** whom they considered to be less righteous than they were, **with contempt.** *Exoutheneō* (**contempt**) means "to despise," "to treat as if of no account," "to consider worthless or of no value." In its only other use in the Gospels, it describes the mocking treatment Jesus received at the hands of Herod and his soldiers (Luke 23:11). In Acts 4:11, Peter used it to describe the Jewish authorities' contemptuous rejection of Jesus.

The Lord's message that people cannot earn their way into the kingdom of God extended beyond His immediate audience. It is universal in scope, and serves as a warning to all who seek salvation through a works-righteousness religion or system of belief.

## THE CONTRASTING ANALOGY

**"Two men went up into the temple to pray, one a Pharisee and the other a tax collector. The Pharisee stood and was praying this to himself: 'God, I thank You that I am not like other people: swindlers, unjust, adulterers, or even like this tax collector. I fast twice a week; I pay tithes of all that I get.' But the tax collector, standing some distance away, was even unwilling to lift up his eyes to heaven, but was beating his breast, saying, 'God, be merciful to me, the sinner!'** (18:10–13)

There is no one a devoutly religious **Pharisee** would have been more contemptuous of than an outcast, irreligious **tax collector** (cf. 3:12; 5:27–30; 7:29, 34; 15:1; 19:2). The two men were polar opposites—they were the most pious and the most impious; the most respected and the most despised members of Jewish society.

In the Lord's story, the **two men went up** the steps **into the temple to pray,** either at the time of the morning (9:00 A.M.), or more likely the evening (3:00 P.M.), sacrifice. After the atoning sacrifices had been made, prayer and worship could be offered. The scene would have been a familiar one to Jesus' hearers; it was only natural for prayers to be offered at the temple, the "house of prayer" (Isa. 56:7; Matt. 21:13).

The **Pharisee stood** as he prayed, since standing was one of the acceptable postures of prayer (Gen. 24:12–14; 1 Sam. 1:26), along with sitting (Judg. 21:2–3; 2 Sam. 7:18; 1 Kings 19:4), kneeling (1 Kings 8:54; Ezra 9:5; Dan. 6:10), bowing (Ex. 34:8–9), lying facedown (Ezek. 9:8; Matt. 26:39), with uplifted hands (Ps. 28:2; 1 Tim. 2:8), looking up (John 11:41; 17:1), and looking down (Luke 18:13). But while praying standing up was acceptable, doing so to be noticed by men was not (cf. Matt. 6:5). The Pharisee's posture was one of self-promoting pride, intended to showcase his supposed spirituality.

His prayer also displayed a hypocritical, self-righteous attitude, as the interesting statement that he **was praying this to himself** reveals. That could mean that he was praying inaudibly, as Hannah did (1 Sam. 1:13). More likely, however, the idea here is that he was focusing his prayer in the direction of himself in a self-congratulatory fashion. This was no prayer to God. He gave Him no praise, and asked nothing from Him; no mercy, grace, forgiveness, or help. His pompous, arrogant declaration, **God, I thank You that I am not like other people,** was sheer hypocrisy. It was an unequivocal declaration to God of his worthiness and self-right- eousness; of what he was and had achieved on his own. It expressed his confidence that his own virtue was sufficient for him to have a relation- ship with God.

To make certain that no one, including God, missed the point, the Pharisee proceeded to compare himself favorably to the riffraff of Jewish society: **swindlers** (robbers), **unjust** (cheaters, dishonest people), and **adulterers** (immoral sexual sinners). Those types of sinful outcasts were frequently associated with tax collectors.

At that moment the Pharisee noticed a perfect example of exactly the kind of person he was not—a **tax collector.** The Pharisee would have kept his distance from such an unclean person, lest he inadvertently touch him and become ceremonially defiled. Such physical isolation was a statement by the Pharisee of his spiritual superiority to the com- mon people the Pharisees considered "accursed" (John 7:49). He and his fellow Pharisees held themselves aloof from the common people, associ- ating only with each other. This one may have wondered why the tax col- lector had not been ushered out with the other impure people (cf. Mishnah, Tamid 5.6).

Not content with saying what he was not, the Pharisee wanted everyone (including God) to know what he was. He then proceeded to list his religious credentials, contrasting himself with the irreligious tax collector. Though the Old Testament prescribed only one fast, in prepara- tion for the Day of Atonement (Lev. 16:29–31), the Pharisees fasted **twice a week** (normally on Monday and Thursday). He was careful to **pay tithes of all that** he received, going beyond the tithing required in the Old Testament law to include such minutiae as "mint and dill and cummin"

(Matt. 23:23) and "rue and every kind of garden herb" (Luke 11:42).

His ostentatious, self-promoting prayer was typical of the Pharisees, as William Hendriksen notes:

> A Pharisaic prayer, dating from about the time Jesus told this parable, runs as follows:
>
>> "I thank thee, Jehovah my God, that thou hast assigned my lot with those who sit in the house of learning, and not with those who sit at street corners [i.e., moneychangers and traders]. For I rise early and they rise early: I rise early to study the words of the Torah, and they rise early to attend to things of no importance. I weary myself and they weary themselves: I weary myself and gain thereby, while they weary themselves without gaining anything. I run and they run: I run toward the life of the age to come, while they run toward the pit of destruction." (*New Testament Commentary: Exposition of the Gospel According to Luke* [Grand Rapids: Baker, 1978], 820)

Jesus condemned praying, fasting, and tithing intended merely to "make a good showing in the flesh" (Gal. 6:12) in the Sermon on the Mount (Matt. 6:1–18).

The second character in Jesus' story manifested a radically different attitude to that of the proud Pharisee. His self-reflection led him to abject humility, which was revealed first by his location. Unlike the Pharisee, who stood as close to the Holy Place as he could get, **the tax collector** was **standing some distance away** on the fringe of the crowd. This man was acutely aware that he was unworthy to be in God's presence, or even in that of the righteous. He was a pariah not only in his own eyes, but more importantly in God's.

The tax collector's posture also manifested his meekness. Unlike the Pharisee, who stood proudly displaying his supposed virtue and spirituality, he **was even unwilling to lift up his eyes to heaven.** Overwhelmed with guilt and shame, he had an overpowering sense of his own unworthiness and alienation from God. His sin, disobedience, and lawlessness brought him pain, along with fear and dread of deserved punishment.

His humility is also seen in his behavior; he was **beating his breast.** When they prayed, the Jewish people sometimes put their hands over their chests and put their eyes down. But this man did something unusual. Clenching his hands into fists, he began pounding his chest rapidly and repeatedly in a gesture used to express the most extreme sorrow and anguish. There is only one other reference in Scripture to this practice. Luke 23:48 records that after Christ's death on the cross "all the crowds who came together for this spectacle, when they observed what had happened, began to return, beating their breasts." The gesture acknowledged that the heart is the source of all evil (cf. Gen. 6:5; 8:21; Jer. 7:24; 16:12; 17:9; Matt. 12:34; 15:19; Luke 6:45).

Finally, the words the tax collector spoke reveal his humility. Unlike the Pharisee, this true penitent actually addressed his prayer to **God.** He referred to himself not as a sinner but as **the sinner.** His words are reminiscent of Paul's declaration in 1 Timothy 1:15, "It is a trustworthy statement, deserving full acceptance, that Christ Jesus came into the world to save sinners, among whom I am foremost of all." The tax collector's unequivocal confession of his extreme and deep sinfulness shows that, compared to others, he viewed himself as the worst sinner of all.

Though they were poles apart in terms of their status in society, the tax collector and the Pharisee had a lot in common in their beliefs. Both understood the Old Testament to be God's revelation; both believed in God as Creator, Lawgiver, and Judge, who is holy and righteous, and at the same time merciful, gracious, and compassionate. Both believed in the sacrificial system, the priesthood, atonement, and God's forgiveness of sin. There was one crucial difference, however: the tax collector repented and sought forgiveness by faith, while the Pharisee did not repent, but sought his forgiveness through his good works.

The tax collector expressed his repentant faith in his plea, **"God, be merciful to me." Merciful** translates a form of the verb *hilaskomai*, which means "to appease," "to make propitiation," and "to make satisfaction." In its only other New Testament use, it describes Christ making propitiation for the sins of His people (Heb. 2:17). He was asking God to be propitious and appeased toward him. This was not a general plea for mercy, but rather that God would provide an atonement for him. That would come in the sacrifice of the Lord Jesus.

## The Confounding Answer

**I tell you, this man went to his house justified rather than the other;** (18:14*a*)

This stunning statement by the Lord shocked the legalists in His audience, absolutely shattering their theological sensibilities. *Dedikaiō-menos* (**justified**) is a perfect passive participle that literally means "having been permanently justified." Moreover, Jesus did not appeal to rabbinic authority; His declaration **I tell you** asserted His absolute divine authority. Here is sound soteriology from God incarnate.

Without any works, merit, worthiness, law keeping, moral achievement, spiritual accomplishment, ritual, penance, good works, or any other meritorious activity, this guilty sinner was pronounced instantly and permanently righteous. The only righteousness acceptable to God is the perfect righteousness that no amount of human effort can earn. Since it cannot be earned, God gives it as a gift to penitent sinners who put their trust in Him. But the self-righteous pride of the Pharisee, and those like him, only increased his alienation from God. His soliloquy merely solidified his confidence in his own righteousness, and he left in a more wretched condition then when he came. Atonement is worthless to the self-righteous.

The work of Jesus on the cross is not mentioned in the story because it had not yet occurred. The salvation of the tax collector was an Old Testament, pre-cross conversion. But in any age, righteousness and justification are granted by God apart from works through the application of Christ's atoning sacrifice before and after His death and resurrection.

## The Central Axiom

**for everyone who exalts himself will be humbled, but he who humbles himself will be exalted."** (18:14*b*)

Jesus closed His story with a truism or proverb. **Exalted** in this context is a synonym for salvation; for being in the spiritual kingdom. In its Old Testament usage, only God is truly exalted and only God can exalt men, who are unable to exalt themselves to His level. Thus, **everyone who exalts himself will be humbled** in the severest sense of the word; crushed in eternal loss and punishment. The path of self-exaltation ends in eternal judgment; "God is opposed to the proud, but gives grace to the humble" (James 4:6).

On the other hand, all who humble themselves and confess that they can do nothing to save themselves will be exalted to eternal glory. The damned think that they are good; the saved know that they are wicked. The damned believe that the kingdom of God is for those worthy of it; the saved know that the kingdom of God is for those who know that they are unworthy of it. The damned believe that eternal life is earned; the saved know it is a free gift. The damned find God's commendation; the saved seek His forgiveness.

# Children and the Kingdom of God (Luke 18:15–17)

## 3

**And they were bringing even their babies to Him so that He would touch them, but when the disciples saw it, they began rebuking them. But Jesus called for them, saying, "Permit the children to come to Me, and do not hinder them, for the kingdom of God belongs to such as these. Truly I say to you, whoever does not receive the kingdom of God like a child will not enter it at all."** (18:15–17)

All Christian parents have been given the responsibility by God to "bring [their children] up in the discipline and instruction of the Lord" (Eph. 6:4). Their greatest concern is their children's eternal destiny; their greatest desire for them is that they spend eternity in heaven, not hell. To that end Christian parents pray for their children's salvation, and work toward that goal by teaching them the gospel in an attitude of love and discipline, while avoiding exasperating and discouraging them (Col. 3:21), and living Christ-loving lives before them.

All of this is to lead children to salvation when they are old enough to repent and believe. But what about before that age comes? How does God see them? This passage is foundational to that understanding. In it the Lord Jesus Christ reveals how God views little children in relation to His kingdom. The text may be examined under four headings: the setting of the text, the scolding by the disciples, the special care for children, and the salvation analogy.

## THE SETTING OF THE TEXT

**And they were bringing even their babies to Him so that He would touch them,** (18:15*a*)

The references to it in verses 16 and 17 show that this section continues the Lord's discussion of the kingdom of God, which began in 17:20. The urgent question that would have arisen in the minds of Christ's hearers is, Who will be in the kingdom? To whom does the kingdom belong? The previous passage (vv. 9–14) answered the question of who will not be in the kingdom. Ironically, it was those who were the most convinced that they would be in it: the religious high achievers, most notably the Pharisees and their followers. They were deceived into believing that their Abrahamic ancestry, self-righteousness, external morality, devotion to observing rituals and ceremonies, and scrupulous keeping of the minutiae of the law guaranteed them entrance into God's kingdom (see the previous chapter of this volume).

But in reality, the opposite is true. Those who enter the kingdom are those who know they cannot achieve righteousness by their own efforts. They are acutely aware of their sinfulness and, like the tax collector in Luke 18, contritely and remorsefully confess their sins and cry to God for forgiveness they do not deserve. Only such people, Jesus declared, will be justified by grace (18:14).

The transition from verse 14 to verse 15 is a natural and logical one. No one better illustrates the reality that only the lowly who have achieved nothing of merit enter the kingdom than infants. No one has achieved less morally and religiously than them; no one has less knowledge of or obedience to the law, or less devotion to God. Thus, infants perfectly illustrate the principle that God saves sinners apart from their achievements. While the proud and self-righteous are excluded from the kingdom, infants—and those who approach the kingdom like infants—are included.

This was yet another stunning rebuke by our Lord of the Pharisees and their works-righteousness religious system, which dominated Jewish culture. In such a system, the idea of a baby entering the kingdom was absurd. Babies neither understood the law nor practiced it, and were thus incapable of performing any meritorious works with which to earn salvation.

This incident, like the previous one, is a real-life story. The significance of this brief account is evident from its inclusion in both Matthew's (19:13–15) and Mark's (10:13–16) gospels, as well as here in Luke. Some parents, concerned about the spiritual well-being of their children, **were bringing even their babies to** Jesus **so that He would touch them.** It was common for Jewish children to receive a blessing from the elders of the synagogue or prominent rabbis. Matthew's account reveals that this incident happened in front of a large crowd, likely numbering in the thousands (Matt. 19:2). According to both Matthew and Mark, the discussion prior to this incident concerned family issues (Matt. 19:3–12; Mark 10:2–12). That being the case, it was natural for the gospel writers to record this story of parents bringing their infants (Gk. *brephos*; a newborn or very young child) to Jesus at that time, hoping that He would pronounce a blessing on them.

The Old Testament reveals God's love for little children, which also pictures His unique love for Israel (Ezek. 16:4–7). Further, God considers all babies to be His (Ezek. 16:20–21). As God incarnate, the Lord Jesus Christ frequently demonstrated divine love for children. For instance, in Matthew 18:1–6 He held a child in His arms (as He did here; cf. Mark 10:16) while teaching the importance of childlike faith. At His triumphal entry, He responded to the indignant Jewish leaders' challenge by quoting the Old Testament saying, "Out of the mouth of infants and nursing babies You have prepared praise for Yourself" (Matt. 21:16). Throughout His ministry Jesus showed compassion to the sick, the grief-stricken, the hungry, and the lost. To fail to show compassion to children, the special object of love for adults, would have undermined all of the compassion that marked His ministry.

Jesus was not simplistically sentimental about children. He knew that they were sinners, and could be peevish, stubborn, selfish, and rebellious. In fact, He not only used them to illustrate the childlike faith that marks those in the kingdom, but also the rebellious stubbornness that marks those who are not (Matt. 11:16–19). But because of His evident compassionate love for children, parents felt very comfortable in bringing their children to Jesus, hoping His blessing would bring divine favor on their lives.

### THE SCOLDING BY THE DISCIPLES

**but when the disciples saw it, they began rebuking them.** (18:15*b*)

Although bringing their children to Jesus was important to the parents, it was nothing but an insignificant obstruction to **the disciples.** They saw it as an intrusive, unnecessary, unimportant interruption to their Lord's ministry, so when they **saw it, they began rebuking** the eager parents. **Rebuking** translates a form of the verb *epitimaō*, which describes a strong rebuke or censure (the related noun *epitimia* is translated "punishment" in 2 Cor. 2:6). The imperfect tense of the verb indicates that the disciples were persistent in rebuking the parents. The disciples had grown up influenced by the Pharisees' teaching that children could not perform any meritorious works that would earn them salvation. Therefore they saw no reason for Jesus to interrupt His discussion of the kingdom for this request.

### THE SPECIAL CARE FOR CHILDREN

**But Jesus called for them, saying, "Permit the children to come to Me, and do not hinder them, for the kingdom of God belongs to such as these.** (18:16)

Overruling the disciples, **Jesus called for** the parents to bring their children to Him. Then He sharply, indignantly (Mark 10:14) rebuked the disciples for their wrong assumptions and efforts to thwart the parents' intention. The Lord emphatically commanded the disciples to allow the children to come to Him, both positively, **"Permit the children to come to Me,"** and negatively, **"Do not hinder them."**

The stunning reason the Lord gave for His special concern for the children is that **the kingdom of God belongs to such as these.** That is an unqualified, unambiguous declaration, allowing for no exceptions or limitations, and opposite the prevailing view of the Jews. Jesus did not limit it to the children of faithful Jews who were part of the covenant, or to circumcised children who manifest the sign of the covenant (or to all children who are baptized). Nor was Jesus by a special sovereign act dispensing salvation only to those infants on that particular occasion, as the use of the word *toioutōn* (**such as these**) instead of *toutois* ("these") indicates. **Children** here refers to all who are unable to believe savingly because they have not reached the condition of personal accountability (the age at which that happens varies from child to child). Until that time when the law and the gospel can do their work, they are under God's special care.

As noted above, that does not mean that children are not sinners; all people are born sinners. "Behold, I was brought forth in iniquity," David said, "and in sin my mother conceived me" (Ps. 51:5). In Psalm 58:3 he added, "The wicked are estranged from the womb; these who speak lies go astray from birth" (cf. Gen. 8:21; 1 Kings 8:46; Ps. 143:2; Prov. 20:9; 22:15; Eccl. 7:20; Isa. 48:8; Jer. 17:9). Everyone inherits the guilt of Adam's sin and the corruption of his nature (cf. Rom. 5:12–21). The reality that children die proves that they are sinners and not morally neutral. But in a child, sin has not yet developed to the degree that it produces conscious resistance to the law and will of God.

The reality that **the kingdom of God belongs to such as these** means that until they reach the condition where they are accountable to God for the work of the law in their conscience and can understand the truth of the gospel, children are in God's gracious care. That care is realized when children die. This is not to say that all children are saved, then lost at the time of accountability. In fact, when Jesus said that **the kingdom of God belongs to such as these,** He was referring to the present form of the kingdom, which is spiritual (the realm of salvation). Children who die before reaching the condition of accountability are then secured in the kingdom forever.

The Bible explicitly supports this implication that children who die before becoming accountable to God are saved and gathered into His presence. Such children are innocent in God's sight. In Deuteronomy 1:39 God referred to Israel's young children as those "who this day have no knowledge of good or evil." He informed Jonah that He was withholding judgment on Nineveh in part because of the children there who were not old enough to "know the difference between their right and left hand" (Jonah 4:11). Such children have no true understanding of good and evil. They have no understanding of God's law, and therefore no sense of disobedience or guilt for violating it. Because they do not know what is right and wrong, they are not culpable for their actions and are innocent before God (cf. Jer. 19:4–5, where God called the infants sacrificed to pagan gods "innocent"). As R. A. Webb wrote,

> If a dead infant were sent to hell on no other account than that of original sin, there would be a good reason to the Divine Mind for the judgment, because sin is a reality. But the child's mind would be a perfect blank as to the reason of its suffering. Under such circumstances, it would know suffering but it would have no understanding of the reason for its suffering. It could not tell itself why it was so awfully smitten, and consequently, the whole meaning and significance of its sufferings, being to it a conscious enigma, the very essence of the penalty would be absent and justice would be disappointed, cheated of its validation. (*The Theology of Infant Salvation* [Richmond, Va.: Presbyterian Committee of Publications, 1907], 42)

Lamenting his misery and suffering, Job said,

> Why did I not die at birth,
> Come forth from the womb and expire?
> Why did the knees receive me,
> And why the breasts, that I should suck?
> For now I would have lain down and been quiet;
> I would have slept then, I would have been at rest,
> With kings and with counselors of the earth,
> Who rebuilt ruins for themselves;
> Or with princes who had gold,
> Who were filling their houses with silver.
> Or like a miscarriage which is discarded, I would not be,
> As infants that never saw light.

> There the wicked cease from raging,
> And there the weary are at rest. (Job 3:11–17)

In light of his suffering, Job felt it would have been better for him to have been a miscarriage or a stillborn child and to have thus entered into heavenly rest.

Perhaps the most helpful illustration in the Old Testament of the salvation of infants who die is found in 2 Samuel 12. After David's horrific sins of committing adultery with Bathsheba and then murdering her husband in a botched attempt to cover it up, he was rebuked by Nathan the prophet. After David confessed his sin (v. 13), Nathan assured him of God's forgiveness, but informed him that one of the consequences of his sin was that his son with Bathsheba would die (v. 14). For seven days, the distraught king fasted and prayed for the life of his son. When he perceived that the child was dead, David "arose from the ground, washed, anointed himself, and changed his clothes; and he came into the house of the Lord and worshiped. Then he came to his own house, and when he requested, they set food before him and he ate" (v. 20). His astonished "servants said to him, 'What is this thing that you have done? While the child was alive, you fasted and wept; but when the child died, you arose and ate food'" (v. 21). David explained that while the child was still alive, there was hope that God would relent and spare his life (v. 22). But after the child died, there was no further point in fasting (v. 23).

Then David confidently said at the end of verse 23, "I will go to him, but he will not return to me." He knew that after his own death, he would be in God's presence (cf. Ps. 17:15), and the certainty that he would be reunited with his son in heaven secured for him comfort and hope.

In contrast, when his rebellious adult son Absalom died, David was inconsolable (2 Sam. 18:33–19:4). He knew that after he died, he would be reunited with his son by Bathsheba. But David knew there was no such hope of a reunion after death with Absalom, the murderer (2 Sam. 13:22–33) and rebel.

By blessing the children on that day, Jesus affirmed the Old Testament's teaching; the Lord blesses those who belong to Him, not to Satan, as all accountable sinners do (John 8:44). When babies die, their souls are received into heaven. Those who do not die live under God's special gracious, compassionate protection until they reach the point where they understand good and evil and become responsible for the law and gospel. Then their eternal destiny will hinge on their repentance and faith, for which God will hold them accountable.

The salvation of infants who die has been the church's teaching for centuries. The great reformer John Calvin wrote,

> Those little children have not yet any understanding to desire his blessing; but when they are presented to him, he gently and kindly receives them, and dedicates them to the Father by a solemn act of blessing.... To exclude from the grace of redemption those who are of that age would be too cruel ... it is presumption and sacrilege to drive far from the fold of Christ those whom he cherishes in his bosom, and to shut the door, and exclude as strangers those whom he does not wish to be forbidden to come to him. (*Commentary On A Harmony of Matthew, Mark, And Luke* [Edinburgh: The Calvin Translation Society, 1845], 2:389, 390, 391)

The noted nineteenth-century theologian Charles Hodge wrote, "Of such [children] He tells us is the kingdom of heaven, as though heaven was, in great measure, composed of the souls of redeemed infants" (*Systematic Theology* [Reprint; Grand Rapids: Eerdmans, 1979], 1:27). B. B. Warfield, the revered and definitive nineteenth-century Princeton theologian, also argued that Scripture teaches the salvation of infants:

> Their destiny is determined irrespective of their choice, by an unconditional decree of God, suspended for its execution on no act of their own; and their salvation is wrought by an unconditional application of the grace of Christ to their souls, through the immediate and irresistible operation of the Holy Spirit prior to and apart from any action of their own proper wills.... And if death in infancy does depend on God's providence, it is assuredly God in His providence who selects this vast multitude to be made participants of His unconditional salvation....This is but to say that they are unconditionally predestined to salvation from the foundation of the world. If only a single infant dying in infancy be saved, the whole Arminian principle is traversed. If all infants dying such are saved, not only the majority of the saved, but doubtless the majority of the human race hitherto, have entered into life by a non-Arminian pathway. (Cited in Loraine Boettner, *The Reformed Doctrine of Predestination* [Phillipsburg, N.J.: Presbyterian and Reformed, 1980], 143–44)

## THE SALVATION ANALOGY

**Truly I say to you, whoever does not receive the kingdom of God like a child will not enter it at all."** (18:17)

This brief analogy is based on the truth illustrated by this incident. Jesus introduced it with the statement of emphasis, **truly I say to you** (cf. Matt. 18:3; 19:14; Mark 10:15). The Lord's point is simple: **whoever does not receive the kingdom of God like a child will not enter it at all.** Children are the best illustration of how people are saved. Like them, the redeemed are saved by God's sovereign grace, despite their spiritual ignorance and lack of any achievements that would merit salvation.

While their young children are under God's special care is the best time for parents to evangelize them. How can they best take advantage of those years? First, by teaching their children the truth of the gospel, as Timothy's mother and grandmother did for him (2 Tim. 1:5). Second, by modeling the truth that they teach. Teaching the truth but not living it is nothing more than counterproductive hypocrisy. Finally, by loving them. Parents love their children by being affectionate, tender, compassionate, sensitive, sacrificial, and generous, and by protecting them from evil influences. Those who train their children in that way form in them lifelong patterns that will not be forgotten (Prov. 22:6).

# The Impossibility of Salvation (Luke 18:18–30)

# 4

A ruler questioned Him, saying, "Good Teacher, what shall I do to inherit eternal life?" And Jesus said to him, "Why do you call Me good? No one is good except God alone. You know the commandments, 'Do not commit adultery, Do not murder, Do not steal, Do not bear false witness, Honor your father and mother.'" And he said, "All these things I have kept from my youth." When Jesus heard this, He said to him, "One thing you still lack; sell all that you possess and distribute it to the poor, and you shall have treasure in heaven; and come, follow Me." But when he had heard these things, he became very sad, for he was extremely rich. And Jesus looked at him and said, "How hard it is for those who are wealthy to enter the kingdom of God! For it is easier for a camel to go through the eye of a needle than for a rich man to enter the kingdom of God." They who heard it said, "Then who can be saved?" But He said, "The things that are impossible with people are possible with God." Peter said, "Behold, we have left our own homes and followed You." And He said to them, "Truly I

**say to you, there is no one who has left house or wife or brothers or parents or children, for the sake of the kingdom of God, who will not receive many times as much at this time and in the age to come, eternal life."** (18:18–30)

The references to eternal life that bracket this passage (vv. 18, 30) reveal that to be the compelling theme with which the story is concerned. All Christians are benefitted by learning from the Lord Himself how to properly respond to those who show interest in their own eternal destiny. The heart of the lesson is that the sinner must be led to understand the cost required to receive eternal life.

Obviously, no one was more concerned about the danger of superficiality than the Lord Jesus was (cf. John 2:23–25; 6:66), and a careful study of the Gospels shows that, in light of that concern, He consistently made clear the difficulty those seeking to enter the kingdom faced (cf. Luke 13:24; Matt. 7:13–14; 10:38; 11:12; Luke 16:24–25). The Lord's encounter with this wealthy, influential young man is a classic account of Him addressing the issue of the true cost of discipleship.

The matter here focuses on repentance and submission to the Lord. The Lord did not accept his superficial interest disconnected from the necessary heart attitudes of penitence and submission, because salvation comes to those who not only have a right understanding of the Savior, but also correctly assess the condition of their sinful, proud hearts and seek forgiveness while offering complete obedience.

The central meaning of this story is clear. No matter what one may believe, no one enters the kingdom without humbly confessing his sinfulness and by faith submitting completely to the sovereign lordship of Jesus Christ. Salvation is more than merely believing the facts concerning the gospel; it involves what people believe concerning their own sinful natures and the Savior's authority. Genuine salvation requires acknowledging that one can hold on to nothing in this temporal, passing world, but must be willing to let go of anything the sovereign Lord demands.

Jesus gave this man the choice between himself and Christ, between self-righteous pride and possessions, and between personal priorities and total abandonment to the Lord's will. Without a proper assessment of his heart and a willingness to forsake his pride in his religious achievements and abandon his worldly possessions and ambitions, he could not be saved. The test the Lord gave him revealed that he loved himself and his possessions more than Christ and hence could not be His disciple (cf. Luke 9:23–25; 14:26–27,33).

The choice he made was surprising, because at first glance this young man appeared to be the perfect seeker (see the discussion below). No pre-evangelism was necessary in his case; the typical obstacles that hinder people from coming to the kingdom of God seem to have already been eliminated. He was ready and eager, and understood his need. Further, he had come to the divine source for an answer by seeking out the Son of God. According to contemporary evangelistic methodology, Jesus should have found the appropriate language and acceptable terms to move this hot prospect to salvation. But instead of finding terms acceptable to him, Jesus introduced terms to him that he found utterly unacceptable. And the amazing part of the story is that as good a prospect as he appeared to be, in reality he was a superficial, illegitimate, self-centered false seeker, who left Jesus rejecting the way to eternal life. And he needed to know that.

The Synoptic Gospels all (cf. Matt. 19:16–30; Mark 10:17–31) record this actual encounter. It is placed in the context of the discussion of the kingdom of God that began in Luke 17:20 to illustrate who enters the kingdom and who does not. The confrontation may be approached from both the human side and the divine side, and concluded with the Lord's commentary on the outcome.

## THE HUMAN SIDE

**A ruler questioned Him, saying, "Good Teacher, what shall I do to inherit eternal life?" And Jesus said to him, "Why do you call Me good? No one is good except God alone.** (18:18–19)

As noted above, this young man seemed to be a surefire prospect, for several reasons.

First, unlike the Pharisee in Luke 18:9–14, he recognized his need.

He was aware that he did not have the eternal life of God in his soul nor the hope of heaven. Despite all of his religious achievements—enough to make him a **ruler** (most likely of a synagogue, and as such the most spiritually, morally, and religiously impressive man in that synagogue)—and his claim to have obeyed the law (v. 21), what he sought by all his religion and morality was absent in his life (cf. Nicodemus in John 3:1–3). Instead of being calm and confident, he was restless and anxious. He wanted relief from the crushing burden of legalism, and the assurance of God's presence that brings hope, peace, joy, contentment, and a confident hope of heaven.

What he sought was **eternal life,** which the Jewish people understood as a kind or quality of life, rather than merely a duration of life. They saw it as that life which God Himself possesses and gives to His children. Eternal life is to possess the life of God, and to have a deep knowledge of Him (John 17:3). Eternal life involves the love of God being poured out in the hearts of His people (Rom. 5:5), the light of the knowledge of God shining in the hearts of believers (2 Cor. 4:6), the peace of God that passes all understanding (Phil. 4:7), and the "joy inexpressible and full of glory" of which Peter wrote (1 Peter 1:8). It is marked by peace, blessing, confidence, assurance, tranquility, satisfaction, and hope. This man was keenly aware that he lacked those realities.

Second, he not only understood his lack, but also urgently, eagerly, and diligently sought to gain what he did not possess. Heedless of his reputation and his dignity, the ruler "ran up to [Jesus] and knelt [in worship] before Him" in full view of everyone walking along the road with Him (Mark 10:17). His question was not a mere abstract theological one, but an honest serious, quest for the solution to his spiritual emptiness.

Third, he came to the right person. Many who seek true spiritual life look for it in the wrong places; the wrong church, wrong religion, or wrong teacher. This man, however, came to the only source of life—the Lord Jesus Christ, who is Himself the eternal life (1 John 5:20).

By respectfully addressing Jesus as **Good** (Gk. *agathos*; good in essence or by nature) **Teacher,** he elevated Him above other teachers and associated Him with God, who alone is good (v. 19). Whatever else he may have known or believed about Him, he affirmed Jesus to be both a teacher and an example of divine truth. Possibly, he hoped Jesus would be the one who could tell him how to possess the eternal life he sought.

Finally in commending him, he came to the point of asking the right question: **"What shall I do to inherit** or take possession of **eternal life?"** In keeping with his legalistic system of self-righteousness, he sought that one elusive good work that would push him over the top to obtain eternal life for himself. When the Lord Jesus was asked a similar question in John 6:28 He replied, "This is the work of God, that you believe in Him whom He has sent" (v. 29). There the issue was the necessity of believing in Him. Here, however, this man was already prepared to believe in Jesus as the source of eternal life if he liked the terms (cf. John 3:3–4).

But the omniscient Lord knew that he had a fatal flaw that would reveal his desire to be false and deceptive. Therefore He answered the man's question with one of His own. **"Why do you call Me good?"** He asked him. **"No one is good except God alone."** Jesus was not, of course, denying His deity, as some of the cults purport. That would have contradicted His direct claims to be God (e.g., John 5:17–18; 8:24, 58; 10:30–33). On the contrary, Jesus was challenging this man to explain why he called Him good, knowing that only God is truly good, unless he was connecting Him to God. And if he did affirm that Jesus was from God, was he then willing to obey Him?

## THE DIVINE SIDE

**You know the commandments, 'Do not commit adultery, Do not murder, Do not steal, Do not bear false witness, Honor your father and mother.'" And he said, "All these things I have kept from my youth." When Jesus heard this, He said to him, "One thing you still lack; sell all that you possess and distribute it to the poor, and you shall have treasure in heaven; and come, follow Me." But when he had heard these things, he became very sad, for he was extremely rich.** (18:20–23)

Speaking to him within the framework of his own legalistic paradigm, Jesus recited some of the **commandments,** specifically the second five of the Ten Commandments, which relate to dealing with other people: **"Do not commit adultery, Do not murder, Do not steal, Do not bear false witness, Honor your father and mother."** But His charge to this young man elicited a response, **"All these things I have kept from my youth,"** evidencing the self-deception of a hypocrite. The Lord's reminder pressed home the point that if salvation comes through keeping the law, and this man had kept the law as he professed, why did he know he had not obtained eternal life? Why was he not satisfied? The truth is that his self-deception was shallow and his heart full of fear over his lack of true spiritual life and love for God.

Two divine requirements implicit in Jesus' words to him reveal his misunderstanding of the law. First, he needed to confess his sin and inability to satisfy God and be reconciled to Him through the law. He had taken the law far too lightly, seeing it primarily as a means to elevate himself. The truth that "whoever keeps the whole law and yet stumbles in one point, he has become guilty of all" (James 2:10) had entirely escaped him. He certainly had not loved the Lord with all his heart, soul, mind, and strength and his neighbor as himself, which sums up the Decalogue. But he viewed the law of God in a corrupted way that allowed him to compare himself favorably to others rather than to God, whose perfect holiness is revealed in the law.

Second, he had also failed to see that the law only renders people sinners; it is unable to save. Self-righteousness had kept the law from doing its work of revealing his sin to him. As a result, he believed that he was more righteous than he really was. Like Israel, he sought to establish his own righteousness instead of submitting to God's righteousness (Rom. 10:3). The Lord pressed home the point that no one can be justified by keeping the law.

This synagogue ruler was in much the same position that Paul had been before his conversion, as he later recalled in Philippians 3:4–6:

> If anyone else has a mind to put confidence in the flesh, I far more: circumcised the eighth day, of the nation of Israel, of the tribe of Benjamin, a Hebrew of Hebrews; as to the Law, a Pharisee; as to zeal, a persecutor of the church; as to the righteousness which is in the Law, found blameless.

But something powerful and dramatic happened to Paul in the process of his conversion, as he noted in Romans 7:7–11:

> What shall we say then? Is the Law sin? May it never be! On the contrary, I would not have come to know sin except through the Law; for I would not have known about coveting if the Law had not said, "You shall not covet." But sin, taking opportunity through the commandment, produced in me coveting of every kind; for apart from the Law sin is dead. I was once alive apart from the Law; but when the commandment came, sin became alive and I died; and this commandment, which was to result in life, proved to result in death for me; for sin, taking an opportunity through the commandment, deceived me and through it killed me.

The apostle had considered himself blameless in regard to the law, spiritually alive and well. But once he came to a true understanding of the law of God, sin became alive and he died. Far from giving him life, the law killed him. That was the turning point in his life; the one who had thought that he would gain eternal life through the law realized that it was in reality rendering him guilty before God. That was the point to which the Lord was directing this young man. That is also the point to which believers need to bring those whom they are evangelizing. Sinners need to determine whether they view themselves as made alive by superficially keeping the law, or killed by profoundly violating it, or in other words, whether they understand that the law cannot save them. The rich young man was unwilling to acknowledge that truth.

Jesus' words to him, **"One thing you still lack; sell all that you possess and distribute it to the poor, and you shall have treasure in heaven; and come, follow Me,"** reveal a second divine requirement. Salvation does not, of course, come through philanthropy, but through humble, self-denying, obedient faith (cf. Luke 9:23–24). But accepting for the sake of argument his misguided claim to have kept the law, and his accurate statement that Jesus' goodness revealed that He was connected to God, the Lord challenged the rich young ruler to submit completely to Him. Jesus gave him a command to abandon all of his earthly priorities and divest himself of everything that mattered to him. Selling all his possessions would not only rid him of everything that he owned, but would also cut him off from his family (cf. Phil. 3:8). They would naturally first be incredulous, then irate that he failed to act responsibly as the steward of his family's wealth, and might disown him. Was he willing to submit to the lordship of Jesus to that degree? Was eternal life valuable enough to him to confess Jesus as Lord and prove it by obedience?

It had all looked so promising for this young man, who now stood at the crossroads of eternal destiny. But as is the case with everyone, his decision hinged on the twin issues of sin and sovereign lordship. He was unwilling to acknowledge that he was a guilty sinner, affirm that his good works could not save him, and cast himself on God's grace. Nor did he value Jesus' terms of sovereign rule in exchange for eternal life. Instead, he clung to his self-righteous legalism, wealth, and relationships. He **became very sad,** but not with the godly sorrow that leads to repentance (2 Cor. 7:10), and "went away grieving" (Matt. 19:22), turning his back on the eternal life he had so hopefully and eagerly sought.

## THE LORD'S COMMENTARY

**And Jesus looked at him and said, "How hard it is for those who are wealthy to enter the kingdom of God! For it is easier for a camel to go through the eye of a needle than for a rich man to enter the kingdom of God." They who heard it said, "Then who can be saved?" But He said, "The things that are impossible with people are possible with God." Peter said, "Behold, we have left our own homes and followed You." And He said to them, "Truly I say to you, there is no one who has left house or wife or brothers or parents or children, for the sake of the kingdom of God, who will not receive many times as much at this time and in the age to come, eternal life." (18:24–30)**

The Lord's comment on this tragic incident may be summarized under two headings. He first described the poverty of riches.

After **Jesus looked at** the rich young ruler walk away, He turned to His disciples (Matt. 19:23) **and said, "How hard it is for those who are wealthy to enter the kingdom of God!"** They were no doubt shocked by that statement, since the idea that wealth was a sign of God's blessing was deeply entrenched in Jewish theology. Accordingly, the rich were thought to have the inside track to salvation, since they had received greater divine blessings and could give more alms. That errant viewpoint was articulated by Job's useless friends. Like the Jews of Jesus' day, they assumed there was a causal connection between wealth and God's blessing. Conversely, they saw suffering as a sure sign of God's punishment for sin, and therefore pressured innocent Job to confess and repent of his sins.

In reality, it is impossible for the rich to buy their way into the kingdom, as the proverbial statement **"For it is easier for a camel to go through the eye of a needle than for a rich man to enter the kingdom of God"** indicates. The Persians expressed impossibility by using a familiar proverb stating that it would be easier for an elephant to go through the eye of a needle. The Jews picked up the proverb, substituting a camel for an elephant, since camels were the largest animals in Palestine.

Some, unwilling to face the stark reality that the saying implies, have attempted to soften it. Noting the similarity between the Greek words *kamelos* (**camel**) and *kamilos* (a large rope or cable), some suggest that a copyist erred by substituting the former for the latter. It is unlikely, however, that all three Synoptic Gospels would have been changed in the same way. Nor would a scribe make the statement harder rather than easier. He might change the wording from "camel" to "cord," but not from "cord" to "camel." But even a rope could no more go through the eye of a needle than a camel could. Others imagine that the reference is to a small gate in Jerusalem's wall that camels could only enter with great difficulty. But there is no evidence that such a gate ever existed. Nor would any person with common sense have attempted to force a camel through such a small gate even if one had existed; they would simply have brought their camel into the city through a larger gate. The obvious point of that picturesque expression of hyperbole is not that salvation is difficult, but rather that it is humanly impossible for everyone by any means, including the wealthy (cf. Mark 10:23–24). Sinners are aware of their guilt and fear, and may even desire a relationship with God that would bring forgiveness and peace. But they cannot hold on to their sinful priorities and personal control and think they can come to God on their own terms. The young man illustrates that reality.

Those who **heard** the Lord's words understood what He meant. They were astonished and exclaimed, **"Then who can be saved?"** The rich could afford to give more alms than other people, and the Jews believed that almsgiving was key to entering the kingdom. The apocryphal book of Tobit expressed that view when it said, "It is better to give alms than to lay up gold: for alms doth deliver from death, and shall purge away all sin. Those that exercise alms and righteousness shall be filled with life" (Tobit 12:8–9; cf. Sirach 3:30).

The Lord's reply, **"The things that are impossible with people are possible with God,"** reiterated the truth that salvation is humanly impossible, and that only a sovereign act of God can change the heart (John 1:11–13; 3:3–8; 6:44; Eph. 2:8–9).

In contrast to the rich young ruler, the disciples had abandoned everything to follow Christ. As Peter noted, **"Behold, we have left our own homes** (no word for **homes** is in the Greek text, so that all their possessions are in view) **and followed You."** Matthew 19:27 records that Peter followed up this statement with the question, "What then will there be for us?" The Lord's reply introduced the second point in His comment on this incident, the riches of poverty.

Peter's comment and question were legitimate, and Jesus did not rebuke him for them. Instead, He gave the wonderful promise, **"Truly I say to you, there is no one who has left house or wife or brothers or parents or children, for the sake of the kingdom of God, who will not receive many times as much at this time and in the age to come, eternal life."** The Lord affirmed that, unlike the rich young ruler, the disciples (and all who forsake everything for **the sake of the kingdom of God**), had been granted by God the full blessings of **eternal life.**

To yield up everything in this life to gain access to the blessings of His kingdom is the greatest wealth (cf. Luke 9:24–25). God, in His lavish grace, promises that the redeemed will **receive many times as much at this time** in addition to receiving, **in the age to come, eternal life.** This is the great exchange: believers receive the treasure hidden in the field (Matt. 13:44) and the pearl of great value (Matt. 13:46) when they willingly give up the right to all that they possess.

Matthew's account adds another dimension to the believers' rewards. In Matthew 19:28 Jesus added, "Truly I say to you, that you who have followed Me, in the regeneration when the Son of Man will sit on His glorious throne, you also shall sit upon twelve thrones, judging the twelve tribes of Israel." In addition to the spiritual blessings God pours out on them in this life, and the full blessings of eternal life in heaven, there is a third sphere in which believers will be blessed. The "regeneration" of which our Lord spoke is His earthly, millennial kingdom, "when the Son of Man will sit on His glorious throne." That kingdom will be the rebirth of the world; paradise regained. Those who have been granted a spiritual rebirth at salvation will participate in the rebirth of the earth; the "times of refreshing" (Acts 3:19) and the "period of restoration of all things" (v. 21). It is the kingdom about which Jesus taught the disciples for forty days between His resurrection and ascension (Acts 1:3). In that kingdom, the apostles will "sit upon twelve thrones, judging the twelve tribes of Israel."

The Lord's answer to the disciples' question, "Lord, is it at this time You are restoring the kingdom to Israel?" (Acts 1:7) is revealing. Instead of rebuking them for failing to understand amillennialism, which teaches that He spoke only of a spiritual kingdom in which the church presently replaces Israel, Jesus affirmed the kingdom coming to Israel when He replied, "It is not for you to know times or epochs which the Father has fixed by His own authority." The apostles were correct in assuming that the kingdom would be an earthly one involving Israel; but the historical time when it would be established was not for them to know.

All the saints from all of redemptive history—the Old Testament saints (Dan. 7:18), New Testament saints (1 Cor. 6:2), and, as noted above, the twelve apostles—are going to be gathered into that glorious kingdom to enjoy all the bounty of paradise regained.

# Jesus Predicts His Sufferings (Luke 18:31–34)

**5**

**Then He took the twelve aside and said to them, "Behold, we are going up to Jerusalem, and all things which are written through the prophets about the Son of Man will be accomplished. For He will be handed over to the Gentiles, and will be mocked and mistreated and spit upon, and after they have scourged Him, they will kill Him; and the third day He will rise again." But the disciples understood none of these things, and the meaning of this statement was hidden from them, and they did not comprehend the things that were said.** (18:31–34)

One of the ways in which pseudo-scholars, critics, and skeptics constantly attack our Lord is by denying that His sufferings were planned and purposeful. They argue that His death was unplanned and accidental; a tragic, unfortunate, bad ending to His life. His death, they insist, resulted from a miscalculation; it was a noble attempt to bring goodness into the world, but ended in an unplanned disaster. Some suggest that Jesus was a naive, well-intentioned, good man, who wanted to elevate people religiously by His ideas, but failed to know when He had gone too far. To others, He was a misguided nationalist, whose efforts at a revolution were hopelessly inept, or an ambitious, self-styled conqueror with delusions of grandeur. There have been those who say He was just another religious fanatic. All such false views of Him imagine that the events of Jesus' life did not go the way He intended them to go. His dream of what He hoped would be a better world ended instead in a nightmare.

But nothing could be further from the truth. The whole trajectory of His life was prophesied 700 years before and included every aspect of His career as the Messiah, Servant of Jehovah:

> Behold, My servant will prosper, He will be high and lifted up and greatly exalted. Just as many were astonished at you, My people, so His appearance was marred more than any man and His form more than the sons of men. Thus He will sprinkle many nations, kings will shut their mouths on account of Him; for what had not been told them they will see, and what they had not heard they will understand. Who has believed our message? And to whom has the arm of the Lord been revealed? For He grew up before Him like a tender shoot, and like a root out of parched ground; He has no stately form or majesty that we should look upon Him, nor appearance that we should be attracted to Him. He was despised and forsaken of men, a man of sorrows and acquainted with grief; and like one from whom men hide their face He was despised, and we did not esteem Him. Surely our griefs He Himself bore, and our sorrows He carried; yet we ourselves esteemed Him stricken, smitten of God, and afflicted. But He was pierced through for our transgressions, He was crushed for our iniquities; the chastening for our well-being fell upon Him, and by His scourging we are healed. All of us like sheep have gone astray, each of us has turned to his own way; but the Lord has caused the iniquity of us all to fall on Him. He was oppressed and He was afflicted, yet He did not open His mouth; like a lamb that is led to slaughter, and like a sheep that is silent before its shearers, so He did not open His mouth. By oppression and judgment He was taken away; and as for His generation, who considered that He was cut off out of the land of the living for the transgression of my people, to whom the stroke was due? His grave was assigned with wicked men, yet He was with a rich man in His death, because He had done no violence, nor was there any deceit in His mouth. But the Lord was pleased to crush Him, putting Him to grief; if He would render Himself as a guilt offering, He will see His offspring, He will prolong His days, and the good pleasure of the Lord will prosper in His hand. As a result of the anguish of His soul, He will see it and be satisfied; by His knowledge the Righteous One, My Servant, will justify the many, as He will

bear their iniquities. Therefore, I will allot Him a portion with the great, and He will divide the booty with the strong; because He poured out Himself to death, and was numbered with the transgressors; yet He Himself bore the sin of many, and interceded for the transgressors. (Isa. 52:13–53:12)

In fulfillment of that prophecy, Jesus said that He came into the world "not to do My own will, but the will of Him who sent Me" (John 6:38). The Father's will was for Him to die. Anticipating the cross, with its sin-bearing and separation from the Father, Jesus said, "Now My soul has become troubled; and what shall I say, 'Father, save Me from this hour'? But for this purpose I came to this hour" (John 12:27).

Jesus was not a well-intentioned victim of a plan that surprised Him when it went horribly wrong. He knew exactly how His life would end, down to the minutest detail, and had known it since before the foundation of the world, when the plan of salvation was formed. The heart of the Christian faith is the death of the Lord Jesus Christ. Everything in the history of redemption in the Old Testament moves toward the cross; everything that has happened since moves from the cross.

The Lord understood every prophetic passage in the Old Testament regarding His death (Luke 24:25–27, 44), which He alluded to throughout His ministry:

And Jesus said to them, "You cannot make the attendants of the bridegroom fast while the bridegroom is with them, can you? But the days will come; and when the bridegroom is taken away from them, then they will fast in those days." (Luke 5:34–35)

"But I have a baptism to undergo, and how distressed I am until it is accomplished!" (Luke 12:50)

And He said to them, "Go and tell that fox [Herod], 'Behold, I cast out demons and perform cures today and tomorrow, and the third day I reach My goal.'" (Luke 13:32)

"O Jerusalem, Jerusalem, the city that kills the prophets and stones those sent to her! How often I wanted to gather your children together, just as a hen gathers her brood under her wings, and you would not have it! Behold, your house is left to you desolate; and I say to you, you will not see Me until the time comes when you say, 'Blessed is He who comes in the name of the Lord!'" (Luke 13:34–35)

> "But first He must suffer many things and be rejected by this genera-tion." (Luke 17:25)

Jesus also made explicit predictions concerning His death:

> But He warned them and instructed them not to tell this to anyone, say-ing, "The Son of Man must suffer many things and be rejected by the elders and chief priests and scribes, and be killed and be raised up on the third day." (Luke 9:21–22)
>
> "Let these words sink into your ears; for the Son of Man is going to be delivered into the hands of men." (Luke 9:44)

The present passage is the third and most complete of the Lord's specific predictions concerning His death recorded by Luke. His words here anticipate His suffering on the cross and His resurrection. They reveal the plan, proportions, power over, and perceptions of His suffering.

## THE PLAN OF SUFFERING

**Then He took the twelve aside and said to them, "Behold, we are going up to Jerusalem, and all things which are written through the prophets about the Son of Man will be accomplished.** (18:31)

As He had been since Luke 9:51, Jesus was on His final journey to Jerusalem. That journey was now nearing its end, as the Lord and the dis-ciples, having crossed the Jordan River from Perea into Judea, approached Jericho, and the steep ascent to Jerusalem from there (Luke 19:1, 11). So that there would be no misunderstanding on their part, Jesus took the Twelve aside to remind them that what was about to happen to Him was God's plan. His suffering and death were no surprise to Him, but rather the eternal purpose of the incarnation.

The Twelve were headed, of course, for Jerusalem because it was time for Passover. What they did not understand was that Jesus would be the Passover Lamb, the only sacrifice for sin that would satisfy God and provide atonement for all the elect. His death brought to an end the entire sacrificial system. One reason that Jesus needed to explain things in advance to them is that the concept of a dying Messiah was completely foreign to their understanding (cf.Luke 9:44–45).The nineteenth-century historian Emil Schürer summarized the Jewish people's expectations regarding the coming of Messiah and the establishing of His kingdom as follows: First, the coming of Messiah would be preceded by a time of tribulation. Second, in the midst of the turmoil an Elijah-like prophet would appear heralding Messiah's coming. Third, Messiah would establish His glorious kingdom, and vindicate His people. Fourth, the nations would ally themselves together to fight Messiah. Fifth, Messiah would destroy all those opposing nations. Sixth, Jerusalem would be restored, and made new and glorious. Seventh, the dispersed Jews scattered all over the world would return to Israel. Eighth, Israel would become the center of the world and all the nations would be subjugated to the Messiah. Finally, the Messiah would establish His kingdom, which would be a time of eternal peace, righteousness, and glory (*A History of the Jewish People in the Time of Jesus Christ* [New York: Scribners, 1896], 2:154–78). There was no place in Jewish messianic theology for a sacrificed, a dead, or even a risen Messiah.

Further, the disciples were aware of the Jewish leaders' intense hatred of Jesus and the hostile reception He would receive from them in Jerusalem.They were amazed and fearful that He seemingly was walking intentionally into the arms of His enemies. Perhaps they had the same attitude that Thomas expressed in John 11:16:"Let us also go, so that we may die with Him."

Knowing their fears, Jesus reassured them that God's plan would be fulfilled **and** that **all things** that were **written through the prophets about the Son of Man** (a messianic title taken from Dan. 7:13) would **be accomplished.** His death would be the culmination of the divine redemptive purpose of God.The cross is the primary event in redemptive history and therefore the primary event in all of history.

The first strains of the symphony of the cross can be heard in Genesis 3. After the fall, Adam and Eve were overwhelmed with guilt. Attempting to hide their shame, they covered themselves with leaves. That was an inadequate human attempt to deal with the guilt of sin, so God killed an animal—the first death in history—and used its skin to cover Adam and Eve. The aftermath of the first sin reveals that sin and guilt are only covered by the death of an innocent sacrifice. The truth that only a blood sacrifice is acceptable to God was reaffirmed in Genesis 4 when God accepted Abel's animal sacrifice, but rejected Cain's offering of the produce of the ground.

Genesis 22 records that God commanded Abraham to offer his son and heir Isaac, through whom the Abrahamic covenant was to be fulfilled, as a sacrifice. After ascending Mount Moriah, Abraham placed his son on the altar. But before he could plunge the knife into him, God stopped him. In place of Isaac, God provided a ram that was caught in a nearby thicket. Here is another strain in the symphony of the cross. Not only is a sacrifice the only way for sinners to be accepted by God, but God Himself will provide the substitute. The name Abraham gave to that place, "The Lord Will Provide" (Gen. 22:14), reinforces that truth.

Similarly, the firstborn of every Jewish household was spared from death by the sacrifice of an unblemished lamb (Ex. 12:1–13, 21–23). Later at Mount Sinai God gave the law, with its complex, elaborate system of sacrifices. All of those constant sacrifices revealed clearly that the final, satisfying, perfect sacrifice had not yet come because

> the Law, since it has only a shadow of the good things to come and not the very form of things, can never, by the same sacrifices which they offer continually year by year, make perfect those who draw near. Otherwise, would they not have ceased to be offered, because the worshipers, having once been cleansed, would no longer have had consciousness of sins? (Heb. 10:1–2)

The Old Testament also contains specific predictions of Christ's death on the cross. Psalm 22 graphically depicts the details of His crucifixion—a form of execution unknown in Israel at that time. The psalm opens with the words our Lord spoke on the cross, "My God, my God, why have You forsaken me?" (v. 1; cf. Matt. 27:46). Verses 6–8 predict the gloating mockery that the Lord received from His enemies:

> But I am a worm and not a man, a reproach of men and despised by the people. All who see me sneer at me; they separate with the lip, they

wag the head, saying, "Commit yourself to the Lord; let Him deliver him; let Him rescue him, because He delights in him." (cf. Luke 23:35–39)

Verses 14–17 describe the physical suffering the Lord endured on the cross:

> I am poured out like water, and all my bones are out of joint; my heart is like wax; it is melted within me. My strength is dried up like a potsherd, and my tongue cleaves to my jaws; and You lay me in the dust of death. For dogs have surrounded me; a band of evildoers has encompassed me; they pierced my hands and my feet. I can count all my bones. They look, they stare at me.

This remarkably accurate prediction even records the detail that His executioners would divide up Jesus' garments: "They divide my garments among them, and for my clothing they cast lots" (v. 18; cf. Luke 23:34).

The marvelous messianic chapter, Isaiah 53, also predicts the events surrounding our Lord's death on the cross. He was "pierced through for our transgressions" (v. 5). Verse 7 predicts Jesus' silence during His mock trials: "He was oppressed and He was afflicted, yet He did not open His mouth; like a lamb that is led to slaughter, and like a sheep that is silent before its shearers, so He did not open His mouth" (cf. Matt. 26:62–63; 27:12–14). Verse 8 says He was "cut off out of the land of the living." Verse 9 notes that although Christ's "grave was assigned with wicked men, yet He was with a rich man in His death." The bodies of crucified victims were usually thrown onto the dump, but Jesus was buried in the tomb of the wealthy Joseph of Arimathea (Matt. 27:57–60). Verse 10 reveals that although Jesus would be put to death by "render[ing] Himself as a guilt offering," He would be resurrected, to "see His offspring" and "prolong His days."

In addition to Psalm 22 and Isaiah 53, Zechariah 12:10 also predicted the crucifixion of Jesus Christ, referring to Him as the one "whom they [Israel] have pierced."

The death of Christ is also pictured by illustrations and types. John 3:14 records that "as Moses lifted up the serpent in the wilderness, even so must the Son of Man be lifted up" (cf. 12:32–33). In John 10:11 Jesus referred to Himself as "the good shepherd [who] lays down His life for the sheep." Jesus knew every detail of His death because it was all ordained in "the predetermined plan and foreknowledge of God" (Acts 2:23).

The Old Testament prophets repeatedly "predicted the sufferings of Christ and the glories to follow" (1 Peter 1:11). Yet some foolishly (cf. Luke 24:25–26) believe that Jesus offered the kingdom to Israel, and would have bypassed the cross and granted them the kingdom if they had accepted Him. But Jesus came to offer the kingdom through the cross, as the detailed Old Testament predictions of the events surrounding His death and resurrection demonstrate (see in addition to the prophecies noted above Zech. 9:9, which describes His triumphal entry into Jerusalem; Ps. 2:1–3, which describes the rage of His enemies; Zech. 13:7, which describes His desertion by His friends; Zech. 11:12, which describes His betrayal for thirty pieces of silver; Ps. 34:20, which says that none of His bones would be broken [cf. Ex. 12:46]; Ps. 69:21, which says that He would be given vinegar to drink; Ps. 16:10, which refers to His resurrection; and Ps. 110:1, which pictures His ascension). Jesus was the "Lamb of God who takes away the sin of the world!" (John 1:29), who was "delivered over [to death] by the predetermined plan and foreknowledge of God" (Acts 2:23).

### THE PROPORTIONS OF SUFFERING

**For He will be handed over to the Gentiles, and will be mocked and mistreated and spit upon, and after they have scourged Him, they will kill Him;** (18:32–33*a*)

Combining these verses with the parallel accounts in Matthew (20:17–19) and Mark (10:32–34) gives the complete record of what the Lord said on this occasion. He would be betrayed to the Jewish authorities (Matt. 20:18; Mark 10:33) and, after a mock trial, condemned by them to death and **handed over to the Gentiles** (since the Jews did not have the authority to execute anyone [John 18:31]), **mocked and mistreated, spit upon, scourged,** and crucified (Matt. 20:19), after which on **the third day He** would **rise again.** His detailed knowledge of what

would happen to Him in the future is another display of Christ's omniscience (cf. His knowledge of people's hearts [John 2:24–25; cf. Luke 6:8;
11:17]; the precise location of where a fish with a coin in its mouth
would be [Matt. 17:27; cf. John 21:5–6]; that a woman whom He had met
for the first time had had five husbands [John 4:18]; where the colt He
would ride in the triumphal entry would be located and what its owners
would say when the disciples took it [Luke 19:30–34]; that the disciples
would meet a man carrying a pitcher who would show them the place
where they would eat the Last Supper [Luke 22:10]; and that Jerusalem
would be destroyed four decades later [Luke 21:20]).

But these verses not only predict Christ's suffering, they also con-
vey the magnitude and intensity of what Jesus, the "man of sorrows" (Isa.
53:3), endured. It is interesting to note that the New Testament frequently
uses the word "suffering" in the plural when it refers to Christ (e.g., 2 Cor.
1:5; Phil. 3:10; Heb. 2:10; 1 Peter 1:11; 4:13; 5:1), while in the Old Testament,
Isaiah 53 reveals the scope and severity of what Jesus would suffer. The
nature of His sufferings can be summarized under five headings.

First, Jesus suffered disloyalty. He was betrayed by Judas Iscariot,
one of those closest to Him, a man into whom He had invested His life
and truth. Exacerbating the suffering it caused the Lord, that betrayal
took place in the intimate setting of the last Passover meal He would eat
with the Twelve. Judas betrayed Christ to the Jewish authorities for a paltry thirty pieces of silver, just as the Scriptures predicted (Ps. 41:9; Zech.
11:12). Cynically, with feigned respect, he pointed out Jesus to His captors
with a kiss (Luke 22:47–48).

Second, Jesus suffered rejection (cf. Isa. 53:3). That rejection
came first of all from Israel. "He came to His own," John wrote, "and those
who were His own did not receive Him" (John 1:11). It was the leaders of
the nation, the chief priests and scribes, who condemned Him to death
and delivered Him to the Romans to be executed. The people also rejected
Him before Pilate, screaming "Crucify Him!" (Matt. 27:22). Jesus was also
rejected by those closest to Him. After His arrest, "all the disciples left Him
and fled" (Matt. 26:56). But the most profound rejection of all was by the
Father, which caused Him to cry out on the cross, "My God, My God, why
have You forsaken Me?" (Matt. 27:46; cf. Ps. 22:1).

Third, Jesus suffered humiliation. The sinless Son of God, in whom "all the fullness of Deity dwells in bodily form" (Col. 2:9), was **mocked and mistreated** and spat **upon.** Luke 22:63 notes that "the men who were holding Jesus in custody were mocking Him and beating Him." Luke 23:11 records that "Herod with his soldiers, after treating Him with contempt and mocking Him, dressed Him in a gorgeous robe and sent Him back to Pilate." While He was on the cross, "the rulers were sneering at Him, saying, 'He saved others; let Him save Himself if this is the Christ of God, His Chosen One.' The soldiers also mocked Him, coming up to Him, offering Him sour wine, and saying, 'If You are the King of the Jews, save Yourself!'" (Luke 23:35–37). Even one of those crucified alongside Him "was hurling abuse at Him, saying, 'Are You not the Christ? Save Yourself and us!'" (v. 39). The reviling and abuse that He had faced throughout His ministry (cf. John 9:28; 1 Peter 2:23) intensified at His death.

Fourth, Jesus suffered injustice. The holy, just, righteous, sovereign second person of the Trinity was falsely accused of sin (John 9:24), sedition, insurrection (Luke 23:13–14), and blasphemy (Matt. 9:3; 26:65; John 10:33). And His trials were monumental demonstrations of injustice at every point.

Finally, Jesus suffered bodily injury. He was brutally scourged with a whip with multiple thongs, at the end of which were tied pieces of glass, bone, rock, or metal. So severe was the damage from such a scourging that many died from it. Crucifixion was the most horrible form of execution. Frederic Farrar wrote,

> For indeed a death by crucifixion seems to include all that pain and death can have of horrible and ghastly—dizziness, cramp, thirst, starvation, sleeplessness, traumatic fever, tetanus, publicity of shame, long continuance of torment, horror of anticipation, mortification of untended wounds—all intensified just up to the point at which they can be endured at all, but all stopping just short of the point which would give to the sufferer the relief of unconsciousness. The unnatural position made every movement painful; the lacerated veins and crushed tendons throbbed with incessant anguish; the wounds, inflamed by exposure, gradually gangrened; the arteries—especially of the head and stomach—became swollen and oppressed with surcharged blood; and while each variety of misery went on gradually increasing, there was added to them the intolerable pang of a burning and raging thirst; and all these physical complications caused an internal excitement and anxiety which made the prospect of death itself—of death, the awful

unknown enemy, at whose approach man usually shudders most—bear the aspect of a delicious and exquisite release. ("The Crucifixion A. D. 30," in Rossiter Johnson, Charles F. Horne, and John Rudd, eds., *The Great Events By Famous Historians* [Project Gutenberg EBook, 2008], 3:47–48)

## THE POWER OVER SUFFERING

**and the third day He will rise again."** (18:33*b*)

Jesus was dead before the sundown that ended the day on Friday, rose early on Sunday morning, and ever lives, in fulfillment of the promise recorded in Psalm 16:10: "For You will not abandon my soul to Sheol; nor will You allow Your Holy One to undergo decay." Although buried in the tomb of a rich man (Isa. 53:9), He would "see His offspring," "prolong His days," and "the good pleasure of the Lord [would] prosper in His hand" (v. 10). That indicates that He would live again after His death. In John 2:19 Jesus said, "Destroy this temple, and in three days I will raise it up," and in John 12:24 He added, "Truly, truly, I say to you, unless a grain of wheat falls into the earth and dies, it remains alone; but if it dies, it bears much fruit." The story would not end with Jesus' death; "He who was delivered over because of our transgressions ... was raised because of our justification" (Rom. 4:25).

## THE PERCEPTION OF SUFFERING

**But the disciples understood none of these things, and the meaning of this statement was hidden from them, and they did not comprehend the things that were said.** (18:34)

Despite Jesus' clear teaching, the disciples failed to perceive the meaning of what He had just taught them. The threefold repetition, that they **understood none of these things, the meaning of this statement was hidden from them, and they did not comprehend the**

**things that were said,** emphasizes their utter lack of understanding (cf. Luke 9:45).

Critics see in this statement proof that Jesus never made this prediction. If He had, they argue, the disciples would surely have understood and not been surprised when what the Lord predicted came to pass. It is true that they did grasp some of the spiritual truth Jesus taught, such as the parables (Matt. 13:16–17). But there was a perfectly good reason that the disciples failed to grasp the Lord's teaching about His suffering and death: it failed to fit their messianic theology. They expected Messiah to be a king, who would defeat Israel's enemies and establish His kingdom. They were looking for a coronation, not a crucifixion; for a messiah who killed His enemies, not one who was killed by His own people. The idea of a crucified Messiah was an absurdity to them. It was so ridiculous that they could not even comprehend it. "The word of the cross is foolishness to those who are perishing," wrote Paul in 1 Corinthians 1:18. Thus "Christ crucified" was "to Jews a stumbling block" (v. 23); a massive barrier that they could not get past.

After His resurrection Christ reaffirmed the veracity of the Old Testament teaching regarding His death and resurrection, and rebuked the disciples for their failure to understand it. On the road to Emmaus, He said to two of them,

> "O foolish men and slow of heart to believe in all that the prophets have spoken! Was it not necessary for the Christ to suffer these things and to enter into His glory?" Then beginning with Moses and with all the prophets, He explained to them the things concerning Himself in all the Scriptures. (Luke 24:25–27; cf. v. 44)

A dying Messiah was not consistent with their theology and their interpretation of the Old Testament, but eventually the disciples came to understand it, believe it, and preach it.

# A Blind Beggar Receives Saving Sight (Luke 18:35–43)

# 6

As Jesus was approaching Jericho, a blind man was sitting by the road begging. Now hearing a crowd going by, he began to inquire what this was. They told him that Jesus of Nazareth was passing by. And he called out, saying, "Jesus, Son of David, have mercy on me!" Those who led the way were sternly telling him to be quiet; but he kept crying out all the more, "Son of David, have mercy on me!" And Jesus stopped and commanded that he be brought to Him; and when he came near, He questioned him, "What do you want Me to do for you?" And he said, "Lord, I want to regain my sight!" And Jesus said to him, "Receive your sight; your faith has made you well." Immediately he regained his sight and began following Him, glorifying God; and when all the people saw it, they gave praise to God. (18:35–43)

During His earthly ministry the Lord Jesus Christ performed countless miracles throughout Palestine. In addition to the three dozen recorded in the Gospels, Jesus performed miracles on an almost daily basis (cf. Mark 6:2; Luke 19:37; John 2:23; 3:2; 6:2; 7:31; 11:47; 12:37; 20:30; 21:25; Acts 2:22). Christ's miracles—which His enemies never denied, but instead blasphemously attributed to satanic power—gave evidence of His supernatural power, and supported His claim to be God incarnate (John 5:36; 10:25, 37–38; 14:11).

Our Lord's miracles revealed His absolute power over demons, disease, death, and nature. As the Son of God, Jesus revealed His power over Satan and the forces of hell by repeatedly casting unwilling demons out of those whom they had infested (Matt. 9:32–33; Mark 7:24–30; Luke 4:33–35; 8:26–33; 9:38–42; 11:14). Christ's countless healings (cf. John 21:25) demonstrated His power over disease, as He banished sickness from Israel during His earthly ministry. As the one by whom "all things were created" (Col. 1:16), Jesus had power over nature (Mark 8:1–9; Matt. 14:25; Luke 5:1–7; 8:22–25; 9:10–17; John 2:1–10; 21:1–6). As the "resurrection and the life" (John 11:25), Jesus exercised power over death (Luke 7:14–15; 8:52–56; John 11:38–44).

As the previous passage (vv. 31–33) indicates, it was time for the Servant of Jehovah to become the suffering Servant; for the anointed one to become the rejected one; for the sovereign Lord to become the sacrificial lamb. Christ's rejection by Israel was set; His death was inevitable. The fickle crowd that hailed Him on His entry into Jerusalem would be the same crowd that a few days later cried for His blood. Israel's apostasy would lead the Jews to execute their own Lord and Messiah. Although that execution was ordained according to God's predetermined plan, they still bore full culpability for that act (Acts 2:23).

After the conversions of the three outcasts in Jericho, the two despised blind men in this passage and the hated tax collector Zaccheus (19:1–10), there are no further accounts of conversions in the Gospels until those of two more outcasts, namely a thief and a Roman soldier, at the cross. The events in Jericho provide the last shining light before the darkness of Christ's suffering begins. There is not one joyful note from the time He walks out of Jericho until He is nailed to the cross.

This is the last of four notable miracles recorded by Luke that took place on Jesus' final journey to Jerusalem, which began in 9:51 (cf. 13:10–17; 14:1–6; 17:11–19). This supernatural sign revolves around the blind man, the Lord Jesus, and the crowd.

## THE SAD PLIGHT OF THE BLIND MAN

**As Jesus was approaching Jericho, a blind man was sitting by the road begging. Now hearing a crowd going by, he began to inquire what this was. They told him that Jesus of Nazareth was passing by. And he called out, saying, "Jesus, Son of David, have mercy on me!" Those who led the way were sternly telling him to be quiet; but he kept crying out all the more, "Son of David, have mercy on me!"** (18:35–39)

The scene was vivid and striking. Jesus, accompanied by a large crowd (Matt. 20:29), **was approaching Jericho** on the way to Jerusalem for Passover. Having come down from Galilee, they detoured, in the normal way, through Perea, east of the Jordan River, to avoid traveling through Samaria (John 4:9). They then recrossed the Jordan near Jericho, from which they would make the six-hour ascent to Jerusalem.

Jericho was located about fifteen miles northeast of Jerusalem and about five miles from the Jordan River. The area was well irrigated so that crops, including almonds, balsam, and most notably date palms, flourished (Judges 1:16 calls Jericho "the city of palms"). Nearby a massive rock formation casts its shadow every night over Jericho as the sun sets. It is a region of steep cliffs, severe drops, and deep canyons. Some think that this rugged, barren land was where Jesus was taken to be tempted by Satan.

There were actually two cities of Jericho, the flourishing New Testament city, and the ruins of the Old Testament city (destroyed during Israel's conquest of the land) east and north of New Testament Jericho. Thus, when Matthew and Mark state that the healing took place while Jesus was leaving Jericho, they may have been referring to the ruined Old Testament city. Luke's statement that Jesus was **approaching** Jericho could also mean simply that He was entering the new city—or simply that He was in the vicinity of Jericho.

The large crowd accompanying Jesus, who had earlier raised Lazarus from the dead in nearby Bethany, would have brought Jericho's inhabitants out of their houses and in from the fields to swell the group of curious onlookers. Jesus, as always, was the focus of their intense interest.

Since He spent one night in Jericho (cf. Luke 19:5), the healing may have taken place on the following day as He was leaving the area.

One of the onlookers in the crowd was a **blind man,** who **was sitting by the road begging.** Matthew notes that there were actually two blind men (Matt. 20:30); Luke focused on one of them, whose name was Bartimaeus (Mark 10:46). That Luke focused only on him and Mark named him suggests that Bartimaeus was, by the time these gospels were written, a well-known member of the early church.

Blindness, whether caused by birth defects, injury, or disease, was common in Israel (cf. Matt. 11:5; 15:30; 21:14), so common that Jesus used it to illustrate spiritual ignorance (e.g., Matt. 15:14; Luke 4:18; 14:13). Beggars also were numerous in Israel (cf. Luke 16:3; Acts 3:2, 10). The blind were despised and reduced to **begging** (cf. John 9:8), since their condition was considered to be God's judgment on their sin (John 9:1–2).

**Hearing a crowd going by,** Bartimaeus sensed that something more significant than the normal flow of Jerusalem-bound pilgrims was happening on the road. He **began to inquire** of the bystanders **what this was,** and they **told him that Jesus of Nazareth was passing by.** It was normal to associate people with the city in which they lived. Although born in Bethlehem, Jesus was associated with Nazareth, where He had lived since childhood (Matt. 2:23; 26:71; John 1:45; Acts 10:38; 26:9; cf. Mark 14:67; Luke 24:19; John 18:5; Acts 2:22; 6:14).

When he heard that the commotion was caused because Jesus was near, Bartimaeus immediately **called out** to Him. But instead of addressing Him in the customary manner as Jesus of Nazareth, he yelled out at the top of his voice (Matthew used a form of the Greek verb *krazō*, which means "to scream"), **"Jesus, Son of David, have mercy on me!"**

**Son of David** is a messianic title (cf. Matt. 12:23; 21:9; 22:42), which indicates more than merely declaring Jesus was a descendant of David. The title describes Him as the heir to the messianic throne and the one who has the right to fulfill the Davidic covenant (2 Sam. 7:12–14). In that covenant, God promised that David would have a greater son, who would reign over an everlasting kingdom. That greater son was not Solomon. Solomon's temporary kingdom ended tragically, since from it came the divided kingdom. The New Testament genealogies trace both Joseph's (Matthew 1) and Mary's (Luke 3) ancestry back to David. Jesus was a true heir to David's throne both by legal right through His father, and by bloodline of descent through His mother.

More than that, He was God's choice out of all David's descendants, so He sent the angel Gabriel to Mary with the message that the child she would bear "will be great and will be called the Son of the Most High; and the Lord God will give Him the throne of His father David; and He will reign over the house of Jacob forever, and His kingdom will have no end" (Luke 1:32–33).

By addressing Jesus as the Son of David, Bartimaeus was affirming his faith in Him as Israel's Messiah. His plea, **"have mercy on me,"** or "be gracious to me," acknowledges that he had no merit. It was the cry of the penitent heart that knows that salvation depends entirely on God's grace and mercy (cf. Pss. 4:1; 41:4; 51:1), among many other passages in the Psalms).

This blind man's plight, however, elicited no sympathy from the crowd. On the contrary, **those who led the way** (i.e., the ones responsible for crowd control), with typical disdain toward an outcast beggar, **were sternly telling him to be quiet.** Nevertheless in an expression of his desperate faith, **he kept crying out all the more, "Son of David, have mercy on me!"** The man could not be brow-beaten into submission; he could not have his passion crushed, nor could he be silenced. The truth concerning Jesus had come home to his heart and he had embraced it. He believed Jesus to be the Messiah and the only one who could heal him physically and spiritually. His heart had seen the light before his eyes did.

## The Savior's Supernatural Power

**And Jesus stopped and commanded that he be brought to Him; and when he came near, He questioned him, "What do you want Me to do for you?" And he said, "Lord, I want to regain my sight!" And Jesus said to him, "Receive your sight; your faith has made you well." Immediately he regained his sight and began following Him, glorifying God;** (18:40–43a)

Jesus performed a miracle that again publicly confirmed His deity and at the same time demonstrated divine compassion on a needy sinner (Matt. 20:34). Hearing the blind beggar's desperate cries, **Jesus stopped and,** reacting opposite to the authorities trying to push Bartimaeus away, **commanded that he be brought to Him.**

Mark adds the detail that at this point some bystanders "called the blind man, saying to him, 'Take courage, stand up! He is calling for you.' Throwing aside his cloak, he jumped up and came to Jesus" (Mark 10:49–50). In his eager faith, he cast away his beggar's cloak, likely the only thing he possessed. His act symbolizes genuine faith, which abandons all to follow Christ.

**When** Bartimaeus **came near,** Jesus asked **him, "What do you want Me to do for you?"** Incredibly, the high King of heaven, the sovereign, creator God of the universe, offered to be the servant of this lowly outcast. Here is an amazing example of God's mercy and grace.

In reply to Jesus' question, Bartimaeus replied, **"Lord, I want to regain my sight!"** He addressed Jesus as *kurie* (**Lord**), likely affirming His deity, and expressing his confidence in Him as the one who dispenses mercy. That he asked to **regain** his sight may imply that he had not been born blind, but had lost his sight at some point in his life.

Jesus' reply, **"Receive your sight,"** was simple and understated. The earth did not shake, there was no trumpet blast from heaven, nor did an angelic chorus appear to announce the miracle. Jesus sometimes healed with a word or a touch (He did both in this case, since Matthew 20:34 adds that He touched the eyes of Bartimaeus and the other blind man), other times the afflicted touched His cloak (Matt. 9:20–22), still other times He used spittle (Mark 8:22–26) or clay (John 9:6). But no matter what gestures accompanied His healings, they were inexplicable in any other way than divine supernatural intervention. Nor were His healings contingent on the faith of the one being healed; many of those He healed manifested no faith prior to their healing.

At this point it is helpful to add that six features characterized Christ's healing ministry.

First, as noted above, Jesus healed with a word, a touch, or some other gesture.

Second, Jesus healed instantly. There were no progressive healings, in which the people He cured gradually got better. Peter's mother-in-law's symptoms vanished at once and she was fully restored to health (Luke 4:38–39). Similarly, the centurion's servant "was healed that very moment" (Matt. 8:13); the woman with the hemorrhage was healed "immediately" (Mark 5:29); the ten lepers were cleansed of their disease as soon as they left to show themselves to the priests (Luke 17:14); after Jesus "stretched out His hand and touched [another leper] ... immediately the leprosy left him" (Luke 5:13); when Jesus commanded the crippled man at the pool of Bethesda, "'Get up, pick up your pallet and walk.' Immediately the man became well, and picked up his pallet and began to walk" (John 5:8–9). Some offer the Lord's healing of the blind man in Bethsaida (Mark 8:22–25) as an example of a progressive healing. But the man's statement, "I see men, for I see them like trees, walking around" (v. 24), merely defined his preexisting condition of blindness. The actual healing was instantaneous (v. 25). Had Jesus' healings not been instantaneous, His critics could have claimed that the people became better as a result of natural processes.

Third, Jesus healed totally. For example, Peter's mother-in-law was cured of all her symptoms and went at once from being bedridden to serving a meal. When Jesus healed a man "covered with leprosy" (Luke 5:12), "the leprosy left him" (v. 13). It was the same with all of Jesus' healings; "the blind received sight and the lame walked, the lepers [were] cleansed and the deaf heard" (Matt. 11:5).

Fourth, Jesus healed everyone. Unlike modern false healers, He did not leave behind long lines of disappointed, distraught people who were not healed. Matthew 4:24 says that "the news about Him spread throughout all Syria; and they brought to Him all who were ill, those suffering with various diseases and pains, demoniacs, epileptics, paralytics; and He healed them." According to Matthew 12:15, "Many followed Him, and He healed them all," while Luke 6:19 notes that "all the people were trying to touch Him, for power was coming from Him and healing them all." So widespread was Jesus' healing that He, in effect, banished disease from Israel during the three years of His ministry.

Fifth, Jesus healed organic disease. He did not heal vague, ambiguous, invisible ailments such as lower back pain, heart palpitations, or headaches. On the contrary, He restored full mobility to paralyzed limbs, full sight to blind eyes, full hearing to deaf ears, and fully cleansed leprous skin. Jesus healed "every kind of disease and every kind of sickness among the people" (Matt. 4:23; cf. 9:35). All of Jesus' healings were undeniable, miraculous signs, as even His most bitter enemies admitted (John 11:47).

Finally, Jesus raised the dead—not those who were in a temporary coma, or whose vital signs fluctuated during surgery, but a young man in his casket on his way to the graveyard (Luke 7:11–15), a young girl whose death was apparent to all (Mark 5:22–24, 35–43), and a man who had been dead for four days (John 11:14–44).

But this was more than physical healing for Bartimaeus and his fellow blind man, since after healing him the Lord told him, **"Your faith has made you well."** The Greek word translated "well" is not *iaomai*, which means "to heal," but *sōzō*, the familiar New Testament term translated "saved" in reference to salvation. While faith was not necessary for someone to be healed, it is absolutely necessary for salvation (Luke 5:20; 7:48–50; 8:46–48; 17:17–19). Further evidence that Jesus was referring to salvation comes from the fact that Bartimaeus (and his companion; Matt. 20:34) **began following Him, glorifying God.** Both are marks of true conversion; **following** refers to obedience, **glorifying** to worship. They undoubtedly were in Jerusalem for the events of Passion Week; the triumphal entry, Christ's cleansing of the temple, perhaps His trial and crucifixion. They may even have been among the 120 gathered in the upper room on the Day of Pentecost. As noted earlier, Mark may have given Bartimaeus's name in his account of this incident (Mark 10:46) because he was well known in the early church.

## THE CROWD'S SPONTANEOUS PRAISE

**and when all the people saw it, they gave praise to God.** (18:43*b*)

Not **all** of the **people** who **saw** the Lord's miraculous healing believed in Him. Yet they could not deny that a miracle had taken place, and therefore **they gave praise to God.** That undoubtedly contributed to the massive outpouring of praise at the triumphal entry.

Five lessons may be learned from this passage.

First, the Lord does not ignore the cry of those who truly call on Him (Matt. 11:28; John 6:37).

Second, the Lord is profoundly compassionate.

Third, the Lord has power over all disease.

Fourth, the Lord came for more than merely to heal disease; He came to save the lost and transform them into obedient worshippers.

Finally, the passage calls for self-examination. Those who express interest in Christ are either among the curious crowd, whose praise is shallow, superficial, and ultimately false, or they are like the two blind men, whose desperation led them to abandon everything to come to Christ for salvation, and who give evidence of that salvation by following Christ obediently and glorifying Him.

# A Sinner Meets the Seeking Savior (Luke 19:1–10)

# 7

He entered Jericho and was passing through. And there was a man called by the name of Zaccheus; he was a chief tax collector and he was rich. Zaccheus was trying to see who Jesus was, and was unable because of the crowd, for he was small in stature. So he ran on ahead and climbed up into a sycamore tree in order to see Him, for He was about to pass through that way. When Jesus came to the place, He looked up and said to him, "Zaccheus, hurry and come down, for today I must stay at your house." And he hurried and came down and received Him gladly. When they saw it, they all began to grumble, saying, "He has gone to be the guest of a man who is a sinner." Zaccheus stopped and said to the Lord, "Behold, Lord, half of my possessions I will give to the poor, and if I have defrauded anyone of anything, I will give back four times as much." And Jesus said to him, "Today salvation has come to this house, because he, too, is a son of Abraham. For the Son of Man has come to seek and to save that which was lost." (19:1–10)

The familiar story of Zaccheus, appearing only in Luke's gospel, is a rich and instructive story with a concluding verse that expresses the most valuable and glorious truth ever revealed. In that closing statement the Lord Jesus Christ summed up the whole purpose of His incarnation —to seek out and redeem lost sinners.

God seeks sinners, because "there is none who seeks for God" (Rom. 3:11). Unless He graciously calls them they will not come (cf. Rom. 1:6–7; 8:28; 11:29; 1 Cor. 1:9, 23–24, 26; Gal. 1:6; Eph. 4:1, 4; Col. 3:15; 1 Thess. 2:12; 2 Thess. 2:14; 2 Tim. 1:9; Heb. 3:1; 1 Peter 2:9, 21; 3:9; 5:10; 2 Peter 1:3). After Adam and Eve sinned and attempted to hide from Him, God called to them, "Where are you?" (Gen. 3:8–9). Throughout history, God has continued to seek for the lost (cf. Ezek. 34:11, 16; Luke 15:4–32). There would be no reconciliation, salvation, forgiveness, or hope of heaven if He did not.

Jesus came into the world not, as some suggest, to be a good teacher, or a moral leader. He did not come to espouse ideas that would raise people's spiritual consciousness. Nor did He come into the world to provide a human example of noble, religious life. The divine Lord Christ came into the world to rescue doomed sinners, because God is a saving God (cf. Ps. 106:21; Isa. 43:11; 45:15, 17, 21, 22). That is the biblical message and the foundation of the gospel. Everything in the Old Testament points to that truth; everything in the New Testament explains it.

That the Son of God came into the world to save sinners was made clear before His birth. In Matthew 1:21, the angel said to Joseph, "[Mary] will bear a Son; and you shall call His name Jesus, for He will save His people from their sins." The apostle John wrote that Jesus "appeared in order to take away sins" (1 John 3:5). Paul testified, "It is a trustworthy statement, deserving full acceptance, that Christ Jesus came into the world to save sinners, among whom I am foremost of all" (1 Tim. 1:15; cf. 4:10; John 4:14, 42; Acts 5:31; 2 Cor. 5:18–21; 2 Tim. 1:10; Titus 2:13).

No inspired gospel writer put more emphasis on this truth than Luke. That emphasis is most clearly and dramatically portrayed in the three parables of Luke chapter 15, in which God likens Himself to a shepherd seeking a lost sheep, a woman seeking a lost coin, and a father seeking a lost son. Those parables not only focus on His seeking, but also express His joy over the salvation of sinners found. God's extreme joy in recovering the lost is also seen in the Old Testament. Isaiah 62:5 says, "For as a young man marries a virgin, so your sons will marry you; and as the bridegroom rejoices over the bride, so your God will rejoice over you." Through the prophet Jeremiah God declared, "I will rejoice over them to do them good and will faithfully plant them in this land with all My heart and with all My soul" (Jer. 32:41).

The story of Zaccheus's conversion is one of the clearest biblical illustrations of God seeking a specific sinner. That man, in the midst of a massive crowd, had a divine appointment with the seeking, saving Lord. Jesus located him, called him by name, and pursued him to salvation.

This profound story may be simply divided into three sections: the sinner, the Savior, and the salvation.

## THE SINNER

**He entered Jericho and was passing through. And there was a man called by the name of Zaccheus; he was a chief tax collector and he was rich. Zaccheus was trying to see who Jesus was, and was unable because of the crowd, for he was small in stature. So he ran on ahead and climbed up into a sycamore tree in order to see Him, for He was about to pass through that way.** (19:1–4)

As noted in the previous chapter of this volume, **Jericho** was located about fifteen miles northeast of Jerusalem and about five miles from the Jordan River. The noted nineteenth-century historian Alfred Edersheim gives a vivid description of Jericho as it was in Jesus' day:

> The ancient City occupied not the site of the present wretched hamlet, but lay about half an hour to the north-west of it, by the so-called Elisha-Spring. A second spring rose an hour further to the north-north-west. The water of these springs, distributed by aqueducts, gave, under a tropical sky, unsurpassed fertility to the rich soil along the 'plain' of Jericho, which is about twelve or fourteen miles wide.... *Josephus* describes it as the richest part of the country, and calls it a little Paradise. Antony had bestowed the revenues of its balsam-plantations as an Imperial gift upon Cleopatra, who in turn sold them to Herod. Here grew palm-trees of various kinds, sycamores, the cypress-flower, the myro-balsamum,

which yielded precious oil, but especially the balsam-plant. If to these advantages of climate, soil, and productions we add, that it was, so to speak, the key of Judæa towards the east, that it lay on the caravan-road from Damascus and Arabia, that it was a great commercial and military centre, and lastly, its nearness to Jerusalem, to which it formed the last 'station' on the road of the festive pilgrims from Galilee and Peræa—it will not be difficult to understand either its importance or its prosperity.

We can picture to ourselves the scene, as our Lord on that afternoon in early spring beheld it. There it was, indeed, already summer, for, as *Josephus* tells us, even in winter the inhabitants could only bear the lightest clothing of linen. We are approaching it from the Jordan. It is protected by walls, flanked by four forts. These walls, the theatre, and the Amphitheatre, have been built by Herod; the new palace and its splendid gardens are the work of Archelaus. All around wave groves of feathery palms, rising in stately beauty; stretch gardens of roses, and especially sweet-scented balsam-plantations—the largest behind the royal gardens, of which the perfume is carried by the wind almost out to sea, and which may have given to the city its name (Jericho, 'the perfumed'). It is the Eden of Palestine, the very fairyland of the old world. And how strangely is this gem set! Deep down in that hollowed valley, through which tortuous Jordan winds, to lose his waters in the slimy mass of the Sea of Judgment. The river and the Dead Sea are nearly equidistant from the town—about six miles. Far across the river rise the mountains of Moab, on which lies the purple and violet colouring. Towards Jerusalem and northwards stretch those bare limestone hills, the hiding-place of robbers along the desolate road towards the City. There, and in the neighbouring wilderness of Judæa, are also the lonely dwellings of anchorites [hermits]—while over all this strangely varied scene has been flung the many-coloured mantle of a perpetual summer. And in the streets of Jericho a motley throng meets: pilgrims from Galilee and Peræa, priests who have a 'station' here, traders from all lands, who have come to purchase or to sell, or are on the great caravan-road from Arabia and Damascus—robbers and anchorites, wild fanatics, soldiers, courtiers, and busy publicans—for Jericho was the central station for the collection of tax and custom, both on native produce and on that brought from across Jordan. (*The Life and Times of Jesus the Messiah* [Reprint; Grand Rapids: Eerdmans, 1971], 2:349–51. Italics in original)

The miracle-working Lord's arrival in Jericho, accompanied by a large crowd of pilgrims bound for Jerusalem, understandably created a sensation. It was to this huge crowd that Jesus declared that He had come to seek and to save the lost, and demonstrated that by bringing salvation to Jericho's most notorious sinner.

One of the many people watching while Jesus **was passing**

**through** the city **was a man called by the name of Zaccheus.** Here is Luke's sixth and final reference to tax collectors (cf. 3:12; 5:27–32; 7:29–34; 15:1; 18:10–13). Although tax collectors were the most hated and despised outcasts in Israel, it was not a crime to be one, since taxation is a divine institution. The theocratic kingdom of Israel in the Old Testament was funded by a detailed taxation system in which every Jewish person paid essentially 23.3 percent of their income to support the government. When some repentant tax collectors asked John the Baptist, "Teacher, what shall we do?" (Luke 3:12), he did not tell them to quit their jobs as tax collectors, but rather charged them, "Collect no more than what you have been ordered to" (v. 13). Jesus commanded that taxes be paid when He said, "Render to Caesar the things that are Caesar's" (Luke 20:25; cf. Rom. 13:7), and He Himself paid the required taxes (Matt. 17:24–27).

What God denounced was abusive or illegitimate taxes, extortion, dishonesty, and taking money from people by use of physical violence, intimidation, and cruelty, as tax collectors in the ancient world did. As I noted in an earlier volume of this series,

> The Roman occupation of Israel involved more than just a military presence; the nation was also subject to Roman taxation. The taxes in Galilee, for example, were forwarded by tax collectors to Herod Antipas, and by him to Rome. Antipas sold tax franchises to the highest bidder, and such franchises were a lucrative business. Tax collectors had a certain amount that they were required to collect, and whatever they collected beyond that they were permitted to keep (cf. Luke 3:12–13). In addition to the poll tax (on everyone, including slaves), income tax (about one percent), and land tax (one tenth of all grain, and one fifth of all wine and fruit), there were taxes on the transport of goods, letters, produce, using roads, crossing bridges, and almost anything else the rapacious, greedy minds of the tax collectors could think of. All of that left plenty of room for larceny, extortion, exploitation, and even loan sharking, as tax collectors loaned money at exorbitant interest to those who were unable to pay their taxes. Tax collectors also employed thugs to physically intimidate people into paying, and to beat up those who refused. (*Luke 1–5*, The MacArthur New Testament Commentary [Chicago: Moody, 2009], 330)

The behavior of tax collectors made them rich, but at the cost of being barred from the synagogue. Because people considered them unclean, they were cut off from social relationships. They could associate only with their fellow tax collectors and the other outcast sinners with whom they associated (15:1; cf. Matt. 9:10–11; 11:19).

Ironically, considering his occupation and reputation, the name **Zaccheus** means "clean," "innocent," "pure," or "righteous." The only other tax gatherer named in the New Testament is Levi (Matthew 9:9; Luke 5:27). Like Bartimaeus (cf. the previous chapter of this volume), Luke may have given his name because he had become well known in the early church (according to tradition, he was appointed bishop of Caesarea by Peter).

Zaccheus was no low-level tax collector. *Architelōnēs* (**chief tax collector**), used only here in the New Testament, means that he was the commissioner of taxes; the head of the region's tax collectors. Zaccheus was at the top of the pyramid; the common tax collectors had to pay him a percentage of what they collected. As a result, **he was rich.**

Like many in the crowd, **Zaccheus was** continually **trying to see who Jesus was.** He, too, was curious about Him, but more than that, he had a dissatisfied heart. Zaccheus knew that he was alienated from God, and lacked eternal life. He was feeling guilty over his sin.

Zaccheus's effort to see Jesus faced two obstacles, however: the **crowd** was large, and **he was small in stature.** With determination and desperation, Zaccheus **ran on ahead** on the path he knew Jesus would take **and climbed up into a sycamore tree in order to see Him, for He was about to pass through that way.** A **sycamore** (or mulberry) tree had a relatively short trunk with low branches that Zaccheus reached. Having climbed into the tree, he waited for Jesus to become visible.

THE SAVIOR

**When Jesus came to the place, He looked up and said to him, "Zaccheus, hurry and come down, for today I must stay at your house." And he hurried and came down and received Him gladly. When they saw it, they all began to grumble, saying, "He has gone to be the guest of a man who is a sinner."** (19:5–7)

**When Jesus came to the place** where Zaccheus sat in the tree waiting, He made some moves that must have shocked him. First, the Lord stopped, then **looked up and** made eye contact with **Zaccheus,** and called him by name, though they had never met (cf. His interaction with Nathanael in John 1:45–48). Finally, and most stunning of all, the Lord commanded Zaccheus to take Him home! He said, **"Hurry and come down, for today I must stay at your house."** The verbs translated **hurry** and **come down** are imperatives, and call for immediate action. The Lord knows not only who He will save, but where and when that salvation will take place (cf. John 3:8). The particle *dei* (**must**) is used throughout Luke's gospel to speak of divine necessity (cf. 2:49; 4:43; 9:22; 13:33; 17:25; 22:37; 24:7, 44). It was predetermined before the foundation of the world that Jesus would stay at Zaccheus's house that day and grant him eternal life.

After Zaccheus overcame his shock and surprise, **he hurried and came down** from his perch in the tree **and received** Jesus **gladly.** This would have been the first time any honorable, ceremonially clean, and respected person had ever come to his house. As the father received the prodigal (Luke 15:11–32), Jesus embraced a sinning hated agent of Rome and reconciled him.

Nothing more clearly illustrates the difference between the heart of God and apostate first-century Judaism than the reaction of outrage by the crowd. **When they saw** that Jesus was going to stay with Zaccheus, **they all began to grumble, saying, "He has gone to be the guest of a man who is a sinner."** The onomatopoeic verb *diagonguzō* (**grumble**) is a strong word, indicating the crowd's intense disapproval of the Lord's action, not only of speaking with Zaccheus, but also of staying the night (the verb translated **gone to be the guest** means to loosen one's clothing in preparation for staying overnight). No self-respecting Jew would ever pollute himself by staying at the house of the chief administrator of Roman taxation. That, however, meant nothing to Jesus, who was on a divine mission, established by divine sovereign electing grace and operating on the divine timetable, to bring this lost sinner to salvation.

THE SALVATION

**Zaccheus stopped and said to the Lord, "Behold, Lord, half of my possessions I will give to the poor, and if I have defrauded anyone of anything, I will give back four times as much." And Jesus said to him, "Today salvation has come to this house, because he, too, is a son of Abraham. For the Son of Man has come to seek and to save that which was lost." (19:8–10)**

Luke does not describe the Lord's presentation of the gospel to Zaccheus, or his response. But the salvation of the man is evident from the transformation of his life, which revealed itself in that part of his life where his sin was most openly manifested. Zaccheus **stopped** (the Greek word is better translated "took a stand"), acknowledged Jesus as **Lord** (cf. Rom. 10:9–10), and expressed his self-denial (cf. Luke 9:23–24) by saying to Him, **"Half of my possessions I will give to the poor"** (cf. 2 Cor. 8:3; James 2:15–16; 1 John 3:17). Further, his statement, **"If I have defrauded anyone of anything, I will give back four times as much,"** declared his intent to make restitution for the wrongs he had committed, in keeping with the maximum amount required by the Old Testament law (Ex. 22:1; cf. vv. 4–14; Num. 5:6–7). The genuineness of Zaccheus's salvation was made evident by the complete transformation of his behavior.

**Jesus** confirmed the reality of Zaccheus's salvation when He **said to him, "Today salvation has come to this house, because he, too, is a son of Abraham."** Zaccheus had, of course, been **a son of Abraham** ethnically all of his life. But as the apostle Paul wrote,

> He is not a Jew who is one outwardly, nor is circumcision that which is outward in the flesh. But he is a Jew who is one inwardly; and circumcision is that which is of the heart, by the Spirit, not by the letter; and his praise is not from men, but from God. (Rom. 2:28–29; cf. 9:6)

> Even so Abraham believed God, and it was reckoned to him as righteousness. Therefore, be sure that it is those who are of faith who are sons of Abraham. The Scripture, foreseeing that God would justify the Gentiles by faith, preached the gospel beforehand to Abraham, saying, "All the nations will be blessed in you." So then those who are of faith

are blessed with Abraham, the believer. . . . And if you belong to Christ, then you are Abraham's descendants, heirs according to promise. (Gal. 3:6–9, 29; cf. John 8:33–44)

Paul had been a zealous Pharisee, proud of his Abrahamic heritage (Phil. 3:4–6). But after his salvation he viewed all of that as "rubbish" (v. 8), and himself as the foremost of all sinners (1 Tim. 1:15).

So complete was Zaccheus's transformation that he instantaneously went from being a thief to being a benefactor; from being selfish to being unselfish, from being a taker to being a giver. He became a true Jew, part of the Israel of God (Gal. 6:16), a Jew who was one inwardly. He was no longer just a son of Abraham by race, but a son of Abraham by faith. That very day he was justified by faith. The one who had been lost was saved and delivered from sin, death, and hell. The Lord gave him life and light to believe and repent and his conduct was transformed.

**Son of Man,** a messianic title taken from Daniel 7:13, was Jesus' most common way of referring to Himself. It describes both His humanity and His deity. The verbs translated **seek** and **save** are infinitives, and express the purpose for which Jesus came into world. To **save** is to rescue from harm and deliver from danger. **Lost** translates a form of the verb *apollumi*, which means "to be ruined," or "destroyed." Sin has devastated all of humanity, leaving lost sinners marred, corrupted, evil, ruined, and headed for eternal damnation (Rom. 3:10–18; Eph. 4:17). But God, in His mercy, grace, and love, sent Christ to seek and to save those who face His own wrath and judgment. In the words of Philip P. Bliss's hymn "Hallelujah, What a Savior!":

> "Man of Sorrows!" what a name
> For the Son of God who came
> Ruined sinners to reclaim!
> Hallelujah, what a Savior!

When a sinner does seek after God (Jer. 29:13; Amos 5:4; Matt. 6:33; 11:28) he does so only because God has first sought him (John 6:44; cf. 1 John 4:19), called him "out of darkness into His marvelous light" (1 Peter 2:9), and shattered his state of death by making him alive (cf. Eph. 2:1–3).

# Fitting Rewards from the Returning King (Luke 19:11–27)

**8**

While they were listening to these things, Jesus went on to tell a parable, because He was near Jerusalem, and they supposed that the kingdom of God was going to appear immediately. So He said, "A nobleman went to a distant country to receive a kingdom for himself, and then return. And he called ten of his slaves, and gave them ten minas and said to them, 'Do business with this until I come back.' But his citizens hated him and sent a delegation after him, saying, 'We do not want this man to reign over us.' When he returned, after receiving the kingdom, he ordered that these slaves, to whom he had given the money, be called to him so that he might know what business they had done. The first appeared, saying, 'Master, your mina has made ten minas more.' And he said to him, 'Well done, good slave, because you have been faithful in a very little thing, you are to be in authority over ten cities.' The second came, saying, 'Your mina, master, has made five minas.' And he said to him also, 'And you are to be over five cities.' Another came, saying, 'Master, here is your mina, which I kept put away in a handkerchief; for I was afraid of you, because you are an exacting man; you take up what you did not lay down and reap what you did not sow.' He said to him, 'By your own words I will judge you, you worthless slave. Did you know that I am an exacting man, taking up what I did not lay down and reaping what I did not sow? Then why did you not put my money in the bank, and having come, I would have collected it with interest?' Then he said to the bystanders, 'Take the mina away from him and give it to the one who has the ten minas.' And they said to him, 'Master, he has ten minas already.' 'I tell you that to everyone who has, more shall be given, but from the one who does not have, even what he does have shall be taken away. But these enemies of mine, who did not want me to reign over them, bring them here and slay them in my presence.'" (19:11–27)

The parables our Lord told were designed to move people from the realm of the familiar to the realm of the unfamiliar. He conveyed spiritual truth that was new and unfamiliar to His hearers by means of analogies, illustrations, and stories about things with which they were familiar. Jesus drew His stories from the customary experiences of everyday life.

This amazing story is no exception. It can be loosely connected to a historical reality, known to the people of Judea, particularly those in Jericho.

Israel in the time of Christ was an occupied nation, under the rule and authority of Rome. The Romans ruled their conquered lands through subordinate rulers, who had to be approved and granted the right to rule by Rome. Herod the Great, the founder of the Herodian dynasty, negotiated with Mark Antony to obtain the right to rule Israel. After his death in 4 B.C., Herod's kingdom was divided among his three sons, and Archelaus was made ruler over Judea. Seeking to intimidate his subjects, he slaughtered three thousand Jews. Not surprisingly, the people hated him, and when he went to Rome to have his rule officially confirmed, they sent a delegation to appeal to Caesar not to make him their ruler. By way of compromise, Augustus granted Archelaus the right to rule, but not to use the title of king until he had gained the favor of the people—which, of course, he never did. Soon, Archelaus's harsh rule created chaos, and the Romans removed him from power. They replaced him with a series of governors, of which Pilate was the fifth. That incident, with which all Jesus' hearers were familiar, provided an historical experience to pave the way for this story.

The Lord's invented story is about an imaginary nobleman who left for a distant country to receive a kingdom, leaving instructions for his servants to fulfill his business responsibilities in his absence. Some of his enemies, however, sent a delegation to the ruler who was to grant him his kingdom, expressing their desire that the nobleman not be appointed ruler over them.

The phrase **while they were listening to these things** refers back to verse 10 and the Lord's comments after the salvation of Zaccheus. The brief statement recorded in that verse was not the entirety of the Lord's sermon, but merely its thesis statement. As they walked along the road on the fifteen or so mile trip to Jerusalem, Jesus continued to teach the large crowd that was accompanying Him, expanding on the significance of His declaration that He had "come to seek and to save that which was lost."

The Lord Jesus did not come to overthrow the Romans and set up the earthly messianic kingdom as the Jewish people anticipated. He will do that when He returns again. Nor was it His goal to bring about social reform, as liberals wrongly believe. If that was His goal, He completely failed to achieve it. Rather, the Lord came to offer salvation to all who would confess their sinful lostness, repent, and believe in Him as Lord and only Savior. The recent healing of the two blind men (18:35–43) and the salvation of Zaccheus reveal Jesus to be the seeking Savior of the lost (as do the three parables He told in chapter 15), but the Jewish people failed to accept His mission and clung to the hope of an earthly messianic kingdom. Even after the resurrection the disciples were still confused. In Acts 1:6 they asked Him, "Lord, is it at this time You are restoring the kingdom to Israel?" (cf. Luke 24:21). Because it ran counter to the Jewish messianic teaching that they had been taught all their lives, they would not accept the Lord's teaching that Messiah's kingdom would be delayed (cf. Matt. 25:5, 19).

**Because** they were **near Jerusalem,** the crowd supposed **that the** earthly **kingdom of God** they fervently longed for **was going to**

**appear immediately.** Their anticipation was growing with each passing mile and is even suggested by the Greek verb translated **appear,** which is a nautical term for something becoming visible on the horizon (cf. Acts 21:3). But that earthly kingdom would be delayed, and Jesus would first be rejected by His people (John 1:11), killed, and raised from the dead to provide the sacrifice for salvation. At His return He will establish His earthly millennial rule (cf. Rev. 20).

To correct their erroneous notions, the Lord created this story about Himself to illustrate the delay in establishing His earthly kingdom. In this **parable,** the **nobleman** represents Jesus; his journey **to a distant country to receive a kingdom for himself** represents Christ's ascension and exaltation to the Father's right hand (Acts 2:33, 36; Phil. 2:9–11) and, after a delay, His **return** to reign (Mark 13:33–37; Luke 21:25–36; Rev. 19:11–21). The **ten slaves** (*doulous* [**slaves**] in this case refers to trustworthy employees given high responsibility) who received the **ten minas** (about three months' wages) represent all who profess to serve Christ. The nobleman charged his slaves to **"do business with this until I come back." Do business** translates a form of the verb *pragmateuomai*, which is related to the noun *pragma*, from which the English word "pragmatic" derives. They were to do something productive and profitable with what he entrusted to them. In so doing they would show their love and respect for their master, and their commitment to the well-being of his household, and be rewarded for their faithfulness when he returned. In application, this is a call to live a life that honors the absent nobleman (Christ), who will hold people accountable for their actions when He returns.

Despite their similarities, this parable is not the same as the parable of the talents that Matthew records (Matt. 25:14–30). Darrell L. Bock outlines

1. The settings are different: Luke has the parable in Jericho, while Matthew has it in Jerusalem.
2. The audiences differ: Luke has the remarks in front of a crowd, while Matthew has it only with disciples.
3. Luke has a number of unique details, including an additional remark in the setting that notes the delay of consummation and a note about the citizens and emissary sent to protest the king's selection.
4. Matthew has a businessman, while Luke has a king.

5. Matthew has three slaves, Luke ten.
6. Matthew gives the servants property and talents (five, two, and one respectively), while Luke gives each servant one mina.
7. The difference in value between a talent and a mina yields a large sum in Matthew and a small sum in Luke.
8. The rewards in Matthew are the same for each servant, while in Luke they are different. (*Luke 9:51–24:53*, Baker Exegetical Commentary on the New Testament [Grand Rapids: Baker, 1996], 1527)

The parable describes three distinct groups: the foes, the faithful servants, and the false servants.

## THE FOES

**But his citizens hated him and sent a delegation after him, saying, 'We do not want this man to reign over us.' . . . 'But these enemies of mine, who did not want me to reign over them, bring them here and slay them in my presence.'"** (19:14, 27)

As had been the case with Archelaus in real life, the **citizens** in the story **hated** the nobleman **and sent a delegation after him, saying** derogatorily, **"We do not want this man to reign over us."** Unlike the historical account of Archelaus, however, nothing in the story indicates that the nobleman gave his citizens any cause to hate him. That illustrates the reality that Jesus was hated without a cause (John 15:25; cf. Ps. 69:4). The Jewish people's attitude toward Archelaus was reasonable; their attitude toward Jesus was blasphemous.

Despite their hatred and rejection of him, the nobleman's enemies in the Lord's story were nonetheless his **citizens.** Everyone—whether they accept Him, reject Him, or ignore Him—is under the sovereign rule of the Lord Jesus Christ (Heb. 2:8). The world is His domain, since He created it (John 1:3; Col. 1:16; Heb. 1:2), and all people are therefore His subjects.

Just as Archelaus's enemies were unable to prevent him from taking the throne, so also Jesus' foes will be unable to keep Him from taking His throne. He has been crowned, and will one day return as the "King of kings and Lord of lords" (Rev. 19:16). When the nobleman returned from being crowned king, he commanded his servants, **"These enemies of mine, who did not want me to reign over them, bring them here and slay** (the Greek verb is a strong word that means "to slay completely," or "to slaughter") **them in my presence."** So also Jesus will judge (Matt. 25:31–46) and destroy (Rev. 19:11–21) His enemies when He returns.

## THE FAITHFUL SERVANTS

**When he returned, after receiving the kingdom, he ordered that these slaves, to whom he had given the money, be called to him so that he might know what business they had done. The first appeared, saying, 'Master, your mina has made ten minas more.' And he said to him, 'Well done, good slave, because you have been faithful in a very little thing, you are to be in authority over ten cities.' The second came, saying, 'Your mina, master, has made five minas.' And he said to him also, 'And you are to be over five cities.'** (19:15–19)

**When he returned, after receiving the kingdom,** the king not only destroyed his foes, but also **ordered that these slaves, to whom he had given the money, be called to him so that he might know what business they had done.** The two groups of servants picture true and false believers.

Verses 15–19 describe the **faithful** believers, and depict the future time when the saints will receive their heavenly rewards (1 Cor. 3:11–15; 4:5; 2 Cor. 5:9–10; Gal. 6:3–5; 2 Peter 1:5–11). When the first servant **appeared** before the king he did not boast of his accomplishment but humbly, respectfully said to him, **"Master, your mina has made ten minas more."** Indirectly, he gave the credit for his success to the king for creating the economic environment that allowed the **mina** to grow so remarkably. The king praised him and **said to him, "Well done, good slave."** Because he had **been faithful in a very little thing,** the king graciously, generously placed him **in authority over ten cities**—a gracious reward incomparably greater than his stewardship of ten minas warranted. In essence, the faithful servant was made a vice-regent ruling over a province or region under the king. That symbolizes believers' responsibility and rule under Christ in His future kingdom (cf. 2 Tim. 2:12; Rev. 1:6; 5:10; 20:4, 6).

Displaying the same humility as the first slave, the **second** slave reported to the king, **"Your mina, master, has made five minas."** Although his results were not the same as the first slave, he was no less faithful. Not everyone has the same gifts, opportunities, or outcomes for ministry. The issue is to faithfully serve the Lord Jesus Christ, maximizing in the power of the Spirit the spiritual privileges that the Lord grants for His honor and His glory.

The Lord is disclosing in this story that there is coming a glorious future reward for those who faithfully serve Him. When the Lord appears He will pour out lavishly on believers eternal blessings vastly and disproportionately beyond what they can ever imagine. In the words of the apostle Paul, "Things which eye has not seen and ear has not heard, and which have not entered the heart of man, all that God has prepared for those who love Him" (1 Cor. 2:9).

## THE FALSE SERVANTS

**Another came, saying, 'Master, here is your mina, which I kept put away in a handkerchief; for I was afraid of you, because you are an exacting man; you take up what you did not lay down and reap what you did not sow.' He said to him, 'By your own words I will judge you, you worthless slave. Did you know that I am an exacting man, taking up what I did not lay down and reaping what I did not sow? Then why did you not put my money in the bank, and having come, I would have collected it with interest?' Then he said to the bystanders, 'Take the mina away from him and give it to the one who has the ten minas.' And they said to him, 'Master, he has ten minas already.' 'I tell you that to everyone who has, more shall be given, but from the one who does not have, even what he does have shall be taken away.' (19:20–26)**

The third slave was very different from the first two, as the Greek word translated **another** indicates. It is not *allos*, which refers to another of the same kind, but *heteros* (the source of the English word "heterodox"), which describes another of a different kind. Unlike the industrious first two slaves, this lazy, indifferent slave took the **mina** the master had entrusted to him, and **kept** it **put away in a handkerchief.** Not only was that an abysmal waste of opportunity to use the master's money for profit, it also put it at risk of being stolen (valuable items were usually buried; cf. Matt. 13:44). He was careless, lazy, and thoughtless, and had no desire to honor or please his master. Instead of being motivated by love, he was driven by fear, and sought to defend himself by shifting the blame to the king. By saying to him, **"I was afraid of you, because you are an exacting** (Gk. *austēros*, from which the English word "austere" derives) **man,"** this wretched slave accused the king of being severe, harsh, strict, and unfair. Taking his blame-shifting one step further, he went on to say, **"You take up what you did not lay down and reap what you did not sow."** Shockingly, he in effect accused his master of being a thief; of stealing crops that he did not plant.

This man had no love or respect for his master, and no real relationship with him. Like a typical legalist, he was merely putting on an outward show. He served him for the money, hoping to get rich from the nobleman turned king.

The king's stern rebuke unmasked the slave's true character. **"By your own words I will judge you, you worthless slave. Did you know that I am an exacting man, taking up what I did not lay down and reaping what I did not sow?"** That he represents false believers is obvious, since Jesus would never refer to any of His beloved children as a **worthless slave.** Continuing his rebuke, the king demanded, **"Then why did you not put my money in the bank** (i.e., take it to the moneylenders), **and having come, I would have collected it with interest?"** If he had any respect for the king, he would have at least invested for minimal gain. The truth is that the wicked slave was indifferent; he had no relationship with the king and did not care about him or his interests. This hypocrite stashed away the money with which he had been entrusted and went on with his own personal interests.

Then the king pronounced judgment on the worthless slave.

Turning to **the bystanders** he commanded them, **"Take the mina away from him and give it to the one who has the ten minas."** Surprised by the king's decision **they said to him, "Master, he has ten minas already."** But illustrating the unceasing, lavish, undiminished nature of God's grace, he declared, **"I tell you that to everyone who has, more shall be given."** On the other hand, the king pronounced concerning the worthless slave, **"From the one who does not have, even what he does have shall be taken away."** He was stripped of every pretense, opportunity, privilege, and position to which he might have aspired.

The worthless slave represents the people who claim to be followers of Christ, are involved with the church, surrounded by the privileges and truth of the gospel, and even make a profession of faith. Yet in reality, they serve the Lord for their own selfish purposes and goals, and have no relationship with Him. Despite their claims, they will hear from Christ's own mouth the shocking, frightening pronouncement of their eternal doom: "I never knew you; depart from Me, you who practice lawlessness" (Matt. 7:23; cf. 25:12; Luke 13:27).

The lesson of the story is clear. There will be rewards for Christ's faithful followers, rejection for the false followers, and retribution for His foes. Every person falls into one of those three categories. The faithful followers are rewarded and lavished with spiritual graces and privileges forever. The day will come when the false followers will be unmasked and all their flimsy pretenses will be unveiled and discounted. The Lord will reject them, and sentence them to perish eternally with His enemies.

# Jesus' Humble Coronation (Luke 19:28–44)

# 9

After He had said these things, He was going on ahead, going up to Jerusalem. When He approached Bethphage and Bethany, near the mount that is called Olivet, He sent two of the disciples, saying, "Go into the village ahead of you; there, as you enter, you will find a colt tied on which no one yet has ever sat; untie it and bring it here. If anyone asks you, 'Why are you untying it?' you shall say, 'The Lord has need of it.'" So those who were sent went away and found it just as He had told them. As they were untying the colt, its owners said to them, "Why are you untying the colt?" They said, "The Lord has need of it." They brought it to Jesus, and they threw their coats on the colt and put Jesus on it. As He was going, they were spreading their coats on the road. As soon as He was approaching, near the descent of the Mount of Olives, the whole crowd of the disciples began to praise God joyfully with a loud voice for all the miracles which they had seen, shouting: "Blessed is the King who comes in the name of the Lord; Peace in heaven and glory in the highest!" Some of the Pharisees

**in the crowd said to Him, "Teacher, rebuke Your disciples." But Jesus answered, "I tell you, if these become silent, the stones will cry out!" When He approached Jerusalem, He saw the city and wept over it, saying, "If you had known in this day, even you, the things which make for peace! But now they have been hidden from your eyes. For the days will come upon you when your enemies will throw up a barricade against you, and surround you and hem you in on every side, and they will level you to the ground and your children within you, and they will not leave in you one stone upon another, because you did not recognize the time of your visitation." (19:28–44)**

On June 28, 1838, the coronation of Queen Victoria took place at Westminster Abbey, with nearly four hundred thousand visitors flocking to London to witness this huge event. A newspaper account from the time described the spectacular scene:

> At this part of the line the crowd was excessive, the dark and heaving masses there, with outstretched necks and full of eager expectation, waited the approach of the procession. At about half-past ten it reached the corner of this street in the precise order in which it left the Palace. The appearance of the resident and foreign ambassadors, in their splendid carriages and gorgeous uniforms, many of which were picturesque and elegant, excited much admiration, and a running comment on the policies of their respective governments was freely indulged in by many who had scarcely indulged in anything else. The good humour of the crowd, however, found a congenial subject in the approach of the Duchess of Kent and attendants, and her Royal Highness was greeted with very unequivocal demonstrations of attachment and respect, and which was cordially transferred to several other members of the Royal Family—particularly the Duke of Sussex, who paid the penalty of his popularity by the warm and affectionate recognition of his people. Her majesty's carriages and attendants, in twelve carriages, each drawn by six beautiful bays, were the subject of much admiration. The Queen's bargemaster, followed by her Majesty's forty-eight watermen, excited much attention; their dresses were novel and pleasing. Except the general admiration bestowed indiscriminately on all that formed the procession, many composing it passed without particular notice or comment, until her Majesty's state carriage approached, this was the signal for the kindliest and most affectionate demonstrations, and a shout echoed and re-echoed along St. James's street and Pall-Mall—deep, fervent—and enthusiastic, was sent up from

immense assemblage. Many an eye gazed upon her with mute and affectionate regard—many a tongue bid God bless as she gracefully bent forward in her splendid state carriage and acknowledged these and many touching demonstrations of loyalty and considerate affection. The windows and balconies were alive with a splendid assemblage of beauty and loveliness, even the roofs had their occupants, and scarfs, handkerchiefs, and hats were waved as her Majesty passed, without intermission—every balcony was a parterre—every window was a bouquet of loveliness and beauty. Her Majesty was visibly affected with these marks of devotion and attachment on the part of the people so warmly and affectionately expressed, and more than once turned to the Duchess of Sutherland to conceal or express her emotions. The police were tolerant and good-humoured, and treated the "pressure from without" with much forbearance. On the top of St. James's Palace, every disposable inch of which was occupied, parties were placed and cheered her Majesty with great cordiality and warmth. On her Majesty's arrival at the Ordnance Office, which looked not unlike a fortress, the band of the Royal Artillery, which had been occasionally enlivening the scene with appropriate airs in the balcony struck up the national anthem, and vivid demonstrations of loyalty and attachment were studiously displayed from the balconies, and windows, from which nods and becks and wreathed smiles were interchanged with some friends in the line of procession. Notwithstanding the vast masses that pressed on all sides, deepening and accumulating as the procession advanced, the utmost order and regularity was observed every where and every individual in that vast assemblage, owing to the firmness and excellent demeanour of the police, was enabled to see everything and everybody with the utmost ease. (A copy of this article may be viewed at http://www.royal.gov.uk/The%20Royal%20Collection%20and%20other %20collections/TheRoyalArchives/QueenVictoriaeducationproject/ QueenVictoriasCoronation1838.aspx)

In contrast to the ornate carriage in which the Queen of the United Kingdom of Great Britain and Ireland rode to her coronation, the King of kings and Lord of lords rode to His coronation "humble, and mounted on a donkey, even on a colt, the foal of a donkey" (Zech. 9:9). Jesus' humble coronation was much like His humble birth. Both were attended by lowly people and ignored by the nobility.

But in spite of His simple coronation, Jesus was nonetheless God's true King (Ps. 2:6). Of all the coronations of earthly rulers that have ever been held, no monarch has come close to deserving the honor that Jesus did. No earthly sovereign is more than a candle compared to the infinite light of His majestic glory. Even this most humble of coronations cannot hide that glory; rather, it displays it.

Earlier, Jesus had just passed through Jericho, where He healed two blind men (18:35–43) and brought salvation to the chief tax collector, Zaccheus (19:1–10). Those startling events caused the already large crowd accompanying Him to Jerusalem for the Passover celebration to swell. Leaving Jericho, Jesus began the arduous ascent of thirty-five hundred feet to Jerusalem (a six to eight hour walk to cover the straight-line distance of fifteen miles) in the midst of this mass of expectant Jews. They were surely buzzing with the hope that He would display messianic power, judge Israel's enemies, and establish the glorious kingdom promised by the Old Testament.

The truth, however, is that Jesus was walking to His death. He was headed to the cross to offer His life as a ransoming, redeeming, reconciling sacrifice. Christ the sinless one had come to bear the punishment for the sins of His elect and thus to satisfy divine law, divine righteousness, and divine wrath. He came to die and then to rise from the dead, not only conquering sin, but also conquering the grave for all who believe in Him (John 11:25). Jesus had come the first time to die to purchase those for whom He would come the second time to reign with.

Up to this point, the Lord had never allowed an open, public declaration that He was the Messiah. In fact, when people sought to do that, He stopped them (cf. Matt. 16:20; John 6:14–15). From the outset of His ministry the religious leaders were intimidated by Jesus and quickly came to hate Him. He knew that any kind of open popular acclaim would escalate the leaders' animosity toward Him and bring about His death prematurely. At this Passover, however, the divinely determined time had come for Him to die, so He accepted such a massive display of popular acclaim (by some estimates, there were one to two million people in Jerusalem and the vicinity for the Passover celebration, and some surmise as many as one hundred thousand may have been involved in the triumphal entry) that the leaders of Israel could not wait any longer to eliminate Him—especially with the possibility that Jesus would lead the crowd in a rebellion against the Roman forces and they would all lose their power and position (John 11:47–50).

Their plan was to seize Jesus and execute Him after the Passover, when the massive crowds had dispersed. They were afraid doing so dur-

ing the festival might trigger a riot (Matt. 26:3–5). But despite His enemies' plan, Jesus would die only at the precise time predetermined by
God (cf. John 10:17–18; 19:10–11; Acts 2:23; 4:27–28; Gal. 4:4–5). Appropri-
ately, God's Lamb would be sacrificed on the same day that the people's
Passover lambs were being sacrificed, because He is "Christ our
Passover" sacrifice (1 Cor. 5:7). The animal slaughter pictured the death of
the one true and only sacrifice for sin (Heb. 7:27; 9:26; 10:12).

Christ's perfect timing also fulfilled one of the most precise Old
Testament prophecies, Daniel's prophecy of the seventy weeks (Dan.
9:24–26):

> The exact day that the Lord chose to enter Jerusalem fulfilled one of
> the most remarkable prophecies of the Old Testament, Daniel's prophe-
> cy of the seventy weeks (Dan. 9:24–26). Through Daniel, the Lord pre-
> dicted that the time from Artaxerxes's decree ordering the rebuilding
> of the Temple (in 445 B.C.) until the coming of the Messiah would be
> "seven weeks and sixty-two weeks" (Dan. 9:25; cf. Neh. 2:6), that is, 69
> weeks total. The literal translation is "seven sevens and sixty-two sev-
> ens," seven being a common designation for a week. In the context of
> the passage, the idea is 69 weeks of years, or 69 times 7 years, which
> comes to a total of 483 Jewish years (which consisted of 360 days each
> as was common in the ancient world). Several different systems of reck-
> oning have endeavored to determine the chronology of the 483 years
> after Artaxerxes's decree, putting the date at either A.D. 30, 32, or 33,
> depending on the actual decree date and the complex calculations
> through those years. Of these explanations, the most detailed are Sir
> Robert Anderson's [book] *The Coming Prince* and Harold Hoehner's
> [book] *Chronological Aspects of the Life of Christ*. Based on all of the
> historical data, it is best to understand the triumphal entry as taking
> place on 9 Nisan, A.D. 30. But even the other dates offered by these
> authors (A.D. 32 or 33), leave one thing remaining undeniably clear:
> whatever may be the precise chronology, Jesus Christ is the only possi-
> ble fulfillment of Daniel's prophetic timetable. (John MacArthur, *John
> 12–21*, The MacArthur New Testament Commentary [Chicago: Moody,
> 2008], 14–15)

Though Jesus knew exactly what He was doing and precisely
where it fit into God's timetable, this was still an experience of indescrib-
able horror, as He contemplated facing not only death, but also the
Father's judgment for sin. Anticipation of that judgment caused Him to
pray in Gethsemane, "Father, if You are willing, remove this cup from Me;
yet not My will, but Yours be done" (Luke 22:42). That prayer did not

reflect any unwillingness on Jesus' part to do God's will, but rather reveals that as a perfectly righteous person, He was repulsed by the reality of sin-bearing.

His arrival at Jerusalem marked the end of the Lord's journey, not just this final journey to Jerusalem that began in Luke 9:51, but of His life's journey from Bethlehem to this moment. Here He faced His greatest challenge and completed the salvation work for which He had come. The people, with no thought of Messiah as a sacrifice for sin (in spite of Isaiah 53), were still focused on the earthly kingdom they fervently hoped He would establish. But there could not be exalted glory until there was shame; there could not be a kingdom until there was a cross; there would be no royal crown without a thorny crown. That would happen at the end of the Passion Week.

The Messiah's dramatic triumphal entry into Jerusalem early in the week unfolds in three scenes: the preparation, the adoration, and the condemnation.

### THE PREPARATION

**After He had said these things, He was going on ahead, going up to Jerusalem. When He approached Bethphage and Bethany, near the mount that is called Olivet, He sent two of the disciples, saying, "Go into the village ahead of you; there, as you enter, you will find a colt tied on which no one yet has ever sat; untie it and bring it here. If anyone asks you, 'Why are you untying it?' you shall say, 'The Lord has need of it.'" So those who were sent went away and found it just as He had told them. As they were untying the colt, its owners said to them, "Why are you untying the colt?" They said, "The Lord has need of it." They brought it to Jesus, and they threw their coats on the colt and put Jesus on it.** (19:28–35)

The phrase **these things** refers to the parable the Lord had told in vv. 11–27. After that instruction, Jesus continued **on ahead** up the road leading from Jericho **up to Jerusalem.** About two miles (John 11:18) east of Jerusalem were the small villages of **Bethphage and Bethany,**

**near the mount that is called Olivet** (the Mount of Olives).When He visited Jerusalem, Jesus had often stayed in **Bethany,** the hometown of Mary, Martha, and Lazarus (John 11:1). The Lord arrived at **Bethany** on the preceding Saturday with Passover coming six days later on Thursday evening through Friday sunset (John 12:1). On the next day, Sunday, Jesus attended a dinner in His honor at the home of Simon the leper (Matt. 26:6–13). Also on that day a "large crowd of the Jews then learned that He was there; and they came, not for Jesus' sake only, but that they might also see Lazarus, whom He raised from the dead" (John 12:9).

His entry into Jerusalem took place the following day (John 12:12), Monday of Passion Week, not on "Palm" Sunday as Christians have traditionally believed. This chronology eliminates the problem of the Gospels having no record of Jesus' activities on Wednesday, which would be the case if the triumphal entry were on Sunday. Since the events of every other day are so carefully accounted for, it would be difficult to explain why there was a day omitted in the account of the most momentous week of Christ's life.

Further evidence that the triumphal entry was on Monday comes from the Law's requirement that the Passover lambs be selected on the tenth day of the first month (Nisan) and sacrificed on the fourteenth day (Ex. 12:2–6). In the year our Lord was crucified, the tenth of Nisan fell on Monday of Passover week. When He entered Jerusalem on that day, Jesus was fulfilling the role as the Father's chosen Lamb (John 1:29, 36) in much the same way the Jewish people chose their Passover lambs. Completing the parallel, Christ was killed on Friday, the fourteenth day of Nisan, with all the thousands of other lambs; but as the one true sacrifice for sin.

The momentous entry of the Messiah was set in motion when Jesus **sent two of the disciples** (possibly Peter and John; cf. Luke 22:8) **saying, "Go into the village ahead of you"** (probably Bethphage). The details of what the two would find there provide an undeniable illustration of the Lord's omniscience (cf. John 1:47–48; 2:25). First, He told them that they would **find a** donkey (John 12:14; cf. Zech. 9:9) **colt** (and its mother; Matt. 21:2) **tied.** Jesus had not been to Bethphage, nor had He sent anyone to arrange for the colt to be available. The detail that the colt was one **which no one** had ever ridden gives further evidence of His omniscience, as does His knowledge that the disciples would be asked, **"Why are you untying it?"**

Just as the Lord had omnisciently foreseen, as the disciples **were untying the colt, its** surprised **owners** asked the obvious question: **"Why are you untying the colt?"** As Jesus had instructed them, they replied. **"The Lord has need of it."** As He also foresaw, when "they spoke to them just as Jesus had told them, [the owners] gave them permission" (Mark 11:6) to take the colt. No further explanation was necessary, since it was widely known that He who had raised Lazarus from the dead and given sight to two blind men in Jericho was staying in Bethany. Having **brought it to Jesus . . . they threw their coats on the colt** to provide a makeshift saddle and **put Jesus on it.**

Though David occasionally rode a mule (cf. 1 Kings 1:38, 44), as Solomon did to his coronation (1 Kings 1:32–40), Jesus was not merely identifying with Davidic tradition. He was specifically fulfilling Old Testament messianic prophecy. According to Matthew 21:4–5, "This took place to fulfill what was spoken through the prophet: 'Say to the daughter of Zion, "Behold your king is coming to you, gentle, and mounted on a donkey, even on a colt, the foal of a beast of burden."'"

Five hundred years before the crowd hailed Him as king, Zechariah (9:9; cf. Isa. 62:11) predicted that Jesus would ride a donkey's colt. He would not come the first time as the conquering hero riding on a white horse; that will happen when He comes again in glory to judge and to reign as King of kings (Rev. 19, 20). The first time He came in humility to give His life a ransom for sinners (Mark 10:45). He did not come in grandeur, but in meekness; not to slay but to save. His coming in incarnation is the time of His humiliation; His second coming in exaltation is the time of His glorification.

### The Adoration

**As He was going, they were spreading their coats on the road. As soon as He was approaching, near the descent of the Mount of Olives, the whole crowd of the disciples began to praise God joyfully with a loud voice for all the miracles which they had seen,**

**shouting: "Blessed is the King who comes in the name of the Lord; Peace in heaven and glory in the highest!"** (19:36–38)

When He was still approaching the city, adoration of Jesus began as the people were **spreading their coats on the road** ahead of Him. By doing so they were expressing their eager submission to Him (cf. 2 Kings 9:13), symbolically placing themselves under His feet as their king. His acceptance of the delirious crowd's adoration and worship was appropriate, for as the Son of God, He was worthy of all praise.

The disciples did not fully grasp the significance of what was happening. As John would later write, "These things His disciples did not understand at the first; but when Jesus was glorified, then they remembered that these things were written of Him, and that they had done these things to Him" (John 12:16).

The little donkey bearing Jesus picked its way through the piles of coats on the road toward the crest, from where Jerusalem would come in view. When the **crowd** saw that Jesus **was approaching, near the descent of the Mount of Olives,** the **disciples,** their fervor inflamed by the sight of the great city, **began to praise God joyfully with a loud voice for all the miracles which they had seen.** Those miracles included the raising of Lazarus and the healing of the two blind men at Jericho, as well as the rest of the miracles Jesus had performed throughout His ministry.

Other people came out from Jerusalem to meet Jesus and those who accompanied Him from Bethany (John 12:12–13). The two great tides of people joined to make one huge throng, some behind Jesus, others in front of Him (Matt. 21:9). While some threw their coats in front of the Lord, others cut palm branches and threw them on the road. Palm branches symbolized victory, joy, and celebration. The apocryphal book of First Maccabees records that when the Jews during the intertestamental period recaptured Jerusalem from the Syrians they "entered it with praise and palm branches" (1 Macc. 13:51; cf. 2 Macc. 10:7). The crowd's messianic hopes reached an apogee and the people began **shouting, "Blessed is the King who comes in the name of the Lord"** (cf. Ps. 118:26), thus acknowledging that Jesus was the promised Messiah **King** who came with the full authority of God. Matthew notes that the crowd also shouted, "Hosanna to the Son of David.... Hosanna in the highest!" (21:9). "Hosanna" means "save now," while "Son of David" is a title for the Messiah (Matt. 12:23; Mark 12:35). The crowd was not pleading for salvation from sin, but from the oppression of Rome and for the establishment of the promises related to Messiah's reign. That hope led them to cry, "Blessed is the coming kingdom of our father David" (Mark 11:10), which they fully expected to appear. They also shouted, **"Peace in heaven and glory in the highest!"** because they could not believe that God's heart could be at peace as long as Jerusalem was not. Not until Messiah came and brought peace and glory to Jerusalem, they believed, could there ever be **peace in heaven and glory in the highest.** It should be noted again that they have no idea of Messiah as the suffering sacrifice for sin as that yet future generation of Jews will who look on the One they pierced, mourn for Him (Zech. 12:10) and confess the very words of Isaiah 53:

> Who has believed our message? And to whom has the arm of the Lord been revealed? For He grew up before Him like a tender shoot, and like a root out of parched ground; He has no stately form or majesty that we should look upon Him, nor appearance that we should be attracted to Him. He was despised and forsaken of men, a man of sorrows and acquainted with grief; and like one from whom men hide their face He was despised, and we did not esteem Him. Surely our griefs He Himself bore, and our sorrows He carried; yet we ourselves esteemed Him stricken, smitten of God, and afflicted. But He was pierced through for our transgressions, He was crushed for our iniquities; the chastening for our well-being fell upon Him, and by His scourging we are healed. All of us like sheep have gone astray, each of us has turned to his own way; But the Lord has caused the iniquity of us all to fall on Him. He was oppressed and He was afflicted, yet He did not open His mouth; like a lamb that is led to slaughter, and like a sheep that is silent before its shearers, so He did not open His mouth. By oppression and judgment He was taken away; and as for His generation, who considered that He was cut off out of the land of the living for the transgression of my people, to whom the stroke was due? His grave was assigned with wicked men, yet He was with a rich man in His death, because He had done no violence, nor was there any deceit in His mouth. But the Lord was pleased to crush Him, putting Him to grief; if He would render Himself as a guilt offering, He will see His offspring, He will prolong His days, and the good pleasure of the Lord will prosper in His hand. As a result of the anguish of His soul, He will see it and be satisfied. (1–11a)

## THE CONDEMNATION

**Some of the Pharisees in the crowd said to Him, "Teacher, rebuke Your disciples." But Jesus answered, "I tell you, if these become silent, the stones will cry out!" When He approached Jerusalem, He saw the city and wept over it, saying, "If you had known in this day, even you, the things which make for peace! But now they have been hidden from your eyes. For the days will come upon you when your enemies will throw up a barricade against you, and surround you and hem you in on every side, and they will level you to the ground and your children within you, and they will not leave in you one stone upon another, because you did not recognize the time of your visitation." (19:39–44)**

Not everyone shared in the joyous excitement, however. Outraged at the crowd's enthusiastic adulation and adoration of Jesus and His acceptance of it, **some of the Pharisees in the crowd,** who considered it all blasphemy, **said to Him, "Teacher, rebuke Your disciples."** Even collectively they knew they were powerless to stop the outpouring of enthusiasm from the huge crowd, so they appealed to Jesus to stop it. It is fitting that in this final mention in Luke of the Pharisees, they manifested the same hostility toward the Lord that had marked them throughout His ministry. His reply to the exasperated Pharisees' request for Jesus to quiet and disperse the crowd marks the dramatic turning point of the event.

Jesus' response reveals the striking difference between the people's expectation of Him and His condemnation of them. The contrast between what the people anticipated and what they would receive is extreme; the contrast between the attitude of the people, one of joy, and the attitude of Jesus, one of sorrow, could not be more opposite. The scene moves from joy to horror. The crowd speaks of peace, He speaks of destruction; they pronounce on Him glory, He pronounces on them doom. The Lord's condemnation manifests His deity both in His authority to pronounce judgment (John 5:22), and in His omniscient knowledge of the precise details of that future judgment. The full judgment on the world of sinners will come at His return in glory, but unbelieving Israel will have a preview very soon.

The statement **I tell you** emphasizes the serious nature of what Jesus was about to say to the Pharisees. The phrase **if these become silent** should be understood not as something that may possibly happen, but as something that will inevitably happen. After the events of Monday, Jesus would receive no more accolades from the crowd. Startlingly, the next time the crowd would be heard from is on Friday, when they would scream for Jesus to be crucified (Luke 23:18–23). Though many Jews have come to salvation in Him and become part of His redeemed church, the nation of Israel offers no praise to Jesus. Their silence is unbroken for two thousand years.

Jesus was saying in effect "if these become silent—and they will —at that point **the stones will cry out!" Cry out** translates the future tense form of the verb *krazō*, which could also be translated "scream." The stones will not cry out in joyful praise to God, but in affirmation of God's judgment on Israel's wickedness (cf. Hab. 2:11–12). That inevitable prospect filled the Lord with a deep sense of sorrow, so **when He approached Jerusalem, He saw the city and wept over it.** The word translated **wept** is the strongest word in the Greek language for weeping. It denotes Jesus' agonized sobbing over their superficiality, hypocrisy, shallowness, and rejection of Him—and the inevitable divine wrath that would follow. The **peace** of which the Lord spoke was not political peace with enemies, or social peace in Israel, but peace with God. The **things** that **make for** that **peace** are repentance, faith in Christ, and believing the message of salvation that He had preached throughout His ministry. **This day** refers not to that Monday, but to the entire time of His presence among them.

Unbelief had blinded them all through His ministry. Most of the people chose to be hard-hearted, self-righteous rejecters of Christ and rebuffed all of His invitations, thereby forfeiting peace with God. Despite the crowd's superficial and short-lived celebration, Jesus, as He had done earlier (Luke 13:34–35), pronounced judgment on them. The truth (Luke 8:10) would be **hidden** from their **eyes.** Willful human blindness would become judicial divine blindness. Again, Israel as a nation will not believe until they "look on [the one] whom they have pierced; and they ... mourn for Him, as one mourns for an only son, and they ... weep bitterly over Him like the bitter weeping over a firstborn" (Zech. 12:10). Then comes the grace of national salvation (Zech. 13:1).

The phrase **the days will come upon you** is an Old Testament expression of coming judgment (cf. Isa. 39:6; Hos. 9:7; Amos 4:2). The judgment of which Jesus spoke would fall four decades later in A.D. 70 when the Roman military crushed the Jewish revolt and destroyed Jerusalem. Revealing His omniscience, the Lord gave five specific features of that judgment: Israel's **enemies** (the Romans) would **throw up a barricade against** Jerusalem, they would **surround** the city, they would **hem** it **in on every side,** they would **level** it **to the ground,** along with its inhabitants, and they would **not leave in** it **one stone upon another.** This would include the temple (Luke 21:6) and with it their religious system (see the discussion of 21:5–7 in chapter 17 of this volume). Those stones lying in the rubble would be the ones that cried out in judgment on the unbelieving nation. All that horrific judgment would come about because Israel refused to **recognize the time of** her **visitation,** when the Lord Jesus Christ, God incarnate, offered them salvation and redemption. "He was in the world, and the world was made through Him, [but] the world did not know Him. He came to His own, and those who were His own did not receive Him" (John 1:10–11).

# The King Confronts Corruption (Luke 19:45–48)

## 10

**Jesus entered the temple and began to drive out those who were selling, saying to them, "It is written, 'And My house shall be a house of prayer,' but you have made it a robbers' den." And He was teaching daily in the temple; but the chief priests and the scribes and the leading men among the people were trying to destroy Him, and they could not find anything that they might do, for all the people were hanging on to every word He said.** (19:45–48)

The event described in this brief, but significant, section of Luke's gospel took place on Tuesday of Passion Week, the final week of our Lord's earthly life. The day before had seen the triumphal entry, Christ's humble coronation when He presented Himself as Israel's true king. The massive throng of people (perhaps as many as one hundred thousand) that had accompanied Jesus hailed Him as the Messiah, the heir to the throne of David's kingdom. After entering Jerusalem through the eastern gate, the celebration ended at the temple, which was just inside the eastern gate. There, "after looking around at everything, He left for Bethany with the twelve, since it was already late" (Mark 11:11).

Bethany, where Jesus most likely stayed in the home of Mary, Martha, and Lazarus, was for Him a place of comfort, love, and much-needed rest. He had had a long, arduous day on Monday, dealing with the enormous crowd at the triumphal entry. Jesus had also had a long day on Sunday, ministering to those who visited Him in Bethany, all following that long, arduous walk from Jericho.

Lodging was a significant problem in Jerusalem and its environs during the Passover celebration. Some calculate that as many as two million Jews would be in and around Jerusalem during that time. There were inns, but they filled up very rapidly, probably mostly with people well-known to the innkeepers, if not their own friends and relatives. The Essenes, Zealots, Pharisees, Sadducees, and other religious groups would accommodate visitors who were a part of their groups. There were probably even a few true believers in Jesus, who housed other believers visiting from Galilee. Foreign synagogues (cf. Acts 6:9) ran hospices for their countrymen who were visiting Jerusalem on this important occasion. There were a number of Jews who were wealthy enough to live somewhere else in Israel, but also own a home in Jerusalem. They would stay in their homes in Jerusalem for Passover and provide housing for friends and guests. Wealthy families who owned great estates in and around Jerusalem could house a number of people.

But when all of that housing was exhausted, there were still masses of people who needed a place to stay. The solution was that Jerusalem became a tent city, with tents erected everywhere around the perimeter of the city, extending the two miles to Bethany, as well as south toward Bethlehem, and in every other direction. Some people pitched their tents near the temple. Although they were forbidden to stay inside the temple grounds, they stayed as close as they could. The temple also had adjacent buildings where places that people could stay were rented out. Jewish law required that those celebrating Passover had to spend at least the night before in Jerusalem. Since that had become impossible because the crowds were too large, during Passover the official boundaries of Jerusalem were extended to encompass the tent cities that surrounded it. In summary, the region was jammed with people beyond its capacity. It was good that Jesus and His disciples had friends in Bethany with a home large enough to accommodate them.

What Jesus saw in the temple grounds in the twilight of Monday evening set the stage for the dramatic confrontation that would take place on Tuesday in an amazing event that would display His kingly credentials. What He did and the response that it generated pointed unmistakably to Him as the Messiah, God's true king and His eternal Son. Five realities in this passage show that Jesus is indeed God's king: He was on a divine mission, He exercised divine authority, He demonstrated a commitment to divine Scripture, He manifested divine compassion, and He fulfilled divine purpose.

## He Was on a Divine Mission

### Jesus entered the temple (19:45a)

What **Jesus** did on that Tuesday of Passion Week was shocking. The crowds that accompanied Him on the triumphal entry fervently hoped that He would be the earthly messiah they were eagerly anticipating. Based on that, they might have expected Jesus to assault the Roman garrison at Fort Antonia, overlooking the temple, or to attack the house of Pilate, the pathetic Roman governor of Judea. To confront the Roman oppressors is what they had wanted Him to do throughout His ministry. John 6:14–15 records that "when the people saw the sign which He had performed, they said, 'This is truly the Prophet who is to come into the world.' So Jesus, perceiving that they were intending to come and take Him by force to make Him king, withdrew again to the mountain by Himself alone."

But instead of attacking the pagan, idolatrous, occupying Romans, Jesus assaulted the doings at temple—the heart of Judaism, the soul of the nation. By doing so, He attacked the respected, elevated, religious leaders of Israel, who claimed to represent God. The Lord was declaring that He was not concerned with Israel's relationship to Rome, but with the nation's relationship to God. The issue that moved Him to action was not Roman oppression, but Jewish religious corruption. That priority had led Him to make such an assault on the temple at the very outset of His ministry:

> The Passover of the Jews was near, and Jesus went up to Jerusalem. And He found in the temple those who were selling oxen and sheep and doves, and the money changers seated at their tables. And He made a scourge of cords, and drove them all out of the temple, with the sheep and the oxen; and He poured out the coins of the money changers and overturned their tables; and to those who were selling the doves He said, "Take these things away; stop making My Father's house a place of business." His disciples remembered that it was written, "Zeal for Your house will consume me." (John 2:13–17)

Again, on this occasion three years later, His earthly ministry ended with Him displaying holy fury on the corrupt temple and its apostate religion. Christ's entire ministry focused on spiritual matters. His concern was always that the true God be worshiped in the true manner as prescribed in His Word. He said to a Samaritan woman, "An hour is coming, and now is, when the true worshipers will worship the Father in spirit and truth; for such people the Father seeks to be His worshipers. God is spirit, and those who worship Him must worship in spirit and truth" (John 4:23–24). Jesus understood that all was not as it should be socially, economically, politically, and in terms of justice and equity. But He also knew that the only way to remedy those injustices was to exchange hypocrisy and works-righteousness for the true relationship with God. Therefore His ministry always focused on the kingdom of God and true worship of Him.

*Hieros* (temple) is the general term for the temple grounds as a whole, the vast complex that was able to accommodate thousands of worshipers. Within this area, surrounded by an outer wall, were several inner courts, progressively smaller, with the innermost being the Holy of Holies and the Holy Place, which were designated by a different word for temple (*naos*). The outer court was the Court of the Gentiles, so named because Gentiles were forbidden to go any further on pain of death. Inside the Court of the Gentiles was the Court of the Women, which was as far as women were permitted to go. That court was entered by a gate known as the Beautiful Gate, which was a popular place for beggars (Acts 3:10). Men could enter the next court, the Court of the Israelites, through Nicanor's Gate, made of Corinthian bronze and so massive that it took twenty men to open and close it. From the Court of the Israelites the assembled worshipers could look through the doorway into the next courtyard, the Court of the Priests. Although they could not enter, they could watch the priests offering incense and sacrificing animals. In the rear of the Court of the Priests was the temple (*naos*) itself; that is, the Holy Place and then the Holy of Holies. The whole large complex, including all the courts, comprised the temple (*hieros*) of God.

What was happening in the Court of the Gentiles was emblematic of the corruption that made the Lord righteously angry. It had essentially been turned into a commerce center, where hundreds of thousands of animals and the other items needed for the sacrifices were sold. Theoretically, people could bring their own animals to be sacrificed. However, those animals had to first be approved by the priests. They had a vested interest in rejecting them, to boost the sales of animals from which the high priests Annas and Caiaphas profited (see below). Money changers had also set up shop there. They provided a needed service. The temple tax could only be paid using Jewish or Tyrian coins, so foreigners had to exchange their money for acceptable coinage. But because they had a monopoly, the money changers charged exorbitant fees for their services (as high as 12.5% [F. F. Bruce, *The Gospel of John* (Grand Rapids: Eerdmans, 1983), 74]).

The merchandising in the Court of the Gentiles had become known as the Bazaar of Annas, after the greedy high priest before whom Jesus would be tried first after His arrest in Gethsemane (John 18:13–23). Although he was no longer the actual high priest, Annas still retained the title and wielded tremendous power and influence behind the scenes. Along with his son-in-law Caiaphas, the current high priest, they ran the temple's business operations, becoming extremely wealthy in the process. They sold franchises to the merchants for exorbitant prices and then skimmed off a huge percentage of the profits that the shop owners made.

All of this had combined to turn the temple of God into a noisy, smelly stockyard. The worshipful atmosphere that was appropriate for the temple, the symbol of God's presence, was missing. Instead of being a place of sacred reverence and adoration, it had become a cacophony of abusive commerce and extortion. The sound of praise and prayers had been replaced by the bawling of oxen, the bleating of sheep, the cooing of doves, and the loud haggling of merchants and their customers.

Jesus, who was not only Lord of the Sabbath (Luke 6:5), but also Lord of the temple, was repulsed by the scene. It was to Israel's hypocritical religion, so vividly portrayed by what He saw, smelled, and heard, that He turned His attention. His divine mission was to assault false worship of the true God; to defend God and His house against those who were blasphemously defiling it.

## HE EXERCISED DIVINE AUTHORITY

**and began to drive out those who were selling,** (19:45*b*)

This first official act of the recognized king was a powerful display of Christ's divine authority. He **began to drive out those who were selling,** singlehandedly shutting down the entire corrupt business operation polluting His Father's house (cf. Luke 2:49; John 2:16). Pandemonium ensued as Jesus physically threw the merchants out, overturning the money changers' tables and sending their coins rolling on the ground. He also yanked the seats out from under the dove sellers (Matt. 21:12) and sent them scrambling out of the temple. Mark 11:16 notes that He also halted the flow of goods being transported through the temple. This was an astonishing display of the force and strength of Jesus, considering the resistance that He must have encountered from the merchants. It reveals in stark clarity that the Lord hates those who pervert worship for their own greed.

## HE DEMONSTRATED A COMMITMENT TO DIVINE SCRIPTURE

**saying to them, "It is written, 'And My house shall be a house of prayer,' but you have made it a robbers' den."** (19:46)

As He evicted the polluting merchants, Jesus was **saying to them, "It is written."** He vindicated His anger by showing its basis in two Old Testament passages. His first quote, **My house shall be a house of prayer,** comes from Isaiah 56:7, "Even those I will bring to My holy mountain and make them joyful in My house of prayer … for My house will be called a house of prayer for all the peoples." The temple was God's house, where people came to commune with and worship Him. Prayer is the essence of worship.

The temple had originally been designed by God to be a place of prayer, a sanctuary of worship, and a place of communion with God (Ps. 65:4), meditation (cf. Ps. 27:4), penitence, confession, and praise, along with the offering of sacrifices. Solomon's prayer at the temple's dedication in 1 Kings 8 expresses that intent, as the following excerpts indicate:

> [Let] …Your eyes … be open toward this house night and day, toward the place of which You have said, "My name shall be there," to listen to the prayer which Your servant shall pray toward this place. (v. 29)

> Listen to the supplication of Your servant and of Your people Israel, when they pray toward this place; hear in heaven Your dwelling place; hear and forgive. (v. 30)

> When Your people Israel are defeated before an enemy, because they have sinned against You, if they turn to You again and confess Your name and pray and make supplication to You in this house, then hear in heaven, and forgive the sin of Your people Israel, and bring them back to the land which You gave to their fathers. (vv. 33–34)

> When the heavens are shut up and there is no rain, because they have sinned against You, and they pray toward this place and confess Your name and turn from their sin when You afflict them, then hear in heaven and forgive the sin of Your servants and of Your people Israel, indeed, teach them the good way in which they should walk. And send rain on Your land, which You have given Your people for an inheritance. (vv. 35–36)

> Whatever prayer or supplication is made by any man or by all Your people Israel, each knowing the affliction of his own heart, and spreading his hands toward this house; then hear in heaven. (vv. 38–39a)

> For they will hear of Your great name and Your mighty hand, and of Your outstretched arm; when he comes and prays toward this house. (v. 42)

> "Let your heart therefore be wholly devoted to the Lord our God, to walk in His statutes and to keep His commandments, as at this day." Now the king and all Israel with him offered sacrifice before the Lord. (vv. 61–62)

Even while making the sacrifices, the greedy priests and merchants had turned it into a circus of blasphemy and **made it a robbers'
den.** The Lord was alluding to Jeremiah 7:11, where God rebuked Israel
for profaning the temple: "'Has this house, which is called by My name,
become a den of robbers in your sight?'" He asked them. "'Behold, I, even
I, have seen it,' declares the Lord." Like the caves where thieves hid, the
temple had become a refuge for robbers, not a sanctuary for worshipers.
Although Jesus' eviction of the robbers was only temporary, the Romans
would completely destroy the temple in A.D. 70. It has never been rebuilt.

## HE MANIFESTED DIVINE COMPASSION

**And He was teaching daily in the temple;** (19:47*a*)

After the opening dramatic demonstration of Christ's holy wrath,
He displayed His compassionate care for souls by **teaching daily in the
temple.** Luke details the content of that teaching in chapters 20 and 21.
Jesus was preaching the gospel, the good news of salvation, forgiveness,
heaven, and eternal life. The desecration of the temple stopped for a few
days, and for a while the Son of God dominated the house of God, teaching there on Tuesday, Wednesday, and Thursday. For one last time the seeking Savior proclaimed the gospel of salvation to a recalcitrant, lost
people.

It is compassionate to preach the gospel; to preach the truth of
God, warn against false leaders, heretics, hypocrites, and coming judgment, and call people to salvation in light of that judgment. But in addition to proclaiming the saving truth to lost sinners, Jesus also
demonstrated His divine compassion by healing the sick. Matthew notes
that "the blind and the lame came to Him in the temple, and He healed
them" (Matt. 21:14). The blind and the lame were often present around
the temple because that is where people went to worship. These beggars
received more than just a few coins, however; they received sight and
motion. The miracles that Jesus performed offer further proof of His deity.

## HE FULFILLED DIVINE PURPOSE

**but the chief priests and the scribes and the leading men among the people were trying to destroy Him, and they could not find anything that they might do, for all the people were hanging on to every word He said.** (19:47b–48)

One might have thought that this glorious display of miracles would seal in the minds of the people that Jesus was truly the Messiah. But the response of the leaders was increased anger, and eventually they turned the crowd against Him. A few days later the people would cry, "Crucify Him, crucify Him!" (Luke 23:21).

The leaders, despite seeing Jesus' miraculous display of compassion, were unmoved in their hatred of Him. Seeing "the children who were shouting in the temple, 'Hosanna to the Son of David,' they became indignant" (Matt. 21:15). In desperation and fear (Mark 11:18), realizing they were losing control of the situation, **the chief priests and the scribes and the leading men among the people were trying to destroy** Jesus.

But that proved, for the moment at least, to be impossible, **for all the people were hanging on to every word He said.** The Greek text literally says that they were hanging on to His lips, a graphic metaphor indicating that they were listening closely to His every word. David Gooding writes concerning their dilemma,

> The temple authorities would have liked to destroy their 'rival' forthwith; but his immense popularity with the people made any immediate attempt at arrest and execution impossible and tactically unwise. To upset the people would have put at risk the very thing for which the battle was to be fought (see 19:47–48). Subtler and more sophisticated tactics would have to be used. (*According to Luke* [Grand Rapids: Eerdmans, 1987], 314–15)

Sadly, in a few days the crowd would turn on Jesus and scream for His blood. After His resurrection, only 120 believers would gather in Judea, with 500 more in Galilee. Jesus was rejected by the nation, and its leaders. But that too fulfilled God's purpose; as Isaiah wrote, "He was despised and forsaken of men, a man of sorrows and acquainted with grief; and like one from whom men hide their face He was despised, and we did not esteem Him" (Isa. 53:3). The Lord Jesus Christ would fulfill God's purpose by dying on Friday as God's chosen sacrificial lamb. As Peter would later proclaim to the Jewish people, "This Man, delivered over by the predetermined plan and foreknowledge of God, you nailed to a cross by the hands of godless men and put Him to death" (Acts 2:23).

# Rejecting the King's Authority (Luke 20:1–8)

# 11

**On one of the days while He was teaching the people in the temple and preaching the gospel, the chief priests and the scribes with the elders confronted Him, and they spoke, saying to Him, "Tell us by what authority You are doing these things, or who is the one who gave You this authority?" Jesus answered and said to them, "I will also ask you a question, and you tell Me: Was the baptism of John from heaven or from men?" They reasoned among themselves, saying, "If we say, 'From heaven,' He will say, 'Why did you not believe him?' But if we say, 'From men,' all the people will stone us to death, for they are convinced that John was a prophet." So they answered that they did not know where it came from. And Jesus said to them, "Nor will I tell you by what authority I do these things." (20:1–8)**

Since this episode ends on the matter of authority, that is a good starting point. In Matthew 28:18 the risen Lord declared, "All authority has been given to Me in heaven and on earth." That reaffirmed His declaration that all things had been placed under His control and rule by the Father (Matt. 11:27; cf. Luke 10:22; John 3:35; 13:3; 17:2; 1 Cor. 15:27; Eph. 1:22; Phil. 2:9–11; Heb. 1:2; 1 Peter 3:22).

Two Greek words translated "authority" in the New Testament reveal the scope of the Lord's dominance. *Dunamis* refers to power or ability; *exousia* to right or privilege. Jesus possesses both aspects of authority infinitely, a clear indication of His deity.

The Lord's authority may be viewed from several perspectives.

First, He possesses authority in Himself. When He spoke, "the crowds were amazed at His teaching; for He was teaching them as one having authority, and not as their scribes," who usually quoted other rabbis as their source of authority (Matt. 7:28–29).

Second, He possesses the authority to forgive sin (Matt. 9:6–8). That direct evidence of His divine nature was not lost on His opponents: "The scribes and the Pharisees began to reason, saying, 'Who is this man who speaks blasphemies? Who can forgive sins, but God alone?'" (Luke 5:21).

Third, He holds authority over the forces of hell. On one occasion when He demonstrated that authority by casting a demon out of a man, "amazement came upon [those who witnessed the miracle], and they began talking with one another saying, 'What is this message? For with authority and power He commands the unclean spirits and they come out'" (Luke 4:36).

Fourth, He has authority to give eternal salvation. "But as many as received Him," the apostle John wrote, "to them He gave the right to become children of God, even to those who believe in His name" (John 1:12).

Fifth, He has authority to judge, since the Father "has given all judgment to the Son" (John 5:22; cf. v. 27).

Finally, He has authority over death and life. In John 10:18 Jesus said, "No one has taken [My life] away from Me, but I lay it down on My own initiative. I have authority to lay it down, and I have authority to take it up again. This commandment I received from My Father," and in Revelation 1:18 He added, "[I am] the living One; and I was dead, and behold, I am alive forevermore, and I have the keys of death and of Hades."

That Jesus presumed to assault the temple operations without regard for the Jewish authorities shocked and outraged them. From their perspective it was bad enough that He physically disrupted their lucrative business operations (see the exposition of 19:45–48 in the previous chapter of this volume). That He did so without first seeking permission from the Jewish hierarchy made the Lord's actions all the more intolerable and outrageous. They were infuriated that He treated the leaders and their religious system with disdain. He ignored the jurisdiction of the Sanhedrin, the high priests, the chief priests, the rabbis, the scribes, and the temple police. He was opposed to the demands of the entire superficial, legalistic system. In fact, He constantly denounced it with His teaching.

The tragic conversation recorded in this passage took place **on one of the days** (Wednesday of Passion Week) when Jesus **was teaching the people in the temple,** which He had attacked with divine, controlled fury on Tuesday. The liars, manipulators, hypocritical false teachers, and greedy merchants He, at least temporarily, evicted. In the vacated space stood Jesus, God's true teacher, to proclaim the truth from heaven and the gospel of salvation.

Jesus would spend most of Wednesday and Thursday teaching (cf. 19:47; 21:37–38); chapter 20 of Luke records what He taught on Wednesday. The content, as always, was **the gospel,** the good news of the kingdom (cf. Matt. 4:23; 9:35; Acts 1:3), as He called the people to repent and believe in Him. Mark 11:27 notes that this particular confrontation took place "as He was walking in the temple."

Christ's teaching likely followed the themes that He had stressed from the start and throughout His ministry—the wretchedness of sin, the folly of hypocritical, legalistic false religion that could not restrain it, and the hopelessness of trying to achieve righteousness by one's own efforts. He may have spoken of the folly of pretentious prayers and superficial religious deeds, performed to be seen by men rather than God (cf. Matt. 6:1–5; 23:5–7). His teaching surely would have included warnings about the inevitability of divine judgment and eternal hell. He would likely have reminded His hearers about the danger of spiritual pride and the need for humility, bankruptcy of spirit, and a broken and contrite heart. He no doubt spoke of the compassionate love of God for sinners, the possibility of forgiveness, peace with God, entrance to His salvation kingdom, eternal life, and the hope of everlasting glory in heaven. He probably reiterated the high cost of following Him in self-denial and for-saking all. His words may have included such themes as the persecution and suffering those who identified with Him would face, the importance of the Word of God, honesty, forgiveness, true riches, faith, grace, and mercy. In short, the Lord's teaching would have touched on everything pertaining to salvation.

This dramatic face-off between Jesus and the Jewish leaders plays out in three scenes: the leaders' confrontation of Jesus, His counter, and His condemnation of them.

THE CONFRONTATION

**the chief priests and the scribes with the elders confronted Him, and they spoke, saying to Him, "Tell us by what authority You are doing these things, or who is the one who gave You this authority?"** (20:1b–2)

Unable to contain their outrage at Him, the Jewish authorities decided once again to make an effort to discredit Jesus. The **chief priests** included the reigning high priest, Caiaphas, and the former high priest Annas, who still wielded heavy influence behind the scenes. Just as American presidents are still referred to by the title "president" after they leave office, so also Annas was still referred to as the high priest. In addition, the **chief priests** included the captain of the temple, who assisted the high priest, and other high-ranking priests. The **scribes,** the mostly Pharisaic theologians who interpreted and taught the law of Moses and the rabbinic tradition, were in the group, along with the **elders.** Essentially this assembly was from the Sanhedrin, the governing body of Judaism. The three groups are frequently mentioned together (cf. Luke 9:22; 22:66; Matt. 27:41; Mark 14:43; 15:1). Though they disagreed on other matters, these diverse lots were united in their determination to execute Jesus.

**Confronted** translates a form of the verb *ephistēmi*, which can have the sense of suddenness, sometimes with hostile intent. In Luke 21:34 it describes the sudden coming of judgment, while in Acts 17:5 it describes the Thessalonian Jews' attack on the house of Jason. That is its emphasis in this context.

The leaders were desperate to stop the Lord from preaching the gospel in the temple, but His popularity with the people restrained them from seizing Him (cf. Luke 19:47–48; 20:19; 22:2). The alternative was to trap Him openly and force Him to discredit Himself publicly. Knowing that Jesus had claimed that His **authority** to do and say what He did in defiance of them came from God, they expected that He would repeat that claim, leading them to accuse Him of blasphemy and call for His execution.

Seeking to implement their plan, they accosted Jesus. **"Tell us by what authority You are doing these things,"** they demanded, **"or who is the one who gave You this authority?"** When He attacked the temple the first time at the start of His ministry, the Jewish authorities had made a similar demand: "The Jews then said to Him, 'What sign do You show us as your authority for doing these things?'" (John 2:18). The phrase **these things** can be stretched beyond Christ's teaching in the temple courts without the approval of the Sanhedrin to include every-thing from His triumphal entry on Monday.

### THE COUNTER QUESTION

**Jesus answered and said to them, "I will also ask you a question, and you tell Me: Was the baptism of John from heaven or from men?" They reasoned among themselves, saying, "If we say, 'From heaven,' He will say, 'Why did you not believe him?' But if we say, 'From men,' all the people will stone us to death, for they are convinced that John was a prophet." So they answered that they did not know where it came from.** (20:3–7)

The Lord's response was devastating. Instead of being snared in their clumsy trap, Jesus' counter question, **"Was the baptism of John from heaven or from men?"** trapped them in a dilemma from which they could not escape. To answer a question with another question was accepted rabbinic practice, the idea being to force the questioner to con-sider the issue at a deeper level. Jesus was not evading the question, but unmasking their hypocrisy. They already knew where He said His authority came from; He had affirmed it many times before. As noted above, their plan was not to gain information, but to lure Him to repeat His claim to divine authority publicly, so they could accuse Him of blasphemy.

The religious authorities, who confidently saw themselves as possessing the deep understanding of all spiritual and theological knowledge, were no match for Jesus, even when facing the simple question that Jesus posed: What was the source of **John** the Baptist's ministry (the **baptism** he performed symbolized John's entire ministry)—was it of divine or human origin?

This query put the Jewish leaders in an impossible quandary. **They** huddled together and **reasoned among themselves** (i.e., deliberated with one another), desperately and futilely seeking a way out. They knew they could not say that John's ministry was from God, for two reasons. First, they themselves did not believe that it was (Luke 7:28–30), and thus did not want to publicly put their seal of approval on the Baptist. Further, to affirm that John was a true prophet of God would leave them with no answer for the question the Lord was sure to ask: **"Why did you not believe him** when he affirmed that I am the Messiah?" (cf. Luke 3:1–18; John 1:26–29; 3:25–30; 5:32–36; 10:41).

On the other hand, to deny the popular view that John was a spokesman for God would have serious and even potentially fatal consequences. **"If we say, 'From men,'"** they reasoned, **"all the people will stone us to death, for they are convinced that John was a prophet."** To reject God's prophet was to reject and blaspheme God Himself. That could make them worthy of death.

The only exit to take to flee the volatile dilemma was to painfully humiliate themselves by pleading ignorance. Therefore **they** condescended grudgingly and **answered that they did not know where** John's ministry **came from.**

### The Condemnation

**And Jesus said to them, "Nor will I tell you by what authority I do these things."** (20:8)

Having silenced His adversaries, Jesus ended the conversation by saying to them, **"Nor will I tell you by what authority I do these things."** After three years of teaching and performing miracles, Jesus had given them sufficient proof that He was the Messiah. No more information would be forthcoming. There was no point in continuing to cast pearls before swine. The Jewish leaders had willfully rejected all the light they had seen; there was no reason to give them more. This was a pronouncement of judgment on the leadership of Israel. At His mock trial two days later, these men demanded of Jesus, "'If You are the Christ, tell us.' But He said to them, 'If I tell you, you will not believe; and if I ask a question, you will not answer. But from now on the Son of Man will be seated at the right hand of the power of God'" (Luke 22:67–69). There was nothing left for them but judgment, and He would sit on that judgment seat to render sentence on them.

There is a limit to God's patience. Those who hard-heartedly reject the light will eventually be abandoned to judicial darkness. God said of the pre-flood world, "My Spirit shall not strive with man forever, because he also is flesh; nevertheless his days shall be one hundred and twenty years" (Gen. 6:3). In a prayer of repentance, the returned exiles from the Babylonian captivity confessed regarding their ancestors, "You bore with them for many years, and admonished them by Your Spirit through Your prophets, yet they would not give ear. Therefore You gave them into the hand of the peoples of the lands" (Neh. 9:30). Isaiah adds, "But they rebelled and grieved His Holy Spirit; therefore He turned Himself to become their enemy, He fought against them" (Isa. 63:10). Through the prophet Jeremiah God reminded wayward Israel, "I solemnly warned your fathers in the day that I brought them up from the land of Egypt, even to this day, warning persistently, saying, 'Listen to My voice.' . . . Therefore thus says the Lord, 'Behold I am bringing disaster on them which they will not be able to escape; though they will cry to Me, yet I will not listen to them'" (Jer. 11:7, 11). Luke 19:41–42 says that "when [Jesus] approached Jerusalem, He saw the city and wept over it, saying, 'If you had known in this day, even you, the things which make for peace! But now they have been hidden from your eyes.'"

The merciful, saving message of the gospel would still be extended to the people, and thousands would be saved on the Day of Pentecost and beyond. But for the hard-hearted leaders, the door of opportunity was shut (cf. Matt. 12:25–32). The Bible warns all people not to follow their example:

> At the acceptable time I listened to you, and on the day of salvation I helped you. Behold, now is "The acceptable time," behold, now is "The day of salvation." (2 Cor. 6:2)

> Therefore, just as the Holy Spirit says, "Today if you hear His voice, do not harden your hearts as when they provoked Me, as in the day of trial in the wilderness, where your fathers tried Me by testing Me, and saw My works for forty years. Therefore I was angry with this generation, and said, 'They always go astray in their heart, and they did not know My ways'; as I swore in My wrath, 'They shall not enter my rest.'" Take care, brethren, that there not be in any one of you an evil, unbelieving heart that falls away from the living God. But encourage one another day after day, as long as it is still called "Today," so that none of you will be hardened by the deceitfulness of sin. (Heb. 3:7–13)

# The Murder of God's Son: A Prophetic Parable (Luke 20:9–18)

**12**

And He began to tell the people this parable: "A man planted a vineyard and rented it out to vine-growers, and went on a journey for a long time. At the harvest time he sent a slave to the vine-growers, so that they would give him some of the produce of the vineyard; but the vine-growers beat him and sent him away empty-handed. And he proceeded to send another slave; and they beat him also and treated him shamefully and sent him away empty-handed. And he proceeded to send a third; and this one also they wounded and cast out. The owner of the vineyard said, 'What shall I do? I will send my beloved son; perhaps they will respect him.' But when the vine-growers saw him, they reasoned with one another, saying, 'This is the heir; let us kill him so that the inheritance will be ours.' So they threw him out of the vineyard and killed him. What, then, will the owner of the vineyard do to them? He will come and destroy these vine-growers and will give the vineyard to others." When they heard it, they said, "May it never be!" But Jesus looked at them and said, "What then

**is this that is written: 'The stone which the builders rejected, this became the chief corner stone'? Everyone who falls on that stone will be broken to pieces; but on whomever it falls, it will scatter him like dust."** (20:9–18)

As noted earlier, from the outset of Christ's ministry, the Jewish religious leaders sought to kill Him. When He attacked their temple the first time (John 2:13–17), they demanded a sign from Him to prove that He had authority for His audacious action. Aware that even at that early stage of His ministry they wanted Him dead, "Jesus answered them, 'Destroy this temple, and in three days I will raise it up'" (v. 19). As verse 21 notes, "He was speaking of the temple of His body"; that is, He was referring to His death and resurrection. After He healed a man on the Sabbath, "the Pharisees went out and immediately began conspiring with the Herodians against Him, as to how they might destroy Him" (Mark 3:6). In Matthew 17:22–23 Jesus said to the disciples, "The Son of Man is going to be delivered into the hands of men; and they will kill Him, and He will be raised on the third day" (cf. 16:21; Luke 18:33). "For this reason therefore the Jews were seeking all the more to kill Him," John wrote, "because He not only was breaking the Sabbath, but also was calling God His own Father, making Himself equal with God" (John 5:18; cf. 7:1, 19, 25; 8:37, 40).

As the Lord's ministry neared its climax, the religious leaders' determination to kill Him intensified. After Jesus raised Lazarus from the dead, "many of the Jews who ... saw what He had done, believed in Him" (John 11:45). The chief priests and Pharisees, alarmed at Jesus' popularity with the people and fearing that it would bring Roman reprisals against them and the nation, held a council. At the urging of the high priest, Caiaphas (vv. 49–50), "from that day on they planned together to kill Him" (v. 53; cf. Mark 14:1). As passionately as they sought it, they were hesitant to carry out their plot because they feared doing so would trigger a riot (Matt. 26:5), until with the assistance of the traitor, Judas Iscariot (Luke 22:3–5), they were able to seize Jesus and work a plan for executing Him.

Jesus, well aware of what His enemies were plotting, told a parable in which He predicted both the murder and the consequences. This prophetic parable, which was told to the people but aimed at the leaders, looks forward to Christ's death as well as backward through Israel's history. It contains four features: the illustration, the explanation, the extension, and the application.

## THE ILLUSTRATION

**And He began to tell the people this parable: "A man planted a vineyard and rented it out to vine-growers, and went on a journey for a long time. At the harvest time he sent a slave to the vine-growers, so that they would give him some of the produce of the vineyard; but the vine-growers beat him and sent him away empty-handed. And he proceeded to send another slave; and they beat him also and treated him shamefully and sent him away empty-handed. And he proceeded to send a third; and this one also they wounded and cast out. The owner of the vineyard said, 'What shall I do? I will send my beloved son; perhaps they will respect him.' But when the vine-growers saw him, they reasoned with one another, saying, 'This is the heir; let us kill him so that the inheritance will be ours.' So they threw him out of the vineyard and killed him. What, then, will the owner of the vineyard do to them? He will come and destroy these vine-growers and will give the vineyard to others."** (20:9–16a)

As was true of all the Lord's parables, this one used imagery from everyday life with which His hearers would be familiar. Vineyards were common in Israel, especially on the terraced hillsides. In this parable **a man planted a vineyard,** making every effort to provide all that was necessary to produce a good crop (the parallel account in Matthew's gospel notes that he built a wall around it, put a wine press in it, and built a tower for added protection against robbers and animals [Matt. 21:33]). As was often done, he **rented it out to vine-growers.** These were tenant farmers, who rented the land from the owner and paid him a percentage of the harvest.

Having leased his vineyard to continue its usefulness and provide income for himself, the owner **went on a journey for a long time.**

This absentee landowner, a common case in Israel and elsewhere, was still away at **harvest time.** To collect his percentage **he sent a slave to the vine-growers, so that they would give him some of the produce of the vineyard.** This, too, was a feature the hearers would have been familiar with.

What occurred next, however, was not at all expected, and utterly outrageous. Instead of giving the slave the agreed-upon share of the crop due to the vineyard owner, **the vine-growers beat him and sent him away empty-handed.** *Derō* (beat) is a strong term; it literally means "to remove the skin," and vividly depicts the savage beating they gave him. The Lord's hearers would have been incensed at such deplorably ungrateful, illegal, and wicked behavior.

Patiently giving the hired vine-growers, who were profiting themselves, multiple opportunities to do what was right, the landowner **proceeded to send another slave,** but the defiant vine-growers **beat him also and treated him shamefully and sent him away empty-handed.** A **third** servant met a similar fate; **this one also they wounded and cast out.** Matthew and Mark note that Jesus had him sending still other slaves, all of whom were either beaten, stoned, or murdered.

The answer to the question the **owner of the vineyard** asked, **"What shall I do?"** would have seemed obvious to Jesus' hearers. Surely they expected him to bring vengeance and just retribution on those criminals. He had given them privileges, and opportunity to benefit from his land. They would have made pledges, promises, and contracts, which they violated by selfish, rebellious, and criminal conduct.

In a generous display of patience and mercy, the vineyard owner hopefully offered one more appeal to the farmers to do what was right. **"I will send my beloved son,"** he reasoned. **"Perhaps they will respect him."** Though they thrashed his slaves, surely they would respect his son. Instead, they saw this as their opportunity to seize full control of the vineyard once and for all, so **when the vine-growers saw** the son, **they reasoned** (i.e., discussed the situation) **with one another.** Their perverse reasoning brought them to deadly violence. **"This is the heir,"** they said to each other. **"Let us kill him so that the inheritance will be ours."** They may have thought that the son was coming to claim his inheritance. According to traditional law, land that remained unclaimed for three years reverted to those who were working it. Therefore if they killed the son, the land could eventually be theirs.

When the son arrived, they **threw him out of the vineyard and killed him.** This act of cold-blooded, premeditated murder was the ultimate outrage to those hearing Jesus spin the story.

The Lord's concluding question to the hearers, **"What, then, will the owner of the vineyard** (who was not dead) **do to them?"** was easy to answer. According to Matthew 21:41 they completed the parable by saying, "He will bring those wretches to a wretched end, and will rent out the vineyard to other vine-growers who will pay him the proceeds at the proper seasons." Jesus agreed with them that **"he will come and destroy these vine-growers and will give the vineyard to others."** Such was an appropriate and just response on the part of the owner.

THE EXPLANATION

**When they heard it, they said, "May it never be!"** (20:16b)

The fact that **when they heard it, they said, "May it never be!"** indicates they had begun to gain clarity on the application our Lord intended. **Heard** translates a form of the Greek verb *akouō*, which refers here (as it does in Rev. 2:7, 11, 17, 29; 3:6, 13, 22) to hearing with understanding. Whether the obvious dawned on the listeners, or Jesus explained it to them, when the full meaning of the parable hit them, they realized Jesus had just condemned their leaders and their nation to destruction.

By then the crowd was processing the component features of the parable: the vineyard owner is God; the vineyard is Israel (cf. Ps. 80:8–16; Isa. 5:7; Jer. 2:21); the vine-growers are the religious leaders of Israel; the extended journey taken by the vineyard owner pictures Old Testament history, which culminated when God returned in the person of His Son; the slaves are the Old Testament prophets, whom Israel mistreated in the same manner as the vine-growers mistreated the vineyard owner's slaves. Alfred Plummer wrote,

"The uniform hostility" of kings, priests, and people to the Prophets is one of the most remarkable features in history of the Jews. The amount of hostility varied, and it expressed itself in different ways, on the whole increasing in intensity; but it was always there. Deeply as the Jews lamented the cessation of Prophets after the death of Malachi, they generally opposed them, as long as they were granted to them. Till the gift was withdrawn, they seemed to have had little pride in this exceptional grace shown to the nation, and little appreciation of it or thankfulness for it. (*An Exegetical Commentary on the Gospel According to S. Matthew* [New York: Scribner's, 1910], 297)

According to tradition, Isaiah was sawn in half with a wooden saw (cf. Heb. 11:37). Jeremiah was constantly mistreated, thrown into a pit (Jer. 38:9), and, according to tradition, stoned to death by the Jews. Ezekiel faced similar hatred and hostility (Ezek. 2:6); Amos was forced to flee for his life (Amos 7:10–13); Zechariah was rejected (Zech. 11:12), and Micaiah was struck in the face (2 Kings 22:24). Both the Old Testament (e.g., Jer. 7:23ff.; 25:4ff.) and the New Testament (e.g., Matt. 23:33–39; Luke 6:22–23; 11:49; 13:34; Acts 7:51–52) rebuked Israel for rejecting and abusing the prophets.

The vineyard owner's son depicts the Lord Jesus Christ. He is distinct from all the rest of God's messengers; He is not God's slave, but God's beloved Son (Matt. 17:5; John 3:16; Col. 1:13; 2 Peter 1:17), the heir of all that He possesses (Heb. 1:2).

By creating this relevant dramatic illustration, Jesus made it clear to His murderers that He knew exactly what they were planning to do to Him. They wanted control of the inheritance; that is, of Israel. Just as the vine-growers **threw** the vineyard owner's son **out of the vineyard and killed him,** so also would the religious leaders throw Jesus out of the nation to the Romans, who killed Him outside Jerusalem.

Backtracking in horror from their earlier declaration that the vineyard owner should destroy the vine-growers **they said, "May it never be!"** (*mē genoito*; the most emphatic negation in the Greek language). But it was to be. Just as the vineyard owner would destroy the rebellious vine-growers, so also would God destroy rebellious Israel. Divine judgment fell on the apostate nation four decades later in A.D. 70, with the Roman destruction of Jerusalem and the temple.

In the Lord's parable, the vineyard owner not only destroyed the vine-growers, but also gave stewardship of the vineyard to others. So also would the custodianship of Israel pass from the hands of the unfaithful, Messiah-rejecting leaders to other stewards. "Therefore I say to you," Jesus declared to them, "the kingdom of God will be taken away from you and given to a people producing the fruit of it" (Matt. 21:43).

Those new leaders of Israel would be the true followers of Jesus Christ. This was the worst-case scenario for the Jewish people, and especially their leaders. They hated Jesus, and they had nothing but disdain, scorn, and ridicule for His followers. They mocked them as unsophisticated Galileans (cf. John 7:52), lacking rabbinic training or credentials (Acts 4:13). The point is not that Gentiles were replacing the Jews, or that the church was replacing Israel. There were Gentile proselytes to Judaism, and there are Jewish believers in the church. But there would be a change in leadership from the corrupt, apostate incumbent rulers of Israel to the apostles and disciples of Jesus Christ.

That transition had already begun. In Luke 9 Jesus "called the twelve together, and gave them power and authority over all the demons and to heal diseases. And He sent them out to proclaim the kingdom of God and to perform healing.... Departing, they began going throughout the villages, preaching the gospel and healing everywhere" (vv. 1–2, 6).

In Luke 10 Jesus sent out seventy more messengers:

> Now after this the Lord appointed seventy others, and sent them in pairs ahead of Him to every city and place where He Himself was going to come. And He was saying to them, "The harvest is plentiful, but the laborers are few; therefore beseech the Lord of the harvest to send out laborers into His harvest. Go; behold, I send you out as lambs in the midst of wolves [the Jewish religious leaders]." ... The seventy returned with joy, saying, "Lord, even the demons are subject to us in Your name." (vv. 1–3, 17)

In Matthew 13:11, Jesus said to the disciples, "To you it has been granted to know the mysteries of the kingdom of heaven, but to them it has not been granted." The disciples had been given knowledge of the mysteries; that is, the now-revealed but formerly hidden truths concerning the kingdom of God contained in the New Testament. They were to be the new custodians of divine truth, and thus the earthly stewards of the kingdom of salvation.

After Peter's affirmation that Jesus is "the Christ [the Messiah], the Son of the living God" (Matt. 16:16),

> Jesus said to him, "Blessed are you, Simon Barjona, because flesh and blood did not reveal this to you, but My Father who is in heaven. I also say to you that you are Peter, and upon this rock I will build My church; and the gates of Hades will not overpower it. I will give you the keys of the kingdom of heaven; and whatever you bind on earth shall have been bound in heaven, and whatever you loose on earth shall have been loosed in heaven." (vv. 17–19)

The disciples were a privileged group to whom God was granting special revelation. They saw things others did not see; they heard and understood what others did not hear and understand (cf. Matt. 13:11–17). The parables that others could not grasp were to them clear and understandable. They exercised power that the leaders of Israel did not have over demons, disease, and death. It was upon the rock of truth revealed to the apostles that Christ would build His church (v. 18; cf. Eph. 2:20).

Though the apostles were a small, nondescript group of unskilled, untrained, and unimpressive men, they were the new leaders of God's vineyard; the stewards of divine revelation and shepherds of the new people of God. Their mission was to "make disciples of all the nations, baptizing them in the name of the Father and the Son and the Holy Spirit" (Matt. 28:19). They accomplished it in a way that turned the world upside down (Acts 17:6 ESV).

As "servants of Christ and stewards of the mysteries of God" (1 Cor. 4:1; cf. Eph. 3:1–11), the apostles were entrusted with the divine revelation of those mysteries in the New Testament Scriptures (John 14:26; 15:26; 16:13; 2 Peter 1:21). Every succeeding generation of pastors, teachers, and evangelists follows in their line (cf. 1 Tim. 4:16; 6:20; 2 Tim. 1:13–14; 2:2).

But as planned from the beginning, God's displacement of Israel is not permanent. "I say then," Paul wrote to the Christians at Rome, "God has not rejected His people, has He? May it never be! For I too am an Israelite, a descendant of Abraham, of the tribe of Benjamin. God has not rejected His people whom He foreknew" (Rom. 11:1–2a; cf. vv. 13–15, 23–30 and the exposition of chapter 11 in *Romans 9–16*, The MacArthur New Testament Commentary [Chicago: Moody, 1994]). There will come a time when "all Israel will be saved" (Rom. 11:26), and again made stewards of

God's truth. In the tribulation, there will be one hundred forty-four thousand Jewish evangelists (Rev. 7:2–8; 14:1–5). The earthly messianic kingdom that the Jewish people expected, and fervently hoped Jesus would establish at His first coming, will be established after His second coming (cf. Isa. 55:3; 56:6–8; 60:1–22; Mic. 4:1–2; Zech. 8:1–8, 14–15, 20–23).

## THE EXTENSION

**But Jesus looked at them and said, "What then is this that is written: 'The stone which the builders rejected, this became the chief corner stone'?** (20:17)

Jesus transitioned directly from the analogy into the reality of Old Testament prophecy. The death of the son cannot be the end of the story. In response to the crowd's horrified response, "May it never be!" **Jesus looked** intently **at them** (the Greek verb literally means "to fix one's gaze on something") **and said, "What then is this that is written"** (in the Old Testament Scriptures [Matt. 21:42]). The reference He quoted, **"The stone which the builders rejected, this became the chief corner stone"** (Ps. 118:22; cf. Dan. 2:34), would have been familiar to them.

And with that reference the imagery of a murdered son had shifted to that of a rejected stone. The **chief corner stone** was the most important part of a stone building, because it properly set every angle for construction. Builders knew that without an absolutely perfect cornerstone, the entire building would drift out of plumb. In the historical context of Psalm 118, the stone rejected by the builders represented Israel, ignored and assaulted by the nations and empires of the world. But that rejected nation will yet become God's cornerstone nation, and the rejected Messiah will be the redeemer and the cornerstone.

The **stone which the builders rejected,** but then **became the chief corner stone,** specifically refers to Jesus Christ, as Peter boldly declared to the Sanhedrin,

Let it be known to all of you and to all the people of Israel, that by the name of Jesus Christ the Nazarene, whom you crucified, whom God raised from the dead—by this name this man stands here before you in good health. He is the stone which was rejected by you, the builders, but which became the chief corner stone. (Acts 4:10–11)

The stone rejected by the Jewish leadership and the nation became the most important stone in the eternal kingdom of God, supporting the whole structure and symmetry of God's glorious kingdom of salvation.

## THE APPLICATION

**Everyone who falls on that stone will be broken to pieces; but on whomever it falls, it will scatter him like dust."** (20:18)

The section concludes with a serious warning against rejecting the Savior. **Everyone who falls on that stone**—that is, who stumbles over Christ in unbelief and rejection (cf. Isa. 8:14–15; Rom. 9:32; 1 Cor. 1:23; 1 Peter 2:6–8)—**will be broken to pieces.** On the other hand, those on whom He **falls** in judgment **will** be scattered **like dust.** In either case the end result is the same: utter, complete, and terrifying destruction.

This is a message of love and warning, though delivering it brought the Lord not joy, but rather intense sorrow moving Him to tears (cf. Luke 19:41). Predictably, but tragically, the leaders rejected His warning and redoubled their efforts to kill Him (Luke 20:19). That same warning applies to everyone: either submit to Christ as Lord and Savior, or be crushed by Him in judgment. Rejecting Jesus Christ is the most tragic choice anyone can ever make. "He who believes in the Son has eternal life; but he who does not obey the Son will not see life, but the wrath of God abides on him" (John 3:36).

# A Diagnosis of the Christ Rejecters (Luke 20:19–26)

# 13

The scribes and the chief priests tried to lay hands on Him that very hour, and they feared the people; for they understood that He spoke this parable against them. So they watched Him, and sent spies who pretended to be righteous, in order that they might catch Him in some statement, so that they could deliver Him to the rule and the authority of the governor. They questioned Him, saying, "Teacher, we know that You speak and teach correctly, and You are not partial to any, but teach the way of God in truth. Is it lawful for us to pay taxes to Caesar, or not?" But He detected their trickery and said to them, "Show Me a denarius. Whose likeness and inscription does it have?" They said, "Caesar's." And He said to them, "Then render to Caesar the things that are Caesar's, and to God the things that are God's." And they were unable to catch Him in a saying in the presence of the people; and being amazed at His answer, they became silent. (20:19–26)

Israel's history, in spite of singular blessings, is a long and relentless account of rebellion against God, indifference to His revelation, and disobedience to His law. God's prophets, sent to call for repentance and proclaim His loving offer of grace, mercy, forgiveness, and salvation, the nation regularly persecuted and killed. That tragic history of wasted privilege is summed up in the dramatic parable Jesus told in the previous section of Luke's gospel (see the exposition of vv. 9–18 in chapter 12 of this volume).

Israel's rebellion against God culminated in their treatment of His Son, the Lord Jesus Christ. In spite of all the Old Testament prophetic revelation that pointed unerringly to Him as Israel's long-awaited king, the generation that saw Him carried out the most unthinkable crime against God—the murder of the divine-human Messiah.

The religious leaders knew of Christ's virgin birth, sinless life, divine words, and power over demons, disease, death, and nature. They had heard His offer of forgiveness, salvation, blessing, and eternal life in the kingdom of God. That Jesus' words and works were the fulfillment of many Old Testament promises and prophecies was obvious. Though the religious leaders never denied Christ's power, miracles, or unequalled wisdom, they rejected Him, because of His attack on their false religion.

Two days before they had Him executed, on Wednesday of Passion Week, one of several confrontations between Jesus and the religious leaders took place. The tide of popularity had not yet faded because the people were hopeful that He was the messiah they envisioned, who would establish His throne in Jerusalem with glory and power. The leaders, who had hated Jesus since His ministry began by His first attack on their temple (John 2), wanted Him dead more than ever. In a remarkable display of diabolical brilliance, they engineered a complete shift in the public attitude toward Jesus. On Friday, the crowd that had enthusiastically shouted, "Hosanna," and hailed Jesus as the Messiah on Monday, changed their shout to "Crucify Him!"

This incident reveals a complex of six motivating sins driving the leaders: hatred, pride, hypocrisy, flattery, deception, and stubbornness.

## HATRED

**The scribes and the chief priests tried to lay hands on Him that very hour,** (20:19a)

So serious was the threat posed by Jesus that the members of the various groups, who often clashed with each other, found unity in their determination to be rid of Jesus. The **scribes,** many of whom were Pharisees, were the experts in the law of Moses and the rabbinic traditions. The **chief priests** included the reigning high priest, Caiaphas; the former high priest, Annas; the captain of the temple, who assisted the high priest; and other high-ranking priests. Many of them were Sadducees. Matthew 22:15 and Mark 12:13 note that despite their animosity toward each other, the Pharisees and Herodians (Jews who supported the Herodian dynasty) were also part of the plot (their collusion went back much earlier in Jesus' ministry; cf. Mark 3:6). All desperately sought to find a way **to lay hands on** (arrest) **Him** and eliminate Him as soon as possible.

The religious coalition, however, could not just seize Jesus openly. Both they and the people understood that the very public parable He had just taught (vv. 9–18) was aimed at them. If they carried out their plot publicly, they would confirm what He had said about them and risk bringing the wrath of the people down on their own heads.

Their strategy was to enlist the aid of their bitter enemies, the Romans. Since Rome was extremely sensitive to the threat of insurrection, particularly during Passover, and could be counted on to take swift action against any rebels, if they could lure Jesus into making an anti-Roman statement, then report Him to the Romans as a political revolutionary, the Romans could have reason to take Him and execute Him. Merely seeing Jesus captured by the Romans would be enough to discredit Him in the eyes of the people, especially if He had no power over His captors.

## PRIDE

**for they understood that He spoke this parable against them.** (20:19b)

As mentioned, the religious leaders **understood** perfectly **that** Jesus **spoke** the **parable** recorded in verses 9–18 **against them,** but were reluctant to take action to kill Him, because the people still held Jesus in high regard (Matt. 21:46). They also feared losing the honor and respect which regularly fed their self-righteous egos. They sought "the place of honor at banquets and the chief seats in the synagogues, and respectful greetings in the market places, and being called Rabbi by men" (Matt. 23:6–7), ostentatiously announced their giving to the poor (Matt. 6:2), and "love[d] to stand and pray in the synagogues and on the street corners so that they [might] be seen by men" (v. 5).

Yet, ironically, these religious hypocrites loathed and despised the very populace whose attention they craved. They derisively referred to them as being ignorant of the law and accursed (John 7:49), and disdainfully refused to associate with them. Utterly without compassion, they "tie[d] up heavy burdens and [laid] them on men's shoulders, but they themselves [were] unwilling to move them with so much as a finger" (Matt. 23:4). Like all false teachers, they ruled by fear and intimidation, threatening that those who did not obey their teaching would miss out on the kingdom of God. Their false teaching led people into eternal ruin, turning them into twice as much sons of hell as they were (Matt. 23:15). These false teachers were neither God-pleasers nor man-pleasers, but self-pleasers, who fed their proud souls on the accolades of those whom they intimidated and abused.

HYPOCRISY

**So they watched Him, and sent spies who pretended to be righteous, in order that they might catch Him in some statement, so that they could deliver Him to the rule and the authority of the governor.** (20:20)

The religious elite's hatred of Jesus and prideful desire to maintain their own elevated status led them to a third sin. Hypocrisy is a hallmark of all false teachers who, like their father Satan (John 8:44), pretend to be righteous (2 Cor. 11:15). Looking for the opportune moment, they

**watched** Jesus, and in addition to keeping Him under general surveillance, **sent spies** from both the Pharisees and the Herodians (Matt. 22:16) to follow Him. Those leaders and spies were hypocrites, **who pretended to be righteous** truth seekers, but in reality sought only to **catch Him in some statement, so that they could deliver Him to the rule and the authority of the** Roman **governor.**

As noted above, the Jewish council's plan was to use the Romans, specifically Pilate, who was in Jerusalem for the Passover season, to execute Jesus. The people expected the messiah to overthrow all Israel's enemies, and establish the nation's superiority and blessing as promised by the prophets in the Old Testament. Therefore the true Messiah would have to view the Romans as idolatrous, blasphemous, pagan intruders to be judged.

To keep up the pretense of being Messiah, the leaders reasoned, Jesus would be forced to take the popular view that the Romans had to be opposed and overthrown. Therefore all they had to do was maneuver Him into a position where He had to say that publicly. Once He was identified as a revolutionary, the Romans would arrest Him. That would prove that they had power over Him and not He over them, and the disappointed people would turn against Him.

FLATTERY

**They questioned Him, saying, "Teacher, we know that You speak and teach correctly, and You are not partial to any, but teach the way of God in truth.** (20:21)

Those who **questioned Him** formally addressed Jesus as **teacher,** a title reserved for the most respected and honored rabbis. Though intended as flattery, what they said about Him was true. Jesus did always **speak and teach correctly,** was **not partial to any,** and did **teach the way of God in truth** and never anything else. The Lord did not adjust His message based on the kind of response He received or who He was talking to. He did not equivocate because of human opinion or possible consequences. This lying sarcasm of their disingenuous flattery was intended to trap Jesus and to destroy Him.

There are two reasons that they spoke to Jesus the way they did. First, they thought He was like them and would respond with feelings of pride so that He would be painfully truthful when questioned to justify their compliment. Second, they wanted to pretend that they agreed with how the people viewed Him. They were hateful flatterers, trying to tempt Jesus to incriminate Himself in a self-serving attempt to avoid contradicting their commendation.

DECEPTION

**Is it lawful for us to pay taxes to Caesar, or not?" But He detected their trickery and said to them, "Show Me a denarius. Whose likeness and inscription does it have?" They said, "Caesar's." And He said to them, "Then render to Caesar the things that are Caesar's, and to God the things that are God's."** (20:22–25)

The greatest admiration that could be paid to an esteemed teacher was to elevate him by asking difficult questions, particularly those regarding the law of God. Assuming that they had Jesus where they wanted Him, His enemies posed a carefully crafted query for Him, **"Is it lawful for us to pay taxes to Caesar, or not?"** By **lawful** they were referring not to Roman law, but to God's law. They thought they knew that the biblically correct answer was negative, and that that was the answer the people would expect. The people believed that the land of Israel and all that it produced belonged to God. Consequently, they hated paying taxes to occupying pagan idolaters.

And there were diverse taxes imposed by the Romans, including income taxes, land taxes, import taxes, and transport taxes. But the tax the Jewish people hated most was the poll tax everyone paid for living under Rome's authority. They found it especially offensive because it suggested that Caesar owned them, while they passionately viewed both themselves and the nation as solely God's possession. Taxation was a constant source of friction between the Jews and Rome, and played a large part in both the rebellion led by Judas of Galilee (A.D. 6–7) and the Jewish revolt of A.D. 66–70, which ended in the utter destruction of Jerusalem by the Roman general Titus.

The leaders thought that they had forced Jesus into an impossible and inescapable dilemma. They were certain that to avoid alienating the people, He would have to affirm the popular view that paying taxes to Rome was violating the law of God. But such a response would leave the very popular Jesus open to the charge of inciting an insurrection against Rome. If He gave that answer to their question, they would dispatch the Herodians to inform the Romans, who would need to seize Jesus, dashing the hopes that He was God's king.

Jesus, however, **detected their** evil attempt at **trickery. "Show Me a denarius,"** He demanded. A **denarius** was a silver coin minted by the authority of the emperor, worth equal to a day's wages for a Roman soldier. In Jesus' day, a denarius would have had the image of Emperor Tiberius's face on the front, and on the reverse side, an imprint of him sitting on his throne wearing priestly robes. Because the Jews considered such images to be a violation of the second commandment (Ex. 20:4), which prohibited idolatry, they avoided carrying such coins. When one was produced, Jesus, without hesitation, asked, **"Whose likeness and inscription does it have?"** The obvious answer was given: **"Caesar's."**

The profundity of Jesus' next statement should not be lost in its simplicity. **"Then render to Caesar the things that are Caesar's,"** He told them, **"and to God the things that are God's."** The Lord's point was that people are to fulfill their obligations, both materially to human government and spiritually to God. **Render** translates a form of the Greek verb *apodidōmi,* which refers to giving back something that is owed.

There are some things that belong, in the providence of God, to the temporal realm. God Himself had brought Israel under Roman rule and Caesar was their earthly ruler. They were to support his rule because all government is ordained by God to protect the innocent, and restrain and punish evil, as Paul noted in Romans 13:1–4:

> Every person is to be in subjection to the governing authorities. For there is no authority except from God, and those which exist are established by God. Therefore whoever resists authority has opposed the

ordinance of God; and they who have opposed will receive condemnation upon themselves. For rulers are not a cause of fear for good behavior, but for evil. Do you want to have no fear of authority? Do what is good and you will have praise from the same; for it is a minister of God to you for good. But if you do what is evil, be afraid; for it does not bear the sword for nothing; for it is a minister of God, an avenger who brings wrath on the one who practices evil.

The Romans did those things. They were powerful militarily, and provided peace, security, and protection. The network of roads and shipping channels they created facilitated the flow of goods and commerce that added to their subjects' prosperity. It was legitimate for them to expect those valuable services to be supported by those who benefitted.

The same is true today. Christians are citizens of this temporal world, under the authority of human government. At the same time, they are subjects of the kingdom of God, under the rule of God and Christ. In the worldly realm, they are to meet their obligations to those governing powers that God, in His sovereign providence, has placed in authority over them. That is true whether they live in a democracy or a dictatorship. In either case, they are to both fear God and honor the king (1 Peter 2:17). Jesus affirmed the right of governments to collect taxes for their support because they are ordained by God for man's well-being and safety. Without such ruling powers, there would be anarchy, chaos, and destruction. When a government, however, commands believers to do what God forbids, or forbids them to do what God commands, it must be legitimately disobeyed (Acts 4:19; 5:29).

On the other hand, Christians are always required to render to **God the things that are God's.** He is the one to whom we belong and whom we serve (Acts 27:23). To Him belong solely our souls, worship, praise, trust, love, and obedience.

STUBBORNNESS

**And they were unable to catch Him in a saying in the presence of the people; and being amazed at His answer, they became silent.** (20:26)

Instead of marveling at Christ's astonishing wisdom and reexamining their obligation to God, the frustrated leaders were **amazed,** but rather than admit that to Jesus, they **became silent.** Their attitude toward Him had not changed.Though they had failed to elicit the incriminating response from Him that they had hoped for, they stubbornly persisted in trying to find another way.When they finally managed to bring Jesus before Pilate, they lied and said, "We found this man misleading our nation and forbidding to pay taxes to Caesar" (Luke 23:2).

Their sinful stubbornness left them in a hopeless, irremediable, unredeemable situation.

# The Savior Silences the Sadducees (Luke 20:27–40)

# 14

Now there came to Him some of the Sadducees (who say that there is no resurrection), and they questioned Him, saying, "Teacher, Moses wrote for us that if a man's brother dies, having a wife, and he is childless, his brother should marry the wife and raise up children to his brother. Now there were seven brothers; and the first took a wife and died childless; and the second and the third married her; and in the same way all seven died, leaving no children. Finally the woman died also. In the resurrection therefore, which one's wife will she be? For all seven had married her." Jesus said to them, "The sons of this age marry and are given in marriage, but those who are considered worthy to attain to that age and the resurrection from the dead, neither marry nor are given in marriage; for they cannot even die anymore, because they are like angels, and are sons of God, being sons of the resurrection. But that the dead are raised, even Moses showed, in the passage about the burning bush, where he calls the Lord the God of Abraham, and the God of Isaac, and the God

**of Jacob. Now He is not the God of the dead but of the living; for all live to Him." Some of the scribes answered and said, "Teacher, You have spoken well." For they did not have courage to question Him any longer about anything.** (20:27–40)

Anticipation of life after death is universal in the human race. Throughout history people in every culture have expressed confident hope that death is not the end of their existence, revealing that God has universally "set eternity in their heart" (Eccl. 3:11). For example, reflecting the ancient Egyptians' belief in life after death, the Book of the Dead contains stories and instructions related to their belief in the afterlife. A solar barge (to be used for transportation in the next life) found in the tomb of Pharaoh Cheops, who died about twenty-five hundred years before Christ was born, reflects that belief. Ancient Greeks sometimes placed a coin in the mouth of a corpse to pay the deceased person's fare across the mystic river of death into the land of resurrection life. Some American Indians buried their dead warriors with useful items (such as their bows, arrows, and horses) that they might need in the next life. The Vikings did similarly. In Greenland, children were sometimes buried with dogs to guide them through the cold wasteland of death. As a young man, Benjamin Franklin (though not a Christian in the biblical sense) composed the following whimsical epitaph:

The Body of
B. Franklin, Printer
Like the Cover of an old Book,
Its Contents torn out,
And stript of its Lettering & Gilding,
Lies here, Food for Worms.
But the Work shall not be lost,
For it will, as he believ'd,
Appear once more,
In a new and more elegant Edition,
Corrected and improved
By the Author

Jewish people have historically had a strong belief in resurrection life, as a gruesome incident recorded in the apocryphal book of 2 Maccabees illustrates. A Jewish elder named Razis was trapped by his enemies, but rather than die at their hands he disemboweled himself with a sword, and "then, standing on a steep rock, as he lost the last of his blood, he tore out his entrails and flung them with both hands into the crowd, calling upon the Lord of life and of spirit to give these back to him again" (14:45–46). Another apocryphal writing, the Apocalypse of Baruch (also known as 2 Baruch), also expresses the traditional Jewish belief in life after death:

> For the earth shall then assuredly restore the dead, [Which it now receives, in order to preserve them]. It shall make no change in their form, but as it has received, so shall it restore them, and as I delivered them unto it, so also shall it raise them. For then it will be necessary to show to the living that the dead have come to life again, and that those who had departed have returned (again). And it shall come to pass, when they have severally recognized those whom they now know, then judgment shall grow strong, and those things which before were spoken of shall come. And it shall come to pass, when that appointed day has gone by, that then shall the aspect of those who are condemned be afterwards changed, and the glory of those who are justified. For the aspect of those who now act wickedly shall become worse than it is, as they shall suffer torment. Also (as for) the glory of those who have now been justified in My law, who have had understanding in their life, and who have planted in their heart the root of wisdom, then their splendour shall be glorified in changes, and the form of their face shall be turned into the light of their beauty, that they may be able to acquire and receive the world which does not die, which is then promised to them. For over this above all shall those who come then lament, that they rejected My law, and stopped their ears that they might not hear wisdom or receive understanding. When therefore they see those, over whom they are now exalted, (but) who shall then be exalted and glorified more than they, they shall respectively be transformed, the latter into the splendour of angels, and the former shall yet more waste away in wonder at the visions and in the beholding of the forms. For they shall first behold and afterwards depart to be tormented. But those who have been saved by their works, and to whom the law has been now a hope, and understanding an expectation, and wisdom a confidence, shall wonders appear in their time. For they shall behold the world which is now invisible to them, and they shall behold the time which is now hidden from them: and time shall no longer age them. For in the heights of that world shall they dwell, and they shall be made like

unto the angels, and be made equal to the stars, and they shall be changed into every form they desire, from beauty into loveliness, and from light into the splendour of glory. (50:2–51:10)

But of far greater significance than the traditional speculation regarding the resurrection life of the age to come is the divine revelation in the Old Testament. In Job 19:25–27 Job expressed his confident hope in the bodily resurrection of the dead: "As for me, I know that my Redeemer lives, and at the last He will take His stand on the earth. Even after my skin is destroyed, yet from my flesh I shall see God; whom I myself shall behold, and whom my eyes will see and not another."

In Psalm 16:9–11 David wrote,

Therefore my heart is glad and my glory rejoices; my flesh also will dwell securely. For You will not abandon my soul to Sheol; nor will You allow Your Holy One to undergo decay. You will make known to me the path of life; in Your presence is fullness of joy; in Your right hand there are pleasures forever.

Psalm 49:15 expresses the psalmist's resurrection hope: "God will redeem my soul from the power of Sheol, for He will receive me," as does Psalm 139:8: "If I ascend to heaven, You are there; if I make my bed in Sheol, behold, You are there." Psalm 73:24, Isaiah 26:19, and Daniel 12:2 also reveal the hope of the resurrection.

The most notable exception to this belief was the Sadducees, who denied any future life at all, either for punishment or reward. They taught that both the soul and the body cease to exist at death. In the incident recorded in this section of Luke's gospel, a huddle of Sadducees confronted Jesus about the resurrection. The passage may be divided into four sections: the approach of the Sadducees, the absurdity of resurrection, the answer of Scripture, and the astonishment of the crowd.

### THE APPROACH OF THE SADDUCEES

**Now there came to Him some of the Sadducees (who say that there is no resurrection),** (20:27)

As noted above, the **Sadducees** were in direct opposition to the common Jewish belief, claiming **that there is no resurrection.** That this idea was a major point of theological controversy is clear from Acts 23:8:"The Sadducees say that there is no resurrection, nor an angel, nor a spirit, but the Pharisees acknowledge them all."The Sadducees scoffed at the Pharisees' crassly literal view of the next life, which imagined it to be essentially the same as the present life (some Pharisees even argued that people would be resurrected in the same clothes in which they were buried, with the same physical defects, and the same interpersonal relationships), rightly viewing it as absurd.

Although few in number, the Sadducees wielded immense influence, because they consisted of the aristocratic, wealthy, and influential religionists, including the high priests, the chief priests (cf. 19:47; 20:1, 19), and most of the Sanhedrin. Holding all the positions of power over the temple compensated for the Sadducees' relatively small number.

Politically, they were eager to cooperate with Rome. Since they rejected any existence after this life, the Sadducees focused all their efforts and attention on the affairs of this present life. They pursued power, wealth, position, and control. If obtaining those things required them to cooperate with their Roman overlords, they were zealous to flatter them.

The Sadducees ran the lucrative business operations located on the temple grounds, and were obviously furious with Jesus for twice disrupting their business (see the exposition of 19:45–48 in chapter 10 of this volume). Jesus' assault on the theology of the Pharisees and the economics of the Sadducees caused those who were separated by their beliefs to unite in hating Him.

In terms of their religious beliefs, the Sadducees were very narrow and strict. While liberal in their denial of the resurrection, angels, and the age to come, they were fundamentalists in rejecting the oral traditions and scribal prescriptions that the Pharisees accepted, and acknowledged only Scripture as authoritative. Further, they interpreted the Mosaic Law more literally than others, and were more fastidious in the matters of ritual purity prescribed in the Law.

They held to the primacy of the Mosaic Law, contained in the Pentateuch (the five books of Moses: Genesis, Exodus, Leviticus, Numbers, and Deuteronomy). All the rest of the Old Testament, they believed, was subordinate to the Mosaic Law, and merely commentary on it. They argued that nowhere in those five books is the resurrection taught, and therefore any writing—even another Old Testament book—that appeared to teach the resurrection must be understood in a different way.

Consistent with their denial of any future life, the Sadducees lived life as if there were no tomorrow. They fastidiously observed the Mosaic Law, but at the same time, like the Pharisees, cruelly oppressed the common people, and used their positions of power and influence to indulge themselves at the expense of the populace.

The Pharisees attempted to destroy Jesus by trapping Him into making an incriminating anti-Roman statement (cf. Luke 20:19–26). The Sadducees, on the other hand, sought to discredit Him in the eyes of the people as ignorant by asking Him a question He could not answer. They decided to stump Him on the issue of marriage relationships after the supposed resurrection. Their question was also designed to make belief in the resurrection appear absurd.

### The Absurdity of Resurrection

**and they questioned Him, saying, "Teacher, Moses wrote for us that if a man's brother dies, having a wife, and he is childless, his brother should marry the wife and raise up children to his brother. Now there were seven brothers; and the first took a wife and died childless; and the second and the third married her; and in the same way all seven died, leaving no children. Finally the woman died also. In the resurrection therefore, which one's wife will she be? For all seven had married her."** (20:28–33)

Feigning a respect for Him that they did not have, like their counterparts, the Sadducees who **questioned Him** flatteringly addressed Jesus as **Teacher,** to raise expectation that He would surely know the answer to their question. Their interrogation involved the instruction regarding levirate marriage in Deuteronomy 25:5–6:

When brothers live together and one of them dies and has no son, the wife of the deceased shall not be married outside the family to a strange man. Her husband's brother shall go in to her and take her to himself as wife and perform the duty of a husband's brother to her. It shall be that the firstborn whom she bears shall assume the name of his dead brother, that his name may not be blotted out from Israel.

The principle predates the Mosaic Law, as the story of Onan (Gen. 38:6–10) indicates. Perhaps the most notable example of levirate marriage in the Old Testament is Boaz's marriage to his relative Elimelech's widowed daughter-in-law, Ruth (Ruth 2:1; 4:1–13).

The Sadducees confronted Jesus with a situation that made the Pharisees' excessively literal view of the life to come seem absurd:

**"Now there were seven brothers; and the first took a wife and died childless; and the second and the third married her; and in the same way all seven died, leaving no children. Finally the woman died also. In the resurrection therefore, which one's wife will she be? For all seven had married her."**

Whether this was a hypothetical situation or one that had actually happened is not known. But in either case, the Sadducees assumed that Jesus' view of the resurrection was the same as that of the Pharisees. They believed that He would be embarrassingly unable to answer their question, and therefore His reputation as an eminent teacher would be diminished.

THE ANSWER OF SCRIPTURE

**Jesus said to them, "The sons of this age marry and are given in marriage, but those who are considered worthy to attain to that age and the resurrection from the dead, neither marry nor are given in marriage; for they cannot even die anymore, because they are like angels, and are sons of God, being sons of the resurrection. But that the dead are raised, even Moses showed, in the passage about the burning bush, where he calls the Lord the God of Abraham, and the God of Isaac, and the God of Jacob. Now He is not the God of the dead but of the living; for all live to Him." (20:34–38)**

Jesus' retort to the Sadducees' attempt to ridicule belief in the resurrection came with a strong rebuke. As Matthew records, He prefaced His reply by saying to them, "You are mistaken, not understanding the Scriptures nor the power of God" (Matt. 22:29). That was a shocking and humiliating statement to make to those who prided themselves on their knowledge of Scripture. But they were void of the truth, bereft of any true spiritual power, and spiritually blind. Had they known the truth concerning the power of God, they would have understood that God will resurrect people without all the supposed absurdities that they delighted in imagining.

In reality, their complicated question was absurd, and the answer simple: there is no marriage in heaven. The **sons of this age** (a Hebraism for those living in this present world; cf. Luke 16:8) **marry and are given in marriage.** But like other family relationships, marriage is for this present life only. The reality is that **those who are considered worthy to attain to** the eternal life that follows **the resurrection from the dead, neither marry nor are given in marriage; for they cannot even die anymore, because they are like angels, and are sons of God, being sons of the resurrection.** There will be no need for marriage and families for the purpose of repopulation, for the obvious reason that those eternally living in God's presence **cannot even die anymore** and hence do not need to be replaced. They will be **like** the **angels,** who were all created at the same time and never die. Nor will there be any need for marriage and family relationships designed to pass truth and righteousness from generation to generation, since everyone is in perfect holy union with the Triune God and each other.

Christ's statement about **those who are considered worthy to attain to that age and the resurrection from the dead** was a warning directly at the Sadducees. They were not worthy of the age to come, since refusing to believe it existed left them with no desire to seek the way to eternal life. Only through faith in the Lord Jesus Christ are people made worthy to be **sons of God** and **sons of the resurrection,** since "all our righteous deeds are like a filthy garment" (Isa. 64:6) and, as a result, "There is none righteous, not even one" (Rom. 3:10). The phrase **sons of** identifies the essential nature or defining quality of something; the essential nature of the **sons of the resurrection** is that they possess the pure, fulfilling life of God. The glorious resurrection body the redeemed will have is described at length in 1 Corinthians 15:35–50 (cf. Phil. 3:21).

Having demonstrated that the Sadducees' objection to the resurrection was irrelevant and based on ignorance regarding life in the age to come, Jesus addressed the issue of their claim that the Pentateuch did not teach the resurrection. Clearly, **Moses** did teach **that the dead are raised,** most notably **in the passage about the burning bush** (Ex. 3:6). In that passage Moses recorded that God called Himself **the God of Abraham, and the God of Isaac, and the God of Jacob.** God used the present tense, saying to Moses, "I am the God of your father, the God of Abraham, the God of Isaac, and the God of Jacob," not the past tense, "I was." Yet the past tense would have been appropriate to use if those men no longer existed (cf. the similar use of the present tense in relation to those who had died in Gen. 26:24; Ex. 3:15–16; 4:5). The God who declared Himself to be the God of Abraham, Isaac, and Jacob does not receive worship from those who no longer exist.

Death does not end a person's existence. All those who belong to God are alive and in union with Him in His presence. "I am the resurrection and the life," Jesus said to Martha. "He who believes in Me will live even if he dies, and everyone who lives and believes in Me will never die" (John 11:25–26).

## THE ASTONISHMENT OF THE CROWD

**Some of the scribes answered and said, "Teacher, You have spoken well." For they did not have courage to question Him any longer about anything.** (20:39–40)

The Lord's reply to the Sadducees was devastating. They had concocted their best assault in a vain attempt, and He had dismantled it. Further, He had exposed their ignorance of the Pentateuch by showing that it, like the rest of Scripture, does teach the reality of the resurrection.

Ironically the scribes, who were against Jesus, were thrilled that He had destroyed the argument of and humiliated their archrivals.

Some of them congratulated Him **and said, "Teacher, You have spoken well."** Matthew notes that "when the crowds heard this, they were astonished at His teaching" (Matt. 22:33). The Sadducees, utterly silenced, **did not have courage to question Him any longer about anything.** The Pharisees, however, went after Him with one last question (Matt. 22:34–45). After He answered it and then asked them a question in return, "No one was able to answer Him a word, nor did anyone dare from that day on to ask Him another question" (Matt. 22:46).

In this passage, Jesus revealed His majestic and invincible wisdom, while affirming the promise of resurrection for all those who put their faith savingly in Him.

# David's Son and Lord (Luke 20:41–44)

**15**

**Then He said to them, "How is it that they say the Christ is David's son? For David himself says in the book of Psalms, 'The Lord said to my Lord, "Sit at My right hand, until I make Your enemies a footstool for Your feet."' Therefore David calls Him 'Lord,' and how is He his son?"** (20:41–44)

The deity of the Lord Jesus Christ has been denied ever since His incarnation. The general consensus in the unbelieving world is that He was a mere man; noble, insightful, wise, devout, and well-intentioned, but nonetheless only a man. That view is consistent with Satan's agenda, since if Jesus was only a man and not also fully God, He was not the Savior, the Bible is not true, and Christianity is a lie. But on the other hand, if Jesus is God, then the Bible is true, and Christianity's truth claims are verified.

Because it is so foundational to salvation, the biblical truth regarding the person of Christ is rejected by satanic cults and false religions. For example the Mormons have succeeded in deceiving many (including some Christians) into believing that they worship the Christ of the Bible. But they teach that the Lord Jesus, the older spirit brother of Lucifer, was one of millions of created spirits born in heaven who became human and attained godhood like many others—including the best Mormons.

Other cults and false religions hold equally aberrant views of Jesus. To the Jehovah's Witnesses, He was Michael the archangel before His birth, lived as nothing more than a perfect man (like Adam before the fall), and was resurrected as a spirit being after His death. The Jesus of Islam was a human prophet of Allah who taught Islamic truth. In Christian Science, Jesus is a man who manifested the Christ idea; to the Bahá'ís He is one of many manifestations of God; to Hindus He is a guru; to Buddhists He is an enlightened teacher; to Spiritists He was a medium, in communication with the spirits of the dead, and is now Himself a spirit with whom people can communicate.

Historically, Jewish people have also refused to acknowledge Jesus as God. In His own day, they expected the messiah to be a notable, powerful, influential man, who would subdue Israel's enemies, establish God's kingdom, in which Israel would play the central role, and fulfill all covenant promises to Abraham and David. The common people accepted that view of the messiah, long taught by their leaders.

His claim to be God was outrageous blasphemy; the most heinous sin imaginable in their view. Jesus' relentless assault on their theology, power, influence, position, and self-righteousness enraged Jerusalem's religious leaders especially. Those assaults culminated during Passion Week, when the Lord cleansed the temple, confronted the religious leaders' corruption, and exposed their hypocrisy, escalating their feverish desire to eliminate Him.

This final conversation between the Lord and the leaders took place late in the day on Wednesday. The Jewish religious authorities' attempts to discredit Him had been utterly unsuccessful, and as a result, "no one would venture to ask Him any more questions" (Mark 12:34). They could not handle His answers, and then it became clear they could not handle His questions either. This dramatic confrontation began when Jesus posed to them a discerning question, to which they gave a deficient answer, and concluded with the Lord presenting a divine reality.

## A Discerning Question

**Then He said to them, "How is it that they say the Christ is David's son?"** (20:41)

The question arises as to why Jesus initiated this dialogue, since by this time in His ministry it was obvious that the leaders and the nation had rejected Him. Why bother to assert once more His true identity? The answer is found in Mark's account of this incident. After Jesus thwarted the Sadducees' crafty attempt to discredit Him by asking a question He could not answer (Mark 12:18–27; cf. the exposition of Luke 20:27–40 in the previous chapter of this volume), a scribe challenged Him to name the greatest commandment in the law (Mark 12:28–34). After the scribe commended His answer, Jesus said to him, "You are not far from the kingdom of God" (v. 34). The dialogue recorded here followed immediately afterward. Jesus' question introduced one final evangelistic appeal to reach those who might be open to the gospel. Despite the virulent hatred of the leaders and the superficial interest of the fickle, indecisive crowds, Jesus still compassionately presented the truth to them. As God incarnate, He had no pleasure in the death of the wicked (Ezek. 33:11). His joy was and is the salvation of sinners (cf. Luke 15:7; John 4:31–42); their destruction brought Him sadness and moved Him to tears (Luke 19:41–44).

But the unmistakably clear testimony of Scripture is that no one will go to heaven who rejects the truth that Jesus Christ is God. John the Baptist testified concerning Him, "He who believes in the Son has eternal life; but he who does not obey the Son will not see life, but the wrath of God abides on him" (John 3:36). In John 5:37–38 Jesus said, "The Father who sent Me, He has testified of Me. You have neither heard His voice at any time nor seen His form. You do not have His word abiding in you, for you do not believe Him whom He sent." In John 8:24 He warned the hostile religious leaders, "Therefore I said to you that you will die in your sins; for unless you believe that I am He, you will die in your sins." Jesus made it clear that there is no other way of salvation when He declared, "I am the way, and the truth, and the life; no one comes to the Father but through Me" (John 14:6). The apostles also proclaimed that truth, declaring of Jesus in Acts 4:12, "There is salvation in no one else; for there is no other name under heaven that has been given among men by which we must be saved." Paul closed his first epistle to the Corinthians by pronouncing a curse on anyone who does not love the Lord Jesus Christ (1 Cor. 16:22). In his first epistle the apostle John wrote, "Who is the liar but the one who denies that Jesus is the Christ? This is the antichrist, the one who denies the Father and the Son. Whoever denies the Son does not have the Father; the one who confesses the Son has the Father also" (1 John 2:22–23). Later in that same epistle he added,

> The one who believes in the Son of God has the testimony in himself; the one who does not believe God has made Him a liar, because he has not believed in the testimony that God has given concerning His Son. And the testimony is this, that God has given us eternal life, and this life is in His Son. He who has the Son has the life; he who does not have the Son of God does not have the life. (1 John 5:10–12)

In his account of this incident, Matthew records that "while the Pharisees were gathered together, Jesus asked them a question: 'What do you think about the Christ, whose son is He?' They said to Him, 'The son of David'" (Matt. 22:41–42). His follow-up rhetorical question, **"How is it that they say the Christ is David's son?"** which reflects their belief that the messiah would be a mere man, challenged them to explain how they arrived at that conclusion.

## A Deficient Answer

As noted above, the religious leaders' answer to the question the Lord asked in Matthew 22:42 was that the Messiah would be the son of David. That was the view taught by the experts in the law (Mark 12:35). And they were correct at that point, since the Old Testament clearly declares that Messiah will be in the line of David. In 2 Samuel 7:12–14 God promised him,

> When your days are complete and you lie down with your fathers, I will raise up your descendant after you, who will come forth from you, and I will establish his kingdom. He shall build a house for My name, and I

will establish the throne of his kingdom forever. I will be a father to him and he will be a son to Me;

In Psalm 89 God declared,

> I have made a covenant with My chosen; I have sworn to David My servant, I will establish your seed forever and build up your throne to all generations.... Once I have sworn by My holiness; I will not lie to David. His descendants shall endure forever and his throne as the sun before Me. It shall be established forever like the moon, and the witness in the sky is faithful. (vv. 3–4, 35–37; cf. Amos 9:11; Mic. 5:2)

That was the common belief in Jesus' day as well. In Matthew 9:27 two blind men followed Him, crying out, "Have mercy on us, Son of David!" (cf. 20:30–31). After the Lord healed a man who was blind and mute, "all the crowds were amazed, and were saying, 'This man cannot be the Son of David, can he?'" (Matt. 12:23). Matthew 15:22 notes that "a Canaanite woman from that region came out and began to cry out, saying, 'Have mercy on me, Lord, Son of David; my daughter is cruelly demon-possessed.'" At His triumphal entry "the crowds going ahead of Him, and those who followed, were shouting, 'Hosanna to the Son of David; blessed is He who comes in the name of the Lord; Hosanna in the highest!'" (Matt. 21:9). There is no question that Jesus was in the line of David, as the genealogies of both Joseph and Mary prove (Matt. 1:1–17; Luke 3:23–38).

None of His opponents ever denied or challenged Christ's Davidic ancestry. The genealogical records in the temple would have verified it. Of course, David had many descendants, but only one of them was the Messiah. But when the people referred to Jesus as the Son of David, the leaders' reaction was hostile, because they were intending to affirm Him as the Messiah.

## A Divine Reality

**For David himself says in the book of Psalms, 'The Lord said to my Lord, "Sit at My right hand, until I make Your enemies a footstool for Your feet."' Therefore David calls Him 'Lord,' and how is He his son?"** (20:42–44)

Before they could reply, the Lord pointed out the inadequacy and incompleteness of the notion that the Messiah would be merely David's son. The testimony comes from **David himself,** who **says in the book of Psalms, "The Lord said to my Lord, 'Sit at My right hand, until I make Your enemies a footstool for Your feet.'"** Jesus quoted Psalm 110, considered to be a messianic psalm. Peter quoted from it in Acts 2:34–35, the writer of Hebrews quoted from it in Hebrews 1:13 and 10:13, and Paul alluded to it in 1 Corinthians 15:25. The psalm reveals that the Messiah will wield God's authority and power, symbolized by sitting at His **right hand.** God will make the Messiah's **enemies a footstool for** His **feet,** a reference to the execution of Messiah's enemies, as the incident recorded in Joshua 10:24–26 illustrates:

> When they brought these kings out to Joshua, Joshua called for all the men of Israel, and said to the chiefs of the men of war who had gone with him, "Come near, put your feet on the necks of these kings." So they came near and put their feet on their necks. Joshua then said to them, "Do not fear or be dismayed! Be strong and courageous, for thus the Lord will do to all your enemies with whom you fight." So afterward Joshua struck them and put them to death, and he hanged them on five trees; and they hung on the trees until evening.

Christ's point is that if the Messiah was merely a man, as the Jews taught, why did David refer to Him as his Lord? No Middle Eastern father, least of all a king, would call his human son Lord. Jesus' simple argument was so powerful and convincing that when it became widely known following the completion of the New Testament, many Jews abandoned the historical view that Psalm 110 was messianic. Instead, some held that it referred somehow to Abraham; others to Melchizedek; and still others to the intertestamental Jewish leader Judas Maccabeus. Contemporary liberal scholars, who deny the deity of Jesus and the veracity of Scripture, have argued that David was simply mistaken in viewing the Messiah as his Lord. However, in Mark's account of this incident Jesus introduced His quote of Psalm 110:1 by saying, "David himself said in the Holy Spirit" (Mark 12:36; cf. Acts 4:25). Thus, to deny what David wrote is also to deny the truthfulness of the testimony by the Holy Spirit to Jesus Christ.

The Lord's logical query, **"Therefore David calls Him 'Lord,' and how is He his son?"** posed an inescapable and terminal dilemma for the religious leaders. Therefore "no one was able to answer Him a word, nor did anyone dare from that day on to ask Him another question" (Matt. 22:46).

As both David's son and David's Lord, Jesus is fully God and fully man. Scripture declares Him to be the eternal Word (John 1:1) who became flesh (v. 14), and His humanity is clearly evident in Scripture. He "was born of a descendant of David according to the flesh" (Rom. 1:3), and "kept increasing in wisdom and stature, and in favor with God and men" (Luke 2:52). The writer of Hebrews says that "since the children share in flesh and blood, He Himself likewise also partook of the same" (Heb. 2:14). Later in that chapter he adds that Jesus "had to be made like His brethren in all things, so that He might become a merciful and faithful high priest in things pertaining to God, to make propitiation for the sins of the people" (Heb. 2:17). Jesus became hungry (Matt. 4:1–2) and thirsty (John 4:7), and got tired (John 4:5–6; cf. Matt. 8:23–24). Jesus experienced the full range of human emotions, including joy (Luke 10:21), grief (Matt. 26:37), love (John 11:5, 36; 15:9), compassion (Matt. 9:36), amazement (Luke 7:9), and anger (Mark 3:5).

But Jesus is also fully God. John 1:1 states that "the Word [Jesus; cf. v. 14] was God." He took for Himself the sacred name of God (YHWH; Ex. 3:14) when He said to His opponents, "Truly, truly, I say to you, before Abraham was born, I am" (John 8:58). That the Jewish leaders (unlike modern cultists) understood clearly what He meant is evident from their reaction: they attempted to stone Him for blasphemy (v. 59; cf. Lev. 24:16). In John 10:30, Jesus claimed to be the same essence as God the Father. Once again the Jews attempted to stone Him for blasphemy, because "being a man [He made Himself] out to be God" (v. 33). When Thomas addressed Him as God (John 20:28), Jesus accepted that affirmation of His deity and praised his faith (v. 29). Philippians 2:6 says that Jesus "existed in the form of God" (i.e., that He is God by nature), and Colossians 2:9 adds that "in Him all the fullness of Deity dwells in bodily form." Titus 2:13 calls Him "our great God and Savior," and 2 Peter 1:1 calls Him "our God and Savior." In Hebrews 1:8 God the Father said to Jesus, "Your throne, O God, is forever and ever."

Many names or titles used in the Old Testament to refer to God are used in the New Testament to refer to Christ:

• YHWH (cf. Isa. 6:5, 10 with John 12:39–41; Jer. 23:5–6)
• Shepherd (cf. Ps. 23:1 with John 10:14)
• Judge (cf. Gen. 18:25 with 2 Tim. 4:1, 8)
• Holy One (cf. Isa. 10:20 with Acts 3:14; cf. Ps. 16:10 with Acts 2:27)
• First and Last (cf. Isa. 44:6; 48:12 with Rev. 1:17; 22:13)
• Light (cf. Ps. 27:1 with John 8:12)
• Lord of the Sabbath (cf. Ex. 16:23, 29; Lev. 19:3 with Matt. 12:8)
• Savior (cf. Isa. 43:11 with Acts 4:12; Titus 2:13)
• I AM (cf. Ex. 3:14 with John 8:58)
• Pierced One (cf. Zech. 12:10 with John 19:37)
• Mighty God (cf. Isa. 10:21 with Isa. 9:6)
• Lord of Lords (cf. Deut. 10:17 with Rev. 17:14)
• Alpha and Omega (cf. Rev. 1:8 with Rev. 22:13)
• Lord of Glory (cf. Ps. 24:10 with 1 Cor. 2:8)
• Redeemer (cf. Isa. 41:14; 48:17; 63:16 with Eph. 1:7; Heb. 9:12)

Jesus Christ possesses the incommunicable attributes of God (those that are unique to God and have no analogy in man):

• Eternalness (Mic. 5:2; Isa. 9:6)
• Omnipresence (Matt. 18:20; 28:20)
• Omniscience (Matt. 11:23; John 16:30; 21:17)
• Omnipotence (Phil. 3:21)
• Immutability (Heb. 13:8)
• Absolute sovereignty (Matt. 28:18)
• Glory (John 17:5; 1 Cor. 2:8; cf. Isa. 42:8; 48:11)

Jesus Christ also did the works that only God can do:

• Creation (John 1:3; Col. 1:16)
• Providence (sustaining the creation) (Col. 1:17; Heb. 1:3)
• Giving life (John 5:21)
• Forgiving sin (Mark 2:7, 10)
• Having His word stand forever (Matt. 24:35; cf. Isa. 40:8)

Finally, Jesus Christ accepted worship, even though He taught that God alone is to be worshiped (Matt. 4:10), and Scripture records that both men (Acts 10:25–26) and angels (Rev. 22:8–9) refused worship:

- Matthew 14:33
- Matthew 28:9
- John 5:23
- John 9:38
- (see also Phil. 2:10 [cf. Isa. 45:23], Heb. 1:6)

Another way of demonstrating Christ's deity is to ask the question, "If God became a man, what would we expect Him to be like?"

First, if God became a man we would expect Him to be sinless, because God is absolutely holy (Isa. 6:3). So is Jesus. Even His bitter enemies could make no reply to His challenge, "Which one of you convicts Me of sin?" (John 8:46). He is "holy, innocent, undefiled, separated from sinners and exalted above the heavens" (Heb. 7:26).

Second, if God became a man we would expect His words to be the greatest words ever spoken, because God is omniscient, is perfectly wise, and has infinite command of the truth and the ability to perfectly express it. Jesus' words demonstrated all that. The officers sent to arrest Him reported back to their superiors, "Never has a man spoken the way this man speaks" (John 7:46; cf. Matt. 7:28–29).

Third, if God became a man we would expect Him to display supernatural power, because God is all powerful. Jesus controlled nature, walked on water, healed the sick, raised the dead, dominated the kingdom of Satan and the demons, supernaturally avoided those who tried to kill Him, and performed miracles too numerous to be counted (John 21:25).

Fourth, if God became a man, we would expect Him to exert a profound influence over humanity. Jesus did. He changed the world like no one else in history.

Fifth, if God became a man, we would expect Him to manifest God's love, grace, kindness, compassion, justice, judgment, and wrath. Jesus did.

Jesus Christ was in every way the exact representation of God's nature (Heb. 1:3). But although they never confounded His infinite wisdom, refuted His matchless words, or denied His powerful miracles, the majority of the Jewish people and their leaders ultimately rejected Him. They failed to hear and obey God incarnate's voice (cf. Heb. 3:7), but instead hardened their hearts against Him, just as their ancestors had done (v. 8). For all those who, like them, "go on sinning willfully after receiving the knowledge of the truth, there no longer remains a sacrifice for sins, but a terrifying expectation of judgment and the fury of a fire which will consume the adversaries" (Heb. 10:26–27). Truly, "it is a terrifying thing to fall into the hands of the living God" (Heb. 10:31).

# Confronting Error with Condemnation, Not Conversation (Luke 20:45–21:4)

**16**

**And while all the people were listening, He said to the disciples, "Beware of the scribes, who like to walk around in long robes, and love respectful greetings in the market places, and chief seats in the synagogues and places of honor at banquets, who devour widows' houses, and for appearance's sake offer long prayers. These will receive greater condemnation." And He looked up and saw the rich putting their gifts into the treasury. And He saw a poor widow putting in two small copper coins. And He said, "Truly I say to you, this poor widow put in more than all of them; for they all out of their surplus put into the offering; but she out of her poverty put in all that she had to live on." (20:45–21:4)**

Emissaries of Satan have always twisted, distorted, and denied God's word. False prophets and false teachers have led millions of people astray from the truth, dooming them to share their own eternal punishment in hell (Matt. 23:15).

The Old Testament records early warnings of the deadly danger false teachers posed to Israel. As they were about to enter the Promised Land, Moses cautioned the nation to be on guard against those who would deceive them with lies:

> If a prophet or a dreamer of dreams arises among you and gives you a sign or a wonder, and the sign or the wonder comes true, concerning which he spoke to you, saying, "Let us go after other gods (whom you have not known) and let us serve them," you shall not listen to the words of that prophet or that dreamer of dreams; for the Lord your God is testing you to find out if you love the Lord your God with all your heart and with all your soul. (Deut. 13:1–3)

But Israel was indifferent to Moses' warnings, so when false prophets arose the people followed their defective doctrine into judgment. "The prophets prophesy falsely," God later said through Jeremiah, "and the priests rule on their own authority; and My people love it so!" (Jer. 5:31). In Jeremiah 14:14 He added, "The prophets are prophesying falsehood in My name. I have neither sent them nor commanded them nor spoken to them; they are prophesying to you a false vision, divination, futility and the deception of their own minds" (cf. 2:8; 6:14).

Through His true and faithful prophets, like Jeremiah, God pronounced judgment on the false prophets and warned His people of their danger:

> "Moreover, among the prophets of Samaria I saw an offensive thing: They prophesied by Baal and led My people Israel astray. Also among the prophets of Jerusalem I have seen a horrible thing: The committing of adultery and walking in falsehood; and they strengthen the hands of evildoers, so that no one has turned back from his wickedness. All of them have become to Me like Sodom, and her inhabitants like Gomorrah. Therefore thus says the Lord of hosts concerning the prophets, 'Behold, I am going to feed them wormwood and make them drink poisonous water, for from the prophets of Jerusalem pollution has gone forth into all the land.'" Thus says the Lord of hosts, "Do not listen to the words of the prophets who are prophesying to you. They are leading you into futility; they speak a vision of their own imagination, not from the mouth of the Lord. They keep saying to those who despise Me, 'The Lord has said, "You will have peace"'; and as for everyone who walks in the stubbornness of his own heart, they say, 'Calamity will not come upon you.' ... I did not send these prophets, but they ran. I did not speak to them, but they prophesied. But if they had stood in My council, then they would have announced My words to My people, and

would have turned them back from their evil way and from the evil of
their deeds.... I have heard what the prophets have said who prophesy
falsely in My name, saying, 'I had a dream, I had a dream!' How long? Is
there anything in the hearts of the prophets who prophesy falsehood,
even these prophets of the deception of their own heart, who intend to
make My people forget My name by their dreams which they relate to
one another, just as their fathers forgot My name because of Baal? The
prophet who has a dream may relate his dream, but let him who has
My word speak My word in truth. What does straw have in common
with grain?" declares the Lord. "Is not My word like fire?" declares the
Lord, "and like a hammer which shatters a rock? Therefore behold, I am
against the prophets," declares the Lord, "who steal My words from each
other. Behold, I am against the prophets," declares the Lord, "who use
their tongues and declare, 'The Lord declares.' Behold, I am against those
who have prophesied false dreams," declares the Lord, "and related
them and led My people astray by their falsehoods and reckless boast-
ing; yet I did not send them or command them, nor do they furnish this
people the slightest benefit," declares the Lord. (Jer. 23:13–17, 21–22, 25–
32; cf. 27:9–10, 14–16)

Ezekiel also recorded God's condemnation of the fraudulent preachers:

Then the word of the Lord came to me saying, "Son of man, prophesy
against the prophets of Israel who prophesy, and say to those who
prophesy from their own inspiration, 'Listen to the word of the Lord'
Thus says the Lord God, "Woe to the foolish prophets who are following
their own spirit and have seen nothing. O Israel, your prophets have
been like foxes among ruins. You have not gone up into the breaches,
nor did you build the wall around the house of Israel to stand in the
battle on the day of the Lord. They see falsehood and lying divination
who are saying, 'The Lord declares,' when the Lord has not sent them;
yet they hope for the fulfillment of their word. Did you not see a false
vision and speak a lying divination when you said, "The Lord declares,"
but it is not I who have spoken?"'" Therefore, thus says the Lord God,
"Because you have spoken falsehood and seen a lie, therefore behold,
I am against you," declares the Lord God. "So My hand will be against
the prophets who see false visions and utter lying divinations. They will
have no place in the council of My people, nor will they be written
down in the register of the house of Israel, nor will they enter the land
of Israel, that you may know that I am the Lord God. It is definitely
because they have misled My people by saying, 'Peace!' when there is
no peace." (Ezek. 13:1–10; cf. 14:9–10; 22:25, 28)

The New Testament also warns of the deadly peril of religious
liars. Jesus told His followers, "Beware of the false prophets, who come to

you in sheep's clothing, but inwardly are ravenous wolves" (Matt. 7:15). Paul cautioned the elders at Ephesus that "savage wolves will come in among you, not sparing the flock; and from among your own selves men will arise, speaking perverse things, to draw away the disciples after them" (Acts 20:29–30). He warned the Corinthians that "such men are false apostles, deceitful workers, disguising themselves as apostles of Christ" (2 Cor. 11:13) when in reality they are "servants [of Satan who] disguise themselves as servants of righteousness" (v. 15). Paul wrote to the churches of Galatia, "I am amazed that you are so quickly deserting Him who called you by the grace of Christ, for a different gospel; which is really not another; only there are some who are disturbing you and want to distort the gospel of Christ" (Gal. 1:6–7; cf. Phil. 3:18–19). In the last inspired letter he penned, the apostle commanded his protégé Timothy, "Avoid worldly and empty chatter, for it will lead to further ungodliness, and their talk will spread like gangrene. Among them are Hymenaeus and Philetus, men who have gone astray from the truth saying that the resurrection has already taken place, and they upset the faith of some" (2 Tim. 2:16–18; cf. 1 Tim. 4:1–3). Jude (Jude 1–19), Peter (2 Peter 2:1–22; 3:15–17), and John (1 John 2:18, 22; 4:3; 2 John 7) also warned their readers to beware of false teachers.

Though always present, at no time in previous history were false teachers more aggressive than during the Lord Jesus Christ's earthly ministry. In a desperate and futile attempt to thwart the gospel purposes of God, Satan unleashed all the power of hell against Jesus. The human agents of the darkness who carried out that assault were the scribes, Pharisees, Sadducees, and Herodians—the political and religious leaders of Israel. Those sects, normally bitterly divided against each other, temporarily set aside their differences and united in their determination to eliminate the disruptive Jesus.

Final confrontation between the Jewish religious leaders and Jesus took place on Wednesday of Passion Week. All of their desperate attempts throughout His ministry to discredit and silence Him had failed, and they had concluded it was useless to ask Him more questions (Luke 20:40). Instead, in a final act of mercy and compassion to show them the truth, He questioned them, challenging them to explain how the Messiah could be both David's son and his Lord as Psalm 110 revealed (vv. 41–44).

After this last confrontation with the elite religionists, the Lord had nothing more to say to them until His trial before the Sanhedrin. He was also finished addressing the crowds, and shifted the direction of His teaching to His disciples. **While all the people were** still **listening** to His teaching, Jesus targeted His words specifically **to the disciples.**

The Lord did not seek common ground with those who rejected the truth. When compassion was exhausted and invitations spurned, He condemned them. Before issuing His condemnation of the religious leaders, Jesus cautioned His hearers of the danger that was hidden in their teaching, gave a characterization of them, condemned them, and pointed to a case that exemplified the threat they posed.

## THE CAUTION

### "Beware of the scribes, (20:46a)

Matthew's account notes that Jesus extended His warning to include the Pharisees (Matt. 23:2). Not all Pharisees were scribes, but the **scribes** were primarily Pharisees, who were interpreters and teachers of the law of Moses and the traditional rabbinic writings. Their teaching provided the theological framework for the Pharisees' legalistic system of works-righteousness. The scribes were the dominant force in Judaism, not only theologically, but socially. Their views affected every aspect of life, and they also handled all legal matters, including property, estates, and contracts. They were revered, and given the respectful title of Rabbi (Matt. 23:7). That title was sometimes given to Jesus because He was a teacher (cf. John 1:38, 49; 3:2, 26; 6:25). It was commonly believed that Moses received the law, then gave it to Joshua, who gave it to the elders, who gave it to the prophets, who gave it to the scribes.

Because of the elevated esteem in which the populace held them, it must have come as a shock when Jesus warned, **"Beware of** ("take heed of"; "guard against") **the scribes."** They posed a soul-killing threat because they did not know God or the way to heaven, nor did they possess true spiritual wisdom. The scribes were destructive agents of Satan who opposed the purposes of God. Although it was not apparent on the outside, on the inside they were vile sinners. In Matthew 23:27 Jesus declared, "Woe to you, scribes and Pharisees, hypocrites! For you are like whitewashed tombs which on the outside appear beautiful, but inside they are full of dead men's bones and all uncleanness" (cf. Luke 11:44). They had nothing beneficial to offer spiritually, and were hypocrites to be avoided. The opening verse of Psalm 1 praises "the man who does not walk in the counsel of the wicked, nor stand in the path of sinners, nor sit in the seat of scoffers!"

### THE CHARACTERIZATION

**who like to walk around in long robes, and love respectful greetings in the market places, and chief seats in the synagogues and places of honor at banquets, who devour widows' houses, and for appearance's sake offer long prayers.** (20:46b–47a)

Jesus gave five illustrations of the scribes' hypocrisy. First, they liked to **walk around in long,** fancy, expensive **robes.** In Numbers 15:38–40 God instructed the Israelites to add tassels to their robes to remind them of His commandments, and Jesus had such tassels on the fringe of His cloak (Matt. 9:20). But the scribes and Pharisees lengthened their tassels in an ostentatious display of their supposed piety.

Second, they loved **respectful greetings in the market places.** As they mingled in public, the scribes expected to be noticed and addressed with dignified titles. The Lord's extended condemnation of them in Matthew 23 reveals that they wanted to be called "Rabbi" (v. 7), a title denoting an exalted, revered teacher. An example of just how revered they were comes from the Mishnah, which states, "It is more culpable to transgress the words of the Scribes than those of the Torah" (cited in Alfred Edersheim, *The Life and Times of Jesus the Messiah* [Grand Rapids: Eerdmans, 1974], 1:625 n. 1). Edersheim went on to relate more outrageous statements regarding the scribes:

> So weighty was the duty of respectful salutation by the title Rabbi, that to neglect it would involve the heaviest punishment.... It reads like a

wretched imitation from the New Testament, when the heathen Governor of Cæsarea is represented as rising up before Rabbis because he beheld "the faces as it were of Angels;" or like an adaptation of the well-known story about Constantine the Great when the Governor of Antioch is described as vindicating a similar mark of respect to the Rabbis by this, that he had seen their faces and by them conquered in battle.... To supply a learned man with the means of gaining money in trade, would procure a high place in heaven. It was said that, according to Prov. viii. 15, the sages were to be saluted as kings; nay, in some respects, they were higher for, as between a sage and a king, it would be duty to give the former priority in redemption from captivity, since every Israelite was fit to be a king, but the loss of a Rabbi could not easily be made up. (Ibid., 5:409)

Incredibly, "a Rabbi went so far as to order that he should be buried in white garments, to show that he was worthy of appearing before his Maker" (ibid., 5:409). Edersheim then gave perhaps the most shocking example of all:

> Perhaps the climax of blasphemous self-assertion is reached in the story, that, in a discussion in heaven between God and the heavenly Academy on a Halakhic question about purity, a certain Rabbi— deemed that most learned on the subject—was summoned to decide the point! As his soul passed from the body he exclaimed: "Pure, pure," which the Voice from Heaven applied to the state of the Rabbi's soul; and immediately afterwards a letter had fallen from heaven to inform the sages of the purpose of which the Rabbi had been summoned to the heavenly assembly, and afterwards another enjoing a week's universal mourning for him on pain of excommunication. (Ibid., 5:410)

Never humble, the scribes also wanted to be called "father," imagining themselves to be the source of spiritual life and truth, and "leader," as befits the ones who determine direction and destiny.

Third, they sought the **chief seats in the synagogues,** which were on the elevated platform at the front. They also sought the **places of honor at banquets,** the ones closest to the host. "Rabbinic writings lay down elaborate directions, what place is to be assigned to the Rabbis, according to their rank, and to their disciples, and how in the College the most learned, but at feast the most aged, among the Rabbis, are to occupy the 'upper seats'" (ibid., 5:409; cf. Matt. 23:1–12).

The first three examples highlighted the scribes' overweening pride. But the next one introduces a more sinister aspect of their hypocrisy—their rapacious greed that led them to prey on the most defenseless members of society. That the scribes would stoop so low as to **devour widows' houses** graphically illustrates the intense desire for wealth that characterizes false teachers (cf. Mic. 3:5, 11; 2 Peter 2:1–3, 14). **Devour** translates a form of the Greek verb *katesthiō*, an intense word that literally means "to eat," and metaphorically, "to devour completely," "to consume," or, "to eat up." The Old Testament teaches that widows are to be protected and cared for (e.g., Ex. 22:22; Deut. 10:18; 14:29; 24:17–21; 27:19; Pss. 68:5; 146:9; Prov. 15:25; Isa. 1:17; Jer. 22:3; Zech. 7:10), but the scribes consumed their meager resources. They took advantage of their hospitality, cheated them out of their estates, mismanaged their property, and took their houses as pledges for debts that they could never repay (cf. Darrell L. Bock, *Luke 9:51–24:53*, The Baker Exegetical Commentary on the New Testament [Grand Rapids: Baker, 1996], 1643).

Finally, **for appearance's sake** they offered **long prayers,** not to call attention to God, but to themselves as pious. Jesus strongly condemned such self-exalting, God-dishonoring prayers in the Sermon on the Mount:

> When you pray, you are not to be like the hypocrites; for they love to stand and pray in the synagogues and on the street corners so that they may be seen by men. Truly I say to you, they have their reward in full. But you, when you pray, go into your inner room, close your door and pray to your Father who is in secret, and your Father who sees what is done in secret will reward you. (Matt. 6:5–6)

## THE CONDEMNATION

**These will receive greater condemnation."** (20:47*b*)

Far from being rewarded for their self-righteous, outwardly moral lives, the scribes would **receive greater condemnation** from God for leading people astray from the truth. His condemnation of them is consistent with the Bible's strong warnings against and denouncing of false teachers, as I noted in an earlier volume of this series:

God's attitude toward false teachers stands in sharp contrast to the inclusiveness and tolerance of error that pervades contemporary evangelicalism. Scripture denounces them as blind men; "mute dogs unable to bark; dreamers lying down who love to slumber"; ignorant (Isa. 56:10); demented fools (Hos. 9:7); reckless, treacherous men (Zeph. 3:4); ravenous wolves (Matt. 7:15); blind guides of the blind (Matt. 15:14; cf. 23:16); hypocrites (Matt. 23:13); fools (v. 17); whitewashed tombs full of bones (v. 27); serpents; a brood of vipers (v. 33); thieves and robbers (John 10:8); savage wolves (Acts 20:29); slaves of their own appetites (Rom. 16:18); hucksters peddling the word of God (2 Cor. 2:17); false apostles; deceitful workers (2 Cor. 11:13); servants of Satan (v. 15); purveyors of a different gospel (Gal. 1:6–8); dogs; evil workers (Phil. 3:2); enemies of the cross of Christ (Phil. 3:18); conceited and understanding nothing (1 Tim. 6:4); men of depraved minds deprived of the truth (v. 5); men who have gone astray from the truth (2 Tim. 2:18); captives of the devil (v. 26); deceivers (2 John 7); ungodly persons (Jude 4); and unreasoning animals (v. 10). As a result, the Bible also pronounces severe judgment on them (Deut. 13:5; 18:20; Jer. 14:15; Gal. 1:8–9; Rev. 2:20–23).

The reason for such seemingly harsh language is the deadly danger false teachers pose because they engage in Satan's most distinctive wickedness and the most devastating sin; they lead people astray from the truth of God's word (Isa. 3:12; 9:16; Jer. 14:13; 23:26–27, 32; 50:6; Matt. 23:13, 15; 24:4–5, 24; Luke 11:46, 52; Rom. 16:17–18; Col. 2:4, 8, 18; 1 Thess. 2:14–16; 2 Tim. 3:13; Titus 1:10; 2 John 7)—including the need for repentance from sin (Jer. 6:14; 8:11; 23:21–22; Lam. 2:14; Ezek. 13:10, 16, 22). Left unchecked, the demon doctrines they peddle (1 Tim. 4:1) will ravage souls and corrupt the church (Acts 20:29–30; 2 Tim. 2:17–18), lulling many into a false sense of security regarding their salvation. (*Luke 6–10*, The MacArthur New Testament Commentary [Chicago: Moody, 2011], 112)

## THE CASE

**And He looked up and saw the rich putting their gifts into the treasury. And He saw a poor widow putting in two small copper coins. And He said, "Truly I say to you, this poor widow put in more than all of them; for they all out of their surplus put into the offering; but she out of her poverty put in all that she had to live on."** (21:1–4)

The previous section ended with a warning of judgment (20:47), and the next section (21:5–36) resumes that theme. The question arises as to how this intervening passage fits into that context. Why did Luke inject this story of a widow giving an offering between a diatribe against false leaders, and a pronunciation of future judgment?

This little vignette is commonly, if oddly, interpreted as a lesson on giving, in which the widow's sacrificial offering is presented as a ray of sunshine in the darkness of hypocrisy and judgment. Not only is such a perspective alien to the context, but also if Jesus is teaching a lesson on giving, is the lesson to give everything you have, go home, and starve? On that, commentators differ.

Some argue that the story teaches that the true measure of a gift is not what was given, but what was withheld; not the amount of the gift, but the amount the giver kept back.

Others insist that a gift should be measured by the giver's self-denial, as reflected by the percentage given.

Another view, related to the first two, is that a gift's value is directly related to the attitude with which it is given. Was it given selflessly? Humbly? As an expression of love and devotion to God? Since the widow had the least amount possible left after her gift, she must have had the attitude most pleasing to God.

The only real option is that the gift that truly pleases God is everything.

All those ideas, however, are imposed on the narrative; Jesus drew no principle regarding giving from her behavior. The text does not record that He condemned the rich for their giving, or commended the widow for hers. There is no judgment made regarding the true nature of her act, nor is anything said about her attitude, or the spirit in which her gift was given. Since Jesus made no point about giving, neither should the interpreter.

To frame this incident as a lesson on giving isolates it from the obvious theme of divine judgment on false religious leaders, their followers, and, ultimately, on the nation as a whole. Such interpretations also assume that Jesus was pleased with the widow's gift, which He does not state or even imply. Further, she was giving to a false, apostate system, not honoring to God. What is clear from the narrative is that the widow's involvement in that system cost her everything she had. That is the obvious lesson. False religion can and does divest the weakest of their resources down to the last coin. That is all the story means. It is an illustration of the corruption that was dominant in the religion.

Mark's account of this incident reveals that the Lord was sitting down near the temple treasury. It was nearing the end of a long, exhausting Wednesday spent in the midst of massive crowds. Jesus had dialogued with the people, taught them, confronted and denounced the religious leaders (Matt. 23:1–36), and lamented the coming judgment on the nation (vv. 37–39). In addition to His physical weariness, Jesus felt deeply the agonizing, sad reality of Israel's coming judgment.

The Lord's eyes must have been downcast as He contemplated the damning false religion that had the nation in its grip, the corruption of the temple, and the divine judgment that would hit the city of Jerusalem and the temple (cf. Luke 21:5–36). As Luke's account opens, Jesus **looked up and saw** the people (Mark 12:41), in particular **the rich, putting their gifts into the treasury.** The **treasury,** located in the Court of the Women, consisted of thirteen trumpet-shaped receptacles into which the people deposited their offerings.

The word translated **rich** (*plousios*) refers to those who have enough; who are fully supplied. But what caught the Lord's attention was not the wealthy **putting their** lavish **gifts into the treasury,** but **a poor widow putting in two small copper coins.** *Penichrōs* (**poor**) describes someone who is poor and needy, but not destitute. Her offering of **two small copper coins** (*lepta*; the smallest denomination of Jewish currency) was a tiny fraction of what the rich would have given. Yet **this poor widow,** hoping to purchase blessing by following the Jewish religious system's legalistic requirements, **put in more than all of them; for they all out of their surplus put into the offering,** while those two small coins were all that she possessed.

This is clearly an example of what the Lord had spoken of earlier (see the discussion of 20:47 above). The legalistic works system had devoured this impoverished widow by taking from her **all that she had to live on.** The second use of **poor** in verse 3 reflects that reality; it is the word *ptōchos*, a different word than the one used in verse 2. *Ptōchos* describes those who have nothing and are reduced to begging. The Old Testament commanded that widows be cared for, as noted above, but the religious leaders set aside those commands for the sake of their traditions (and their greed). Mark 7:9–13 records Jesus' condemnation of them for another practice that set aside the clear teaching of the Old Testament:

> He was also saying to them, "You are experts at setting aside the commandment of God in order to keep your tradition. For Moses said, 'Honor your father and your mother'; and, 'He who speaks evil of father or mother, is to be put to death'; but you say, 'If a man says to his father or his mother, whatever I have that would help you is Corban (that is to say, given to God),' you no longer permit him to do anything for his father or his mother; thus invalidating the word of God by your tradition which you have handed down; and you do many things such as that."

As the story of this widow reveals, deceptive, self-righteous religion preys on the weak, the desperate, and the defenseless. Far from being pleased with her giving, Jesus was angry that the so-called worship she had bought into had taken her last cent. The Lord would go on to pronounce judgment on that very apostate Judaism in the next section.

Money has always been at the heart of satanic religion (cf. Luke 16:14; 19:46; 1 Peter 5:2), consequently abuse of the poor by false religious systems has continued from our Lord's day down to our own. For example, the medieval Roman Catholic Church defrauded the desperate by selling indulgences, purportedly to free the purchasers' loved ones from purgatory. Like modern religious hucksters, those who sold them used fear tactics to relieve the poor of their money.

One very successful seller of indulgences was the Dominican friar Johann Tetzel. In the fall of 1517, Tetzel began selling indulgences in Germany, raising money to help build the Sistine Chapel and St. Peter's Basilica. Historian James M. Kittleson describes a typical Tetzel sales pitch:

> "Do you not hear the voices of your dead relatives and others, crying out to you and saying, 'Pity us, pity us, for we are in dire punishment and torment from which you can redeem us for a pittance'? And you will not?" Finally, there was the appeal: "Will you not then for a quarter of a florin receive these letters of indulgence through which you are able to lead a divine and immortal soul safely and securely into the homeland of paradise?" A money chest, a supply of blank indulgences, a scale to make certain that people's coins were good, and the scribes were all ready and in their places. Then came Tetzel's last exhortation: "Once the coin into the coffer clings, a soul from purgatory heavenward springs!"

The transactions were finished quickly. Soon the entourage was on its way to the next town. (*Luther the Reformer* [Minneapolis: Augsburg, 1986], 103–104)

To Martin Luther, such "pious defrauding of the faithful" (Kittleson, 104) was intolerable. Like any true pastor, Luther was outraged at this fleecing of his flock. In response, he railed against indulgences and posted his famous Ninety-Five Theses condemning them along with other deadly aberrations. That act sparked the Reformation.

This passage is instructive in today's context, as it reveals how Jesus dealt with those who did not believe the truth. His approach was radically different from that of today's evangelical trends. The charismatic movement leads the list in taking money from the most desperate, weak, sick, and poor on the promise of health, wealth, and prosperity. The means is to send the minister "seed" money and wait for the Lord to fulfill all desires. Instead, like any Ponzi scheme, only the false teacher becomes rich.

Jesus taught in this passage that those who are purveyors of false religion will face the most severe divine condemnation. They are not fellow truth seekers, to be engaged in "conversation," but dangerous opponents of biblical truth (cf. Matt. 7:15; Acts 20:29). While Christians are to compassionately present the gospel to them, pray for their salvation, and grieve when they reject the truth and are eternally lost, the true church of Jesus Christ must warn them and all who follow them of the grave and eternal danger awaiting.

# Signs of Christ's Return—Part 1: Jesus' Description of the Temple's Destruction (Luke 21:5-7)

**17**

**And while some were talking about the temple, that it was adorned with beautiful stones and votive gifts, He said, "As for these things which you are looking at, the days will come in which there will not be left one stone upon another which will not be torn down." They questioned Him, saying, "Teacher, when therefore will these things happen? And what will be the sign when these things are about to take place?" (21:5-7)**

The Son of God, the Lord Jesus Christ, came into the world to redeem lost sinners from judgment and hell. Before His birth an angel told His father Joseph, "You shall call His name Jesus, for He will save His people from their sins" (Matt. 1:21). Jesus defined His mission when He said that He had "come to seek and to save that which was lost" (Luke 19:10). In Matthew 20:28 He told the disciples that "the Son of Man did not come to be served, but to serve, and to give His life a ransom for many." When the scribes and Pharisees complained that He associated with tax collectors and sinners, Jesus replied, "It is not those who are well who need a physician, but those who are sick. I have not come to call the righteous but sinners to repentance" (Luke 5:31–32). He told the preeminent Jewish teacher Nicodemus that "God did not send the Son into the world to judge the world, but that the world might be saved through Him" (John 3:17). In John 12:47 Jesus said, "If anyone hears My sayings and does not keep them, I do not judge him; for I did not come to judge the world, but to save the world."

The rest of the New Testament also teaches that Jesus came to redeem sinners. John the Baptist declared of Him, "Behold, the Lamb of God who takes away the sin of the world!" (John 1:29). Paul wrote, "It is a trustworthy statement, deserving full acceptance, that Christ Jesus came into the world to save sinners, among whom I am foremost of all" (1 Tim. 1:15). After He brought salvation to the village of Sychar, the Samaritans declared that Jesus was "the Savior of the world" (John 4:42). In his first epistle the apostle John wrote:

> You know that He appeared in order to take away sins.... By this the love of God was manifested in us, that God has sent His only begotten Son into the world so that we might live through Him. In this is love, not that we loved God, but that He loved us and sent His Son to be the propitiation for our sins.... We have seen and testify that the Father has sent the Son to be the Savior of the world. (1 John 3:5; 4:9–10, 14)

Christ's redemptive mission clearly fulfilled Old Testament prophecy, most notably that of Isaiah 53:

> But He was pierced through for our transgressions, He was crushed for our iniquities; the chastening for our well-being fell upon Him, and by His scourging we are healed. All of us like sheep have gone astray, each of us has turned to his own way; but the Lord has caused the iniquity of us all to fall on Him. He was oppressed and He was afflicted, yet He did not open His mouth; like a lamb that is led to slaughter, and like a sheep that is silent before its shearers, so He did not open His mouth. By oppression and judgment He was taken away; and as for His generation, who considered that He was cut off out of the land of the living for the transgression of my people, to whom the stroke was due? His grave was assigned with wicked men, yet He was with a rich man in His death, because He had done no violence, nor was there any deceit in His mouth. But the Lord was pleased to crush Him, putting Him to grief; if He would render Himself as a guilt offering, He will see His offspring,

He will prolong His days, and the good pleasure of the Lord will prosper in His hand. As a result of the anguish of His soul, He will see it and be satisfied; by His knowledge the Righteous One, My Servant, will justify the many, as He will bear their iniquities. Therefore, I will allot Him a portion with the great, and He will divide the booty with the strong; because He poured out Himself to death, and was numbered with the transgressors; yet He Himself bore the sin of many, and interceded for the transgressors. (vv. 5–12)

But although He was sent ultimately to redeem the "lost sheep of the house of Israel" (Matt. 15:24), Jesus pronounced judgment on that nation when it rejected Him. At both the beginning (John 2:13–22) and the end (Mark 11:15–18) of His ministry, He struck a blow against Israel's false religious system by attacking the corrupt operations of the temple during Passover. Further, He upbraided the cities of Chorazin, Bethsaida, and Capernaum for their unbelief, and warned that Capernaum faced more severe judgment than Sodom because of it (Matt. 11:20–24). He rebuked the entire wicked generation that rejected Him for refusing to repent, in contrast to the people of Nineveh and the Queen of Sheba (Matt. 12:41–42). He told the disciples that those who willfully reject the truth will be judicially deprived of it (Luke 8:9–18). Though He was moved to tears by the judgment that Israel's stubborn rejection of Him would bring (Luke 13:34–35; 19:41–44), He gave a blistering denunciation of the scribes and Pharisees and those who followed them and did so with another lamentation over Israel's (represented by Jerusalem) fate (Matt. 23:37–39).

This section of Luke's gospel records Christ's final pronouncement of judgment on Israel in particular, as well as the world in general. This last of His great discourses is commonly known as the Olivet Discourse, because the Lord taught this truth to His disciples while sitting on the Mount of Olives, across the Kidron Valley looking back at the temple (Matt. 24:3).

It was Wednesday evening of Passion Week. All of the scribes', Pharisees', and Sadducees' attempts to publicly discredit and destroy Jesus had utterly failed, and they were forced to silence (Luke 20:40) by His answers. The Lord had preached His last sermon to the crowds, condemning the religious leaders (Matt. 23:1–36) and warning the people of the deadly influence of their hypocrisy. After watching a poor widow give all that she possessed to the apostate religious system, Jesus and the disciples left the temple (see the exposition of 21:1–4 in the previous chapter of this volume) for the mount.

As they were leaving, some of the disciples were commenting on the magnificence of the temple (v. 5). When Christ replied that the coming judgment on the nation would include the destruction of the temple (v. 6), His followers asked Him when that judgment would take place and what signs would precede both it (v. 7) and His return (Matt. 24:3). Jesus' reply, beginning in verse 8, is the longest recorded answer He ever gave to any question, establishing its importance.

This preliminary section introduces Luke's account of the Olivet Discourse, and may be divided into two parts: judgment's coming predicted, and judgment's timing questioned.

## JUDGMENT'S COMING PREDICTED

**And while some were talking about the temple, that it was adorned with beautiful stones and votive gifts, He said, "As for these things which you are looking at, the days will come in which there will not be left one stone upon another which will not be torn down."** (21:5–6)

As noted above, when Jesus and the disciples left the temple grounds, **some** of the disciples **were** admiring **the temple.** The construction of that stunning, magnificent structure, one of the architectural wonders of the ancient world, had been started half a century earlier by Herod the Great, but was still ongoing when the Romans destroyed the temple in A.D. 70. It was built with brilliant white stone, polished like marble, and contained numerous rooms, porticos, colonnades, plazas, and patios, as well as caves, cisterns, and pits for water storage. The highest of its many levels towered hundreds of feet above the Kidron Valley. The eastern wall of the temple's main structure was covered in plates of gold, which shone brilliantly in the rays of the morning sun coming over Olivet.

The disciples noted in particular that the massive stone block walls were also **adorned with beautiful stones,** donated by the wealthy as their ancestors had done for Solomon's temple (1 Chron. 29:8). **Votive gifts** were given as offerings symbolizing a vow made by the giver. Such consisted of plaques, sculptures, and other artistic treasures (including a nearly six-foot-high golden vine with golden grapes, donated by Herod), found throughout the temple.

It must have seemed inconceivable to the disciples that such an enduring, massive, ornate structure, prized so highly for its magnificence and value, would ever be destroyed. Yet the temple could not escape the coming judgment on the unbelieving nation. **"As for these things which you are looking at,"** Jesus told them, **"the days will come in which there will not be left one stone upon another which will not be torn down."** His words would be fulfilled literally in A.D. 70, when the Romans, the human means of divine wrath, erected scaffolds around the walls of the temple and its buildings, filled them with wood and other flammable material, and set them on fire. The intense heat from the fires caused the stones to crumble. After it was further dismantled and sifted to find all the melted gold, the rubble was thrown down into the Kidron Valley. Only the huge foundation stones remained largely intact. Those stones, however, were not part of the temple itself, but supports for the retaining wall.

The disciples could have remembered from the Old Testament that there would be judgment on Israel's enemies associated with the Messiah's coming. In Zechariah 12:8–9 God said,

> In that day the Lord will defend the inhabitants of Jerusalem, and the one who is feeble among them in that day will be like David, and the house of David will be like God, like the angel of the Lord before them. And it will come about in that day I will set about to destroy all the nations that come against Jerusalem.

In distinction to the destruction of the nation's enemies, they would likely have known Israel was promised salvation.

> I will pour out on the house of David and on the inhabitants of Jerusalem, the Spirit of grace and of supplication, so that they will look

on Me whom they have pierced; and they will mourn for Him, as one mourns for an only son, and they will weep bitterly over Him like the bitter weeping over a firstborn....In that day a fountain will be opened for the house of David and for the inhabitants of Jerusalem, for sin and for impurity. (v. 10; 13:1)

All that would be followed by the glorious reign of Messiah in the kingdom on earth. "The Lord will be king over all the earth; in that day the Lord will be the only one, and His name the only one" (14:9).

But looking more carefully at Zechariah's prophecy, it was also predicted that before the time of Israel's salvation, Jerusalem will be destroyed: "For I will gather all the nations against Jerusalem to battle," the Lord declared, "and the city will be captured, the houses plundered, the women ravished and half of the city exiled, but the rest of the people will not be cut off from the city" (14:2). So Messiah's coming will produce both judgment and destruction as well as final restoration and salvation for Israel.

## Judgment's Timing Questioned

**They questioned Him, saying, "Teacher, when therefore will these things happen? And what will be the sign when these things are about to take place?" (21:7)**

In light of the Lord's prediction of coming judgment, the disciples had two questions: When would the judgment of which He spoke take place? And what would be the sign of His coming (or "presence"; Matt. 24:3), which will usher in the judgment?

They were not completely without knowledge about elements of the coming of the messiah, since the Jewish people had a well-developed system of eschatology, as the following summary indicates:

(i) Before the Messiah came there would be a time of terrible tribulation. There would be a Messianic travail. It would be the birth-pangs of a new age. Every conceivable terror would burst upon the world; every standard of honour and decency would be torn down; the world would become a physical and moral chaos.

"And honour shall be turned into shame,
And strength humiliated into contempt.
And probity destroyed,
And beauty shall become ugliness ...
And envy shall rise in those who had not thought aught of
    themselves,
And passion shall seize him that is peaceful,
And many shall be stirred up in anger to injure many,
And they shall rouse up armies in order to shed blood,
And in the end they shall perish together with them." (2 *Baruch* 27.)

There would be "quakings of places, tumult of peoples, schemings of nations, confusion of leaders, disquietude of princes." (4 Ezra 9:3.)

"From heaven shall fall fiery words down to the earth. Lights shall come, bright and great, flashing into the midst of men; and earth, the universal mother, shall shake in these days at the hand of the Eternal. And the fishes of the sea and the beasts of the earth and the countless tribes of flying things and all the souls of men and every sea shall shudder at the presence of the Eternal and there shall be panic. And the towering mountain peaks and the hills of the giants he shall rend, and the murky abyss shall be visible to all. And the high ravines in the lofty mountains shall be full of dead bodies and rocks shall flow with blood and each torrent shall flood the plain. ...And God shall judge all with war and sword, and there shall be brimstone from heaven, yea stones and rain and hail incessant and grievous. And death shall be upon the four-footed beasts....Yea the land itself shall drink of the blood of the perishing and beasts shall eat their fill of flesh." (the *Sibylline Oracles* 3:363 ff.)

The Mishnah enumerates as signs that the coming of the Messiah is near,

"That arrogance increases, ambition shoots up, that the vine yields fruit yet wine is dear. The government turns to heresy. There is no instruction. The synagogue is devoted to lewdness. Galilee is destroyed, Gablan laid waste. The inhabitants of a district go from city to city without finding compassion. The wisdom of the learned is hated, the godly despised, truth is absent. Boys insult old men, old men stand in the presence of children. The son depreciates the father, the daughter rebels against the mother, the daughter-in-law against the mother-in-law. A man's enemies are his house-fellows."

The time which preceded the coming of the Messiah was to be a time when the world was torn in pieces and every bond relaxed. The physical and the moral order would collapse.

(ii) Into this chaos there would come Elijah as the forerunner and herald of the Messiah. He was to heal the breaches and bring order into the chaos to prepare the way for the Messiah. In particular he was to mend disputes. In fact the Jewish oral law laid it down that money and property whose ownership was disputed, or anything found whose owner was unknown, must wait "till Elijah comes." When Elijah came the Messiah would not be far behind.

(iii) Then there would enter the Messiah. The word *Messiah* and the word *Christ* mean the same thing. *Messiah* is the Hebrew and *Christ* is the Greek for *the Anointed One.* A king was made king by anointing and the Messiah was God's Anointed King. It is important to remember that *Christ* is not a *name*; it is a *title*. Sometimes the Messiah was thought of as a king of David's line, but more often he was thought of as a great, divine, superhuman figure crashing into history to remake the world and in the end to vindicate God's people.

(iv) The nations would ally themselves and gather themselves together against the champion of God.

> "The kings of the nations shall throw themselves against this land bringing retribution on themselves. They shall seek to ravage the shrine of the mighty God and of the noblest men whensoever they come to the land. In a ring round the city the accursed kings shall place each one his throne with his infidel people by him. And then with a mighty voice God shall speak unto all the undisciplined, empty-minded people and judgment shall come upon them from the mighty God, and all shall perish at the hand of the Eternal." (*Sibylline Oracles* 3:363–372.)

> "It shall be that when that the nations hear his (the Messiah's) voice, every man shall leave his own land and the warfare they have one against the other, and an innumerable multitude shall be gathered together desiring to fight against him." (4 *Ezra* 13:33–35.)

(v) The result would be the total destruction of these hostile powers. Philo said that the Messiah would "take the field and make war and destroy great and populous nations."

> "He shall reprove them for their ungodliness,
> Rebuke them for their unrighteousness,
> Reproach them to their faces with treacheries—
> And when he has rebuked them he shall destroy them." (4 *Ezra* 12:32, 33.)

> "And it shall come to pass in those days that none shall be saved,
> Either by gold or by silver,

And none shall be able to escape.
And there shall be no iron for war,
Nor shall one clothe oneself with a breastplate.
Bronze shall be of no service,
And tin shall not be esteemed,
And lead shall not be desired.
And all things shall be destroyed from the surface of the earth."
(*Enoch* 52:7–9.)

The Messiah will be the most destructive conqueror in history, smashing his enemies into utter extinction.

(vi) There would follow the renovation of Jerusalem. Sometimes this was thought of as the purification of the existing city. More often it was thought of as the coming down of the new Jerusalem from heaven. The old house was to be folded up and carried away, and, in the new one, "All the pillars were new and the ornaments larger than those of the first." (*Enoch* 90:28, 29.)

(vii) The Jews who were dispersed all over the world would be gathered into the city of the new Jerusalem. To this day the Jewish daily prayer includes the petition, "Lift up a banner to gather our dispersed and assemble us from the four ends of the earth." The eleventh of the *Psalms of Solomon* has a noble picture of that return.

"Blow ye in Zion on the trumpet to summon the saints,
Cause ye to be heard in Jerusalem the voice of him that bringeth good tidings;
For God hath had pity on Israel in visiting them.
Stand on the height, O Jerusalem, and behold thy children,
From the East and the West, gathered together by the Lord;
From the North they come in the gladness of their God,
From the isles afar off God hath gathered them.
High mountains hath he abased into a plain for them;
The hills fled at their entrance.
The woods gave them shelter as they passed by;
Every sweet-smelling tree God caused to spring up for them,
That Israel might pass by in the visitation of the glory of their God.
Put on, O Jerusalem, thy glorious garments;
Make ready thy holy robe;
For God hath spoken good for Israel forever and ever,
Let the Lord do what he hath spoken concerning Israel and Jerusalem;
Let the Lord raise up Israel by His glorious name.
The mercy of the Lord be upon Israel forever and ever."

*181*

It can easily be seen how Jewish this new world was to be. The nationalistic element is dominant all the time.

(viii) Palestine would be the centre of the world and the rest of the world subject to it. All the nations would be subdued. Sometimes it was thought of as a peaceful subjugation.

> "And all the isles and the cities shall say, How doth the Eternal love those men! For all things work in sympathy with them and help them.... Come let us all fall upon the earth and supplicate the eternal King, the mighty, everlasting God. Let us make procession to His Temple, for He is the sole Potentate." (*Sibylline Oracles* 3:690 ff.)

More often the fate of the Gentiles was utter destruction at which Israel would exult and rejoice.

> "And He will appear to punish the Gentiles,
> Then, thou, O Israel, shalt be happy.
> And He will destroy all their idols.
> And thou shalt mount upon the necks and the wings of the eagle
> (i.e., Rome, the eagle, is to be destroyed)
> And they shall be ended and God will exalt thee.

> "And thou shalt look from on high
> And see thine enemies in Gehenna,
> And thou shalt recognize them and rejoice."
> (*Assumption of Moses* 10:8–10.)

It was a grim picture. Israel would rejoice to see her enemies broken and in hell. Even the dead Israelites were to be raised up to share in the new world.

(ix) Finally, there would come the new age of peace and goodness which would last forever. (William Barclay, *The Gospel of Mark*, rev. ed. [Philadelphia: Westminster, 1975], 194–198; cf. Emil Schürer, *A History of the Jewish People in the Time of Jesus Christ* [New York: Scribners, 1896], 2:154–178)

But that general knowledge did not provide the disciples with the answers they sought to their specific questions, so Jesus gave them a detailed answer in verses 8–36. The truths He presented regarding His coming are critically important. The end of history is the reason for history; the consummation is the reason for the creation; the story that began in Genesis reaches its glorious climax in Revelation. In the next several chapters of this volume we will learn from our Lord Himself the reasons that necessitate His coming, the preliminary signs and events leading up to His coming, and how believers are to prepare for His coming.

Indifference to our Lord's eschatology is unacceptable, and so is ignorance. The end of the story matters for our comfort and God's glory. And it is not vague or unclear. We must hold to the precision of sound doctrine on this subject as we do on any category of divine revelation in Scripture.

The book of Revelation, the most comprehensive prophecy of the end times, begins with a call to such understanding and blessing:

> The Revelation of Jesus Christ, which God gave Him to show to His bond-servants, the things which must soon take place; and He sent and communicated it by His angel to His bond-servant John, who testified to the word of God and to the testimony of Jesus Christ, even to all that he saw. Blessed is he who reads and those who hear the words of the prophecy, and heed the things which are written in it; for the time is near. (Rev. 1:1–3)

# Signs of Christ's Return—Part 2: Why Jesus Must Return to Earth (Luke 21:8)

# 18

**And He said, "See to it that you are not misled; for many will come in My name, saying, 'I am He,' and, 'The time is near.' Do not go after them.** (21:8)

By some estimates, future predictive prophecy comprises one fifth of Scripture. Of that one fifth, one third refers to the second coming of the Lord Jesus Christ. Of the approximately 300 Old Testament prophecies regarding the coming of Christ, approximately one third were fulfilled at His first coming, leaving about 200 still to be fulfilled at His second coming. The New Testament also predicts Christ's return (some of the Old and New Testament predictions are listed below).

But despite the abundant biblical evidence, proud scoffers have always denied the reality that the Lord Jesus Christ will one day return to earth—just as the Bible predicts they would. Peter warned, "Know this first of all, that in the last days [which began with Christ's first coming; cf. Heb. 9:26; 1 John 2:18] mockers will come with their mocking, following after their own lusts, and saying, 'Where is the promise of His coming? For ever since the fathers fell asleep, all continues just as it was from the beginning of creation'" (2 Peter 3:3–4). They deny the second coming because they deny the deity of the Lord Jesus, and reject any idea that He is the judge and executioner of humans for their sins who will return to judge. The simplistic argument Peter answers invokes the principle of uniformitarianism: Christ has not returned, "all continues just as it was from the beginning of creation," they say, therefore He never will return. But to claim that something cannot happen because it has not yet happened is obviously foolish.

Further, that convenient, if faulty, reasoning ignores the obvious reality that things have not continued uniformly from the beginning, namely the destruction of the world by the flood of Noah's day, "through which the world at that time was destroyed, being flooded with water" (v. 6). Peter then pointed out that the cosmic judgment of the flood serves as a model for the even more catastrophic judgment yet to come:

> By His word the present heavens and earth are being reserved for fire, kept for the day of judgment and destruction of ungodly men.... But the day of the Lord will come like a thief, in which the heavens will pass away with a roar and the elements will be destroyed with intense heat, and the earth and its works will be burned up. (vv. 7, 10)

In the preceding verses, Jesus had told the disciples that judgment —including the destruction of the temple—was coming on Israel. That judgment, which began with the Roman destruction of Jerusalem and the temple in A.D. 70, will continue until Christ's second coming. His men would never have expected that such judgment of which Jesus spoke would last as long as it has. They likely would have expected it in Jesus' lifetime, and that it would be followed immediately by the restoration of Israel and the setting up of Messiah's earthly kingdom. Even after Jesus' death and resurrection they asked Him, "Lord, is it at this time You are restoring the kingdom to Israel?" (Acts 1:6).

The first hint that such expectation was wrong and that Christ's return would be delayed is His warning, **"See to it that you are not misled."** That warning would have been unnecessary while He was still with them to protect them. Because of their eager anticipation of His return, believers will be in danger of being deceived by the **many** false messiahs who will **come in** His **name, saying, "I am He," and, "The time is near."** The Lord's followers are **not** to **go after them.** Subsequent history would prove the timeliness of His warning:

> The passing centuries have seen false messiahs, each claiming to be the one so eagerly anticipated by the Jewish people. Of these self-proclaimed deliverers, some were simply self-deceived, while others were purposefully exploitative; some sought personal prestige, others to rescue their people from oppression; some advocated violence, others prayer and fasting; some professed to be political deliverers, others to be religious reformers. But though their motives, methods, and claims varied, they all had one thing in common—they were satanic counterfeits of the true Messiah, Jesus of Nazareth.
>
> About A.D. 44 Theudas (not the same individual mentioned in Acts 5:36) promised his followers that he would part the Jordan River. But before he was able to do so, Roman troops attacked and massacred many of his followers. The Egyptian for whom Paul was mistaken (Acts 21:38) had boasted that he would command the walls of Jerusalem to fall down. But, like Theudas, his plans were also foiled by Roman soldiers. Although the Egyptian managed to escape his attackers, several hundred of his followers were killed or captured (Josephus, *Antiquities* 20.8.6; *Wars* 2.13.5). In the second century Simon Bar Cochba ("son of a star"; cf. Num. 24:17), who was identified as the Messiah by the leading rabbi of the time, led a major Jewish uprising against Rome, conquering Jerusalem for three years, where he was called king and messiah. The Romans crushed the rebellion, retook Jerusalem, and massacred Bar Cochba and five to six hundred thousand of his followers. A fifth-century false messiah on the island of Crete promised to part the Mediterranean Sea so his followers could walk to Palestine on dry land. But the sea refused to part and some of his followers drowned. In the seventeenth century Shabbethai Zebi proclaimed himself "king of the kings of the earth," and attracted a widespread following among the Jews of western Europe. Zebi later converted to Islam and was eventually executed. (John MacArthur, *John 12–21*, The MacArthur New Testament Commentary [Chicago: Moody, 2008], 11–12)

The long parade of charlatans claiming to be Christ will culminate in the ultimate deceiving false messiah, the Antichrist, the

> man of lawlessness ... the son of destruction, who opposes and exalts himself above every so-called god or object of worship, so that he takes his seat in the temple of God, displaying himself as being God ... [the] lawless one ... whom the Lord will slay with the breath of His mouth and bring to an end by the appearance of His coming; that is, the one

whose coming is in accord with the activity of Satan, with all power and signs and false wonders, and with all the deception of wickedness for those who perish, because they did not receive the love of the truth so as to be saved. (2 Thess. 2:3, 4, 8, 9, 10; cf. Rev. 13:1–18)

There will be no mistaking Christ's return. Jesus said, "For just like the lightning, when it flashes out of one part of the sky, shines to the other part of the sky, so will the Son of Man be in His day" (Luke 17:24).

Not only must believers be wary of false christs, but they must also be ready for Jesus' return. Earlier in Luke's gospel Jesus told His followers,

Be dressed in readiness, and keep your lamps lit. Be like men who are waiting for their master when he returns from the wedding feast, so that they may immediately open the door to him when he comes and knocks. Blessed are those slaves whom the master will find on the alert when he comes; truly I say to you, that he will gird himself to serve, and have them recline at the table, and will come up and wait on them. Whether he comes in the second watch, or even in the third, and finds them so, blessed are those slaves. But be sure of this, that if the head of the house had known at what hour the thief was coming, he would not have allowed his house to be broken into. You too, be ready; for the Son of Man is coming at an hour that you do not expect. (12:35–40)

In Luke 17:22 "He said to the disciples, 'The days will come when you will long to see one of the days of the Son of Man, and you will not see it.'"

Despite the denials and mocking of the scoffers, the Lord Jesus Christ will return to earth. Before examining in detail His discourse on the events leading up to His return, it will be helpful to generally consider the reasons why He must return. As I have pointed out in each of the gospel treatments of the Olivet Discourse, Jesus must return to earth because God's person, program, and priorities demand it.

## GOD'S PERSON DEMANDS CHRIST'S RETURN

### THE PROMISES OF THE FATHER DEMAND IT

God is the "God of truth" (Ps. 31:5; Isa. 65:16), who abounds in truth (Ex. 34:6) and whose words are truth (2 Sam. 7:28). God cannot lie

(1 Sam. 15:29; Titus 1:2), therefore all of His promises will certainly be fulfilled (Num. 23:19; 1 Kings 8:56).

God made numerous promises concerning Jesus' first coming, including that He would be born of a virgin (Isa. 7:14), that He would be born in Bethlehem (Mic. 5:2), that God would call Him from Egypt (where His parents had taken Him to avoid Herod; Matt. 2:13–15) (Hos. 11:1), that He would be a descendant of Jesse, David's father, and would be anointed with the Holy Spirit (Isa. 11:1–2), that He would enter Jerusalem riding on a colt, the foal of a donkey (Zech. 9:9), that He would be betrayed by a close associate with whom He had shared a meal (Ps. 41:9), that He would be forsaken by His disciples (Zech. 13:7), and that the exact amount Judas would receive for betraying Him would be thirty pieces of silver, which he would throw into the temple (Zech. 11:12–13).

The Old Testament also predicted the specific details of Christ's death. Isaiah 50:6 says that He would be beaten and spit upon. David recorded the details of His crucifixion (a form of execution unknown in Israel in Old Testament times), including the piercing of His hands and feet, His final cry to the Father, and the dividing of His garments by lot among His executioners (Ps. 22). Psalm 34:20 notes that none of His bones would be broken, while Zechariah 12:10 predicted that His side would be pierced. Psalms 2:7 and 16:10 allude to His resurrection.

All of those promises regarding the Lord's first coming were fulfilled literally; they were not just spiritual ideals or subjective principles. Their fulfillment set the standard and pattern for the prophecies yet to be fulfilled at His second coming. As noted above, approximately two thirds of the Old Testament prophecies regarding His return were still unfulfilled after His first coming. For instance, Genesis 49:10 predicts that when Messiah comes, the people of the world will obey Him. But when Jesus came the first time, "He was in the world, and the world was made through Him, and the world did not know Him. He came to His own, and those who were His own did not receive Him" (John 1:10–11).

Psalm 2 describes Messiah's earthly reign (v. 6), when God "will surely give [Him] the nations as [His] inheritance, and the very ends of the earth as [His] possession," and "[He will] break them with a rod of iron" and "shatter them like earthenware" (vv. 8–9). But Christ's earthly rule was not established at His first coming.

The familiar text of Isaiah 9:6–7 merges both Messiah's first and second comings. The prediction that "a child will be born to us, a son will be given to us" (v. 6) clearly was fulfilled in Christ's incarnation. But the rest of the passage was not:

> And the government will rest on His shoulders; and His name will be called Wonderful Counselor, Mighty God, Eternal Father, Prince of Peace. There will be no end to the increase of His government or of peace, on the throne of David and over his kingdom, to establish it and to uphold it with justice and righteousness from then on and forevermore.

Jesus did not assume the throne of David in a literal sense; in fact, He Himself declared that it is only "when the Son of Man comes in His glory, and all the angels with Him, [that] He will sit on His glorious throne" (Matt. 25:31).

Micah predicted that Messiah "will judge between many peoples and render decisions for mighty, distant nations. Then they will hammer their swords into plowshares and their spears into pruning hooks; nation will not lift up sword against nation, and never again will they train for war" (Mic. 4:3). The literal fulfillment of that prophecy awaits Christ's return. Jeremiah 23:5 also predicts Christ's future earthly rule: "'Behold, the days are coming,' declares the Lord, 'when I will raise up for David a righteous Branch; and He will reign as king and act wisely and do justice and righteousness in the land,'" as does Daniel 7:13–14:

> I kept looking in the night visions, and behold, with the clouds of heaven one like a Son of Man was coming, and He came up to the Ancient of Days and was presented before Him. And to Him was given dominion, glory and a kingdom, that all the peoples, nations and men of every language might serve Him. His dominion is an everlasting dominion which will not pass away; and His kingdom is one which will not be destroyed.

THE STATEMENTS OF JESUS DEMAND IT

Jesus repeatedly said that He would return, and gave a detailed description of the second coming in the Olivet Discourse (Matt. 24, 25;

Mark 13; Luke 21:5–36; cf. 17:20–37). After telling the disciples that He was leaving, Jesus comforted them with the promise, "If I go and prepare a place for you, I will come again and receive you to Myself, that where I am, there you may be also" (John 14:3). At His trial before the Sanhedrin the Lord boldly declared, "You shall see the Son of Man sitting at the right hand of power, and coming with the clouds of heaven" (Mark 14:62)—a promise He repeated several times in Revelation (2:5, 16; 3:11; 22:7, 12, 20). Jesus also told parables that illustrated the second coming (e.g., Matt. 24:45–51; 25:1–13; 14–30, Luke 12:35–40, 41–48; 19:11–27). If the Lord Jesus Christ does not return to earth, His word was not true.

### THE GUARANTEE OF THE HOLY SPIRIT DEMANDS IT

The Spirit-inspired authors of the New Testament epistles also spoke of Jesus Christ's return to earth. Paul commended the Corinthians for "awaiting eagerly the revelation of our Lord Jesus Christ" (1 Cor. 1:7). To the Philippians he wrote, "Our citizenship is in heaven, from which also we eagerly wait for a Savior, the Lord Jesus Christ" (Phil. 3:20). The apostle reminded the Colossians that "when Christ, who is our life, is revealed, then you also will be revealed with Him in glory" (Col. 3:4). In 1 Thessalonians 4:16–17 he wrote,

> The Lord Himself will descend from heaven with a shout, with the voice of the archangel and with the trumpet of God, and the dead in Christ will rise first. Then we who are alive and remain will be caught up together with them in the clouds to meet the Lord in the air, and so we shall always be with the Lord. (cf. Heb. 9:28; James 5:7–8; 1 Peter 1:13; 5:4; 1 John 3:2)

Like that of the Father and the Son, the credibility of the Holy Spirit will be undermined if Jesus does not return to earth. An errant, incapable, or unfaithful Triune God would be a devil more powerful than Satan.

## GOD'S PROGRAM DEMANDS CHRIST'S RETURN

### GOD'S PROGRAM FOR THE CHURCH DEMANDS IT

The Jerusalem council, recorded in Acts 15, decided the momentous issue of whether salvation is by law or grace. After there had been extensive debate, Peter reminded those assembled that it was in response to revelation from God that he had taken the gospel to the Gentiles (vv. 7–11). Paul and Barnabas then related the mighty works of salvation that God had done through their ministry among the Gentiles (v. 12). Finally James, the Lord's brother and head of the Jerusalem church (cf. Acts 12:17; 21:18; the apostle James, the brother of John, had already been executed [Acts 12:2]), brought the council to a conclusion (vv. 13–21). He cited Amos 9:11–12, which prophesied that after the setting aside of Israel (Rom. 11), God would call a people for Himself from the Gentiles (the church; cf. Matt. 16:18; Acts 2:1–41). It is only after that gathering is completed (cf. 2 Peter 3:9) that Christ will return.

The second coming of Christ includes a series of events stretching from the rapture to the new heaven and the new earth. The first event, the rapture, is the catching away of the church to heaven (John 14:1–3; 1 Cor. 15:51–54; 1 Thess. 4:13–18; Rev. 3:10). In John 14:3 Jesus promised, "I will come again and receive you to Myself, that where I am, there you may be also." The absence of any reference to judgment, both here and in the other rapture passages, is significant. That omission indicates that those passages do not refer to Christ's coming to judge the wicked and set up His millennial kingdom (Matt. 13:36–43, 47–50; 24:29–44; 25:31–46; Rev. 19:11–15), but rather to His prior meeting believers to take them into heaven (cf. 1 Thess. 4:13–18; 1 Cor. 15:51–57).

Further differences between the two events reinforce that truth. At the second coming angels gather the elect (Matt. 24:30–31), but in John 14 Jesus told the disciples He would come for them personally. At the second coming believers will return with Christ (Rev. 19:8, 14) as He comes to set up His earthly kingdom (Rev. 19:11–20:6); in John 14 He promises to return for them. Between the rapture and the second coming, the church will celebrate the marriage supper of the Lamb (Rev. 19:7–10), and believers will receive their rewards (1 Cor. 3:10–15; 4:5;

2 Cor. 5:10). When Jesus returns in judgment and kingdom glory, the saints will come with Him (Rev. 19:7, 11–14).

GOD'S PROGRAM FOR THE NATIONS DEMANDS IT

The rampant wickedness that marks the present world cannot go on indefinitely. It is true that God is "patient toward [sinners], not wishing for any to perish but for all to come to repentance" (2 Peter 3:9). But His patience will one day give way to judgment; God is not only a God of love, grace, and mercy, but also of justice, holiness, and wrath against sin.

Joel's prophecy records the judgment on the sinful nations that will take place when Christ returns:

> For behold, in those days and at that time, when I restore the fortunes of Judah and Jerusalem, I will gather all the nations and bring them down to the valley of Jehoshaphat. Then I will enter into judgment with them there on behalf of My people and My inheritance, Israel, whom they have scattered among the nations; and they have divided up My land. . . . Proclaim this among the nations: Prepare a war; rouse the mighty men! Let all the soldiers draw near, let them come up! Beat your plowshares into swords and your pruning hooks into spears; let the weak say, "I am a mighty man." Hasten and come, all you surrounding nations, and gather yourselves there. Bring down, O Lord, Your mighty ones. Let the nations be aroused and come up to the valley of Jehoshaphat, for there I will sit to judge all the surrounding nations. Put in the sickle, for the harvest is ripe. Come, tread, for the wine press is full; the vats overflow, for their wickedness is great. Multitudes, multitudes in the valley of decision! For the day of the Lord is near in the valley of decision. The sun and moon grow dark and the stars lose their brightness. The Lord roars from Zion and utters His voice from Jerusalem, and the heavens and the earth tremble. But the Lord is a refuge for His people and a stronghold to the sons of Israel. Then you will know that I am the Lord your God, dwelling in Zion, My holy mountain. So Jerusalem will be holy, and strangers will pass through it no more. (3:1–2, 9–17; cf. Rev. 14:14–20)

Jesus described this same judgment in Matthew 25:31–46.

GOD'S PROGRAM FOR ISRAEL DEMANDS IT

Christ's return will bring not only judgment on the Gentile nations, but also salvation for the believing remnant of Israel (Rom. 11:25–27; cf. Luke 1:72–75), as the Old Testament promised:

> "As I live," declares the Lord God, "surely with a mighty hand and with an outstretched arm and with wrath poured out, I shall be king over you. I will bring you out from the peoples and gather you from the lands where you are scattered, with a mighty hand and with an outstretched arm and with wrath poured out; and I will bring you into the wilderness of the peoples, and there I will enter into judgment with you face to face. As I entered into judgment with your fathers in the wilderness of the land of Egypt, so I will enter into judgment with you," declares the Lord God. "I will make you pass under the rod, and I will bring you into the bond of the covenant; and I will purge from you the rebels and those who transgress against Me; I will bring them out of the land where they sojourn, but they will not enter the land of Israel. Thus you will know that I am the Lord." (Ezek. 20:33–38)

> "It is not for your sake, O house of Israel, that I am about to act, but for My holy name, which you have profaned among the nations where you went. I will vindicate the holiness of My great name which has been profaned among the nations, which you have profaned in their midst. Then the nations will know that I am the Lord," declares the Lord God, "when I prove Myself holy among you in their sight. For I will take you from the nations, gather you from all the lands and bring you into your own land. Then I will sprinkle clean water on you, and you will be clean; I will cleanse you from all your filthiness and from all your idols. Moreover, I will give you a new heart and put a new spirit within you; and I will remove the heart of stone from your flesh and give you a heart of flesh. I will put My Spirit within you and cause you to walk in My statutes, and you will be careful to observe My ordinances. You will live in the land that I gave to your forefathers; so you will be My people, and I will be your God. Moreover, I will save you from all your uncleanness; and I will call for the grain and multiply it, and I will not bring a famine on you. I will multiply the fruit of the tree and the produce of the field, so that you will not receive again the disgrace of famine among the nations. Then you will remember your evil ways and your deeds that were not good, and you will loathe yourselves in your own sight for your iniquities and your abominations. I am not doing this for your sake," declares the Lord God, "let it be known to you. Be ashamed and confounded for your ways, O house of Israel!" Thus says the Lord God, "On the day that I cleanse you from all your iniquities, I will cause the cities to be inhabited, and the waste places will be rebuilt. The desolate land will be cultivated instead

of being a desolation in the sight of everyone who passes by. They will say, 'This desolate land has become like the garden of Eden; and the waste, desolate and ruined cities are fortified and inhabited.' Then the nations that are left round about you will know that I, the Lord, have rebuilt the ruined places and planted that which was desolate; I, the Lord, have spoken and will do it." (Ezek. 36:22–36)

God's covenant promises to Israel of salvation, restoration to their land, and the kingdom can only be fulfilled by the return of Jesus Christ.

## GOD'S PRIORITIES DEMAND CHRIST'S RETURN

### THE HUMILIATION OF CHRIST DEMANDS IT

The last view the world has of the Lord of glory cannot be of Him hanging on a cross between two criminals. The world did not see Jesus after the resurrection, since He appeared only to believers (1 Cor. 15:4–8). The writer of Hebrews said that "Christ also, having been offered once to bear the sins of many, will appear a second time for salvation without reference to sin, to those who eagerly await Him" (Heb. 9:28). Having come the first time to offer Himself as a sacrifice for sin, Jesus will come again in triumphant salvation glory.

Only a relatively small group of people watched Jesus die on a hill outside Jerusalem. When He returns, however, the whole world will see Him:

Immediately after the tribulation of those days the sun will be darkened, and the moon will not give its light, and the stars will fall from the sky, and the powers of the heavens will be shaken. And then the sign of the Son of Man will appear in the sky, and then all the tribes of the earth will mourn, and they will see the Son of Man coming on the clouds of the sky with power and great glory. (Matt. 24:29–30)

### THE EXALTATION OF SATAN DEMANDS IT

Satan is at present the "god of this world" (2 Cor. 4:4; cf. Luke 4:6; John 12:31; 16:11; 1 John 5:19), a usurper permitted by God to reign temporarily. When He returns, Jesus will end Satan's rule, destroy his kingdom, and take back what is rightfully His.

In Revelation 5, the apostle John describes a startling, dramatic scene in heaven just prior to Christ's return. In his vision John "saw in the right hand of Him who sat on the throne a book written inside and on the back, sealed up with seven seals" (v. 1). This book, or scroll, is the title deed to the earth. As the vision continued he "saw a strong angel proclaiming with a loud voice, 'Who is worthy to open the book and to break its seals?'" (v. 2). To John's dismay, "no one in heaven or on the earth or under the earth was able to open the book or to look into it" (v. 3), and he "began to weep greatly because no one was found worthy to open the book or to look into it" (v. 4). But "one of the elders said to [him], 'Stop weeping; behold, the Lion that is from the tribe of Judah, the Root of David, has overcome so as to open the book and its seven seals'" (v. 5). John "saw between the throne (with the four living creatures) and the elders a Lamb standing, as if slain, having seven horns and seven eyes, which are the seven Spirits of God, sent out into all the earth" (v. 6). The Lamb, the Lord Jesus Christ, "came and took the book out of the right hand of Him who sat on the throne" (v. 7), at which the heavenly host burst forth in praise (vv. 8–14).

Then in verse 1 of chapter 6, Christ began breaking the book's seals, unleashing a series of catastrophic judgments that will devastate the world and destroy Satan's kingdom. After those judgments have run their course, Jesus will return to take back what is rightfully His (Rev. 11:15; 19:11–21), and imprison Satan for the duration of the millennial kingdom (Rev. 20:1–3), before sending him forever to the lake of fire (Rev. 20:10).

History will not end with Satan on any throne. The Son of God will be vindicated, and reign over this universe as He is entitled to.


THE EXPECTATION OF THE SAINTS DEMANDS IT


The saints' "blessed hope" of "the appearing of the glory of our great God and Savior, Christ Jesus" (Titus 2:13) will not prove to be in vain. Jesus, who has ascended into heaven, will come again (Acts 1:11) to rescue His people from God's eternal wrath against sin (1 Thess. 1:10), judge the wicked (2 Thess. 1:7–9), and receive glory (v. 10).

How should believers respond to the certain return of Jesus Christ? First, they are to long for it. Paul characterized Christians as those "who have loved [Christ's] appearing" (2 Tim. 4:8; cf. Heb. 9:28), and in 1 Corinthians 16:22 used the word "Maranatha," which means "Oh Lord, come!" (cf. John's exclamation, "Come, Lord Jesus" [Rev. 22:20]).

Second, believers must watch for it, since the launch event, the rapture, is a signless event and could happen at any moment. "You too, be ready," Jesus warned, "for the Son of Man is coming at an hour that you do not expect" (Luke 12:40; cf. Matt. 24:44). Mark concludes his account of the Olivet Discourse with the Lord's warning,

> Take heed, keep on the alert; for you do not know when the appointed time [for Christ's return] will come. It is like a man away on a journey, who upon leaving his house and putting his slaves in charge, assigning to each one his task, also commanded the doorkeeper to stay on the alert. Therefore, be on the alert—for you do not know when the master of the house is coming, whether in the evening, at midnight, or when the rooster crows, or in the morning—in case he should come suddenly and find you asleep. What I say to you I say to all, "Be on the alert!" (Mark 13:33–37)

Finally, believers are to be prepared for it. Peter exhorted his readers, "Therefore, beloved, since you look for these things, be diligent to be found by Him in peace, spotless and blameless" (2 Peter 3:14). Paul gave similar counsel:

> The night is almost gone, and the day is near. Therefore let us lay aside the deeds of darkness and put on the armor of light. Let us behave properly as in the day, not in carousing and drunkenness, not in sexual promiscuity and sensuality, not in strife and jealousy. But put on the Lord Jesus Christ, and make no provision for the flesh in regard to its lusts. (Rom. 13:12–14)

The promise to those who are prepared is that "when [Christ] appears, [they will] have confidence and not shrink away from Him in shame at His coming" (1 John 2:28).

# Signs of Christ's Return—Part 3: Birth Pains (Luke 21:8–19)

19

And He said, "See to it that you are not misled; for many will come in My name, saying, 'I am He,' and, 'The time is near.' Do not go after them. When you hear of wars and disturbances, do not be terrified; for these things must take place first, but the end does not follow immediately." Then He continued by saying to them, "Nation will rise against nation and kingdom against kingdom, and there will be great earthquakes, and in various places plagues and famines; and there will be terrors and great signs from heaven. But before all these things, they will lay their hands on you and will persecute you, delivering you to the synagogues and prisons, bringing you before kings and governors for My name's sake. It will lead to an opportunity for your testimony. So make up your minds not to prepare beforehand to defend yourselves; for I will give you utterance and wisdom which none of your opponents will be able to resist or refute. But you will be betrayed even by parents and brothers and relatives and friends, and they will put some of you to death, and you will be hated by

**all because of My name. Yet not a hair of your head will perish. By your endurance you will gain your lives.** (21:8–19)

The currently popular questioning of the perspicuity (clarity) of Scripture has led many to view the biblical prophecies regarding the future as especially mysterious, hidden, and obscure. Some think themselves noble for considering prophecy as unfathomable and incomprehensible. That view, however, is seriously troubling. What the Bible says about the future is as clear and accessible as what it says about the present or the past. To argue that prophecy cannot be understood is to deny both the clarity of Scripture, and its importance (cf. 2 Tim. 3:16–17; Rev. 1:3).

The foundational interpretive question of how the recipients of biblical revelation would have understood it applies to prophecy just as it does to the rest of Scripture. Biblical revelation was given in specific historical and cultural settings; therefore the correct interpretation of any text—including prophetic texts—must be consistent with how the original author and hearers understood it and thus apply the normal grammatical principles.

The Lord did not give this prophetic sermon, known as the Olivet Discourse, to the theological elite of Israel. The disciples were plain, simple, straightforward men, who had not been educated in the rabbinical schools. They would have found the bizarre, esoteric, mysterious interpretations of this sermon that some have invented to be inconceivable and incomprehensible. Since Jesus obviously intended for the disciples to understand what He was saying, such interpretations cannot be correct. Walter C. Kaiser notes a further difficulty with rejecting the literal approach to interpreting prophecy:

> Who or what will arbitrate among the various [non-literal] meanings suggested and decide which are to be accepted as authoritative and which are spurious? Short of saying that every person's fancy is his or her own rule, there does not appear to be any final court of appeal.... There simply are no justifiable criteria for setting boundaries once the interpreter departs from the normal usage of language. (*Back Toward the Future* [Grand Rapids: Baker, 1989], 129–30)

The disciples were familiar with the Jewish eschatology of their day, which emphasized Messiah's coming to destroy the Gentile nations and establish His kingdom, in which Israel would be the centerpiece (for a summary of the Jewish eschatology of the time, see chapter 17 of this volume). They eagerly anticipated that Jesus would fulfill all their messianic expectations at His first coming. But by the time this sermon was given (Wednesday of Passion Week) that hope had faded. Rather than the pagan nations, Jesus had publicly assaulted Israel by attacking the temple. In a series of conversations with the leaders of Jewish religion, He had refuted their attempts to discredit Him, and unmasked their hypocrisy. He had also predicted His death at their hands. Certainly Jesus had not done what the disciples expected Messiah to do, leaving them wondering if and when He would display His glory, judge Israel's enemies, and establish the promised kingdom.

Many who observe the way the world is going today fear what may happen in the future. The world seems to be careening toward ultimate apocalyptic disaster, leading some to wonder if God has lost control. After all, Jesus promised to build His church and not allow the gates of hell to prevail against it. He is the risen, death-conquering Lord, who has ascended to the Father, and His kingdom is steadily progressing toward its glorious consummation at His second coming (cf. Luke 13:18–21). In light of that, should everything not be getting better and better, as postmillennialists believe, until Jesus returns to reign over the kingdom that the spread of Christianity has inaugurated? Has something gone terribly wrong with God's plan? Not at all.

In this text, Jesus told His followers what to expect in the interval between His first and second comings. His predictions demonstrate His deity by revealing both His knowledge of and control over future events. The present era between the Lord's two comings will be marked by deceivers, disasters, and distress, which, like the birth pains of a pregnant woman, will intensify as the time of His coming draws near.

## Deceivers

**And He said, "See to it that you are not misled; for many will come in My name, saying, 'I am He,' and, 'The time is near.' Do not go after them.** (21:8)

As noted in the previous chapter of this volume, false messiahs and false teachers have been around since the time of Christ. Through the centuries, they have led millions of people onto the broad road that leads to destruction (Matt. 7:15–20; cf. the discussion of false teachers in chapter 16 of this volume). Religious deceivers and the lies they propagate will increase as the return of the Lord Jesus draws near (cf. Matt. 24:11).

DISASTERS

**When you hear of wars and disturbances, do not be terrified; for these things must take place first, but the end does not follow immediately." Then He continued by saying to them, "Nation will rise against nation and kingdom against kingdom, and there will be great earthquakes, and in various places plagues and famines; and there will be terrors and great signs from heaven.** (21:9–11)

The alarming and dangerous conditions in the present world will continue unabated for the rest of human history. They do not signal that the **end** will **follow immediately**; however, disasters will increase and worsen as the end approaches, just as a woman's birth pains intensify as the time for birth draws near.

Human history is largely the history of **wars,** which have increased in number and intensity over the centuries. By some estimates there were seventy significant wars before the time of Christ, fifty in the first one thousand years after Him, one hundred between A.D. 1000 and 1500, two hundred fifty between 1500 and 1800, and five hundred since 1800. Those numbers do not include the numerous lesser conflicts that took place during those time periods. The wars mankind has engaged in have resulted in the deaths of millions of people (approximately seventy-five million in World Wars 1 and 2 alone).

But all the wars of human history are insignificant in comparison to the devastating conflicts that will take place during the tribulation, when, on a scale never before seen in history, **nation will rise against nation and kingdom against kingdom.** In Revelation 6:3–4 John wrote, "When [Christ] broke the second seal, I heard the second living creature saying, 'Come.' And another, a red horse, went out; and to him who sat on it, it was granted to take peace from the earth, and that men would slay one another; and a great sword was given to him." This world-wide conflict, and the famine and disease that will accompany it (vv. 5–6, 8), will kill one fourth of the earth's population (v. 8). By way of comparison, less than 3 percent of the world's population perished in World War 2.

Revelation chapters 16 and 19 describe the final, climactic battle of the tribulation:

> The sixth angel poured out his bowl on the great river, the Euphrates; and its water was dried up, so that the way would be prepared for the kings from the east. And I saw coming out of the mouth of the dragon and out of the mouth of the beast and out of the mouth of the false prophet, three unclean spirits like frogs; for they are spirits of demons, performing signs, which go out to the kings of the whole world, to gather them together for the war of the great day of God, the Almighty.... And they gathered them together to the place which in Hebrew is called Har-Magedon. (16:12–14, 16)

Under the influence of three particularly foul and vile demons, pictured here as "frogs," the rulers of the east and their armies will march to "Har-Magedon" (Armageddon) to meet their doom. Armageddon refers to the plain of Megiddo, about sixty miles north of Jerusalem, and the site of many historical battles (cf. Judg. 4–5 [cf. 5:19], 7; 2 Chron. 35:22). While Megiddo and the nearby Plain of Esdraelon will be the focal point of the battle, the fighting will stretch throughout the length of Israel, including the vicinity of Jerusalem (Zech. 14:1–3).

But this final battle will be brought to an abrupt end by the return of the Lord Jesus Christ. The world's armies, under the command of Antichrist (Rev. 19:19), will be annihilated, and Antichrist and his henchman, the false prophet, cast alive into the lake of fire (v. 20). So great will the carnage be that blood of the slain will be splattered several feet high, and perhaps run in streams in places, across two hundred miles (Rev. 14:20). The battle will end in a slaughter, when Christ returns to judge and execute His enemies (19:17–21).

In addition to the manmade disaster of war, **disturbances** in the natural world have also caused great damage and loss of life. There have been many severe **earthquakes** in recorded history, both in magnitude and in terms of fatalities. Since the invention of the Richter scale, there have been thirty-five with a recorded or estimated magnitude of 8.5 or greater. The most powerful earthquake ever recorded took place in Chile in 1960, registering a magnitude 9.5. A dozen other earthquakes with a magnitude of 8.5 or greater have also taken place in Chile. The 1964 Alaska earthquake measured 9.2, the 2004 earthquake in the Indian Ocean near Sumatra measured 9.1, and an earthquake in 1952 on the Kamchatka Peninsula in far eastern Russia and the 2011 earthquake in the Pacific Ocean off the coast of Japan both measured 9.0.

Earthquakes have also resulted in massive loss of life. An earthquake in China in 1556 killed an estimated 830,000 people. Another earthquake in China in 1920 resulted in the deaths of nearly 275,000 people, while a third Chinese earthquake, this one in 1976, caused a quarter of a million fatalities. The 2004 Sumatra earthquake, mentioned above, killed more than 230,000 people, while a 1923 earthquake in the Kanto region of Japan took the lives of more than 140,000 people. Earthquakes in Sicily in 1908, Turkmenistan in 1948, and Japan in 1703 also killed more than 100,000 people.

But as is the case with wars, the unparalleled earthquakes that will devastate the earth during the tribulation will dwarf all previous ones. The sixth seal judgment will unleash one of those earthquakes:

> I looked when He broke the sixth seal, and there was a great earthquake; and the sun became black as sackcloth made of hair, and the whole moon became like blood; and the stars of the sky fell to the earth, as a fig tree casts its unripe figs when shaken by a great wind. The sky was split apart like a scroll when it is rolled up, and every mountain and island were moved out of their places. (Rev. 6:12–14)

So terrifyingly powerful will that earthquake be that in John's vision

> the kings of the earth and the great men and the commanders and the rich and the strong and every slave and free man hid themselves in the caves and among the rocks of the mountains; and they said to the mountains and to the rocks, "Fall on us and hide us from the presence

of Him who sits on the throne, and from the wrath of the Lamb; for the great day of their wrath has come, and who is able to stand?" (vv. 15–17)

Another earthquake will destroy one tenth of the city of Jerusalem (Rev. 11:13). But the most catastrophic earthquake that will ever strike the earth is described in Revelation 16:18–20:

> There was a great earthquake, such as there had not been since man came to be upon the earth, so great an earthquake was it, and so mighty. The great city was split into three parts, and the cities of the nations fell. Babylon the great was remembered before God, to give her the cup of the wine of His fierce wrath. And every island fled away, and the mountains were not found.

This devastating, unprecedented earthquake will drastically alter the topography of the entire planet.

**Plagues and famines** have ravaged mankind throughout history. The play on words in the Greek text, *loimos* (plagues) and *limos* (famines), shows that the two are often connected. Epidemics of various diseases, including smallpox, measles, typhus, influenza, and, most notoriously, bubonic plague, have struck repeatedly throughout history. There were plagues in Athens in the fifth century B.C., and various locations in the Roman and Byzantine empires in the second, third, sixth, seventh, and eighth centuries A.D. The notorious pandemic outbreak of bubonic plague known as the Black Death, which took place in the middle of the fourteenth century, killed an estimated one third to one half of Europe's population. There were other bubonic plague epidemics in European countries in the sixteenth, seventeenth, and eighteenth centuries, including Italy, England (most notably, the great plague that ravaged London in 1665–1666), Spain, Austria, France, and Russia. A prolonged pandemic of bubonic plague, which began in China in the middle of the nineteenth century and lasted until the middle of the twentieth century, killed millions. Recent decades have witnessed outbreaks of severe acute respiratory syndrome (SARS), bird flu, and AIDS.

Often associated with and resulting from plagues and wars, **famines** have also been common throughout history. According to some sources, there have been more than 1,800 famines of varying degrees of severity in China alone, and ninety-five famines in Britain during the Middle Ages. There were famines in Rome in the fifth century B.C., India in the eleventh, fourteenth, seventeenth, eighteenth, nineteenth, and twentieth centuries, and Spain in the eighth and sixteenth centuries. A severe famine lasting from the ninth through the eleventh centuries helped destroy the Mayan civilization, and the Great Famine in nineteenth-century Ireland (also called the Potato Famine) changed the course of that nation's history. Far greater famine will mark the tribulation period (Rev. 6:5–6), and contribute to the deaths of one fourth of the earth's population (v. 8).

**Terrors** is a broad term encompassing events and experiences other than wars, earthquakes, plagues, and famine that produce fear. Among those terrors are the deadly fires that have always been a destructive part of human experience. Fires have damaged or destroyed numerous cities, including Rome, Constantinople, London (in 1135, 1212, 1666), Chicago, Amsterdam, Copenhagen, Washington, D.C. (burned by the British during the War of 1812), Moscow, Montreal, Tokyo, New York, Detroit, Pittsburgh, Boston, Vancouver, Seattle, and Shanghai, among many others. In addition, bombing raids during the Second World War caused fires that severely damaged such cities as London, Rotterdam, Hamburg, Dresden, Tokyo, Hiroshima, and Nagasaki (the latter two caused by atomic bombs), as well as numerous other cities, primarily in Germany and Japan.

Wildfires have also scorched the planet with destruction. On the same day that the infamous urban Chicago fire started (October 8, 1871), the most deadly rural wildfire in US history, the Peshtigo Fire in Wisconsin, broke out. It burned an estimated one million to three and a half million acres, destroyed the town of Peshtigo and a dozen other villages, and took the lives of an estimated fifteen hundred people. Also on that same day, a series of fires known collectively as the Great Michigan Fire damaged or destroyed several cities, towns, or villages. More than a million and a half acres were burned, and hundreds of people were killed. Ten years later another wildfire in that same part of Michigan burned over one million acres and took the lives of nearly three hundred people. A fire in 1910 burned more than three million acres in Idaho and Montana. Fires in 1982–1983 in Indonesia burned more than seven million acres;

another outbreak in 1997–1998 consumed a staggering 24 million acres. The 1988 fire in Yellowstone National Park and the surrounding region scorched one and a half million acres. In the summer of 2011, more than twenty-one thousand fires raged across Texas, burning nearly four million acres and destroying approximately seven thousand homes.

Vast, incinerating fires, unprecedented in extent, will also be a weapon of God's judgment during the tribulation. As a result of the first three trumpet judgments, fires will destroy one third of the earth, one third of the trees, and all the green grass, and will pollute one third of the sea and one third of the planet's sources of fresh water (Rev. 8:6–11). Fire associated with the sixth trumpet will contribute to the deaths of one third of mankind (Rev. 9:17–18). Ultimately, evil angels and wicked men will be cast into the ultimate eternal fire of hell (Rev. 19:20; 20:10, 15).

The Lord also warned of **great signs from heaven.** Those signs include objects falling to earth from space, such as meteors or comet showers (Rev. 8:8, 10), along with atmospheric events, such as tornadoes, hurricanes, severe thunderstorms with large hail, flooding rains, blizzards, and lightning strikes. During the tribulation, those and even more terrifying signs will take place:

> I looked when He broke the sixth seal, and there was a great earthquake; and the sun became black as sackcloth made of hair, and the whole moon became like blood; and the stars of the sky fell to the earth, as a fig tree casts its unripe figs when shaken by a great wind. The sky was split apart like a scroll when it is rolled up. (Rev. 6:12–14)

> The fourth angel sounded, and a third of the sun and a third of the moon and a third of the stars were struck, so that a third of them would be darkened and the day would not shine for a third of it, and the night in the same way. (Rev. 8:12)

> The sun will be turned into darkness and the moon into blood before the great and awesome day of the Lord comes. (Joel 2:31)

> Behold, the day of the Lord is coming, cruel, with fury and burning anger, to make the land a desolation; and He will exterminate its sinners from it. For the stars of heaven and their constellations will not flash forth their light; the sun will be dark when it rises and the moon will not shed its light. (Isa. 13:9–10)

Do not expect things to get better, Jesus warned. Conditions in the world will deteriorate as ours is a scarred, stained, cursed planet, suffering the consequences of the fall and groaning for its redemption (Rom. 8:22).

## DISTRESS

**But before all these things, they will lay their hands on you and will persecute you, delivering you to the synagogues and prisons, bringing you before kings and governors for My name's sake. It will lead to an opportunity for your testimony. So make up your minds not to prepare beforehand to defend yourselves; for I will give you utterance and wisdom which none of your opponents will be able to resist or refute. But you will be betrayed even by parents and brothers and relatives and friends, and they will put some of you to death, and you will be hated by all because of My name. Yet not a hair of your head will perish. By your endurance you will gain your lives.** (21:12–19)

**Before all these things** about which Jesus had just warned the disciples, the final, apocalyptic wars, earthquakes, plagues, famines, fires, and signs from heaven—the birth pains presaging His return—will come the persecution of believers. That persecution came first to those in the first century who heard this message.

And it came first from the Jewish people. As He had earlier done (Matt. 10:17), Jesus warned the disciples, **"They** (the Jews) **will lay their hands on you** (i.e., arrest them) **and will persecute you."** The **synagogues** served as the local Jewish courts, and handled both civil and criminal cases. To be brought before the synagogue court was considered to be a humiliating and degrading experience. In those courts, Christ's followers were to be flogged (Acts 5:40; 2 Cor. 11:24) and imprisoned (Acts 5:18; 8:3).

The early church faced Jewish persecution from the outset, as the book of Acts records. After Peter's miraculous healing of a congenitally lame man (3:1–11) and the powerful evangelistic sermon that followed

(vv. 12–26), the Jewish authorities arrested Peter and John, and imprisoned them (4:1–3). Threatened and jealous of the apostles' continued
popularity, the high priest and the Sadducees again "laid hands on the
apostles and put them in a public jail" (Acts 5:18). Stephen was falsely
accused (Acts 6:8–11), put on trial before the Sanhedrin (6:12–7:56), and
stoned to death (7:57–60). In the aftermath of Stephen's death, persecution, spearheaded by Saul of Tarsus, broke out against the church in
Jerusalem (8:1–3). Currying favor with the Jews, Herod Agrippa I "laid
hands on some who belonged to the church in order to mistreat them.
And he had James the brother of John put to death with a sword. When
he saw that it pleased the Jews, he proceeded to arrest Peter also" (12:1–
3). Paul faced persecution from his fellow Jews throughout his ministry
(Acts 9:23–24, 29; 13:6–8; 45; 14:2, 19; 17:5, 13; 18:6, 12–16; 19:8–9; 20:3, 19;
21:27–32; 23:12–22; 25:2–3; 28:23–28; cf. 2 Cor. 11:24, 26).

Not only would Christ's followers be persecuted by the Jews, but
also by the Gentiles, as the phrase **kings and governors** indicates. Paul
was imprisoned at least five times by the Romans (at Philippi [Acts
16:23–24], Jerusalem [Acts 22:24–29; 23:10, 18], Caesarea [Acts 23:35;
24:27], and twice at Rome [Acts 28:16–31; 2 Tim. 1:8]). Writing at the end
of the first century, the church father Clement of Rome reported that the
apostle had been imprisoned seven times. In addition to the floggings he
received at the hands of the Jews, Paul was judicially sentenced to being
beaten by the Romans at least three times (2 Cor. 11:25), only one of
which is recorded in Acts (16:22, 37; cf. 1 Thess. 2:2). The last apostle was
also brought before other pagan rulers, including the chief magistrates at
Philippi (Acts 16:19–22), the proconsul Gallio at Corinth (Acts 18:12–16),
the commander of the Roman cohort stationed in Jerusalem (Acts
21:31–33; 22:24–29), the Roman governors Felix (Acts 24:1–22) and Festus (Acts 25:1–12), King Herod Agrippa II (Acts 26:1–32), and Emperor
Nero (Acts 25:11–12, 21; 27:24; 2 Tim. 4:16–17).

Official persecution of Christians began with the Romans. As I
explained in an earlier volume in this series,

> The Romans persecuted Christians for several reasons. At first, they
> viewed Christianity as merely another Jewish sect. Since Judaism was
> a legally tolerated religion (*religio licita*), the Romans left the Christians
> alone. Thus, when the Jews at Corinth accused Paul before the Roman

proconsul Gallio, he refused to intervene, deeming the matter an internal dispute within Judaism (Acts 18:12–15).

Eventually the Jews' hostility toward the Christians and the influx of Gentiles into the church led the Romans to recognize Christianity as distinct from Judaism. Christianity then became an illegal religion, proscribed by the Roman government. In addition to Christianity's illegal status, several factors prompted Roman persecution. Politically, the Christians' allegiance to Christ above Caesar aroused suspicions that they were disloyal to the state. To maintain control over their vast empire, the Romans required that their subjects' ultimate loyalty be to the emperor as the embodiment of the Roman state. And since "there was a union of religion and state in ancient Rome … refusal to worship the goddess Roma or the divine emperor constituted treason" (Howard F. Vos, *Exploring Church History* [Nashville: Thomas Nelson, 1994], 26). Because the Christians refused to make the required sacrifice offered in worship to the emperor, they were seen as traitors. They also proclaimed the kingdom of God, which caused the Romans to suspect them of plotting to overthrow the government. To avoid harassment by government officials, Christians often held their meetings in secret and at night. That heightened the Romans' suspicions that they were hatching an anti-government plot. That Christians generally refused to serve in the Roman army also caused them to be viewed as disloyal.

The Romans also persecuted Christians for religious reasons. They allowed their subjects to worship whatever gods they liked, as long as they also worshiped the Roman gods. But Christians preached an exclusive message that there is only one God and only one way of salvation. That, coupled with their evangelistic efforts to win converts from other religions, went against the prevailing atmosphere of religious pluralism. Christians were denounced as atheists because they rejected the Roman pantheon of gods, and because they worshiped an invisible God, not an idol. The secrecy of the Christians' meetings led to lurid, false rumors of gross immorality. Misunderstanding about what was meant by eating and drinking the elements during the Lord's Supper led to charges of cannibalism. The Christians' practice of greeting each other with a holy kiss (Rom. 16:16; 1 Cor. 16:20; 2 Cor. 13:12; 1 Thess. 5:26; cf. 1 Peter 5:14) gave rise to allegations of incest and other sexual perversions.

Socially, the leaders of Roman society feared the influence of the Christians on the lower classes, from whose ranks the church drew many of its members (cf. 1 Cor. 1:26). Haunted by the ever-present specter of slave revolts, the wealthy aristocrats felt especially threatened by the Christians' teaching that all people are equal (Gal. 3:28; Col. 3:11; cf. Paul's letter to Philemon), though the church did not openly oppose slavery. Christians also held themselves aloof from much of the public life of the time. For obvious reasons, they could not be involved in the idolatrous temple worship that was such an important part of social life. But even sporting and theatrical events involved sacrifices to pagan deities that Christians could not participate in. The purity of their lives rebuked the debauched lifestyles of rich and poor alike and provoked further hostility (cf. 1 Peter 4:3–4).

Economic factors played an often overlooked role in the persecution of the early believers. Paul's exorcism of a demon from a fortune-telling slave girl at Philippi caused her masters, incensed by the loss of the revenue she brought them, to stir up hostility against him (Acts 16:16–24). Economic factors also played a significant role in provoking the riot at Ephesus (Acts 19:23–27). Early in the second century Pliny, the Roman governor of Bithynia, lamented in a letter to Emperor Trajan that the spread of Christianity had caused the pagan temples to be deserted and sales of sacrificial animals to plummet. In that superstitious age people also attributed plague, famine, and natural disasters to the Christians' forsaking of the traditional gods, prompting the Christian apologist Tertullian to remark sarcastically, "If the Tiber reaches the walls, if the Nile does not rise to the fields, if the sky doesn't move or the earth does, if there is famine, if there is plague, the cry is at once, 'Christians to the lion!' What, all of them to one lion?" (*Apology* 40.2, as cited in M. A. Smith, *From Christ to Constantine* [Downers Grove, Ill.: InterVarsity, 1973], 86).

For these and other reasons, Christianity became a hated and despised religious sect in the Roman Empire. In his letter to Emperor Trajan, Pliny scorned Christianity as a "depraved and extravagant superstition." Pliny went on to complain that "the contagion of this superstition [Christianity] has spread not only in the cities, but in the villages and rural districts as well" (cited in Henry Bettenson, ed., *Documents of the Christian Church* [London: Oxford University Press, 1967], 4). The Roman historian Tacitus, a contemporary of Pliny, described Christians as "a class hated for their abominations" (cited in Bettenson, *Documents*, 2) while Suetonius, another contemporary of Pliny, dismissed them as "a set of men adhering to a novel and mischievous superstition" (cited in Bettenson, *Documents*, 2).

The first official persecution of Christians by the Roman government came during the reign of Emperor Nero. In July of A.D. 64 a fire ravaged Rome, destroying or damaging much of the city. Popular rumors pinned the blame for the fire on Nero. Though the rumors were probably not true, Nero sought for scapegoats to shift the suspicion away from himself. He therefore blamed the Christians, who were already despised by the populace (as the quotes in the preceding paragraph indicate), and began to savagely persecute them. Christians were arrested, cruelly tortured, thrown to wild animals, crucified, and burned as torches to light

Nero's gardens at night. The official persecution apparently was confined to the vicinity of Rome. But attacks on Christians undoubtedly spread, unchecked by the authorities, to other parts of the empire. According to tradition, Peter and Paul were martyred during Nero's persecution.

Three decades later, during the reign of Emperor Domitian, another government-sponsored persecution of Christians broke out. Little is known of the details, but it extended to the province of Asia (modern Turkey). The apostle John was banished from Ephesus to the island of Patmos, and among those martyred was a man (probably a pastor) named Antipas (Rev. 2:13).

In the second century and the first half of the third century, official persecution of Christians was sporadic. During the reign of Emperor Trajan early in the second century, Pliny, in the letter mentioned earlier, asked Trajan how to deal with the Christians in his region. Trajan replied that they were not to be sought out, but if accused (Trajan instructed Pliny to ignore anonymous accusations), they were to be brought to trial. Those who refused to recant were to be punished. Though Trajan's policy did not result in widespread persecution, it did result in the martyrdom of some, most notably the famous church father Ignatius. Trajan's policy remained in force for several decades, until the reign of Marcus Aurelius. Under his rule the state took a more active role in ferreting out Christians. During his reign the famous Christian apologist Justin Martyr was executed, and a savage persecution broke out against the Christians in Lyons and Vienne in Gaul (modern France).

The first empire-wide persecution of the church took place under Emperor Decius in A.D. 250. Rome at that time faced serious internal (an economic crisis and various natural disasters) and external (barbarian incursions) problems. Decius was convinced that those difficulties resulted from the neglect of Rome's ancient gods. He issued an edict requiring everyone to offer a sacrifice to the gods and to the emperor and to obtain a certificate attesting that they had done so. Those who refused faced arrest, imprisonment, torture, and execution. Thankfully for the church, Decius's persecution was cut short by his death in battle in July, A.D. 251.

The final and most violent empire-wide persecution of the church began in A.D. 303, during the reign of Diocletian. This persecution was nothing less than an all-out attempt to exterminate the Christian faith. Diocletian issued a series of edicts ordering that churches be destroyed, all copies of the Bible be burned, and all Christians offer sacrifices to the Roman gods on pain of death. The persecution subsided when Constantine and his co-emperor Licinius issued the Edict of Milan (A.D. 313), granting freedom of worship to members of all religions. But Licinius reneged on the agreement and persecution continued in some parts of the empire. It was not until Constantine became sole emperor in A.D. 324 that Roman persecution of Christians ended permanently. (*John 12–21*, The MacArthur New Testament Commentary [Chicago: Moody, 2008], 167–70)

But persecution of believers did not end with the fall of the Roman Empire:

> Under the Roman Catholic Church, which replaced Imperial Rome as the dominant power during the Middle Ages, persecution broke out anew. Ironically, this time the persecution against true believers came from those who called themselves "Christian." The horrors of the Inquisition, the St. Bartholomew's Day Massacre, and the martyrdoms of many believers, epitomized the Roman Church's effort to suppress the true gospel of Jesus Christ. More recently, believers have been brutally repressed by Communist and Islamic regimes. In fact, it has been estimated by none other than a Roman Catholic source that, in all of church history, roughly 70 million Christians have been killed for their profession of faith, with two-thirds of those martyrdoms occurring after the start of the twentieth century (Antonio Socci, I *Nuovi Persequitati* [The New Persecuted] Casale Montferrato: Edizioni Piemme, 2002). The actual number is likely much greater. The Catholic journalist cited in this news article estimates that an average of 100,000 Christians have been killed every year since 1990. (*John 12–21*, 170)

Christ's warning of the persecution to come shocked the disciples, who were still expecting Him to inaugurate the golden age of the messianic kingdom. Incredibly, the very next evening, during the Last Supper they, unable to shake the persistent hope of the kingdom, bickered over which of them would be elevated to the greatest honor in the kingdom (Luke 22:24). There was no place in their theology or their minds for Messiah to be killed and His followers persecuted.

But persecution of Christians would have an outcome opposite what the enemies of Christ intended. Far from destroying the Christian faith, it would help spread the gospel by leading **to an opportunity for** believers' gospel **testimony**. Over the centuries persecution has provided opportunities to proclaim the gospel, purified the church, and demonstrated the triumph of saving faith. As the late second and early third century Christian apologist Tertullian triumphantly wrote, "The oftener we are mown down by you, the more in number we grow; the blood of Christians is seed" (Apology, chap. 50).

To those who might fear that they will not know what to say when on trial for their faith, Jesus promised, **"Make up your minds not to prepare beforehand to defend yourselves; for I will give you utterance and wisdom which none of your opponents will be able to resist or refute"** (cf. Matt. 10:17; Mark 13:11; Luke 12:11–12). That promise has been fulfilled repeatedly throughout history. The confident manner in which Peter and John addressed them amazed the Sanhedrin (Acts 4:13). Facing martyrdom Polycarp, the second-century bishop of Smyrna, when urged by the proconsul to deny Christ, replied, "Eighty and six years have I served Him, and He never did me any injury: how then can I blaspheme my King and my Saviour?" (*The Encyclical Epistle of the Church at Smyrna Concerning the Martyrdom of the Holy Polycarp*, chap. 9).

As he was about to be burned at the stake, the Czech reformer John Huss confidently proclaimed,

> The Lord Jesus Christ, my Redeemer, was bound with a harder chain, and I, a miserable sinner, am not afraid to bear this one, bound as I am for his name's sake. . . . In the same truth of the Gospel which I have written, taught, and preached, drawing upon the sayings and positions of the holy doctors, I am ready to die today. (David S. Schaff, *John Huss, His Life, Teachings and Death After Five Hundred Years* [New York: Scribners, 1915], 257)

As he stood before the emperor and the Diet (general assembly) of the Holy Roman Empire, having been ordered to recant his teaching, Martin Luther boldly declared,

> Since then your serene majesty and your lordships seek a simple answer, I will give it in this manner, neither horned nor toothed: Unless I am convinced by the testimony of the Scriptures or by clear reason (for I do not trust either in the pope or in councils alone, since it is well known that they have often erred and contradicted themselves), I am bound by the Scriptures I have quoted and my conscience is captive to the Word of God. I cannot and I will not retract anything, since it is neither safe nor right to go against conscience. I cannot do otherwise, here I stand, may God help me, amen. (Cited in Lewis W. Spitz, *The Protestant Reformation 1517–1559* [New York: Harper & Row, 1985], 75)

The persecution believers endure, Jesus said, would be for His **name's sake.** The risen, glorified Lord whom His enemies hate is beyond their reach. Driven by their animosity toward Him, they lash out instead at His followers. Even those closest to believers will turn against them; they **will be betrayed even by parents and brothers and relatives and friends.** Their persecutors will **put some of** them **to death, and** they **will be hated by all because of** the **name** of Jesus (cf. Matt. 10:22; Luke 6:22; John 15:18; 16:1–4).

In light of the deceivers, disasters, and distress in the form of persecution that Jesus warned were coming, the disciples must have wondered if their faith and cause would survive. So in the brief closing verses of this section, Jesus reassured them, and by extension all Christians, that it absolutely would. Despite the trials they would face, the Lord pledged to them, **"Not a hair of your head will perish. By your endurance you will gain your lives."**

Those words introduce the vitally important subject of the permanence of salvation. The issue is whether a true believer, genuinely forgiven and granted regeneration and salvation by God from sin, death, and hell, can then behave in such a way as to have that salvation taken away by Him. Can a true believer forfeit the eternal life granted by God? The Westminster Confession of 1646, one of the most important doctrinal statements ever compiled, sums up the biblical teaching on this issue: "They, whom God has accepted in His Beloved, effectually called, and sanctified by His Spirit, can neither totally nor finally fall away from the state of grace, but shall certainly persevere therein to the end, and be eternally saved."

Jesus repeatedly emphasized the permanence of salvation. In the familiar words of John 3:16–18, He made it clear that eternal life can never end. Those who possess it will neither perish, nor be judged. He told the Samaritan woman at the well, "Everyone who drinks of this water will thirst again; but whoever drinks of the water that I will give him shall never thirst; but the water that I will give him will become in him a well of water springing up to eternal life" (John 4:13–14). In John 5:24 He declared, "Truly, truly, I say to you, he who hears My word, and believes Him who sent Me, has eternal life, and does not come into judgment, but has passed out of death into life." Jesus is the bread of life, and those who come to Him for salvation will never again hunger or thirst spiritually (John 6:35). He unequivocally declared, "All that the Father gives Me will come to Me, and the one who comes to Me I will certainly not cast out" (v. 37), because it is "the will of [the] Father, that everyone who beholds the Son and believes in Him will have eternal life, and [Christ Himself] will raise him up on the last day" (v. 40). His sheep have eternal life and will never perish, because no one has the power to take them away from either Him or the Father (John 10:27–29). Christ's prayer to the Father that He keep those whom He had given to Him (John 17:11) is being answered.

The apostles also affirmed the truth that salvation is forever. Paul reminded the Corinthians that God "will also confirm you to the end, blameless in the day of our Lord Jesus Christ" (1 Cor. 1:8). To the Thessalonians he wrote, "Now may the God of peace Himself sanctify you entirely; and may your spirit and soul and body be preserved complete, without blame at the coming of our Lord Jesus Christ. Faithful is He who calls you, and He also will bring it to pass" (1 Thess. 5:23–24). In Romans 8:30 he described the unbreakable progression from predestination to effectual calling to justification to glorification, and eloquently pointed out the impossibility that anyone whose faith is genuine could ever be lost (vv. 31–39). In his first epistle Peter revealed the promise from the Holy Spirit that saving faith results in obtaining "an inheritance which is imperishable and undefiled and will not fade away, reserved in heaven for [those] who are protected by the power of God through faith for a salvation ready to be revealed in the last time" (1:4–5). Though they may be "distressed by various trials," their faith, "even though tested by fire, [will] be found to result in praise and glory and honor at the revelation of Jesus Christ" (vv. 6–7); Jude's epistle concludes with a marvelous benediction that emphasizes the reality that salvation is absolutely permanent: "Now to Him who is able to keep you from stumbling, and to make you stand in the presence of His glory blameless with great joy, to the only God our Savior, through Jesus Christ our Lord, be glory, majesty, dominion and authority, before all time and now and forever. Amen" (vv. 24–25).

Like all other elements of salvation, saving faith is a gift from God (Eph. 2:8–9). It is permanent, unfailing, and undying. Unlike human faith in the routine aspects of everyday life, which is based on natural experience, saving faith is supernatural and divine, so that it cannot wane or die; the nature or essence of the gift of faith is that it endures.

But just as there have always been false believers, so also will there be in the future. In Matthew's account of the Olivet Discourse, Jesus warned, "Because lawlessness is increased, most people's love will grow cold" (Matt. 24:12). John characterized those who appear to lose their faith as never truly possessing it: "They went out from us, but they were not really of us; for if they had been of us, they would have remained with us; but they went out, so that it would be shown that they all are not of us" (1 John 2:19).

Jesus' promise to those whose faith is genuine, **"Not a hair of your head will perish,"** is a proverbial saying expressing safety and protection (cf. 1 Sam. 14:45; 2 Sam. 14:11; 1 Kings 1:52; Acts 27:34). Since He had just warned that believers would die in the coming persecutions, this cannot be a guarantee of absolute physical protection. The point of the saying is metaphoric—that though they may die physically, true believers will not perish spiritually.

Some have interpreted the Lord's concluding statement, **"By your endurance you will gain your lives,"** as a reference to physical survival. That, however, reduces it to a meaningless tautology, saying in effect that those who do not die will not die. What Jesus was actually pointing out is that those whose trust in Christ endures to the end (cf. Matt. 10:22; 24:13), so that they do not fall away, prove that their faith is the authentic gift from God. Such will receive the final aspect of salvation, glorification, and live forever in the joy of God's glorious kingdom.

# Signs of Christ's Return—Part 4: The End Is Near (Luke 21:20–24)

# 20

**But when you see Jerusalem surrounded by armies, then recognize that her desolation is near. Then those who are in Judea must flee to the mountains, and those who are in the midst of the city must leave, and those who are in the country must not enter the city; because these are days of vengeance, so that all things which are written will be fulfilled. Woe to those who are pregnant and to those who are nursing babies in those days; for there will be great distress upon the land and wrath to this people; and they will fall by the edge of the sword, and will be led captive into all the nations; and Jerusalem will be trampled under foot by the Gentiles until the times of the Gentiles are fulfilled.** (21:20–24)

The end of history has already been written by God and revealed in the Bible. Mankind is not headed for a utopia, such as those envisioned by Plato, Thomas More, Karl Marx, or others, but rather faces increasing chaos, devastation, and disaster until the end. Humans will create no Shangri-La. Our planet and its occupants also face a terrifying future—far worse than even the most pessimistic environmentalist could ever be willing to imagine.

Ever since the fall, the human race has battled the devastating effects of sin and the consequent curse on individuals, society, and the environment (cf. Rom. 8:20–22). As noted in the previous chapter of this volume, because of that divine curse, there have always been deceivers who twist and pervert the truth, natural disasters that bring destruction and death, and distress in the form of persecution of Christians.

But what lies ahead as the return of the Lord Jesus Christ draws near will be unimaginably worse than anything that has happened in the past, or will happen before the birth pains. Religious deceivers, natural catastrophes, and persecution of believers will escalate to a level never seen. Jesus described the last three and one half years of the final time of tribulation immediately preceding His return as "a great tribulation, such as has not occurred since the beginning of the world until now, nor ever will" (Matt. 24:21; cf. Rev. 7:14).

Wickedness will be collective and unrestrained, dominating life on earth as never before. The Holy Spirit, who currently holds back evil, will no longer do so, permitting sin to run rampant (2 Thess. 2:7). Further, Satan will be allowed to release demons who are presently bound in hell (Rev. 9:1–2) to unleash one final, futile onslaught against God and Christ. At the same time, in addition to wickedness causing chaos, God's wrath will be poured out with sustained deadly force on the world and its population.

As the tribulation accelerates, events will get progressively worse as God's judgments intensify. They will consist of three sets of seven judgments each, beginning with the seal judgments (Rev. 6). As the Lord Jesus Christ unrolls the scroll that symbolizes the title deed to the earth (Rev. 5:7) He will break each seal, unleashing a specific judgment on the earth. Out of the seventh seal will come the rapid-fire seven trumpet judgments; out of the seventh trumpet will come the still more rapid-fire seven bowl judgments. The bowl judgments are God's final outpouring of wrath (Rev. 16:1), and will be followed by the return of the Lord Jesus Christ to destroy the surviving ungodly and gather His saints into His earthly kingdom. He will return to earth visibly and the whole world will see Him (Rev. 1:7). His feet will touch the Mount of Olives in Jerusalem

(Zech. 14:4), which will split open and water will flow out and create a river that will run down from Jerusalem into the desert (vv. 8, 10, 11). That will initiate the restoration and renovation of the planet, turning it into paradise regained.

While anticipating Christ's glorious return is joy to the believer, it should be a terrifying reality for those who reject Him. He will come not only to establish His kingdom, into which those who belong to Him will be gathered alive, but also to kill the ungodly, who will then be condemned to eternal punishment in hell (cf. Matt. 25:31–46). The realization of those dual realities brought the apostle John's consideration of the Lord's coming both sweetness and bitterness (Rev. 10:9–10).

The time of tribulation will also be both bitter and sweet. It will not only be a time of unprecedented judgment and wrath, but also of God's grace in global salvation. The gospel will be preached all over the world by one hundred forty-four thousand zealous Jewish evangelists (Rev. 7), as well as being proclaimed by an angel (Rev. 14:6). The result will be a worldwide revival in which multitudes will be converted to Christ (Rev. 7:9–10).

The credibility of God the Father and the Lord Jesus depend upon the exact fulfillment of the prophecies of Christ's return. The precise predictions of the events at the second coming recorded in both the Old and New Testaments reflect God's knowledge of the future. In several passages in Isaiah, God challenged the idols worshiped by Israel to demonstrate their deity by predicting the future:

> "Present your case," the Lord says. "Bring forward your strong arguments," the King of Jacob says. Let them bring forth and declare to us what is going to take place; as for the former events, declare what they were, that we may consider them and know their outcome. Or announce to us what is coming; declare the things that are going to come afterward, that we may know that you are gods; indeed, do good or evil, that we may anxiously look about us and fear together. (41:21–23)

> "Thus says the Lord, the King of Israel and his Redeemer, the Lord of hosts: 'I am the first and I am the last, and there is no God besides Me. Who is like Me? Let him proclaim and declare it; yes, let him recount it to Me in order, from the time that I established the ancient nation. And let them declare to them the things that are coming and the events that are going to take place.'" (44:6–7)

Gather yourselves and come; draw near together, you fugitives of the nations; they have no knowledge, who carry about their wooden idol and pray to a god who cannot save. Declare and set forth your case; indeed, let them consult together. Who has announced this from of old? Who has long since declared it? Is it not I, the Lord? And there is no other God besides Me, a righteous God and a Savior; there is none except Me. (45:20–21)

To whom would you liken Me and make Me equal and compare Me, that we would be alike? Those who lavish gold from the purse and weigh silver on the scale hire a goldsmith, and he makes it into a god; they bow down, indeed they worship it. They lift it upon the shoulder and carry it; they set it in its place and it stands there. It does not move from its place. Though one may cry to it, it cannot answer; it cannot deliver him from his distress. Remember this, and be assured; recall it to mind, you transgressors. Remember the former things long past, for I am God, and there is no other; I am God, and there is no one like Me, declaring the end from the beginning, and from ancient times things which have not been done, saying, "My purpose will be established, and I will accomplish all My good pleasure." (46:5–10)

God stakes His credibility on His Word's prophesying the future.

The rampant wickedness and the escalation of God's wrath spoken of in this chapter will be general signs that Christ's return is near. But in addition, our Lord predicts two specific signs: Jerusalem will be surrounded by armies, and the abomination of desolation will be set up.

## JERUSALEM WILL BE SURROUNDED BY ARMIES

**But when you see Jerusalem surrounded by armies, then recognize that her desolation is near. Then those who are in Judea must flee to the mountains, and those who are in the midst of the city must leave, and those who are in the country must not enter the city; because these are days of vengeance, so that all things which are written will be fulfilled. Woe to those who are pregnant and to those who are nursing babies in those days; for there will be great distress upon the land and wrath to this people; and they will fall by the edge of the sword, and will be led captive into all the nations; and Jerusalem will be trampled under foot by the Gentiles until the times of the Gentiles are fulfilled.** (21:20–24)

**Jerusalem** has been **surrounded by armies** repeatedly through-out its history. As one writer notes:

> There have been at least 118 separate conflicts in and for Jerusalem during the past four millennia—conflicts that ranged from local reli-gious struggles to strategic military campaigns and that embraced everything in between. Jerusalem has been destroyed completely at least twice, besieged twenty-three times, attacked an additional fifty-two times, and captured and recaptured forty-four times. It has been the scene of twenty revolts and innumerable riots, has had at least five sep-arate periods of violent terrorist attacks during the past century, and has only changed hands completely peacefully twice in the past four thou-sand years. (Eric H. Cline, *Jerusalem Besieged* [Ann Arbor, Mich.: University of Michigan Press, 2004], 2)

In A.D. 70, forty years after our Lord spoke these words, His prediction that Jerusalem would suffer **desolation** was fulfilled. The Romans laid siege to Jerusalem, sacked the city, burned the temple, and slaughtered thou-sands of people.

But no previous assault, including the destruction of Jerusalem in A.D. 70, is what Jesus referred to here. It is true that during that Roman siege there were those **in Judea** who did **flee to the** nearby **mountains,** and others **who** were **in the midst of the city** did manage to **leave** be-fore the city was surrounded, while **those who** were **in the country** nat-urally did **not enter the city** once that massacre and destruction had begun.

The events of A.D. 70, however, were nothing like the **days of vengeance** of which Jesus spoke. **All things which are written** were not **fulfilled** (cf. such unfulfilled prophecies as Zech. 12:1–9; 14:1–11 and the unprecedented outpouring of God's wrath described in Rev. 6–19). Nor did Jesus visibly return to earth (Zech. 14:4; Acts 1:9–11), judge the wicked (Matt. 25:31–46), and establish His absolute rule here (Rev. 20:4–6).

The phrase **days of vengeance** is an Old Testament expression that speaks of divine vengeance in the end times (cf. Isa. 34:8; 35:4; 61:2; 63:4; Mic. 5:15), specifically the tribulation, the time of Jacob's distress (Jer. 30:7; cf. Dan. 12:1). It describes God's final, eschatological judgment, and is the equivalent of the familiar Old Testament term the Day of the Lord (Isa. 2:12; 13:6, 9; Ezek. 13:5; 30:3; Joel 1:15; 2:1, 11, 31; 3:14; Amos 5:18, 20; Obad. 15; Zeph. 1:7, 14; Zech. 14:1; Mal. 4:5).

When those days come, it will be especially difficult for **those who are pregnant and . . . those who are nursing babies.** Encumbered as they are, such women will find it difficult to escape the **distress upon the land and** the **wrath** poured out on its **people.** The mass exodus from Jerusalem will mark the end of evangelism, as the believing remnant, protected by God, flees into hiding.

Not all who flee will escape, however. Many Christian martyrs and Jewish unbelievers **will fall by the edge of the sword,** while others **will be led captive into all the nations.** In addition, **Jerusalem will be trampled under foot by the Gentiles until the times of the Gentiles** (the period from 586 B.C., when Israel first went into captivity, until Christ returns to establish His kingdom) **are fulfilled.** The **times of the Gentiles** obviously did not end in A.D. 70; they will not end until the future day of God's final vengeance and judgment comes.

## THE ABOMINATION OF DESOLATION WILL BE SET UP

The second sign that the Lord's coming is near appears in Matthew's parallel account of the Olivet Discourse, where Jesus referred to "the abomination of desolation which was spoken of through Daniel the prophet, standing in the holy place" (Matt. 24:15). That event, coming at the midpoint of the tribulation, will trigger the severest cataclysms— the time that Jesus, as noted above, called the "great tribulation."

The word "abomination" refers to something disgusting, repulsive, detestable, and abhorrent to God. In the Old Testament, it describes immoral practices that God hates (e.g., Lev. 18:22–29; Deut. 22:5; 25:13–16; 1 Kings 14:24; 2 Kings 16:3; Prov. 11:1; 12:22; 15:8–9; 20:23; Jer. 13:27). According to Revelation 21:27, "no one who practices abomination" will enter heaven. The ultimate false religion that arises in the end times is represented by a woman

> clothed in purple and scarlet, and adorned with gold and precious stones and pearls, having in her hand a gold cup full of abominations and of the unclean things of her immorality, and on her forehead a name was written, a mystery, "Babylon the great, the mother of harlots and of the abominations of the earth." (Rev. 17:5)

The "abomination of desolation" has its roots in the book of Daniel, where it was referred to three times (9:27; 11:31; 12:11). The prophecy of the seventy weeks describes sixty-nine weeks of seven years each (483 years), culminating in Christ's first coming and crucifixion (9:24–26) with the seventieth week (seven years) separated and yet to come in the future. At the outset of that seven-year tribulation, the final Antichrist "will make a firm covenant with [Israel] for [that] one week" (v. 27). He will offer to provide protection for Israel and, engulfed by an increasingly deadly world, the nation will accept his offer.

But "in the middle of the week," Antichrist will show his true colors. "He will put a stop to sacrifice and grain offering; and on the wing of abominations will come one who makes desolate" (v. 27). The New Testament adds that Antichrist will oppose God and exalt "himself above every so-called god or object of worship, so that he takes his seat in the temple of God, displaying himself as being God" (2 Thess. 2:4). Most likely, he will defile the temple by installing an idol of himself inside it (cf. Rev. 13:15). The term "abomination" was used in the Old Testament in reference to idolatry (e.g., Deut. 7:25; 27:15; 29:17; 32:16; Isa. 44:19; Ezek. 7:20; 18:12), and this unparalleled example of blasphemy will be the ultimate act of idolatry.

It will not, however, be without historical precedent. Daniel 11 records an amazingly detailed prophecy that would be fulfilled more than three centuries after Daniel revealed it. The prophecy highlights the career of the Seleucid king of the intertestamental period, Antiochus IV.

> Antiochus bestowed on himself the title "Epiphanes," meaning "manifest one" or "splendid one." It was for all practical purposes a claim of deity for himself. But his enemies, varying the word slightly, nicknamed him "Epimanes," meaning "madman."
>
> Pretending to be the defender of Jerusalem, Antiochus went to war against Egypt, then used spoils plundered from Egypt to win support from influential people in Israel. This seems to be precisely what Daniel prophesied in 11:24: "He shall enter peaceably, even into the richest places of the province; and he shall do what his fathers have not done, nor his forefathers: he shall disperse among them the plunder, spoil, and riches; and he shall devise his plans against the strongholds, but only for a time."

History records that as he prepared to launch a final assault against Egypt in 160 B.C., he received orders from Rome via Cyprus (where the Roman fleet was anchored at the time) that he was not to make war against the Ptolemies. Antiochus, humiliated but unwilling to go against both Rome and Egypt, reluctantly withdrew from Egypt, and on his way back to Syria he decided to vent his rage against Jerusalem. That is precisely what Daniel had foretold more than three centuries before: "Ships from Cyprus shall come against him; therefore he shall be grieved, and return in rage against the holy covenant, and do damage" (11:30).

Two Apocryphal books, 1 and 2 Maccabees, record Antiochus' treachery. He entered Jerusalem under the pretense of peace. He then waited until the Sabbath and ordered his army of more than 250,000 to carry out wholesale slaughter against the Jews. They met with very little resistance because of the Jews' rigid observance of the Sabbath laws (2 Maccabees 5:24–26). Antiochus then deliberately set several Jewish apostates (enemies of Israel's covenant with Jehovah) in power over the occupied city, again fulfilling Daniel's prophecy to the letter: "So he shall return and show regard for those who forsake the holy covenant" (Dan. 11:30). He set out deliberately to defile the temple, and this he did by sacrificing a pig (an unclean and forbidden animal, according to Lev. 11:7) on the altar and forcing the priests to eat its flesh.

His design, moreover, was to set up a new religion of his own, a thoroughly pagan kind of worship that was a mockery of Judaism.

> King Antiochus wrote to his whole kingdom, that all should be one people, and every one should leave his laws: so all the heathen agreed according to the commandment of the king. Yea, many also of the Israelites consented to his religion, and sacrificed unto idols, and profaned the Sabbath. For the king had sent letters by messengers unto Jerusalem and the cities of Judah that they should follow the strange laws of the land, and forbid burnt offerings, and sacrifice, and drink offerings, in the temple; and that they should profane the Sabbaths and festival days: and pollute the sanctuary and holy people: set up altars, and groves, and chapels of idols, and sacrifice swine's flesh, and unclean beasts: that they should also leave their children uncircumcised, and make their souls abominable with all manner of uncleanness and profanation: to the end they might forget the law, and change all the ordinances, and whosoever would not do according to the commandment of the king, he said, he should die. (1 Maccabees 1:41–50)

In other words, it was forbidden for anyone to observe the Old Testament dietary laws, the Sabbath laws, circumcision, or anything else distinctly Jewish. Notice that Antiochus' stated goal was "that all should be one people." In other words, he wanted to establish a new one world religion, beginning at Jerusalem. Under the pretense of "unity," this megalomaniacal madman sought to found a religion that was an amalgam of many religions, but in which he was the ultimate object of worship. And there is little doubt that his real goal was eventually to conquer the whole world and impose his religion everywhere.

It was at this time that Antiochus committed the act usually associated with the abomination of desolation: "Now the fifteenth day of the month Chislev, in the hundred forty and fifth year, they set up the abomination of desolation upon the altar" (1 Maccabees 1:54). History records that this was an image of Zeus and an altar to Zeus, built right on the Jews' altar of the burnt offering. This put an end to the daily sacrifices to Jehovah in the temple.

Again, history accords precisely with Daniel's prophecy: "Forces shall be mustered by him, and they shall defile the sanctuary fortress; then they shall take away the daily sacrifices, and place there the abomination of desolation" (Dan. 11:31). (John MacArthur, *The Second Coming* [Wheaton, Ill.: Crossway, 1999], 108–10)

The ultimate eschatological meaning of Daniel's prophecy was foreshadowed, but not at all fulfilled, by the degradations carried out by Antiochus IV. The final abomination of desolation of which Jesus spoke awaits fulfillment in the middle of the seventieth week, three and one half years into the tribulation.

At the same time that the abomination of desolation is set up, Jerusalem will be under massive assault from the world's armies, under the leadership of Antichrist. The attacking force will be huge, extending from Jerusalem to Megiddo, about sixty miles to the north. This massive assault will cause many professing believers to abandon their faith (Matt. 24:9–12), but not true believers, who will persevere to the end (v. 13). It will also be a time of savage atrocities against the Jewish people, two thirds of whom will be killed, while the rest will call on the Lord and be redeemed (Zech. 13:8–9; cf. Jer. 30:1–8). Zechariah describes the siege and judgment, but also promises the salvation of the nation of Israel (12:1–13:1).

As noted above, the terrors of the great tribulation, initiated by Antichrist's setting up of the abomination of desolation, will last for three and one half years. That fact is confirmed by several passages of Scripture. Daniel 12:7 says that it will last "for a time [one year], times [two years], and half a time [half a year]," and verse 9 makes it clear that the reference is to an event in the end times. Revelation 11:2 and 13:5 set its length at forty-two months; 11:3 and 12:6 at 1,260 days, all of which add up to three and one half years (1,260 days equals three and one half years based on a 360 day year). A comparison of Daniel 12:12 and 13 reveals that there will be an additional seventy-five days between Christ's destruction of the forces of Antichrist at the battle of Armageddon and the establishment of His kingdom, perhaps to clean up the remains of the carnage.

Though they will not know the exact day or hour (Matt. 24:36), the twin signs of Jerusalem being surrounded by armies and the setting up of the abomination of desolation will give clear warning to those alive at that time that the return of the Lord Jesus Christ is near.

The church will be spared the unimaginable horrors of the entire tribulation period, being raptured before it begins (John 14:1–3; 1 Cor. 15:51–52; 1 Thess. 4:15–18; Rev. 3:10). Just as the church was not in the first sixty-nine weeks of Daniel's prophecy regarding Israel, so also it will not be in the seventieth. (For a defense of the pretribulation rapture, see *1 & 2 Thessalonians*, The MacArthur New Testament Commentary [Chicago: Moody, 2002], chap. 11.)

In the meantime, Christians are to be prepared for Christ's return:

> Since all these things are to be destroyed in this way, what sort of people ought you to be in holy conduct and godliness, looking for and hastening the coming of the day of God, because of which the heavens will be destroyed by burning, and the elements will melt with intense heat! But according to His promise we are looking for new heavens and a new earth, in which righteousness dwells. Therefore, beloved, since you look for these things, be diligent to be found by Him in peace, spotless and blameless, and regard the patience of our Lord as salvation; just as also our beloved brother Paul, according to the wisdom given him, wrote to you, as also in all his letters, speaking in them of these things, in which are some things hard to understand, which the untaught and unstable distort, as they do also the rest of the Scriptures, to their own destruction. You therefore, beloved, knowing this beforehand, be on your guard so that you are not carried away by the error of unprincipled men and fall from your own steadfastness, but grow in the grace and knowledge of our Lord and Savior Jesus Christ. To Him be the glory, both now and to the day of eternity. Amen. (2 Peter 3:11–18)

# Signs of Christ's Return—Part 5: Celestial Signs of the Coming Savior (Luke 21:25–28)

# 21

**There will be signs in sun and moon and stars, and on the earth dismay among nations, in perplexity at the roaring of the sea and the waves, men fainting from fear and the expectation of the things which are coming upon the world; for the powers of the heavens will be shaken. Then they will see the Son of Man coming in a cloud with power and great glory. But when these things begin to take place, straighten up and lift up your heads, because your redemption is drawing near." (21:25–28)**

The second coming of the Lord Jesus Christ will not only be the most significant event in history, but also the most widely viewed one. His birth was witnessed by only a few people: Mary, Joseph, the shepherds, and perhaps a few others in Bethlehem. But when Christ returns, the whole world will see Him. "Behold, He is coming with the clouds," John wrote, "and every eye will see Him" (Rev. 1:7).

Five key words aid in summarizing our Lord's teaching in this section regarding His second coming: sequence, staging, shock, sign, and saints.

SEQUENCE

**There will be** (21:25*a*)

The Greek word *kai* (left untranslated by the New American Standard) at the beginning of verse 25 connects this passage with what the Lord had already taught the disciples. Jesus gave this discourse in response to their question about the signs of His coming (v. 7). He replied by describing the period between His first and second comings. That long era would be characterized first of all by a proliferation of deceiving, lying false teachers claiming to be Christ (v. 8). Those false messiahs and the specious misrepresentations of Christianity they spawn and spew will lead millions astray from the truth, so that false believers will always outnumber true ones (cf. Matt. 7:13–14).

There will also be disasters in the natural world. Wars on a scale without precedent in human history will cause widespread death and destruction (vv. 9–10). Powerful earthquakes, deadly plagues and desperate famines, destructive fires, terrifying signs from the sky (possibly comet or meteor impacts), violent hurricanes, tornadoes, torrential rains that produce floods, and blizzards will ravage the planet (v. 11). Those deadly catastrophes, unparalleled in scope, will escalate as the time of Christ's return draws near. But long centuries before all those things even start, His followers would face persecution, soon from the Jews, and later from the Gentiles, beginning with the Romans (vv. 12–17). That persecution will preview on a small scale the zenith of persecution during the tribulation.

In addition to those general characteristics of the period between Christ's two comings, there will be two specific sign events that will declare the second coming is finally at hand: First, Jerusalem will be surrounded by the world's armies under the leadership of Antichrist (v. 20), and second, the final Antichrist will set up the "abomination of desolation" in the temple (Matt. 24:15). Those events take place during the last three and one half years of the tribulation judgments, called the "great tribulation" (Matt. 24:21; Rev. 7:14). As this passage opens in verse 25, those are all past, and the sequence of events advances to the final signs of the Lord's return at the end of the tribulation (Matt. 24:29; Mark 13:24).

## STAGING

**There will be signs in sun and moon and stars . . . the roaring of the sea and the waves . . . the powers of the heavens will be shaken.** (21:25*a, c*, 26*b*)

History's most momentous and widely viewed event demands a correspondingly dramatic backdrop. God will set the stage for Christ's return by extinguishing all the celestial lights (Matt. 24:29; cf. Zech. 14:6–7), plunging the heavens into total darkness. With all of the world's attention focused on the blackness, Jesus will descend out of the darkened sky in blazing glory. His return to this earth will be like His departure. As the disciples stared transfixed into the sky watching Him ascend to heaven in a cloud (Acts 1:9), two angels said to them, "Men of Galilee, why do you stand looking into the sky? This Jesus, who has been taken up from you into heaven, will come in just the same way as you have watched Him go into heaven" (v. 11). Revelation 1:7, as noted above, also reveals that Jesus will come in the clouds, which the Old Testament describes as God's chariots (Ps. 104:3; Isa. 19:1). Daniel "kept looking in the night visions, and behold, with the clouds of heaven One like a Son of Man was coming, and He came up to the Ancient of Days and was presented before Him" (Dan. 7:13). Clouds are also associated with Christ's gathering up His church in the rapture (1 Thess. 4:17).

Adding to the glory and majesty of the dramatic scene, "the Lord Jesus will be revealed from heaven with His mighty angels in flaming fire, dealing out retribution to those who do not know God and to those who do not obey the gospel of our Lord Jesus" (2 Thess. 1:7–8). In addition to bringing fiery judgment on unbelievers, Jesus "comes to be glorified in His saints on that day, and to be marveled at among all who have believed" (v. 10).

Immediately preceding Christ's arrival there will be vast cosmic catastrophes that will cause unimaginable destruction. **There will be signs in sun and moon and stars, the roaring of the sea and the waves,** and the powers of **the heavens will be shaken.** In his book *Earth in Upheaval*, Immanuel Velikovsky speculated as to what might happen if the approach of a heavenly body toward the earth caused it to tilt on its axis:

At that moment an earthquake would make the globe shudder. Air and water would continue to move through inertia; hurricanes would sweep the earth and the seas would rush over continents, carrying gravel and sand and marine animals, and casting them on the land. Heat would be developed, rocks would melt, volcanoes would erupt, lava would flow from fissures in the ruptured ground and cover vast areas. Mountains would spring up from the plains and would travel and climb on the shoulders of other mountains, causing faults and rifts. Lakes would be tilted and emptied, rivers would change their beds; large land areas with all their inhabitants would slip under the sea. Forests would burn and the hurricanes and wild seas would wrest them from the ground on which they grew and pile them, branch and root, in huge heaps. Seas would turn into deserts, their waters rolling away. ([Garden City, N.Y.: Doubleday, 1955], 136)

The Lord did not explain these **signs** and the disciples did not ask Him about them, because they understood them from the Old Testament. The judgment on Babylon predicted in Isaiah 13 provides an illustration of the final divine reckoning that will come on the whole earth:

Wail, for the day of the Lord is near! It will come as destruction from the Almighty. Therefore all hands will fall limp, and every man's heart will melt [cf. Luke 21:26]. They will be terrified, pains and anguish will take hold of them; they will writhe like a woman in labor, they will look at one another in astonishment, their faces aflame. Behold, the day of the Lord is coming, cruel, with fury and burning anger, to make the land a desolation; and He will exterminate its sinners from it. For the stars of heaven and their constellations will not flash forth their light; the sun will be dark when it rises and the moon will not shed its light. Thus I will punish the world for its evil and the wicked for their iniquity; I will also put an end to the arrogance of the proud and abase the haughtiness of the ruthless. I will make mortal man scarcer than pure gold and mankind than the gold of Ophir. Therefore I will make the heavens tremble, and the earth will be shaken from its place at the fury of the Lord of hosts in the day of His burning anger. (Isa. 13:6–13)

The twenty-fourth chapter of Isaiah further describes God's future retribution:

Behold, the Lord lays the earth waste, devastates it, distorts its surface and scatters its inhabitants. And the people will be like the priest, the servant like his master, the maid like her mistress, the buyer like the seller, the lender like the borrower, the creditor like the debtor. The earth will be completely laid waste and completely despoiled, for the Lord has spoken this word. The earth mourns and withers, the world fades and withers, the exalted of the people of the earth fade away. The earth is also polluted by its inhabitants, for they transgressed laws, violated statutes, broke the everlasting covenant. Therefore, a curse devours the earth, and those who live in it are held guilty. Therefore, the inhabitants of the earth are burned, and few men are left.... Then it will be that he who flees the report of disaster will fall into the pit, and he who climbs out of the pit will be caught in the snare; for the windows above are opened, and the foundations of the earth shake. The earth is broken asunder, the earth is split through, the earth is shaken violently. The earth reels to and fro like a drunkard and it totters like a shack, for its transgression is heavy upon it, and it will fall, never to rise again. So it will happen in that day, that the Lord will punish the host of heaven on high, and the kings of the earth on earth. They will be gathered together like prisoners in the dungeon, and will be confined in prison; and after many days they will be punished. Then the moon will be abashed and the sun ashamed, for the Lord of hosts will reign on Mount Zion and in Jerusalem, and His glory will be before His elders. (vv. 1–6, 18–23)

The prophet Joel adds more.

Blow a trumpet in Zion, and sound an alarm on My holy mountain! Let all the inhabitants of the land tremble, for the day of the Lord is coming; surely it is near, a day of darkness and gloom, a day of clouds and thick darkness. As the dawn is spread over the mountains, so there is a great and mighty people; there has never been anything like it, nor will there be again after it to the years of many generations.... Before them the earth quakes, the heavens tremble, the sun and the moon grow dark and the stars lose their brightness.... I will display wonders in the sky and on the earth, blood, fire and columns of smoke.... For behold, in those days and at that time, when I restore the fortunes of Judah and Jerusalem, I will gather all the nations and bring them down to the valley of Jehoshaphat. Then I will enter into judgment with them there on behalf of My people and My inheritance, Israel. ... Multitudes, multitudes in the valley of decision! For the day of the Lord is near in the valley of decision. The sun and moon grow dark and the stars lose their brightness. The Lord roars from Zion and utters His voice from Jerusalem, and the heavens and the earth tremble. But the Lord is a refuge for His people and a stronghold to the sons of Israel. Then you will know that I am the Lord your God, dwelling in Zion, My holy mountain. So Jerusalem will be holy, and strangers will pass through it no more. And in that day the mountains will drip with sweet wine, and the hills will flow with milk, and all the brooks of Judah will flow with water; and a spring will go out from the house of the Lord to water the valley of Shittim. (2:1–2, 10, 30; 3:1–2, 14–18)

Judgments described in Ezekiel 38:19–23 are identical to those that will take place during the last half of the tribulation (Rev. 6:12–17; 11:19; 16:17–21; 19:11–21). Haggai (2:6–7) and Zephaniah (1:14–18) also predict God's final temporal fury.

SHOCK

**on the earth dismay among nations . . . perplexity . . . men fainting from fear and the expectation of the things which are coming upon the world** (21:25*b*, 26*a*)

The devastating judgments that come **on the earth** will inflict incredible trauma on the unbelieving **nations.** *Sunochē* (**dismay**) appears only here and in 2 Corinthians 2:4, where it describes Paul's anguish and consternation over the troubled church at Corinth. The word refers to severe emotional stress; an overwhelming, overpowering sense of acute, unrelieved fear and torment.

*Aporia* (**perplexity**) appears only here in the New Testament. It has connotations of distress, dismay, discomfort, being at a loss, uncertainty. For example, the related verb *aporeō* is used to describe Herod's bewilderment regarding John the Baptist (Mark 6:20), the women's perplexity at finding the empty tomb after the resurrection (Luke 24:4), the disciples' being at a loss as to who would betray Jesus (John 13:22), Festus's uncertainty of how to handle the Jews' charges against Paul (Acts 25:20), and Paul's being at his wit's end over the Galatians (Gal. 4:20).

*Apopsuchō* (**fainting**) also appears only here in the New Testament. It literally means "to breathe out," "to stop breathing," and hence "to expire." People will literally be scared to death; they will be frightened to death because of what is happening around them. The radical alteration of the world and its environment at the end of the tribulation will be the culmination and climax of all the terrifying events of that period. Isaiah 13:8 says humanity "will be terrified, pains and anguish will take hold of them; they will writhe like a woman in labor, they will look at one another in astonishment, their faces aflame." Reacting to the sixth seal judgment, the kings of the earth and the great men and the commanders and the rich and the strong and every slave and free man hid themselves in the caves and among the rocks of the mountains; and they said to the mountains and to the rocks, "Fall on us and hide us from the presence of Him who sits on the throne, and from the wrath of the Lamb; for the great day of their wrath has come, and who is able to stand?" (Rev. 6:15–17)

Revelation 9:6 warns that "in those days men will seek death and will not find it; they will long to die, and death flees from them." When

the fourth angel poured out his bowl upon the sun ... it was given to it to scorch men with fire. Men were scorched with fierce heat; and they blasphemed the name of God who has the power over these plagues, and they did not repent so as to give Him glory. Then the fifth angel poured out his bowl on the throne of the beast, and his kingdom became darkened; and they gnawed their tongues because of pain, and they blasphemed the God of heaven because of their pains and their sores; and they did not repent of their deeds. (Rev. 16:8–11)

The eighteenth chapter of Revelation describes the disintegration of life in the final days:

"For this reason in one day [Babylon's] plagues will come, pestilence and mourning and famine, and she will be burned up with fire; for the Lord God who judges her is strong. And the kings of the earth, who committed acts of immorality and lived sensuously with her, will weep and lament over her when they see the smoke of her burning, standing at a distance because of the fear of her torment, saying, 'Woe, woe, the great city, Babylon, the strong city! For in one hour your judgment has come.' And the merchants of the earth weep and mourn over her, because no one buys their cargoes any more—cargoes of gold and silver and precious stones and pearls and fine linen and purple and silk and scarlet, and every kind of citron wood and every article of ivory and every article made from very costly wood and bronze and iron and marble, and cinnamon and spice and incense and perfume and frankincense and wine and olive oil and fine flour and wheat and cattle and sheep, and cargoes of horses and chariots and slaves and human lives. The fruit you long for has gone from you, and all things that were luxurious and splendid have passed away from you and men will no longer find them. The merchants of these things, who became rich from her, will stand at a distance because of the fear of her torment, weeping and mourning, saying, 'Woe, woe, the great city, she who was clothed in fine linen and purple and scarlet, and adorned with gold and precious stones and pearls; for in one hour such great wealth has been laid waste!' And every shipmaster and every passenger and sailor, and as many as make their living by the sea, stood at a distance, and were crying out as they saw the smoke of her burning, saying, 'What city is like the great city?' And they threw dust on their heads and were crying out, weeping and mourning, saying, 'Woe, woe, the great city, in which all who had ships at sea became rich by her wealth, for in one hour she has been laid waste!' Rejoice over her, O heaven, and you saints and apostles and prophets, because God has pronounced judgment for you against her." Then a strong angel took up a stone like a great millstone and threw it into the sea, saying, "So will Babylon, the great city, be thrown down with violence, and will not be found any longer. And the sound of harpists and musicians and flute-players and trumpeters will not be heard in you any longer; and no craftsman of any craft will be found in you any longer; and the sound of a mill will not be heard in you any longer; and the light of a lamp will not shine in you any longer; and the voice of the bridegroom and bride will not be heard in you any longer; for your merchants were the great men of the earth, because all the nations were deceived by your sorcery." (vv. 8–23)

The catastrophic end of human history will shock the unbelieving world. People will understand that what is happening is the wrath of God, due to hearing the preaching of the 144,000 Jewish evangelists (Rev. 7:2–8), the two witnesses (Rev. 11:3), testimony of those saved in that time, and even flying angels (Rev. 14:6–8). Some will believe, but most will refuse to repent, and blaspheme God (Rev. 16:11, 21). Many who reject the truth will die; the others will wish they were dead; those who survive the succession of judgments will be killed by the Lord Jesus Christ when He arrives (Rev. 19:11–15).

SIGN

**Then they will see the Son of Man coming in a cloud with power and great glory.** (21:27)

The final sign of Christ's arrival is not another event that points to the **Son of Man**; it is the Son of Man Himself. The subjective genitive in Matthew's parallel account could be translated, "The sign which is the Son of Man" (Matt. 24:30). The ultimate sign will not be a blazing cross, or a visible manifestation of God's Shekinah glory, but the Lord Jesus Christ, bodily returning in **a cloud** of blazing divine glory (see the discussion above), previewed in His transfiguration (Matt. 17:1–2).

The most detailed description of His appearance, His unveiling, and His apocalypse is recorded in Revelation 19:11–15:

> And I saw heaven opened, and behold, a white horse, and He who sat on it is called Faithful and True, and in righteousness He judges and wages war. His eyes are a flame of fire, and on His head are many diadems; and He has a name written on Him which no one knows except Himself. He is clothed with a robe dipped in blood, and His name is called The Word of God. And the armies which are in heaven, clothed in fine linen, white and clean, were following Him on white horses. From His mouth comes a sharp sword, so that with it He may strike down the nations, and He will rule them with a rod of iron; and He treads the wine press of the fierce wrath of God, the Almighty.

The "white horse" symbolizes power and authority; victorious Roman generals rode on white horses through the streets of Rome in their triumphal processions. White also symbolizes the spotless, unblemished, absolutely holy nature of the Lord Jesus Christ. Because He is "Faithful and True," He keeps His word and must act against sin; therefore "in righteousness He judges and wages war." His judgment is absolutely accurate, because "His eyes are a flame of fire," a reference to His omniscience. "On His head are many diadems," because He is the sole ruler; the "King of kings and Lord of lords" (Rev. 19:16). He has a unique "name written on Him which no one knows except Himself." This name (representing all that He is) transcends human comprehension as the nature of God transcends all ideas. No one can fully understand Christ's majesty, authority, glory, power, or the fullness of His other attributes. That "He is clothed with a robe dipped in blood" signifies that this will not be His first battle. His robe bears the blood of enemies whom He has already conquered, and it will shortly bear the blood of those He is about to destroy.

Accompanying "the Word of God," the Son who existed from all eternity (John 1:1) and "became flesh, and dwelt among us" (v. 14), will be the "armies which are in heaven, clothed in fine linen, white and clean . . . following Him on white horses." This heavenly force includes the believers from the church age (Rev. 19:7–8), believers from the Old Testament (Jude 14–15), and those martyred earlier in the tribulation (Rev. 7:9, 13–14), as well as the holy angels (Matt. 25:31).

Christ's judgment will be instantaneous and accurate. "From His mouth comes a sharp sword," symbolizing the death-dealing power of His word (cf. 1:16; Isa. 11:4), "so that with it He may strike down the nations." Having done so, Jesus "will rule them with a rod of iron" (cf. Ps. 2:8–9; Rev. 12:5). The vivid imagery of Christ treading "the wine press of the fierce wrath of God, the Almighty" pictures Him crushing sinful humanity like one would crush grapes to make wine (cf. Isa. 63:1–4).

Unlike His first coming, when He came in humility to die as a sacrifice for sin, Jesus will come again to kill **with power and great glory** (cf. Matt. 26:64). He will manifest His power by both destroying and renewing the world; defeating and judging Satan, the demons, Antichrist, and his forces; and eliminating all the unregenerate, at the same time establishing His kingdom for those who belong to Him (Matt. 25:34).

SAINTS

**But when these things begin to take place, straighten up and lift up your heads, because your redemption is drawing near."** (21:28)

When the signs that indicate that the Lord's return is near (cf. chapter 20 of this volume) **begin to take place,** the believers alive at that time are to **straighten up and lift up** their **heads.** Although they cannot know the exact day Jesus will arrive, the events indicate their **redemption is drawing near** and that "He is near, right at the door" (Matt. 24:33).

How extensive will this coming of the Son of God be? Every person who has ever lived will play a role in history's most dramatic event. Believers from the Old Testament and church eras and those martyred during the tribulation will participate with joy in the glory and bliss of heaven. They will return with Christ to His earthly kingdom, along with those believers who survive the tribulation. On the other hand, those alive who refuse to repent and believe in the Lord Jesus Christ will face temporal death followed immediately by eternal hell.

The urgent message to unbelievers then and now is, "Seek the Lord while He may be found; call upon Him while He is near. Let the wicked forsake his way and the unrighteous man his thoughts; and let him return to the Lord, and He will have compassion on him, and to our God, for He will abundantly pardon" (Isa. 55:6–7; cf. 2 Cor. 6:2; Heb. 3:7–13; 4:7). Delaying a response to God's call to repent and be saved risks the missed opportunity that results in eternal tragedy (cf. Luke 13:24–27; 17:26–33; Acts 24:25).

# Signs of Christ's Return—Part 6: The Final Generation (Luke 21:29–33)

# 22

**Then He told them a parable: "Behold the fig tree and all the trees; as soon as they put forth leaves, you see it and know for yourselves that summer is now near. So you also, when you see these things happening, recognize that the kingdom of God is near. Truly I say to you, this generation will not pass away until all things take place. Heaven and earth will pass away, but My words will not pass away.** (21:29–33)

All who love the Lord and are concerned about His glory, desire His return. They wait eagerly for "[God's] Son from heaven, whom He raised from the dead, that is Jesus" (1 Thess. 1:10) and are "looking for the blessed hope and the appearing of the glory of our great God and Savior, Christ Jesus" (Titus 2:13). Paul referred to Christians as those "who have loved [Christ's] appearing" (2 Tim. 4:8). At the close of the book of Revelation the apostle John responded to Christ's promise, "Yes, I am coming quickly," by saying, "Amen. Come, Lord Jesus" (Rev. 22:20). Believers also anticipate the glory that will be revealed in them; the glorious manifestation of the sons of

God that will take place at Christ's return with the redemption of the body (Rom.8:18–23).

The second coming is the most important of all subjects, because all other biblical truths find their culmination in it.The return of Jesus Christ marks the consummation of redemptive history; it brings to conclusion God's glorious purpose in His eternal plan of salvation. Indifference to it or ignorance of its revealed features is inexcusable and robs the Lord of due honor.

Not surprisingly, then, the truth of Christ's return is a major theme in the New Testament, including Jesus' own teaching. His most complete and comprehensive exposition of the event took place on Wednesday of Passion Week, in response to the disciples' questions about the signs of His coming, the end of the present age, and the establishment of His earthly kingdom.This treatment of His return has been traditionally known as the Olivet Discourse, because the Lord revealed it to His disciples while they were on the Mount of Olives (Matt. 24:3; Mark 13:3).Its truths have been the subject of Luke's gospel since verse 7 of this chapter.

As noted in the previous chapters of this volume, the period between Christ's first and second comings will be marked by three general categories of signs: deception (false Christians, false teachers, and a false church), disasters (both manmade and natural), and persecution of the true followers of Jesus Christ. All of those things will become increasingly severe as the time of Christ's return draws near.

In addition to those general signs, there will be two specific ones. Midway through the tribulation, Antichrist, who had pretended to be Israel's protector and benefactor, will desecrate the temple in Jerusalem by setting up the "abomination of desolation" (Dan. 11:31; 12:11; Matt. 24:15; cf. 2 Thess. 2:3–4)—a blasphemous image of himself that everyone will be required to worship or be killed (Rev. 13:14–15; 14:9, 11).That act will trigger the severe outpouring of divine wrath and judgment that marks the second half of the tribulation, which Jesus referred to as the "great tribulation" (Matt. 24:21; cf. Rev. 7:14). That intense and unparalleled three and a half years of devastation, destruction, and death will reach its climax when Antichrist's forces surround Jerusalem (Luke 21:20) to face their destruction.

The simple, straightforward story the Lord told in this passage is not an allegory, or a mystery with hidden meaning. It is an analogy, parable, or illustration couched in uncomplicated and unmistakable language. The disciples, who after all were plain, ordinary working men, not sophisticated theologians, would have easily understood its meaning. Jesus' story may be discussed under three headings: the simple analogy, the specific application, and the supernatural authority.

## THE SIMPLE ANALOGY

**Then He told them a parable: "Behold the fig tree and all the trees; as soon as they put forth leaves, you see it and know for yourselves that summer is now near.** (21:29–30)

As He frequently did, Jesus **told** an agrarian **parable,** the elements of which were familiar to them, to clarify unfamiliar spiritual truth (cf. 8:4–15; 13:6–9, 18–19; 15:3–7; 20:9–19; Matt. 13:24–30; 20:1–16; Mark 4:26–29). **The fig tree,** a common sight in Israel, is often used in Scripture in spiritual analogies. In Judges 9:10–11 Jotham used the fig tree in his analogy rebuking Israel for making Abimelech king. Hosea used the fig tree to represent the patriarchs (Hos. 9:10). Jeremiah used good and bad figs to illustrate good and bad people (Jer. 24:1–10), while Joel used the fig tree to represent Israel (Joel 1:6–7).

Fig trees, like **all the** rest of the **trees, put forth** their **leaves** in the spring. Everyone understands the obvious reality that the budding trees of spring indicate **that summer is near.** The Lord's point is that events in the present can anticipate what will happen in the future.

## THE SPECIFIC APPLICATION

**So you also, when you see these things happening, recognize that the kingdom of God is near. Truly I say to you, this generation will not pass away until all things take place.** (21:31–32)

Just as the appearance of leaves on trees signifies that summer is near, **so you also,** Jesus declared, **when you see these things**—the signs of His return that He had delineated in the preceding verses—**happening, recognize that the kingdom of God is near.** The twice-repeated word **you** (the people alive when the final signs of His return begin to take place) is the bridge between the general principle expressed in Christ's analogy and its specific application.

The word **truly** (*amēn*) is emphatic, and indicates that what Jesus was about to say is a vital, unequivocal truth (cf. Matt. 5:18; 6:2, 5, 16; 8:10; 11:11; 18:3; 19:23; Mark 3:28; 10:15; John 3:3, 5; 5:24–25; 6:47; 8:51, 58; 16:23).

The identity of the **generation** to whom Jesus was referring has been much discussed. One common view is that the Lord was referring to the disciples; that He was telling them that they would live to see His second coming. But if that was what He meant, Jesus was wrong, since He obviously did not return in their lifetimes. Some, seeking to deny His deity and thus undermine His divine authority over their lives, argue just that. They misuse Jesus' words in Mark 13:32, "But of that day or hour no one knows, not even the angels in heaven, nor the Son, but the Father alone," in an attempt to support their point. Since He Himself admitted His ignorance, they argue, it should come as no surprise that He was wrong. But though Jesus voluntarily set aside the full use of His divine attributes during His incarnation (Phil. 2:5–7), doing so never caused Him to err. So this view is unacceptable.

Another view argues that Jesus was referring to the destruction of Jerusalem in A.D. 70. According to that view, the people of whom the Lord spoke included not only the disciples, but also that entire generation. While it is true that Jerusalem was surrounded by the Roman army in A.D. 70, the other signs of Christ's return that He had referred to earlier in this discourse—worldwide catastrophes on a scale unprecedented in history and Antichrist's setting up of the abomination of desolation—did not take place. Nor, most importantly, did Jesus return to earth following the events of A.D. 70. The generation alive at that time did **pass away** before He returned.

It should be noted that some (proponents of the view known as full or hyper-preterism) are forced to argue that Jesus did return in A.D.

70—but not in a literal, bodily sense. Hyper-preterists believe that all of biblical prophecy—including the second coming of Christ—was fulfilled by A.D. 70. That radical error sets in motion a series of disastrous consequences. Denying the literal, bodily return of Christ means denying His bodily ascension, since, as the angels told the apostles, "This Jesus, who has been taken up from you into heaven, will come in just the same way as you have watched Him go into heaven" (Acts 1:11). Further, if the resurrection of all believers is a past event, it must of necessity be a spiritual, not bodily one. Even more alarming, to deny the bodily resurrection of believers is to deny the bodily resurrection of Christ, since the two events are inseparably linked (1 Cor. 15:13, 16). Shockingly, some hyper-preterists take the extreme view that Christ's resurrection was also a spiritual, not a physical one.

The truth is that denying the bodily resurrection destroys the Christian faith. In 1 Corinthians 15 the apostle Paul bluntly warned the Corinthian believers, some of whom were denying the bodily resurrection (v. 12), of six dire consequences of that denial:

- Preaching Christ would be pointless (v. 14)
- Faith in Christ would be in vain (v. 14)
- All who preached and taught the resurrection would be liars (v. 15)
- No one would be redeemed from sin (v. 17)
- Believers who had already died would have perished (v. 18)
- A hope in Christ that is for this present life only would make Christians "of all men most to be pitied" (v. 19)

To deny the future, bodily resurrection of believers is, like Hymenaeus and Philetus, to "have gone astray from the truth" (2 Tim. 2:18). (For a more detailed critique of hyper-preterism, see my book *The Second Coming* [Wheaton, Ill.: Crossway, 1999], 9–13.)

A third view sees the generation of which the Lord spoke as the Jewish race, His point being that the Jews would survive until the end. But that would not have told the disciples anything they did not already know. They understood from the Old Testament that God had made an eternal covenant with Israel. In Jeremiah 31:35–37 God declared,

Thus says the Lord, who gives the sun for light by day and the fixed order of the moon and the stars for light by night, who stirs up the sea so that its waves roar; the Lord of hosts is His name: "If this fixed order departs from before Me," declares the Lord, "then the offspring of Israel also will cease from being a nation before Me forever." Thus says the Lord, "If the heavens above can be measured and the foundations of the earth searched out below, then I will also cast off all the offspring of Israel for all that they have done," declares the Lord.

Later in Jeremiah He added,

"For thus says the Lord, 'David shall never lack a man to sit on the throne of the house of Israel; and the Levitical priests shall never lack a man before Me to offer burnt offerings, to burn grain offerings and to prepare sacrifices continually.'" The word of the Lord came to Jeremiah, saying, "Thus says the Lord, 'If you can break My covenant for the day and My covenant for the night, so that day and night will not be at their appointed time, then My covenant may also be broken with David My servant so that he will not have a son to reign on his throne, and with the Levitical priests, My ministers. As the host of heaven cannot be counted and the sand of the sea cannot be measured, so I will multiply the descendants of David My servant and the Levites who minister to Me.'" … "Thus says the Lord, 'If My covenant for day and night stand not, and the fixed patterns of heaven and earth I have not established, then I would reject the descendants of Jacob and David My servant, not taking from his descendants rulers over the descendants of Abraham, Isaac and Jacob. But I will restore their fortunes and will have mercy on them.'" (33:17–22, 25–26; cf. Gen. 17:7–8, 19; 2 Sam. 23:5; Jer. 32:40; Ezek. 37:25; Luke 1:72–73; Acts 3:25; Heb. 9:15)

It would have been pointless for Jesus to introduce this topic to the disciples. The everlasting nature of God's covenant with Israel was not an issue for them, and has nothing to do with their original question about the signs of the Lord's return (Luke 21:7).

The notion that the word **generation** refers to evil people in general (cf. Matt. 12:39, 45; 16:4) is similarly pointless. That there will always be wicked people until Christ returns is self-evident and communicates nothing new or definitive. It would also fail to relate to the analogy of the fig tree budding being a sign of summer.

Still another view (popularized by Hal Lindsey's 1970 book *The Late Great Planet Earth*) sees the **generation** as the one alive when Israel was restored as a nation in 1948. Its proponents interpret the fig tree as an allegorical picture of Israel, and its budding as a reference to Israel's rebirth as a nation. Because they teach that a biblical generation is forty years in length, the logical conclusion of that view is that Christ had to return before 1988. Obviously, that did not happen. Further, Luke's inclusion of the phrase **all the trees** indicates that Jesus was not identifying the fig tree with Israel, but merely using trees in general to illustrate His point, as noted above.

All of those interpretations fail either to explain the meaning of **generation** in the context of the parable, or to show how Jesus' reply answered the disciples' question (v. 7). It is best to understand the **generation** of which Jesus spoke to be the one that will be alive when the signs come to pass. Just as the appearing of leaves on the trees indicates that summer is near, so also will those signs reveal to that generation that the coming of the Son of Man to establish the earthly, millennial **kingdom of God** is near. That also answers the disciples' question that prompted the Lord's discourse. Christ's return will come soon after the appearance of the final signs.

The final **generation** will be limited to those saved after the rapture of the church, which will take place before the tribulation begins. Several lines of evidence support the pretribulational view of the rapture.

First, the flow of thought in the book of Revelation suggests that the church will not be on earth during the tribulation. The church appears repeatedly on earth in chapters 1 to 3. In chapters 4 and 5 the scene shifts to heaven where the church, represented by the twenty-four elders (4:4, 10; 5:8; cf. 11:16; 19:4), appears (for evidence that the twenty-four elders represent the church, see *Revelation 1–11*, The MacArthur New Testament Commentary [Chicago: Moody, 1999], 148–50). Then in chapters 6–18, which record the events of the tribulation, the church is not mentioned. In chapter 19 the church returns with Christ (19:14; cf. v. 8).

Second, there are no warnings or instructions in Scripture addressed to the church that tell it how to live during the devastating divine judgments of the tribulation.

Third, the passages that describe the rapture (John 14:1–3; 1 Cor. 15:51–52; 1 Thess. 4:13–18) make no mention of judgment, which features prominently in the passages that describe Christ's return (e.g., Matt. 13:34–50; 24:29–44; Rev. 19:11–21).

Fourth, a posttribulational rapture is pointless. Why rapture believers to meet Christ in the air (1 Thess. 4:17), only to have them immediately return to earth with Him? Why not just gather them together to meet Him when He arrives on earth? Commenting on the pointlessness of a posttribulational rapture Thomas R. Edgar asks,

> What can be the purpose for keeping a remnant alive through the tribulation so that some of the church survive and then take them out of their situation and make them the same as those who did not survive? Why keep them for this? [The] explanation that they provide an escort for Jesus does not hold up. Raptured living saints will be exactly the same as resurrected dead saints. Why cannot the dead believers fulfill this purpose? Why keep a remnant alive [through the Tribulation], then rapture them and accomplish no more than by letting them die? There is no purpose or accomplishment in [such] a rapture....
>
> With all the saints of all the ages past and the armies [of angels] in heaven available as escorts and the fact that [raptured] saints provide no different escort than if they had been killed, why permit the church to suffer immensely, most believers [to] be killed, and spare a few for a rapture which has no apparent purpose, immediately before the [Tribulation] period ends? ... Is this the promise? You will suffer, be killed, but I will keep a few alive, and take them out just before the good times come. Such reasoning, of course, calls for some explanation of the apparent lack of purpose for a posttribulational rapture of any sort.
>
> We can note the following:
>
> (1) An unusual, portentous, one-time event such as the rapture must have a specific purpose. God has purposes for his actions. This purpose must be one that can be accomplished only by such an unusual event as a rapture of living saints.
>
> (2) This purpose must agree with God's general principles of operation.
>
> (3) There is little or no apparent reason to rapture believers when the Lord returns and just prior to setting up the long-awaited kingdom with all of its joyful prospects.
>
> (4) There is good reason to deliver all who are already believers from the tribulation, where they would be special targets of persecution.
>
> (5) To deliver from a period of universal trial and physical destruction such as the tribulation requires a removal from the earth by death

or rapture. Death is not appropriate as a promise in Rev. 3:10.

(6) Deliverance from the tribulation before it starts agrees with God's previous dealings with Noah and Lot and is directly stated as a principle of God's action toward believers in 2 Pet. 2:9. ("Robert H. Gundry and Revelation 3:10," *Grace Theological Journal* 3 [Spring 1982]: 43–44)

Fifth, if at the end of the tribulation all unbelievers are judged and executed, and all living believers raptured and given their glorified bodies, who would be left alive to populate the millennial kingdom (cf. Isa. 65:20–23)?

Sixth, the promise to the church in Revelation 3:10 is that it will be kept out of the tribulation, not preserved in the midst of it (see *Revelation 1–11*, 124–25).

Finally, there are notable differences between the rapture and the second coming, in addition to the issue of judgment noted earlier. At the rapture, the church meets Christ in the air; at the second coming, the church returns with Christ to the earth. At the rapture, the church goes to heaven; at the second coming, it returns to earth. At the rapture, the Mount of Olives is untouched; at the second coming it is touched and split. At the rapture, living saints are translated; at the second coming, no one is translated into heaven. At the rapture the world is not judged, and sin gets worse; at the second coming, sin is judged, and the world is ruled by righteousness. At the rapture the body goes to heaven; at the second coming it comes to earth. The rapture is imminent and signless; the second coming has distinct signs preceding it. The rapture involves only the saved; the second coming involves both the saved and the lost.

## The Supernatural Authority

**Heaven and earth will pass away, but My words will not pass away.** (21:33)

The opening phrase of this verse is not mere hyperbole; **heaven and earth will** indeed **pass away.** After Christ's thousand-year earthly kingdom comes to an end, God will destroy the present heaven and earth and create a new heaven and earth. In his second epistle Peter described the destruction of the present universe:

> But by His word the present heavens and earth are being reserved for fire, kept for the day of judgment and destruction of ungodly men.... But the day of the Lord will come like a thief, in which the heavens will pass away with a roar and the elements will be destroyed with intense heat, and the earth and its works will be burned up. Since all these things are to be destroyed in this way, what sort of people ought you to be in holy conduct and godliness, looking for and hastening the coming of the day of God, because of which the heavens will be destroyed by burning, and the elements will melt with intense heat! But according to His promise we are looking for new heavens and a new earth, in which righteousness dwells. (2 Peter 3:7, 10–13)

In his vision of the great white throne judgment, John wrote, "Then I saw a great white throne and Him who sat upon it, from whose presence earth and heaven fled away, and no place was found for them" (Rev. 20:11; cf. 21:1; Isa. 65:17; 66:22).

In contrast, the **words** of Jesus **will not pass away.** They are not ephemeral like flowers or grass (Isa. 40:8), but permanent. His word can neither be added to nor taken away from (cf. Deut. 4:2; Matt. 5:17–19; Luke 16:17; Rev. 22:18–19). The Word of God is the same unassailable, unchanging truth whether it speaks of the past, present, or future. Just as Christians were "born again ... through the living and enduring word of God" (1 Peter 1:23) and are being sanctified by the "word of His grace" (Acts 20:32), so also will they in the future be glorified, according to the promises of the Word (Rom. 8:17, 30).

# Signs of Christ's Return—Part 7: The Believer's Gift to Christ (Luke 21:34–36)

**23**

**Be on guard, so that your hearts will not be weighted down with dissipation and drunkenness and the worries of life, and that day will not come on you suddenly like a trap; for it will come upon all those who dwell on the face of all the earth. But keep on the alert at all times, praying that you may have strength to escape all these things that are about to take place, and to stand before the Son of Man."** (21:34–36)

The birth of Jesus Christ is the most familiar event of ancient history and the most well-known story in all of Western culture. Christmas is ostensibly the celebration of the incarnation. In reality, however, it has long been confused with and obscured by unrelated cultural baggage, pagan features, and winter themes. The syncretistic amalgam is the largest, longest, most elaborate, and most expensive celebration in the Western world, and in the center of all the confusion is the acknowledgment that the Son of God was born.

But though the world sees (if in a jaded way) the first coming of the Lord Jesus Christ as a good reason for an endless party, there will be no partying when He comes the second time:

> Then a strong angel took up a stone like a great millstone and threw it into the sea, saying, "So will Babylon, the great city, be thrown down with violence, and will not be found any longer. And the sound of harpists and musicians and flute-players and trumpeters will not be heard in you any longer; and no craftsman of any craft will be found in you any longer; and the sound of a mill will not be heard in you any longer; and the light of a lamp will not shine in you any longer; and the voice of the bridegroom and bride will not be heard in you any longer; for your merchants were the great men of the earth, because all the nations were deceived by your sorcery." (Rev. 18:21–23)

As popular as it is to sentimentalize the arrival of the baby in Bethlehem, it is correspondingly unpopular to proclaim His arrival to execute final judgment. The world is eager to embrace an infant in a manger, but has no tolerance for a sovereign Lord coming in power, glory, and judgment. Jesus came to earth the first time in humility to save sinners; He will return in the full display of His deity and glory to judge sinners, establish His kingdom for the saints, and bring to reality the eternal state, finally populating heaven and hell.

The most dramatic revelation regarding our Lord's return comes from the detailed teaching He Himself gave the disciples two days before His execution. That teaching, commonly known as the Olivet Discourse, is found in Matthew 24 and 25, Mark 13, and Luke 21. In His discourse, Jesus described the signs that would lead up to His coming (cf. the exposition of Luke 21:7–33 in the previous chapters of this volume).

What He did not reveal, however, was the exact time of His return. Instead, He warned believers, "Be on the alert then, for you do not know the day nor the hour" (Matt. 25:13; cf. Luke 12:40). No signs precede the rapture, which is the next event on the prophetic calendar. It is imminent; that is, Christ could return for His church at any time. This truth of imminence is demonstrated by many statements from Paul, such as when he commended the Corinthian believers because they were "awaiting eagerly the revelation of our Lord Jesus Christ" (1 Cor. 1:7) that will take place when He returns, and the Thessalonian Christians for "wait[ing] for His Son from heaven, whom He raised from the dead, that is Jesus, who rescues us from the wrath to come" (1 Thess. 1:10). In his second inspired letter to the Thessalonians, Paul wrote as if believers' "gathering together to [Christ]" (2 Thess. 2:1) could take place at any time. Three times in the last chapter of the Bible, Jesus personally promised that He was coming suddenly (Rev. 22:7, 12, 20).

The reality of the many features which are part of the second coming is a source of comfort for Christians; it is their "blessed hope" (Titus 2:13). As noted above, the Corinthian church was "awaiting eagerly the revelation of our Lord Jesus Christ" (1 Cor. 1:7). After presenting the truth about the rapture to the Thessalonians, Paul wrote, "Therefore comfort one another with these words" (1 Thess. 4:18). James exhorted his readers, "You too be patient; strengthen your hearts, for the coming of the Lord is near" (James 5:8). The apostle John's reply to Jesus' promise that He would return, "Amen. Come, Lord Jesus" (Rev. 22:20), expresses the longing and anticipation that has characterized all who love the Lord Jesus Christ.

This portion of Luke's account of the Olivet Discourse contains Jesus' final extended teaching regarding His return. Relating to the Christmas gifts of the wise men, it may be summarized as four gifts Christians can give Him when He returns: vigilant anticipation, spiritual separation, evangelistic occupation, and faithful continuation.

## VIGILANT ANTICIPATION

**Be on guard . . . But keep on the alert at all times** (21:34a, 36a)

Since the first event of the apocalypse, the signless rapture of the church, is imminent, believers are to live their lives in the expectation that Jesus may return for His body at any moment. The church at Thessalonica modeled the constant vigilance, watchfulness, and readiness that is to mark all Christians by continuing to "wait for His Son from heaven, whom He raised from the dead, that is Jesus, who rescues us from the wrath to come" (1 Thess. 1:10). Believers must always **be on guard** and **keep on the alert at all times,** since the Lord's coming will be as unexpected as the arrival of a thief (Luke 12:39; 2 Peter 3:10; Rev. 3:3; 16:15).

Matthew's account of the Olivet Discourse contains three illustrations that emphasize the need to be ready. The first is the historical account of the global flood:

> For the coming of the Son of Man will be just like the days of Noah. For as in those days before the flood they were eating and drinking, marrying and giving in marriage, until the day that Noah entered the ark, and they did not understand until the flood came and took them all away; so will the coming of the Son of Man be. Then there will be two men in the field; one will be taken and one will be left. Two women will be grinding at the mill; one will be taken and one will be left. Therefore be on the alert, for you do not know which day your Lord is coming. (Matt. 24:37–42; cf. Luke 17:26–27)

During the one hundred twenty years that Noah spent building the ark, life went on as usual, as indicated by the matter-of-fact statement that people were "eating and drinking, marrying and giving in marriage" (v. 38). They paid no attention to the constant warnings of coming judgment proclaimed by Noah, who is called "a preacher of righteousness" (2 Peter 2:5). In their skepticism and unbelief, they rejected the truth that judgment was coming "until the flood came and took them all away" (Matt. 24:39). The same thing happened on a local scale "in the days of Lot: they were eating, they were drinking, they were buying, they were selling, they were planting, they were building; but on the day that Lot went out from Sodom it rained fire and brimstone from heaven and destroyed them all" (Luke 17:28–29). Further illustrating the sudden unexpectedness of His return He said, "There will be two men in the field; one will be taken and one will be left. Two women will be grinding at the mill; one will be taken and one will be left" (vv. 40–41). People will ignore all the warnings and life will go on as usual until it is too late and divine judgment falls on the unprepared world.

A second illustration of Matthew's account is the hypothetical story of a man whose house was robbed. Obviously, "if the head of the house had known at what time of the night the thief was coming, he would have been on the alert and would not have allowed his house to be broken into" (v. 43). No thief would be foolish enough to announce in advance when he was going to rob someone; therefore homeowners have to be prepared at all times. Applying the principle to His return,

Jesus said, "For this reason you also must be ready; for the Son of Man is coming at an hour when you do not think He will" (v. 44).

A final analogy contrasts a faithful slave with a wicked one. The "faithful and sensible slave whom his master put in charge of his household [gave his fellow slaves] their food at the proper time" (v. 45). Because he faithfully carried out his duties in his master's absence, Jesus said of him, "Blessed is that slave whom his master finds so doing when he comes. Truly I say to you that he will put him in charge of all his possessions" (vv. 46–47).

On the other hand, the "evil slave [said] in his heart, 'My master is not coming for a long time,' and [began] to beat his fellow slaves and eat and drink with drunkards" (vv. 48–49). But "the master of that slave will come on a day when he does not expect him and at an hour which he does not know" (v. 50), and the price for his unpreparedness for his master's return will be severe. His master "will cut him in pieces and assign him a place with the hypocrites; in that place there will be weeping and gnashing of teeth" (v. 51).

It is not surprising that unbelievers live indifferently and irresponsibly, with no regard for the Lord's coming; that they say mockingly, "Where is the promise of His coming? For ever since the fathers fell asleep, all continues just as it was from the beginning of creation" (2 Peter 3:4). But it is inexcusable for believers to disregard the second coming and live careless lives. To do so is to face the loss of eternal rewards (2 John 8).

SPIRITUAL SEPARATION

**Be on guard, so that your hearts will not be weighted down with dissipation and drunkenness and the worries of life, and that day will not come on you suddenly like a trap; for it will come upon all those who dwell on the face of all the earth.** (21:34)

Vigilant anticipation of the Lord's return produces the fear that leads to holiness and virtue in believers, since it motivates separation from worldliness and sin. *Mēpote* (**so that**) introduces a result clause that expresses the expected outcome of vigilantly anticipating the second coming. Those who eagerly watch for the Lord's return will not have their **hearts . . . weighted down with dissipation and drunkenness and the worries of life,** so **that day will not come on** them **suddenly like a trap.**

Believers seem to be in view here because they are differentiated from **those who dwell on . . . the earth.** They are to live in such a manner that they can present to Christ a heart that is not **weighted down** with sin. *Bareō* (**weighted down**) means "to be burdened," "to be troubled," or "to be overcome." In Matthew 26:43 it describes the eyes of Peter, James, and John as being heavy with sleep, and in Luke 9:32 it refers to the same three being overcome with sleep at the transfiguration. The word is used figuratively in 2 Corinthians 1:8 of Paul's affliction, and in 2 Corinthians 5:4 to speak of the crushing burden of sin and affliction that believers experience in this life.

Jesus then gave three examples of sins that can weigh people down. *Kraipalē* (**dissipation**) literally refers to the nausea associated with drinking and debauchery. **Drunkenness** and the vile behavior that accompanies it has been a problem throughout history. After the flood Noah "became drunk, and uncovered himself inside his tent" (Gen. 9:21). Nabal, whose name means "foolish," lived up to his name (1 Sam. 25:25) by getting drunk at a feast after scorning and turning away David's messengers (v. 36). While Elah, king of the northern kingdom of Israel, "was at Tirzah drinking himself drunk in the house of Arza, who was over the household at Tirzah [1 Kings 16:9] ... Zimri went in and struck him and put him to death ...and became king in his place" (v. 10; cf. 20:16). Shockingly, some of the Corinthians actually got drunk at the Lord's Supper (1 Cor. 11:21). The Bible repeatedly warns against drunkenness (Rom. 13:13; 1 Cor. 5:11; 6:10; Gal. 5:21; Eph. 5:18; 1 Peter 4:3).

The **worries of life** are the issues, struggles, temptations, and cares of this fallen world. In the parable of the sower, Jesus pictured those consumed with them as "the ones on whom seed was sown among the thorns; these are the ones who have heard the word, but the worries of the world, and the deceitfulness of riches, and the desires for other things enter in and choke the word, and it becomes unfruitful" (Mark 4:18–19). In the Sermon on the Mount Jesus told those listening,

For this reason I say to you, do not be worried about your life, as to what you will eat or what you will drink; nor for your body, as to what you will put on. Is not life more than food, and the body more than clothing? Look at the birds of the air, that they do not sow, nor reap nor gather into barns, and yet your heavenly Father feeds them. Are you not worth much more than they? And who of you by being worried can add a single hour to his life? And why are you worried about clothing? Observe how the lilies of the field grow; they do not toil nor do they spin, yet I say to you that not even Solomon in all his glory clothed himself like one of these. But if God so clothes the grass of the field, which is alive today and tomorrow is thrown into the furnace, will He not much more clothe you? You of little faith! Do not worry then, saying, "What will we eat?" or "What will we drink?" or "What will we wear for clothing?" For the Gentiles eagerly seek all these things; for your heavenly Father knows that you need all these things. But seek first His kingdom and His righteousness, and all these things will be added to you. So do not worry about tomorrow; for tomorrow will care for itself. Each day has enough trouble of its own. (Matt. 6:25–34; cf. Phil. 4:19)

The truth that Christians are to live holy lives in light of Christ's imminent return is repeated several times in the New Testament. In Romans 13:11–14 Paul exhorted,

Do this, knowing the time, that it is already the hour for you to awaken from sleep; for now salvation [not our past justification or our present sanctification, but our future glorification when Christ returns] is nearer to us than when we believed. The night is almost gone, and the day is near. Therefore let us lay aside the deeds of darkness and put on the armor of light. Let us behave properly as in the day, not in carousing and drunkenness, not in sexual promiscuity and sensuality, not in strife and jealousy. But put on the Lord Jesus Christ, and make no provision for the flesh in regard to its lusts.

"Now, little children, abide in Him," John wrote, "so that when He appears, we may have confidence and not shrink away from Him in shame at His coming" (1 John 2:28). Later in that same epistle he added,

Beloved, now we are children of God, and it has not appeared as yet what we will be. We know that when He appears, we will be like Him, because we will see Him just as He is. And everyone who has this hope fixed on Him purifies himself, just as He is pure. (3:2–3)

Living in the hope of the rapture and second coming produces vigilance and separation from sin, and avoids the sin that leads to shame now and later the loss of eternal reward (2 John 8).

EVANGELISTIC OCCUPATION

**for it will come upon all those who dwell on the face of all the earth.** (21:35)

Anticipation of the glorious arrival of the Lord Jesus Christ not only stimulates believers to personal holiness, but also compels them to warn the lost. The Lord's return will produce universal judgment **upon all those who dwell on the face of all the earth.** Sentence and execution will fall on all who have rejected Jesus Christ and the true gospel. That fearful reality should terrify unbelievers and motivate Christians to carry out the great commission to "go therefore and make disciples of all the nations, baptizing them in the name of the Father and the Son and the Holy Spirit" (Matt. 28:19).

The fact that the ante-diluvian world ignored the preaching of Noah and were judged so cataclysmically and eternally and the unmistakable warnings of God that pledge that all who reject the gospel will fall to divine judgment (Luke 17:26–30; cf. Matt. 25:1–13) should move the church to compassion for the lost and perishing, just as Jesus wept over Jerusalem (Matt. 23:37; Luke 13:34) and God takes no pleasure in the death of the wicked (Ezek. 33:11).

But the church today, often abandoning the truth of judgment and hell, is losing its effectiveness in evangelism. Not because people do not talk about Jesus and salvation, but because there is a tendency within evangelicalism to affirm in the name of love and tolerance that anyone who professes even a vague belief in God or Jesus Christ is headed to heaven. Some professing evangelicals go further and claim that even those who do not believe in Jesus or the God of the Bible will go to heaven, if they do their best religiously or morally and sincerely worship God in their own way. Such notions eviscerate evangelism, because they no longer view those who accept only a superficial, truncated form of the gospel as doomed, damned, perishing sinners.

Also contributing to the church's loss of serious gospel evangelism is the belief among many churches that the only way to reach the lost is to give them what they want. Such churches view boldly confronting sin and judgment and proclaiming the gospel of repentance and faith as an archaic, ineffective method of winning the world. Instead, they seek to make people feel comfortable, and to cater to their whims and desires. The idea is to get sinners to embrace Jesus by making His message less offensive to them.

Such teaching relegates God and His Word to a subordinate role in the church and elevates entertainment over biblical preaching and worship. But the great commission is not a marketing manifesto. Evangelism does not require slick salesmen, but bold, fearless proclaimers of divine truth. (I critique this tendency of some churches in my book *Ashamed of the Gospel* [Wheaton, Ill.: Crossway, 1993.)

FAITHFUL CONTINUATION

**But keep on the alert at all times, praying that you may have strength to escape all these things that are about to take place, and to stand before the Son of Man." (21:36)**

Jesus concluded His message with an urgent exhortation to perseverance; commanding believers to **keep on the alert at all times, praying that** they **may have strength.** Throughout the New Testament saints are instructed to continue in the faith and warned not to turn back (e.g., Matt. 24:13; John 8:31; Col. 1:21–23; Heb. 3:6, 14; 10:39). Two promises are given to those who faithfully persevere.

First, they will **escape all these things that are about to take place**; that is, the future and eternal judgments associated with Christ's second coming in power and glory (1 Thess. 1:10; 5:9). The believers of the church age will be raptured before the tribulation begins and thus escape the future judgments (cf. Rev. 3:10); those alive during the tribulation will be protected from the outpouring of God's wrath on unbelievers.

Second, having escaped divine judgment, they will **stand before**

**the Son of Man,** receiving acceptance, approval, and welcome from Him. No one can do so in his own strength. Confronted by a vision of God "sitting on a throne, lofty and exalted" (Isa. 6:1), Isaiah cried out, "Woe is me, for I am ruined! Because I am a man of unclean lips, and I live among a people of unclean lips; for my eyes have seen the King, the Lord of hosts" (Isa. 6:5). Confronted by his inability to keep God's law, Paul cried out, "Wretched man that I am! Who will set me free from the body of this death?" (Rom. 7:24). Only through the imputed righteousness of Christ (2 Cor. 5:21), purchased at the cross (Col. 1:20), can anyone stand before Him pardoned, cleansed, and accepted (Jude 24–25), "protected by the power of God through faith for a salvation ready to be revealed in the last time" (1 Peter 1:5).

# Preparation for the Cross
(Luke 21:37–22:13)

# 24

Now during the day He was teaching in the temple, but at evening He would go out and spend the night on the mount that is called Olivet. And all the people would get up early in the morning to come to Him in the temple to listen to Him. Now the Feast of Unleavened Bread, which is called the Passover, was approaching. The chief priests and the scribes were seeking how they might put Him to death; for they were afraid of the people. And Satan entered into Judas who was called Iscariot, belonging to the number of the twelve. And he went away and discussed with the chief priests and officers how he might betray Him to them. They were glad and agreed to give him money. So he consented, and began seeking a good opportunity to betray Him to them apart from the crowd. Then came the first day of Unleavened Bread on which the Passover lamb had to be sacrificed. And Jesus sent Peter and John, saying, "Go and prepare the Passover for us, so that we may eat it." They said to Him, "Where do You want us to prepare it?" And He said to them, "When you have

**entered the city, a man will meet you carrying a pitcher of water; follow him into the house that he enters. And you shall say to the owner of the house, 'The Teacher says to you, "Where is the guest room in which I may eat the Passover with My disciples?"' And he will show you a large, furnished upper room; prepare it there." And they left and found everything just as He had told them; and they prepared the Passover.** (21:37–22:13)

This passage marks a major point in Luke's gospel, beginning its final and most significant section. That section, which covers the death and resurrection of Jesus Christ, is the climax to which all that preceded it has been headed.

Since the cross is the high point of redemptive history, everything that came before it looked forward to it; everything that comes after it looks back to it. The apostle Paul proclaimed the centrality of the cross when he wrote to the Corinthian believers, "We preach Christ crucified" (1 Cor. 1:23), and "I determined to know nothing among you except Jesus Christ, and Him crucified" (2:2). Apart from Christ's death and resurrection there would be no forgiveness of sin, no salvation, and no hope of heaven.

The glory of the cross is foreshadowed in the death of the first animal, slain by God to make coverings for Adam and Eve, the acceptable sacrifice Abel offered to God, the ark that delivered Noah and his family from the divine destruction of the world, the sacrifice of the ram that became a substitute for Isaac on Mount Moriah, and the Passover lambs in Egypt, whose blood was applied to the doorposts and the cross-piece so that the angel of death would pass by and not slaughter the firstborn. All the countless sacrifices offered in obedience to the Old Testament law pointed to the final sacrifice of the Lord Jesus Christ. The glory of the cross is also prefigured by the serpent lifted up in the wilderness, to which people could look and be delivered from death. The cross and the redemption provided there is also typified by Boaz, the kinsman redeemer.

From the outset, the Old Testament clearly revealed that the soul that sins will pay with death and that the only hope of escaping eternal death and punishment is the forgiveness of God. God is willing and by nature a forgiver (Ex. 34:6–7), but in turn requires an acceptable sacrifice to bear the punishment for the sinner's iniquities. It is clear throughout the Old Testament, however, that there was never an animal sacrifice sufficient to satisfy God's wrath and divine justice (Heb. 10:1–2, 11).

The people of Israel, daily offering symbolic sacrifices, hoped for a final, real sacrifice, which would atone for sin, satisfy divine justice, propitiate divine wrath, and end all sacrifices. Thus, it was a monumental moment in Israel's history when John the Baptist identified Jesus as "the Lamb of God who takes away the sin of the world!" (John 1:29; cf. v. 36). He was the true sacrifice, of which all the Old Testament sacrifices were but shadows, pictures, figures, and symbols.

The New Testament also points to the cross. The central truth of the Gospels is the cross. The book of Acts records the preaching of the cross, specifically that Messiah had to suffer, be crucified, and rise again. The epistles expound the rich theological meaning of the Messiah's death, and its application to believers' salvation, sanctification, and glorification. Before the unfolding visions of His triumphant return to judge the world and establish His earthly kingdom, Revelation presents Jesus as the Lamb who was slain (5:6, 12; cf. 13:8).

Although with this passage the focus of Luke's gospel shifts to the historical events of the cross and the resurrection, this is not the first time Luke records those realities. In 9:22 Jesus said, "The Son of Man must suffer many things and be rejected by the elders and chief priests and scribes, and be killed and be raised up on the third day," while in verse 44 He added, "Let these words sink into your ears; for the Son of Man is going to be delivered into the hands of men." Later,

> He took the twelve aside and said to them, "Behold, we are going up to Jerusalem, and all things which are written through the prophets about the Son of Man will be accomplished. For He will be handed over to the Gentiles, and will be mocked and mistreated and spit upon, and after they have scourged Him, they will kill Him; and the third day He will rise again." (18:31–33)

But as this passage opens, the long-awaited sacrifice is imminent. It was Wednesday evening of Passion Week, less than two days before the crucifixion of God's Lamb. The preparation for the cross, already underway, involved five individuals or groups: the deity, the devout, the devil, the defector, and the disciples.

## THE DEITY

**Now during the day He was teaching in the temple, but at evening He would go out and spend the night on the mount that is called Olivet. And all the people would get up early in the morning to come to Him in the temple to listen to Him. Now the Feast of Unleavened Bread, which is called the Passover, was approaching.** (21:37–22:1)

This portion is at once a concise summary of the last days of Jesus' public ministry and a transition into the features of His death and resurrection.

Although He is not named or identified in any other way, God was providentially and purposefully at work behind the scenes. His divine timetable had reached its climax, and the other parties involved, both human and satanic, were moved to act under His sovereign power. Just as Jesus' life had been controlled by the Father (John 4:34; 5:30; 6:38; 8:29; 14:31; 15:10; 17:4), so also would His death come on God's schedule. John's gospel repeatedly declares that Jesus would not die until His hour—the hour predetermined by God—arrived (John 7:30; 8:20; 12:23, 27; 13:1; 17:1).

After finishing the discourse on His second coming, Jesus moved back to the conclusion of His first coming. The theme of the second coming was not completely dropped, however; He would return to it again in 22:16, 18, 29, 30, and 24:25–26. But the primary emphasis from this point forward was His death.

On Monday, Tuesday, and Wednesday Jesus had, **during the day, been teaching in the temple . . . and all the people would get up early in the morning to come to Him in the temple to listen to Him.** He did not stay overnight in the city, however, **but at evening He would go out and spend the night on the mount that is called Olivet** (the Mount of Olives). To remain in Jerusalem was too dangerous, as was staying in Bethany at the home of His friends Mary, Martha, and Lazarus. The Jewish authorities might have seized Him if they had been able to find Jesus away from the crowds, then held Him until after the Passover until the crowds had dispersed, and had Him executed (cf. Luke 19:47–48; 22:2).

The **Feast of Unleavened Bread, which is called the Passover,** was one of the three major feasts in Israel, along with Pentecost (called the Feast of Weeks in the Old Testament) and the Feast of Booths (Deut. 16:16; 2 Chron. 8:13). It commemorated God's deliverance of Israel from Egypt, as described in the book of Exodus. The Feast of Unleavened Bread was celebrated from the fifteenth day to the twenty-first day of the Jewish month Nisan, which corresponds to April in the Western (Gregorian) calendar. The **Passover**, which commemorated the destroying angel's (Ex. 12:23) passing over the Israelites' houses because of the blood sprinkled on the doorposts and lintels (v. 22), was celebrated the day before the Feast of Unleavened Bread began. Over time, the two terms came to be used interchangeably.

On Thursday night, Jesus would eat the Passover meal with His disciples and, while eating, transform it into the new memorial—the Lord's Supper (cf. chapter 25 of this volume). Instead of commemorating the deliverance of Israel from bondage in Egypt, the Lord's Supper celebrates the infinitely greater deliverance from the bondage and guilt of sin through the Savior's death.

Despite the claims of unbelieving skeptics and critics, Christ's death was not an unplanned, unexpected, unfortunate event. He was not a misguided martyr, a well-intentioned spiritual visionary whose ideals were ahead of His time. Neither was He a delusionary madman who wrongly believed He was God, nor a failed political revolutionary. All such blasphemous notions are false, for several reasons.

First, Jesus predicted His death and resurrection. In Mark 8:31 "He began to teach [the disciples] that the Son of Man must suffer many things and be rejected by the elders and the chief priests and the scribes, and be killed, and after three days rise again." Later "He was teaching His disciples and telling them, 'The Son of Man is to be delivered into the hands of men, and they will kill Him; and when He has been killed, He will rise three days later'" (Mark 9:31). On the final journey to Jerusalem Jesus

> took the twelve aside and began to tell them what was going to happen to Him, saying, "Behold, we are going up to Jerusalem, and the Son of Man will be delivered to the chief priests and the scribes; and they will condemn Him to death and will hand Him over to the Gentiles. They will mock Him and spit on Him, and scourge Him and kill Him, and three days later He will rise again." (Mark 10:32–34)

After the resurrection, Jesus rebuked the two disciples on the road to Emmaus for being "foolish men and slow of heart to believe in all that the prophets have spoken! Was it not necessary," He chided them, "for the Christ to suffer these things and to enter into His glory?" (Luke 24:25–26). At the empty tomb the two angels asked the women,

> Why do you seek the living One among the dead? He is not here, but He has risen. Remember how He spoke to you while He was still in Galilee, saying that the Son of Man must be delivered into the hands of sinful men, and be crucified, and the third day rise again. (Luke 24:5–7)

Even the Jewish leaders, His bitter enemies, affirmed that Jesus had made those predictions. "Sir," they said to Pilate, "we remember that when He was still alive that deceiver said, 'After three days I am to rise again'" (Matt. 27:63).

Second, Jesus had absolute authority and power over His life. In John 10:17–18 He said, "I lay down My life so that I may take it again. No one has taken it away from Me, but I lay it down on My own initiative. I have authority to lay it down, and I have authority to take it up again." Overestimating his own importance Pilate said to Jesus, "Do You not know that I have authority to release You, and I have authority to crucify You?" (John 19:10). "You would have no authority over Me," Jesus replied, "unless it had been given you from above" (v. 11).

Third, the numerous attempts to kill Jesus before it was God's time for Him to die all failed. Shortly after He was born the paranoid sociopath Herod the Great tried to eliminate the child-king of the Jews of whom the magi had spoken, fearing He might be a rival to his throne. Uncertain of the newborn king's identity, Herod brutally ordered the slaughter of all the boys two and under in the vicinity of Bethlehem (Matt. 2:16). Though the slaughter was accomplished, Jesus had been taken safely to Egypt by Joseph and Mary (vv. 13–15). Outraged when in a sermon He offended their spiritual pride by describing them as spiritually poor, blind, captive, and oppressed (Luke 4:18), the very people of His hometown synagogue in Nazareth tried to kill Jesus by throwing Him off a cliff (vv. 28–29)."But passing through their midst, He went His way" (v. 30). Throughout Christ's ministry the Jewish religious leaders sought unsuccessfully to take His life (Matt. 26:3–4; Mark 3:6; Luke 19:47; John 7:1,25; 11:53),so much so that people began referring to Him as "the man whom they are seeking to kill" (John 7:25).

At the divinely decreed time, however, Jesus would die as it had been determined (Luke 22:22)—not by the will of men, but "by the predetermined plan and foreknowledge of God" (Acts 2:23). He was God's chosen sacrificial Lamb, who was led to the slaughter on God's schedule, and did not open His mouth in protest (Isa.53:7; cf.Acts 8:32–35).He was the "lamb unblemished and spotless ... foreknown before the foundation of the world" (1 Peter 1:19–20). He is "the Lamb that was slain," and worthy "to receive power and riches and wisdom and might and honor and glory and blessing" (Rev.5:12).

From the human viewpoint, the death of Christ was a horrific injustice. No human victim has ever been perfectly innocent and sinless as Christ was.Yet both men and God punished Him for sins He did not commit. On the Jews' part, He was falsely accused of blasphemy, but from God's perspective He was executed to truly bear the sins of His people— none of whom deserve it. He "died for sins once for all, the just for the unjust, so that He might bring us to God" (1 Peter 3:18), "for the demonstration ... of [God's] righteousness at the present time, so that He would be just and the justifier of the one who has faith in Jesus" (Rom. 3:26). God "made Him who knew no sin to be sin on our behalf, so that we might become the righteousness of God in Him" (2 Cor. 5:21).

This was a sacrifice infinitely greater than any other. Jesus was not killed because the plan went wrong, or the revolution failed. He did not die simply because of human hate or human injustice, nor because God acted unjustly or could not prevent it.What might appear to be an act of injustice or impotence on the part of God is in reality an act of divine power and justice motivated by pure love and grace. Christ's death was God's provision for the redemption of sinners, and no one who rejects that truth can be saved from judgment.

## The Devout

**The chief priests and the scribes were seeking how they might put Him to death; for they were afraid of the people.** (22:2)

The **chief priests, the scribes,** and the elders who collectively made up the religious leadership of Israel are frequently mentioned together (cf. Luke 9:22; 22:66; Matt. 27:41; Mark 14:43; 15:1). They were, in their own estimation, the most devoutly religious of all the Jewish people (cf. Matt. 23:1–7). The **chief priests** included the reigning high priest, Caiaphas, and the former high priest Annas, who still wielded significant influence behind the scenes. The **chief priests** also included the captain of the temple, who assisted the high priest, and other high-ranking priests. Most of them were Sadducees. The **scribes** (primarily Pharisees) were theologians who interpreted and taught the law of Moses and the rabbinic tradition. Members of the elders (family and tribal heads), the chief priests, and the scribes made up the Sanhedrin, the governing body (under the ultimate authority of the Romans) of Israel.

While they were united in their hatred of Jesus, these groups had different motives for opposing Him. Caiaphas, the chief priests, and the Sadducees opposed Him on political and economic grounds. Caiaphas expressed their political concerns in John 11:47–50:

> Therefore the chief priests and the Pharisees convened a council, and were saying, "What are we doing? For this man is performing many signs. If we let Him go on like this, all men will believe in Him, and the Romans will come and take away both our place and our nation." But one of them, Caiaphas, who was high priest that year, said to them, "You know nothing at all, nor do you take into account that it is expedient for you that one man die for the people, and that the whole nation not perish."

They feared that Jesus' popularity might provoke a response by the Romans that would cause them to lose their privileged and tenuous positions under Rome's tolerance, or even cause the forces of Caesar to destroy the entire nation. They also opposed Jesus for economic reasons. Caiaphas and his henchmen oversaw the merchandising on the temple grounds, and the Lord had twice attacked and disrupted their business interests (see the exposition of 19:45–48 in chapter 10 of this volume). The scribes and Pharisees, on the other hand, hated Jesus because of His relentless assault on their false, legalistic religious system, as well as His constant exposure of their hypocrisy.

Despite that hostility, the blame the Jews have borne over the centuries for Christ's death is unconscionable. Some who call themselves Christians have derided and persecuted them as "Christ-killers." But it was Jews in first-century Israel who wanted Jesus dead and blackmailed Pilate into executing Him. That provides no justifiable reason for unscrupulous people to persecute the entire Jewish race. To use what people in that generation did to Jesus as justification for hate crimes, pogroms, and holocausts against the Jewish people is anything but Christian. Such bigotry does not come from God, who loves and will one day redeem Israel (Jer. 31:31–34; Ezek. 36:25–27; Zech. 12:10–13:1; Rom. 11:26), and who pronounces a curse on those who curse Israel (Gen. 12:3). Nor does it characterize true Christians; it is anti-Christian and evil. It is true that the leaders and people of that era bore responsibility for Christ's death, and if they did not repent and confess Him as Lord, they were judged by God for their rejection of the Son. But the same can be said for the Romans, and for every other person, Jew or Gentile, who rejects Jesus Christ. And ultimately, as noted above, Christ's death was according to God's plan (Isa. 53:10; Acts 2:23).

By this time the Jewish leaders **were** desperately **seeking how they might put** Jesus **to death.** But they could not arrest Him during the day **for they were afraid of the people** (cf. Matt. 26:5). Nor could they find Him at night, when He withdrew to the secluded area of the Mount of Olives. They needed an insider to betray Him and tip them off as to where they could locate Him away from the crowds. They were surprised and pleased when, prompted by Satan, one volunteered—Judas Iscariot.

THE DEVIL

**And Satan entered into Judas** (22:3a)

Whatever restraint Judas may have felt due to his association with Jesus no longer held him back. **Satan entered into** him and put it into his heart to betray the Lord (John 13:2). Like the religious leaders (John 8:44), he too was a child of the devil.

The question arises as to why Satan would want Judas to betray Jesus to those who sought His death, knowing that His death would accomplish God's salvation plan. That Satan did not want Christ to die as a sacrifice for sin and thus "destroy the works of the devil" (1 John 3:8) by rescuing sinners from his domain (Col. 1:13) is clear from the Lord's rebuke of Peter for opposing His death (Matt. 16:22–23), and thus acting as a mouthpiece for Satan. In Gethsemane, Satan would again tempt Jesus to abandon God's plan for His death. On the other hand, he hated the Savior and surely wished Him dead. As the most corrupt of all beings, it is not surprising that Satan's rational powers are corrupt, causing him to think inconsistently.

Whatever may have motivated Satan, he acted as he did because he could not do anything other than what his wickedness longed for and, at the same time, what God willed (Luke 22:31; Job 1:12; 2:6). He willingly took the role in the death of Jesus that God had determined for him. This time was the "hour and the power of darkness" (Luke 22:53).

## THE DEFECTOR

**who was called Iscariot, belonging to the number of the twelve. And he went away and discussed with the chief priests and officers how he might betray Him to them. They were glad and agreed to give him money. So he consented, and began seeking a good opportunity to betray Him to them apart from the crowd.** (22:3b–6)

Judas, **who was called Iscariot,** is history's most notorious traitor. He had the incalculable privilege of **belonging to the number of the twelve,** the apostles of the Lord Jesus Christ. He lived and walked with the Son of God daily for more than three years, heard His preaching and teaching, and witnessed the miraculous signs He performed—a privilege shared by only eleven other men. Yet shockingly, after all that he experienced with the Lord Jesus, Judas sold Him to His enemies for a mere thirty pieces of silver (Zech. 11:12)—the price of a slave (Ex. 21:32).

Despite his significant role in Christ's death, the New Testament says little about Judas's background. His surname, **Iscariot,** suggests that he was from the village of Kerioth in the far southern region of Israel. That makes him the only one of the Twelve who was not from Galilee, making him and his family unfamiliar to the others. That fact may help explain why none of the other disciples had any reason to suspect that he was the betrayer (John 13:22). Jesus recognized Judas's evil heart from the beginning (John 6:64, 70). The Synoptic Gospels describe him as the one who betrayed Christ (e.g., Matt. 10:4; 26:25; 27:3; Mark 3:19; Luke 6:16); John notes that he was a thief (John 12:6), and Jesus called him a devil (John 6:70–71).

The Old Testament predicted Judas's betrayal of Christ. In Psalm 41:9 David wrote prophetically, "Even my close friend in whom I trusted, who ate my bread, has lifted up his heel against me." Psalm 55:12–14 also looks ahead to Messiah's betrayal:

> For it is not an enemy who reproaches me, then I could bear it; nor is it one who hates me who has exalted himself against me, then I could hide myself from him. But it is you, a man my equal, my companion and my familiar friend; we who had sweet fellowship together walked in the house of God in the throng.

Zechariah, as noted above, predicted the paltry amount Judas would receive for his betrayal. Zechariah also noted that the money would be used to buy the Potter's Field after Judas's unsuccessful attempt to return it to the Jewish authorities:

> I said to them, "If it is good in your sight, give me my wages; but if not, never mind!" So they weighed out thirty shekels of silver as my wages. Then the Lord said to me, "Throw it to the potter, that magnificent price at which I was valued by them." So I took the thirty shekels of silver and threw them to the potter in the house of the Lord. (Zech. 11:12–13; cf. Matt. 27:3–10)

The most chilling comment in Luke's brief introduction of Judas is that he belonged **to the number of the twelve**—a truth mentioned by all four of the gospel writers (cf. 22:47; Matt. 26:14, 47; Mark 14:10; 14:43; John 6:71). Judas's crime against privilege and opportunity is equaled only by Adam's sin. But while Adam was redeemed, Judas was not.

Once Satan entered into the betrayer, the plan was set into motion. Judas **went away,** most likely that Wednesday night, **and discussed with the chief priests and officers how he might betray** Jesus **to them. They,** of course, **were glad,** since this was the answer to their dilemma of how to seize Jesus privately, **and agreed to give** Judas the **money** he sought. Matthew notes that Judas asked them, "What are you willing to give me to betray Him to you?" He was seeking some compensation for what he now regarded as three wasted years spent following Jesus. But the best deal he could negotiate was not a good one; thirty pieces of silver, as noted above, was an insignificant sum. Nevertheless Judas **consented,** taking what he could get, **and began seeking a good opportunity to betray Him to them apart from the crowd.**

THE DISCIPLES

**Then came the first day of Unleavened Bread on which the Passover lamb had to be sacrificed. And Jesus sent Peter and John, saying, "Go and prepare the Passover for us, so that we may eat it." They said to Him, "Where do You want us to prepare it?" And He said to them, "When you have entered the city, a man will meet you carrying a pitcher of water; follow him into the house that he enters. And you shall say to the owner of the house, 'The Teacher says to you, "Where is the guest room in which I may eat the Passover with My disciples?"'" "And he will show you a large, furnished upper room; prepare it there." And they left and found everything just as He had told them; and they prepared the Passover.** (22:7–13)

In verse 7, the scene shifts from Wednesday evening to Thursday, **the first day of Unleavened Bread on which the Passover lamb**

**had to be sacrificed.** The hour of Jesus' death was near (Matt. 26:18). The Jewish leaders, Satan, and Judas were in action in preparation for the cross, in accordance with the purposes of God. Now it was time for the disciples to begin to act.

The design of God was that Jesus would die on Friday afternoon during the period between the two evenings (Ex. 12:6; "twilight" literally means "between the two evenings"). At that time (between approximately three in the afternoon and sunset) tens of thousands of lambs would be being sacrificed. Jesus would die then because He is, as Paul wrote in 1 Corinthians 5:7, our Passover; "the Lamb of God who takes away the sin of the world!" (John 1:29).

The Lord knew that Judas intended to betray Him (John 6:71), and that the Passover meal would be the perfect opportunity to do so. It would take place in the evening, at a time when few people would be outside in the streets, in a secluded location where He could be seized by the authorities without risking a riot. To thwart that plan, Jesus arranged for the Passover meal to be held in a secret location. **Peter and John** were sent on a clandestine mission to **prepare the Passover;** the Lord's instructions to them contained no names or locations, so that Judas could not know in advance where Jesus and the Twelve would eat the Passover meal (since Peter and John evidently did not return) and thus could not tip off the Jewish leaders. And once the supper began, he would have had no plausible reason to leave until it was over.

Peter and John, along with James, constituted the innermost circle of the Twelve, the ones closest to Jesus. Perhaps James did not accompany them because according to tradition, no more than two men were permitted to bring each sacrificial animal to the temple. After the two disciples **entered the city,** they would meet a man **carrying a pitcher of water.** Since carrying water was traditionally done by women, he would stand out. They were to **follow him into the house that he** entered and **say to the owner of the house, "The Teacher says to you, 'Where is the guest room in which I may eat the Passover with My disciples?'"** He would then **show** them **a large, furnished upper room** where they could **prepare** the Passover meal.

Preparing the Passover supper involved far more than taking the lamb to the temple to be slaughtered and then roasting it. Numerous other items had to be obtained, including unleavened bread, wine, bitter herbs, and the apples, dates, pomegranates, nuts, and sometimes sticks of cinnamon that made up the thick paste into which the unleavened bread was dipped.

The question arises as to how Jesus and the Twelve could have eaten the Passover supper on Thursday night when the Passover lambs were slain on Friday. I wrote the following concerning this issue in my commentary on the gospel of John:

> An apparent discrepancy exists at this point between John's chronology and that of the Synoptic Gospels. The latter clearly state that the Last Supper was a Passover meal (Matt. 26:17–19; Mark 14:12–16; Luke 22:7–15). John 18:28, however, records that the Jewish leaders "led Jesus from Caiaphas into the Praetorium, and it was early [Friday morning; the day of the Crucifixion]; and they themselves did not enter into the Praetorium so that they would not be defiled, but might eat the Passover." Further, according to John 19:14 Jesus' trial and Crucifixion took place on "the day of preparation for the Passover," not the day after the eating of the Passover meal. Thus the Lord was crucified at the same time that the Passover lambs were being killed (cf. 19:36; Ex. 12:46; Num. 9:12). The challenge, then, is to explain how Jesus and the disciples could have eaten the Passover meal on Thursday evening if the Jewish leaders had not yet eaten it on Friday morning.
>
> The answer lies in understanding that the Jews had two different methods of reckoning days. Ancient Jewish sources suggest that Jews from the northern part of Israel (including Galilee, where Jesus and most of the Twelve were from) counted days from sunrise to sunrise. Most of the Pharisees apparently also used that method. On the other hand, the Jews in the southern region of Israel counted days from sunset to sunset. That would include the Sadducees (who of necessity lived in the vicinity of Jerusalem because of their connection with the temple). Though no doubt confusing at times, that dual method of reckoning days would have had practical benefits at Passover, allowing the feast to be celebrated on two consecutive days. That would have eased the crowded conditions in Jerusalem, especially in the temple, where all the lambs would not have had to be killed on the same day.
>
> Thus, there is no contradiction between John and the synoptics. Being Galileans, Jesus and the Twelve would have viewed Passover day as running from sunrise on Thursday to sunrise on Friday. They would have eaten their Passover meal on Thursday evening. The Jewish leaders (the Sadducees), however, would have viewed it as beginning at sunset on Thursday and ending at sunset on Friday. They would have

eaten their Passover meal on Friday evening. (For a further discussion of this issue, see Harold W. Hoehner, *Chronological Aspects of the Life of Christ* [Grand Rapids: Zondervan, 1977], 74–90; Robert L. Thomas and Stanley N. Gundry, *A Harmony of the Gospels* [Chicago: Moody, 1979], 321–22). (*John 12–21*, The MacArthur New Testament Commentary [Chicago: Moody, 2008], 62–63)

Many people were involved in the death of the Lord Jesus Christ: the seemingly devout, but hypocritical, Jewish religious leaders, who rejected their Messiah and manipulated the Romans into executing Him; the fickle crowds, that enthusiastically welcomed Him as the Messiah at the triumphal entry, then turned on Him and screamed for His blood; Judas, who after being discipled by Jesus for three years became a traitor and betrayed Him; Satan, the malevolent, supremely sinister being who prompted Judas's defection and betrayal; Pilate, the cowardly governor who disgraced the proud tradition of Roman justice by sentencing a man he had repeatedly declared innocent to death.

But ultimately, Jesus went to the cross because it was the "predetermined plan ... of God ... to do whatever [His] hand and [His] purpose predestined to occur" (Acts 2:23; 4:28; cf. Luke 22:22, 37; 24:44–46). The "things which God announced beforehand by the mouth of all the prophets, that His Christ would suffer, He ... fulfilled" (Acts 3:18; cf. 13:27; Matt. 26:24).

# The Final Passover, The First Communion (Luke 22:14–20)

**25**

When the hour had come, He reclined at the table, and the apostles with Him. And He said to them, "I have earnestly desired to eat this Passover with you before I suffer; for I say to you, I shall never again eat it until it is fulfilled in the kingdom of God." And when He had taken a cup and given thanks, He said, "Take this and share it among yourselves; for I say to you, I will not drink of the fruit of the vine from now on until the kingdom of God comes." And when He had taken some bread and given thanks, He broke it and gave it to them, saying, "This is My body which is given for you; do this in remembrance of Me." And in the same way He took the cup after they had eaten, saying, "This cup which is poured out for you is the new covenant in My blood." (22:14–20)

Among the many unforgettable statements the Lord Jesus Christ made was His declaration,

> For this reason the Father loves Me, because I lay down My life so that I may take it again. No one has taken it away from Me, but I lay it down on My own initiative. I have authority to lay it down, and I have authority to take it up again. (John 10:17–18)

No one took Jesus' life. He gave it up. He was not a victim, but willingly offered His life in complete agreement with and submission to God the Father. He died according to the divine plan, orchestrating every act of both enemies and friends to accomplish God's purpose. He died as the true Passover lamb, whose sacrifice paid the full penalty for the sins of all who would ever believe.

There are many compelling figures surrounding the death of Jesus Christ, including the current high priest Caiaphas; the powerful and influential former high priest Annas; the Jewish leaders—the Sadducees, Pharisees, Herodians, and the Sanhedrin—who plotted and carried out the death of the Messiah; the puppet king Herod Antipas, not a Jew but an Idumean; the wretched Judas Iscariot, who betrayed Christ; the woeful puppet Pilate, who ordered Jesus' execution despite having declared Him innocent; and the cowardly disciples, who at His arrest deserted Him.

Those characters will act freely and yet carry out their divinely assigned roles as the drama of the cross unfolds. The central figure is, of course, the Lord Jesus Christ, who eclipses all the others just as the blazing noon-day sun eclipses the stars. He appears as humiliated and yet majestic; suffering and yet exalted; punished and yet innocent; hated and yet loving; subjected and yet sovereign. Far from being a victim, Jesus moved through the events surrounding His death controlled by the Father's will, kept by the Spirit's power, and acting on the heavenly timetable, which was established before the world began.

The setting for this section of Luke's gospel was Thursday night of Passion Week, the beginning of the eight-day-long celebration of Passover and the Feast of Unleavened Bread. It was also the night before Christ's crucifixion, and His final gathering with the apostles before His death, since He would be arrested later that evening after the Passover meal. This section of Luke's gospel marks the major turning point of redemptive history. Jesus brought the Old Covenant to an end and inaugurated the New Covenant. Thus, He and the disciples celebrated the last legitimate Passover, and the first Lord's Supper. Jesus culminated the celebration looking back to God's miraculous historical deliverance of Israel from Egypt and inaugurated a new memorial, looking to the cross and the eternal deliverance accomplished for His people there.

### THE FINAL PASSOVER

**When the hour had come, He reclined at the table, and the apostles with Him. And He said to them, "I have earnestly desired to eat this Passover with you before I suffer; for I say to you, I shall never again eat it until it is fulfilled in the kingdom of God." And when He had taken a cup and given thanks, He said, "Take this and share it among yourselves; for I say to you, I will not drink of the fruit of the vine from now on until the kingdom of God comes."** (22:14–18)

The message of Passover is that God delivers through the judgment of sin by the death of an innocent substitute. All the Old Testament sacrifices were symbols of that reality. But those animal sacrifices were not, in themselves, sufficient substitutes, or such offerings would have ceased (Heb. 10:1–2). No person has ever been delivered from divine judgment by the death of an animal (Heb. 10:4). Through the centuries, the people of Israel waited for the sacrifice that would be satisfactory to God, the one to which all the countless animal sacrifices had pointed.

That long-awaited sacrifice would be offered the next day, Friday, while countless thousands of lambs were again being sacrificed on the Passover. At that very time, God offered His sacrifice. He poured out His wrath against sinners on an innocent substitute—the "Lamb of God who takes away the sin of the world" (John 1:29). Jesus was the perfect, final, and complete sacrifice for sin, making this the last Passover approved by God. Symbolic animal sacrifices pointing to the true sacrifice were no longer necessary once the Savior had been offered.

Luke's treatment of Passover and the Lord's Supper is brief, since the Old Testament contains a lot of information about Passover, and Paul had already described the Lord's Supper in detail at least five years before Luke's gospel when he wrote 1 Corinthians (see chapters 10 and 11). The precise sequence of the many features (e.g., the Passover meal, the institution of the Lord's Supper, Christ's washing of the disciples' feet, upper room discourse [John 13–16], high priestly prayer [John 17], prediction of Peter's denials, and dismissal of Judas) that took place in the upper room that evening is not known. The **hour** they commenced, however, was sunset, the time when Passover always officially began. As was customary, Jesus **reclined at the table, and the apostles with Him,** lying on cushions with their heads near the table and their feet away from it. That Jesus and the Twelve reclined in such a manner indicates that this was a prolonged meal. The custom had changed since the original Passover celebration, a hurried affair before Israel fled from Egypt.

There were several stages in the Passover celebration, spread out over a period of hours and interspersed with conversation. The event opened with a prayer thanking God for His preservation, deliverance, protection, goodness, and blessing. Next came the first of four cups of diluted red wine, known as the cup of blessing. That was followed by a ceremonial washing of the hands, symbolizing the need for cleansing from sin. It was most likely at this point that the disciples began arguing among themselves about who was the greatest (Luke 22:24). In response, Jesus washed their feet (John 13:3–5) and instructed them concerning humility. The next element was the eating of bitter herbs, dipped along with pieces of bread into a paste made from fruit and nuts. That act symbolized the bitterness of Israel's slavery in Egypt. Then the participants sang Psalms 113 and 114, the first two of the Hallel Psalms (113–118), after which they drank the second cup of wine. After that the father of the family, or as in this case Jesus as the head of the table, explained the meaning of Passover. Then came the main meal, consisting of the roasted sacrificial lamb and unleavened bread, after which they drank the third cup of wine. The ceremony closed with the singing of the remainder of the Hallel Psalms (115–118), and the drinking of the fourth cup of wine.

Christ's words to the disciples in verse 15, **"I have earnestly desired to eat this Passover with you before I suffer,"** likely were spoken just after the men had reclined at the table. They are intensive and forceful; the Greek text could be translated, "With desire I have desired." These words indicate that this final Passover would be the fulfillment of a most powerful, emotional longing in the heart of the Lord. In a few hours He would go from eating again a sacrificial lamb to dying as the one true Lamb of God to validate the New Covenant. His whole life He had anticipated this hour, surely with increasing emotion.

The Lord's next statement, **"For I say to you, I shall never again eat it until it is fulfilled in the kingdom of God,"** reveals that although this was the final Passover of His life, there will be another time when He celebrates the Passover with His own. That will take place **in the kingdom of God** (cf. vv. 18, 28–30; 1 Cor. 11:26). According to Ezekiel's description of the future millennial temple, Passover will be celebrated in the millennial kingdom (Ezek.45:21)—not remembering the exodus, but the cross. Until then, there are no divinely authorized Passovers. The regular celebration of Passover by the Jews is an expression of their rejection of their Messiah.

Jesus' promise was wonderful news to the apostles. He had taught them the previous evening on the Mount of Olives what would happen in the future (Luke 21:7–36). Now in this reference to His kingdom He reassured them that His death was not the end of the story. He will rise and return to establish His promised kingdom in which His true followers will join with Him.

Jesus' taking **a cup and** giving **thanks** (*eucharisteō,* from which the English word "eucharist" derives) marked the beginning of the Passover celebration. This **cup,** which He then commanded the disciples to **take . . . and share . . . among** themselves, was the first cup, called the cup of blessing. The apostle Paul referred to it in his instructions to the Corinthian church regarding communion (1 Cor. 10:16). The head of the table extolled God for His goodness, mercy, and provision through the years. Traditionally, he would also extol the glory and righteousness of Israel. But Jesus in all likelihood did not do that, since apostate Israel's apostasy had reached its apex in eagerness to crucify the Messiah.

His words in verse 18, **"For I say to you, I will not** (*ou mē;* the strongest form of negation in Greek) **drink of the fruit of the vine from now on until the kingdom of God comes,"** emphasize once again that this was the final Passover until it is reinstated in the millennial kingdom. These were words of comfort and hope for the disciples.

The **fruit of the vine** is a symbol of fruitfulness, blessing, and joy, reflecting God's goodness to His people in delivering them from bondage. There will be a future salvation for the believing remnant of Israel (Rom. 11:1–32), when they and all believers will celebrate the Passover with Christ and extol the goodness of God. The cup of blessing here looks past the judgment that would fall on Jerusalem in the holocaust of A.D. 70, in which the Romans would utterly destroy both the city and the temple and scatter the people, to Israel's ultimate salvation and blessing.

THE FIRST COMMUNION

**And when He had taken some bread and given thanks, He broke it and gave it to them, saying, "This is My body which is given for you; do this in remembrance of Me." And in the same way He took the cup after they had eaten, saying, "This cup which is poured out for you is the new covenant in My blood.** (22:19–20)

It is impossible to overstate the monumental change these few simple phrases introduce. Christ's words signaled the end of the Old Covenant, with its social, ceremonial, dietary, and Sabbath laws, and installed the New Covenant. With these words, Jesus marked the end of all the rituals and sacrifices, the priesthood, the holy place, and the Holy of Holies, the curtain of which God would soon split from top to bottom, throwing it wide open (Mark 15:38). All that the Old Covenant symbolism pointed toward would be fulfilled in the sacrifice of the Lord Jesus Christ.

Jesus' taking of the **bread** and giving **thanks** took place after the singing of the first part of the Hallel (Pss. 113, 114), followed by the second cup of wine, and the explanation of the meaning of Passover, while they were eating the main meal (Matt. 26:26).

Having taken the **bread,** Jesus then **broke it and gave it to them.** The bread was no longer the Passover "bread of affliction" (Deut. 16:3), nor was the breaking of the loaf a figure of Christ's death, since none of His bones were broken (John 19:36; cf. Ex. 12:46). The disciples' all partaking of the same loaf symbolized the unity of the body of Christ.

The Roman Catholic doctrine of transubstantiation perverts the intent of Jesus' reference to the bread as **My body.** According to that doctrine, during the mass the substance (though not the outward appearance) of the bread and wine are changed into the actual body and blood of Christ. The Lutheran notion of spiritual presence (known as consubstantiation) is also an errant view of our Lord's words. According to that view

> the molecules [of the bread and wine] are not changed into flesh and blood; they remain bread and wine. But the body and blood of Christ are present "in, with, and under" the bread and wine. It is not that the bread and wine have become Christ's body and blood, but that we now have the body and blood in addition to the bread and wine. (Millard J. Erickson, *Christian Theology* [Grand Rapids: Baker, 1985], 3:1117)

Christ's statement is no more to be taken literally than are His references to Himself as a door (John 10:9), vine (John 15:1, 5), and bread (John 6:35, 48). Such language is figurative, symbolically conveying spiritual truth using everyday items. Bread pictures things that are earthly, fragile, and subject to decay, symbolizing the reality that the Son of God took on human form and became subject to death.

The phrase **which is given for you** introduces the most important truth in the Bible—substitutionary atonement. As noted above, Passover conveyed the twin truths that divine wrath and justice can only be satisfied by death, but that death can be the death of innocent substitutes for the guilty. The millions of lambs that were slain throughout the centuries were all innocent. Animals are incapable of sinning, since they are not persons, and have no morality or self-consciousness. Jesus, however, is both innocent and a person—fully man as well as God. Therefore His substitutionary atonement death was acceptable to God to satisfy His holy condemnation of sin. Isaiah wrote, "He was pierced through for our transgressions, He was crushed for our iniquities; the chastening for our well-being fell upon Him, and by His scourging we are healed" (Isa. 53:5; cf. v. 12). Jesus "bore our sins in His body on the cross, so that we might die to sin and live to righteousness; for by His wounds [we] were healed" (1 Peter 2:24). God "made Him who knew no sin to be sin on our behalf, so that we might become the righteousness of God in Him" (2 Cor. 5:21).

Then **in the same way** (that is, with thanks; cf. v. 19) Jesus **took the cup after they had eaten, saying, "This cup which is poured out for you is the new covenant in My blood."** The **cup** was the third cup, which came after the meal. That it was **poured out for you** "for forgiveness of sins" (Matt. 26:28) is another declaration of Christ's death as a substitute for all who would believe. Sin can only be forgiven when satisfactory payment to God in the form of the death of the perfect sacrifice has been rendered. The Lord Jesus' death was that payment. As the infinite God incarnate, He was actually able to bear the sins of and suffer God's wrath for those sins on behalf of all who would ever believe, rescuing them from divine judgment by fully satisfying the demands of God's justice.

His death inaugurated the **new covenant** which, like the Old Covenant, was ratified by the shedding of blood (Ex. 24:8; Lev. 17:11; Heb. 9:18–20). The New Covenant (Jer. 31:31–34; cf. Ezek. 36:25–27) is a covenant of forgiveness (Jer. 31:34) and the only saving covenant. As noted above, it was ratified by the blood of Christ, whose death as an innocent substitute satisfied the demands of God's justice. (For a detailed discussion of the New Covenant, see *2 Corinthians*, The MacArthur New Testament Commentary [Chicago: Moody, 2003], chaps. 7 and 8.)

Regular observance of the Lord's Supper is to be a constant reminder to Christians of the Lamb of God, chosen by God, sacrificed for sinners, whose death satisfied the demands of God's justice, and whose life was poured out on our behalf so that our sins can be fully and forever forgiven. Paul summarized the significance of the Lord's Supper when he wrote to the Corinthian believers,

> For I received from the Lord that which I also delivered to you, that the Lord Jesus in the night in which He was betrayed took bread; and when He had given thanks, He broke it and said, "This is My body, which is for you; do this in remembrance of Me." In the same way He took the cup also after supper, saying, "This cup is the new covenant in My blood; do this, as often as you drink it, in remembrance of Me." For as often as you eat this bread and drink the cup, you proclaim the Lord's death until He comes. (1 Cor. 11:23–26)

# Table Talk on Trouble and Triumph (Luke 22:21–38)

# 26

"But behold, the hand of the one betraying Me is with Mine on the table. For indeed, the Son of Man is going as it has been determined; but woe to that man by whom He is betrayed!" And they began to discuss among themselves which one of them it might be who was going to do this thing. And there arose also a dispute among them as to which one of them was regarded to be greatest. And He said to them, "The kings of the Gentiles lord it over them; and those who have authority over them are called 'Benefactors.' But it is not this way with you, but the one who is the greatest among you must become like the youngest, and the leader like the servant. For who is greater, the one who reclines at the table or the one who serves? Is it not the one who reclines at the table? But I am among you as the one who serves. You are those who have stood by Me in My trials; and just as My Father has granted Me a kingdom, I grant you that you may eat and drink at My table in My kingdom, and you will sit on thrones judging the twelve tribes of Israel. Simon, Simon, behold, Satan has demanded permission to sift you like wheat; but I have prayed for you, that your faith may not fail; and you, when once you have turned again, strengthen your brothers." But he said to Him, "Lord, with You I am ready to go both to prison and to death!" And He said, "I say to you, Peter, the rooster will not crow today until you have denied three times that you know Me." And He said to them, "When I sent you out without money belt and bag and sandals, you did not lack anything, did you?" They said, "No, nothing." And He said to them, "But now, whoever has a money belt is to take it along, likewise also a bag, and whoever has no sword is to sell his coat and buy one. For I tell you that this which is written must be fulfilled in Me, 'And He was numbered with transgressors'; for that which refers to Me has its fulfillment." They said, "Lord, look, here are two swords." And He said to them, "It is enough." (22:21–38)

Ever since Adam and Eve sinned in the garden, trouble has defined this fallen world. After the fall God declared to Adam,

> Cursed is the ground because of you; in toil you will eat of it all the days of your life. Both thorns and thistles it shall grow for you; and you will eat the plants of the field; by the sweat of your face you will eat bread, till you return to the ground, because from it you were taken; for you are dust, and to dust you shall return. (Gen. 3:17–19)

Job 5:7 notes that "man is born for trouble, as sparks fly upward," while Job 14:1 adds, "Man, who is born of woman, is short-lived and full of turmoil" (cf. 3:1–16). After Solomon's "wives turned his heart away after other gods; and his heart was not wholly devoted to the Lord his God" (1 Kings 11:4), he came to view life as troublesome and futile:

> So I hated life, for the work which had been done under the sun was grievous to me; because everything is futility and striving after wind.... For what does a man get in all his labor and in his striving with which he labors under the sun? Because all his days his task is painful and grievous; even at night his mind does not rest. This too is vanity. (Eccl. 2:17, 22–23)

The history of redemption is the story of God triumphing over trouble, overcoming sin and evil to achieve His glorious salvation purposes. He does not require a perfect world to accomplish His perfect ends, but will bring them to pass in an imperfect one, despite the strength of His enemies, and the weakness of His friends.

The Bible establishes that God is the ultimate sovereign and able to accomplish all His plans both in spite of and through fallen beings—both saints and sinners. In Deuteronomy 32:39 He declared, "See now that I, I am He, and there is no god besides Me; it is I who put to death and give life. I have wounded and it is I who heal, and there is no one who can deliver from My hand." In Isaiah 46:9–10 He said, "I am God, and there is no other; I am God, and there is no one like Me, declaring the end from the beginning, and from ancient times things which have not been done, saying, 'My purpose will be established, and I will accomplish all My good pleasure.'" Hannah praised God because He

> kills and makes alive; He brings down to Sheol and raises up. The Lord makes poor and rich; He brings low, He also exalts. He raises the poor from the dust, He lifts the needy from the ash heap to make them sit with nobles, and inherit a seat of honor; for the pillars of the earth are the Lord's, and He set the world on them. (1 Sam. 2:6–8)

David also extolled God's absolute sovereignty:

> Yours, O Lord, is the greatness and the power and the glory and the victory and the majesty, indeed everything that is in the heavens and the earth; Yours is the dominion, O Lord, and You exalt Yourself as head over all. Both riches and honor come from You, and You rule over all, and in Your hand is power and might; and it lies in Your hand to make great and to strengthen everyone. (1 Chron. 29:11–12)

In Psalm 115:3 the psalmist wrote, "But our God is in the heavens; He does whatever He pleases." "The Lord has made everything for its own purpose," Solomon noted, "even the wicked for the day of evil" (Prov. 16:4). "Who is there who speaks and it comes to pass," asked Jeremiah rhetorically, "unless the Lord has commanded it? Is it not from the mouth of the Most High that both good and ill go forth?" (Lam. 3:37–38; cf. Job 2:10; Isa. 45:5–7; Amos 3:6).

God allows evil that opposes His purposes so that He may in triumphing over it display His glory. By permitting evil, God is able to display

His righteousness in contrast to sin. Allowing evil also demonstrates His amazing love toward wicked and utterly unworthy sinners. God's love for His enemies reached its apex when Christ laid down His life for their eternal salvation from hell (Rom. 5:6–8). Even the most evil act in history, the murder of the Lord Jesus Christ, was ordained by God (Isa. 53:10; Acts 2:23; 4:27–28), to fulfill His gracious plan for the everlasting blessing of His chosen enemies.

As the Son of God approached the triumph of the cross and resurrection, He was engulfed in severe tribulation from all sides. The assaults came from Judas, the apostles, Satan, Peter, and the unbelieving world.

TROUBLE AND TRIUMPH WITH THE BETRAYER

**"But behold, the hand of the one betraying Me is with Mine on the table. For indeed, the Son of Man is going as it has been determined; but woe to that man by whom He is betrayed!" And they began to discuss among themselves which one of them it might be who was going to do this thing.** (22:21–23)

The setting was still the upper room on Thursday evening of Passion Week. Jesus had just finished celebrating the final Passover meal and inaugurated the first Lord's Supper with the apostles when He stunned them by saying, **"Behold, the hand of the one betraying Me is with Mine on the table."** The strong exclamation **behold** introduces something surprising and shocking. The disciples, of course, knew that the Jewish leaders hated Jesus and wanted Him dead; they had observed that firsthand over the years of His ministry. They also knew that during Passion Week He had avoided being prematurely seized by those leaders by mingling with the crowds during the day and withdrawing to the Mount of Olives at night. The disciples were aware of the steps that had been taken to keep the location of this Passover celebration secret. All but Judas Iscariot expected Jesus to be out of danger in that place of security, surrounded only by His innermost circle of apostles.

However, as the present tense of the Greek participle translated

**betraying** reveals, the danger was imminent and already in progress. Satan had previously entered Judas (Luke 22:3) and put it into his heart to betray the Lord (John 13:2), so that he had already cut a deal with the Jewish leaders (Luke 22:4–5). He was ready for the moment of opportunity he had been seeking (Luke 22:6) to actually hand Jesus over to them, but he was trapped in that room, feeling unable to leave without giving himself away.

Judas's treachery did not escape the omniscient Lord, who knew from the beginning who the traitor was (John 6:70–71). That **the hand of the one betraying** Jesus was **with** His **on the table** made Judas's crime all the more heinous and despicable. Eating with someone symbolized security, peace, friendship, and loyalty. For a person to betray someone with whom he had eaten a meal (let alone many meals) was unthinkable. Yet, that was exactly what Psalm 41:9 predicted would happen when Judas betrayed Jesus: "Even my close friend in whom I trusted, who ate my bread, has lifted up his heel against me."

Unbelieving critics who see Judas as the anti-hero who brought Jesus down, ending His noble effort at Jewish renewal, ignore this prophecy. They view the resurrection as a fiction produced by the apostles' imagination. Thus, for them His death was the end of everything. Jesus, they argue, never expected or planned for the terminal trouble Judas caused Him.

But they could not be more wrong. **Indeed, the Son of Man** (a messianic title taken from Dan. 7:13 that Jesus frequently applied to Himself) would go to His death **as it** had **been determined**—but not by Judas, the Jewish leaders, the Romans, Herod, or Pilate. Jesus would die "by the predetermined plan and foreknowledge of God" (Acts 2:23; cf. 4:24–28). Judas, acting like an atheist, foolishly imagined that he was operating freely, according to his own will for his own benefit. But no one acts independent of the sovereign plan and purpose of God, who overrules every human act or decision for His own ends and glory.

Jesus' death should have come as no surprise, since it was also predicted in the Old Testament. He is the suffering servant whose biography and death are the subject of Isaiah 53; the crucified one spoken of in Psalm 22; the pierced one foretold in Zechariah 12:10; and the true Passover lamb pictured by all the lambs sacrificed in the Old Testament sacrificial system. Jesus did not go to the cross because of Judas or the machinations of human agents, but so that the Word of God would be fulfilled (Matt. 26:54; Luke 24:44).

But although Judas acted in consistency with God's sovereign will, he was nevertheless fully responsible for his actions. Jesus said of him, **"woe** (damned, cursed, consigned to hell) **to that man by whom He is betrayed!"** Judas chose to do what he did and is fully culpable for that choice. This is another example of the interface between divine sovereignty and human responsibility. It is only an apparent paradox, not an actual one, which faith accepts while reason rejects. Human reason is finite and cannot fully comprehend the infinite mind of God (Rom. 11:33). But faith humbly accepts what God's Word reveals, even if the human mind lacks the capacity to understand it.

Judas had been present during the Passover meal, celebrating God's redemption of Israel from slavery in Egypt. He had also heard Jesus declare that from now on His body and blood given on the cross will be the new symbol of redemption. But his hypocrisy was so deep-seated, his heart so hardened, that he was unmoved by those realities or anything else that was said that evening. When Jesus announced that one of those present would betray Him, all the disciples "began to say to Him, 'Surely not I, Lord?' (Matt. 26:22). Instead of keeping quiet and not drawing attention to himself, the emboldened hypocrite "Judas, who was betraying Him, said, 'Surely it is not I, Rabbi?'" along with the rest (v. 26). He continued his hard-hearted hypocrisy to the end, when "Jesus [privately] said to him, 'You have said it yourself,'" and then eventually dismissed him (cf. John 13:27–30).

Unlike Judas, however, the rest of the disciples were deeply troubled at the thought of betrayal. They understood their weakness and realized the possibility that their own doubting, vacillating hearts could be capable of such treachery. So convincing was Judas's hypocrisy that the disciples suspected themselves rather than him. With that barest self-doubt, **they began to discuss among themselves which one of them it might be who was going to do this thing.** Not coming to any conclusion, Peter signaled to John to ask Jesus who the betrayer was (John 13:24), to which the Lord replied, "That is the one for whom I shall dip the morsel and give it to him" (v. 26). Evidently only John heard Jesus' reply, because even "when He had dipped the morsel, [and given] it to Judas, the son of Simon Iscariot" (v. 26) and then dismissed him (v. 27), the rest of the disciples still did not realize that Judas was the betrayer (vv. 28–29).

TROUBLE AND TRIUMPH WITH THE APOSTLES

**And there arose also a dispute among them as to which one of them was regarded to be greatest. And He said to them, "The kings of the Gentiles lord it over them; and those who have authority over them are called 'Benefactors.' But it is not this way with you, but the one who is the greatest among you must become like the youngest, and the leader like the servant. For who is greater, the one who reclines at the table or the one who serves? Is it not the one who reclines at the table? But I am among you as the one who serves. You are those who have stood by Me in My trials; and just as My Father has granted Me a kingdom, I grant you that you may eat and drink at My table in My kingdom, and you will sit on thrones judging the twelve tribes of Israel.** (22:24–30)

Jesus was genuinely and profoundly agitated with grief over Judas's betrayal. As I wrote in an earlier volume in this series,

> Several things troubled the Lord; His unrequited love for Judas, Judas's ingratitude for all the kindness He had shown him, the malevolent presence of Satan, who would shortly possess Judas (v. 27), the fearful fate that awaited Judas in hell, and the knowledge that the betrayal would lead Him to the cross, with its sin-bearing (2 Cor. 5:21) and separation from the Father (Matt. 27:46). "In the present passage, Jesus' emotions are shown to be in a state of turmoil, his whole inner self convulsing at the thought of one of his closest followers betraying him to his enemies" (Andreas J. Köstenberger, *John*, Baker Exegetical Commentary on the New Testament [Grand Rapids: Baker, 2004], 413). Such would be the terrible consequences of the betrayal Jesus now openly declared. (*John 12–21*, The MacArthur New Testament Commentary [Chicago: Moody, 2008], 78)

The disciples, however, were oblivious to the Lord's grief, and focused instead on the matter of who was the betrayer. But that discussion soon degenerated into the familiar long-running, selfish **dispute among them as to which one of them was regarded to be greatest** (cf. 9:46–48; Matt. 18:1–5; Mark 10:35–45). Instead of showing sympathy to the Lord, the disciples again manifested pride, and ambition. Considering that this was the night before the cross, this may have been their most humiliating and disappointing moment.

The disciples' eschatology was correct; there would be an earthly messianic kingdom in which they would hold places of honor (Matt. 19:28). But they still failed to understand that before the establishing of that kingdom in the distant future (cf. the exposition of Luke 21:5–36 in chapters 17–23 of this volume), there would be suffering, beginning with their Messiah's own death on the cross.

Instead of a stern rebuke, however, Jesus' response to His disciples was gracious, kind, and gentle. He loved them to the infinite capacity of divine love (John 13:1), even though they were often so troubling to Him. The introductory phrase, **And He said to them,** appears seven times in Luke's account of the upper room, stressing the Lord's emphasis on teaching (cf. John 13–17). His instruction to the disciples contains three elements.

First, He pointed them to a familiar principle. The world operates on the basis of autocratic power, dominance, and dictatorship; **the kings of the Gentiles lord it over them; and those who have authority over them are called "Benefactors"** (i.e., people of influence. The Greek word was often used as a title of honor for prominent public leaders).

But that is not the way the kingdom operates. Instead, **the one who is the greatest . . . must become like the youngest, and the leader like the servant.** Leaders in the kingdom are not to dominate others by force, intimidation, or fear, nor boast because of their position or influence. Those who are truly great in the kingdom will be humble. They will be like the **youngest,** who were the least honored people in Jewish society, since honor was associated with age. Opposite from acting like a worldly dictator, a **leader** in God's kingdom will be a **servant** (cf. Matt. 20:26–27).

To further illustrate that truth, Jesus posed a question, **"For who is greater, the one who reclines at the table or the one who serves?"** and then a second one giving the obvious answer: **"Is it not the one who reclines at the table?"** The **one who reclines at the table** is either a guest or the host; the **one who serves** is the slave who waited on him. Unquestionably, the one eating at the table is greater than the one serving. Leaders in God's kingdom are to have the attitude of a slave and seek to serve, not to be served.

Jesus then offered Himself as the pattern for that servanthood, reminding the disciples, **"I am among you as the one who serves"** (cf. Matt. 20:28). The Lord was referring specifically to His washing of their feet earlier that evening:

> Jesus, knowing that the Father had given all things into His hands, and that He had come forth from God and was going back to God, got up from supper, and laid aside His garments; and taking a towel, He girded Himself. Then He poured water into the basin, and began to wash the disciples' feet and to wipe them with the towel with which He was girded. So He came to Simon Peter. He said to Him, "Lord, do You wash my feet?" Jesus answered and said to him, "What I do you do not realize now, but you will understand hereafter." Peter said to Him, "Never shall You wash my feet!" Jesus answered him, "If I do not wash you, you have no part with Me." Simon Peter said to Him, "Lord, then wash not only my feet, but also my hands and my head." Jesus said to him, "He who has bathed needs only to wash his feet, but is completely clean; and you are clean, but not all of you." For He knew the one who was betraying Him; for this reason He said, "Not all of you are clean." So when He had washed their feet, and taken His garments and reclined at the table again, He said to them, "Do you know what I have done to you? You call Me Teacher and Lord; and you are right, for so I am. If I then, the Lord and the Teacher, washed your feet, you also ought to wash one another's feet. For I gave you an example that you also should do as I did to you. Truly, truly, I say to you, a slave is not greater than his master, nor is one who is sent greater than the one who sent him. If you know these things, you are blessed if you do them." (John 13:3–17)

Finally, Jesus gave them a promise. But first, He commended them for being **those who** had **stood by** Him **in** His **trials.** Despite their pride, indifference ambition, and failure to capitalize on their opportunities, the disciples (with the exception of Judas) had remained faithful to Him (cf. John 6:66–69).

Because of their faithfulness, Jesus declared to them, **"Just as My Father has granted Me a kingdom** (the messianic kingdom, which had been postponed, but not cancelled) **I grant you that you may eat and drink at My table in My kingdom, and you will sit on thrones judging the twelve tribes of Israel."** At the culmination of redemptive history, the apostles (including Matthias; Acts 1:15–26) will be rewarded. They will be the most honored and noble guests, seated at Christ's own table in His earthly kingdom, and granted rule over the **twelve tribes of Israel** (cf. Matt. 19:27–28). Although in a few hours they all would abandon Christ and flee in panic, and Peter would verbally deny Him multiple times, they all would be restored. It would then be their privilege and honor to proclaim the gospel, beginning the proclamation of the good news of salvation to the ends of the earth (Matt. 28:19–20).

## TROUBLE AND TRIUMPH WITH THE DEVIL

**Simon, Simon, behold, Satan has demanded permission to sift you like wheat; but I have prayed for you, that your faith may not fail;** (22:31–32a)

Jesus triumphed over trouble with a human enemy in Judas, and with His human friends, the apostles. He also triumphed over the trouble caused by His supernatural adversary Satan. The setting is still the upper room, as is John's description of this conversation between the Lord and Peter (13:31–38). Matthew (26:30–35) and Mark (14:26–31) record a similar conversation that took place later on the Mount of Olives. Only Luke notes that Satan **demanded permission to sift** the disciples (the pronoun translated **you** is plural). *Exaiteō* (**demanded**) appears only here in the New Testament. It is an intensified form of the verb *aiteō,* which means "to ask." The verb is reflexive, indicating that Satan was demanding Peter and the rest for himself.

Though he continually assaults believers (as he did Paul; cf. 2 Cor. 12:7; 1 Thess. 2:18; 2 Cor. 2:11), the devil can operate only within the parameters and limitations established by God, and hence needed His permission to attack the disciples (cf. Job 1:6–12; 2:1–6; Zech. 3:1–5).

What the devil intended to do with them was **sift** them **like wheat.** When wheat was harvested, the wheat and the chaff were shaken and tossed into the air. The wind would blow away the lighter chaff, leaving behind the good grain. Satan wanted to violently shake the disciples to see if their faith remained. He would assault them with a severe trial a short time later in Gethsemane, which, in fulfillment of Zechariah 13:7, would cause them to forsake Jesus and flee.

But the disciples' defection would not be permanent. After Christ's resurrection, they would be restored and meet Him in Galilee (Matt. 26:32). Their restoration from temporary fear was guaranteed by the Lord's promise, **"I have prayed for you, that your faith may not fail"** (or be eclipsed; cf. Luke 23:45). Jesus, their great high priest, continually intercedes for believers (Heb. 7:25; cf. Rom. 8:33–34; Jude 24–25 and the example of His intercessory praying in John 17:6–19), and His prayers are always answered, since He always prays according to God's will. The saving faith of Peter and the other apostles was the genuine gift of God, and, like Job's faith, Satan's best efforts would not destroy it.

## TROUBLE AND TRIUMPH WITH PETER

**and you, when once you have turned again, strengthen your brothers." But he said to Him, "Lord, with You I am ready to go both to prison and to death!" And He said, "I say to you, Peter, the rooster will not crow today until you have denied three times that you know Me."** (22:32b–34)

Satan had been assaulting Peter, at least as far back as his foolish attempt to dissuade Jesus from going to the cross (Matt. 16:22–23). Despite having given him the name Peter (Mark 3:16), Jesus almost always addressed him as **Simon,** the lone exception being here in verse 34. Since Peter so often acted like his old self, Jesus usually addressed him by his old name. The twofold intensive repetition, **Simon, Simon,** reveals pathos, disappointment, and sadness on the Lord's part over his behavior.

Unfazed by Jesus' warning, Peter brashly declared, **"Lord, with**

**You I am ready to go both to prison and to death!"** His overconfi-
dent bravado expressed a sincere love for the Lord. But it was based on
the assumption that Jesus would be present, as the prepositional phrase
**with You** indicates. Since Peter had witnessed firsthand countless examples of Christ's limitless power, he was sure he could withstand anything,
as long as Jesus was there. That confidence was revealed a few hours
later in Gethsemane, when he fearlessly took on the force sent to arrest
Jesus. Confident in his Lord's power to rescue him, Peter evidently intended
to hack his way through the entire detachment, if necessary, beginning
with the high priest's slave (22:50).

Shortly afterward, however, away from Christ's presence in the
high priest's courtyard, Peter would cringe in cowardly fear and deny his
Lord (Luke 22:54–62), fulfilling Jesus' warning, **"I say to you, Peter, the
rooster will not crow today until you have denied three times
that you know Me."**

Peter eventually would be imprisoned (Acts 12:3–11) and later
executed. According to tradition, he was crucified upside down because
he declared himself unworthy to be crucified in the same manner as his
Lord. Despite his denial under the threat of the events surrounding Jesus'
arrest, Peter's faith would not ultimately fail. When he was **turned** around
by divine grace, he would be able to **strengthen** his **brothers.** Having
been through such an unusual temptation and trial and experienced the
enduring character of saving faith, Peter would be able to strengthen and
encourage others. He could gratefully tell them that Christ upheld,
restored, and commissioned him (John 21:15–19; cf. 1 Peter 1:3–9). Peter
would later write his first epistle as a revelation from the Holy Spirit to
strengthen others in their trials. His recovery demonstrates the indestruc-
tible power of the saving faith that God graciously grants to His own.

TROUBLE AND TRIUMPH FROM THE HOSTILE WORLD

**And He said to them, "When I sent you out without money belt
and bag and sandals, you did not lack anything, did you?" They
said, "No, nothing." And He said to them, "But now, whoever has
a money belt is to take it along, likewise also a bag, and whoever**

**has no sword is to sell his coat and buy one. For I tell you that this which is written must be fulfilled in Me, 'And He was numbered with transgressors'; for that which refers to Me has its fulfillment." They said, "Lord, look, here are two swords." And He said to them, "It is enough."** (22:35–38)

The final source of trouble over which the Lord will triumph is the hostile world of unbelievers, who reject God and serve Satan. Trouble from the world would fall first on the Lord Jesus Christ Himself, and after His resurrection and ascension, it would be extended to His followers, beginning with the apostles.

The phrase **and He said** appears seven times in verses 10 to 38, indicating the emphasis Jesus put on teaching during this final time with the disciples before His death. He began by reminding them of the generally favorable reception they had received on previous preaching tours. **"When I sent you out without money belt and bag and sandals,"** He asked them, **"you did not lack anything, did you?" They said, "No, nothing."** Because people had opened their homes to them, the apostles had not needed to provide for themselves (Luke 9:3–4; cf. 10:1–8).

Being welcomed by Jewish society (and even some Gentiles) reinforced their view that all was on track for the arrival of the messianic kingdom (cf. Luke 19:11). Despite Jesus' teaching on Wednesday evening that His return and the establishing of His kingdom would not happen until the distant future, the disciples still clung stubbornly to their imbedded ideas. Even after Christ's resurrection they still expected Him to immediately establish His kingdom (Acts 1:6).

Jesus' words **But now** signal that things will be different in the future. His arrest and death would trigger persecution of His followers, because having rejected Christ, the nation would no longer welcome His disciples. Instead, they would be hated and persecuted—just as Jesus had warned them (9:23–24; 12:11–12; 14:26–33; cf. Matt. 5:10; John 15:18–25; 16:1–4, 33; 2 Tim. 3:12).

Because from now on they would have to supply their own needs, Jesus told them, **"Whoever has a money belt is to take it along, likewise also a bag."** Since the people would be hostile toward them, they would have to provide for and protect themselves; hence the

Lord's command, **"Whoever has no sword is to sell his coat and buy one."** The reference is figurative, and not to an actual sword. When Peter attacked the high priest's slave with a sword, Jesus said, "Stop! No more of this" (22:51). Nor is there any record in Acts of the apostles using force to defend themselves.

As was the case with the trouble He faced from Judas, the apostles, Satan, and Peter, Jesus and His people will also triumph over the hostile world. The hatred that Christ and His followers would face did not come as a surprise to Him, but was the direct fulfillment of Scripture. The Lord made that clear by bracketing His quote of Isaiah 53:12 with the statements, **"this which is written must be fulfilled in Me"** and **"for that which refers to Me has its fulfillment"** (there are at least five other New Testament references to Jesus fulfilling Isaiah 53 [Matt. 8:17; John 12:38; Acts 8:32–33; Rom. 10:16; 1 Peter 2:22]).

That **He was numbered with transgressors** does not refer to Christ's being crucified with two criminals, or associating with sinners during His earthly ministry. It refers specifically to His death in the place of sinners (cf. 2 Cor. 5:21; Gal. 3:10–13; 1 Peter 2:24). The fifty-third chapter of Isaiah teaches that God categorized Jesus as a transgressor and then punished Him as a substitute for sinners. That thought is repeated in different forms twenty times in the chapter, and thus this statement quoted by the Lord summarizes the entire chapter.

Isaiah 53 records the lament of penitent Jews in the future, who will recognize that Israel had killed the Messiah (cf. Zech. 12:10). They will realize that He died as a substitute for them, punished by God for their sins. They will recognize Him as the scarred substitute (Isa. 52:14; 53:2–3), the suffering substitute (vv. 4–6), the submissive substitute (vv. 7–9), and the sovereign substitute (vv. 10–12).

Although Christ would triumph over the hostile world, the faltering apostles could not be sure that they would. Therefore **they said, "Lord, look, here are two swords."** Jesus' reply, **"It is enough,"** meaning "Enough of that kind of talk," indicates that the disciples' future protection would not depend on them, but on God, who would empower and guard them (John 14:12–18, 23, 25–27; 15:16; 16:7, 12–15, 23, 24, 26, 27, 32, 33; cf. Jesus' prayer in John 17:6–26).

# Four Features of Triumphant Prayer (Luke 22:39-46)

## 27

**And He came out and proceeded as was His custom to the Mount of Olives; and the disciples also followed Him. When He arrived at the place, He said to them, "Pray that you may not enter into temptation." And He withdrew from them about a stone's throw, and He knelt down and began to pray, saying, "Father, if You are willing, remove this cup from Me; yet not My will, but Yours be done." Now an angel from heaven appeared to Him, strengthening Him. And being in agony He was praying very fervently; and His sweat became like drops of blood, falling down upon the ground. When He rose from prayer, He came to the disciples and found them sleeping from sorrow, and said to them, "Why are you sleeping? Get up and pray that you may not enter into temptation."** (22:39-46)

As Isaiah prophesied He would be, the Messiah our Lord was "a man of sorrows and acquainted with grief" (Isa. 53:3). The Gospels record that He grieved over Israel's hardness of heart (Mark 3:5), the plight of a deaf man (Mark 7:34), the superficiality of Israel's religious leaders (Mark

8:12), at the tomb of Lazarus (John 11:35), and over Jerusalem (Luke 19:41).

But the extremity of Christ's grief came in Gethsemane on the night before His death, when He "offered up both prayers and supplications with loud crying and tears to the One able to save Him from death, and He was heard because of His piety" (Heb. 5:7). Christ's sorrow in facing death as the sin bearer is beyond comprehension. It defies description and surpasses understanding, because what Jesus endured is absolutely unique and without any parallel in human experience. The account of His temptation in the garden confronts those who read it with an incalculable mystery. It leaves them awestruck over Christ's agony in facing the Father's anger at the cross and stunned by the intensity of this greatest of all battles against temptation.

Satan's objective throughout Christ's life was to keep Him from going to the cross where, in fulfillment of God's preordained plan, He would die as the substitute for sinners. That was the devil's goal when he tempted Jesus at the beginning of His ministry (Matt. 4:1–11; Luke 4:1–13). In each of the three temptations, Satan offered to give Him what was rightfully His apart from suffering, death, and divine wrath. Preventing the Lord from getting to the cross was also his goal in this final and most severe temptation.

Satan would have his hour, called "the hour and the power of darkness" (v. 53). In the sovereign purposes of God this was the predetermined time for him to make his supreme effort to keep the Son of God from His propitiatory sacrifice. So intense was the conflict that in Mark 14:34 Jesus said, "My soul is deeply grieved to the point of death." But when the battle was over, Satan would be vanquished. Jesus would emerge triumphant and a few hours later be nailed to the cross.

It was at the very end of Thursday or early Friday morning when Jesus **came out** from the upper room **and proceeded as was His custom** (cf. John 18:2) **to the Mount of Olives; and the** eleven remaining **disciples also followed Him.** It would have been warm enough during Passover to rest or sleep in the seclusion of the **Mount of Olives,** located just east of Jerusalem across the Kidron Valley (John 18:1). On the Mount of Olives was a garden (John 18:1) called Gethsemane (Matt. 26:36), which means "olive press." It was a private garden, likely owned by a wealthy follower of Jesus who allowed the Lord and the disciples to sleep there. Behind the scene is another nameless individual who showed sympathy to Jesus during Passion Week, as did the owners of the donkey's colt He rode on during the triumphal entry (Luke 19:33–35), the man carrying the water pitcher who led Him to the upper room (Luke 22:10), and the owner of the upper room (Luke 22:11–12). There was no longer any need to avoid Judas, who knew where Jesus and the apostles would be (John 18:2), since the divinely ordained time for the Lord's arrest was at hand.

Christ's supernatural conflict with Satan and His prayer to the Father are marked by four vital elements: anticipation, affliction, submission, and restoration.

## ANTICIPATION

**When He arrived at the place, He said to them, "Pray that you may not enter into temptation."** (22:40)

Jesus prayed in anticipation of and all the way through His temptation, which was real, since although He was incapable of sinning (John 5:19, 30), He could be tempted (Heb. 2:17–18; 4:15). The temptation the Lord faced, however, was different from that of believers. Christians are new creations (2 Cor. 5:17), incarcerated in unredeemed flesh (Rom. 7:18–25) and easily seduced by the remnants of their fallenness. Satan tempts them to hold on to sin and not mature. They fight against their attraction to sin, and to abandon it and embrace righteousness, holiness, and purity.

But Satan's temptation of Christ was just the opposite. He was perfectly pure and righteous, and His absolute holiness motivated His every thought, word, and deed. While believers struggle to abandon sin and embrace holiness, Jesus struggled to set aside His holiness and embrace sin-bearing. He was not fighting against sinful impulses to become holy, but against holy impulses to allow Himself to be made sin for believers (2 Cor. 5:21). Satan tempts Christians to cling to sin; he tempted Jesus to cling to holiness.

Christ had always known it would be the greatest struggle of His pure, sinless eternal life to be separated from the Father and bear His wrath against sin. In His prayer recorded in John 17 He asked, "Father, glorify Me together with Yourself, with the glory which I had with You before the world was" (v. 5). Thus He prayed that the Father would strengthen Him through the coming ordeal, and restore Him to eternal glory.

Although He was fully focused on the conflict, Jesus was still concerned about the apostles. He knew that they, too, would struggle with severe temptation that night, and that they needed to be ready to face it. Just as He prepared Himself through prayer, so also did they need to pray. Therefore **when He arrived at** Gethsemane **He said to them, "Pray that you may not enter into temptation."** Leaving eight of the apostles at the entrance to the garden (Matt. 26:36), He took Peter, James, and John (Mark 14:33) in with Him. Jesus then left the three and went to pray alone, returning to them later and again charging them to pray that they not fall to temptation (v. 38; cf. Matt. 26:41).

Here is an example of the ever-present balance between divine sovereignty and human responsibility. Jesus had already prayed that the apostles' faith would not fail (Luke 22:32), but that did not relieve them of their responsibility to pray. At least twice in the past Jesus had taught them to pray specifically that they would not be led into temptation (Matt. 6:13; Luke 11:4).

The lesson is clear. If even Christ did not face temptation without prayer, how much more did the apostles, and all Christians, need to do the same? Those who would pray properly must empty themselves of all self-confidence (which Peter and the apostles had already exhibited; Mark 14:31), spiritual pride, and over-estimation of their strength, and call for divine help. Jesus' words are a warning against being caught prayerless when the full force of temptation hits, and are a promise that help awaits those who pray.

AFFLICTION

**And He withdrew from them about a stone's throw, and He knelt down and began to pray** (22:41)

Luke's account is brief, and does not include some of the details provided by Matthew and Mark. The latter reveal that after Jesus initially **withdrew** from Peter, James, and John and prayed, He returned to them twice, finding them asleep both times (Matt. 26:39–45; Mark 14:35–42). Luke notes that having moved **about a stone's throw away** from the three apostles to a place where He would be alone, Jesus **knelt down and began to pray.** Standing was the customary posture for prayer (Matt. 6:5; Mark 11:25; Luke 18:11), but the Lord **knelt**, then "fell on His face and prayed" (Matt. 26:39). Mark adds that this was because He "began to be very distressed and troubled" (Mark 14:33), and the writer of Hebrews says that "He offered up both prayers and supplications with loud crying and tears" (Heb. 5:7). Taken together, those passages reveal the intense agony of Christ's struggle. This was the Man of Sorrows in His most sorrowful conflict.

A number of things depressed Jesus into such sorrow, including His rejection by the nation, the defection of the betrayer, Judas, the dissension among the remaining apostles and their imminent desertion of Him, His repudiation and denial by Peter, as well as the injustice of men, whereby the sinless Prince of truth and justice, the lover and source of righteousness, would be condemned in a corrupt court and slain by evil men. But all those things paled in comparison to the reality that the wrath of His Father against the sins of the elect would fall on His sinless being at the cross.

Triumphing over temptation involves experiencing sin's painful assault, being repulsed by it, and agonizing in prayer to be delivered from it. Only loving holiness, hating sin, and feeling its agony can produce prayer that leads to triumph over temptation.

Submission

**saying, "Father, if You are willing, remove this cup from Me; yet not My will, but Yours be done."** (22:42)

The goal of all true prayer is that God's will be done. Those who genuinely feel the affliction caused by sin and temptation are motivated to submit to Him. In Psalm 40:8 David exclaimed, "I delight to do Your will, O my God," while in Psalm 143:10 he pleaded, "Teach me to do Your will, for You are my God; let Your good Spirit lead me on level ground." Jesus' model prayer teaches those who address God in prayer to say, "Your will be done, on earth as it is in heaven" (Matt. 6:10; cf. Luke 11:2). The apostle John wrote, "This is the confidence which we have before Him, that, if we ask anything according to His will, He hears us. And if we know that He hears us in whatever we ask, we know that we have the requests which we have asked from Him" (1 John 5:14–15). Submission to God's will is foundational to prayer.

Jesus' request, **"Father, if You are willing,"** highlights once again the contrast between His temptation and those of believers. He submitted to the Father's will that He be made sin; believers pray that they might submit to God's will by forsaking sin and embracing holiness. Mark records that Jesus addressed the **Father** using the intimate, endearing, affectionate term "Abba" (Mark 14:36), revealing the earnestness and intensity of His plea. No Jew would ever call God Father, let alone Abba. But the Lord uses this affectionate, personal term to refer to God, pleading for His intimate love to rescue Him if He wills.

The word "cup" is frequently associated with judgment in the Old Testament (Pss. 11:6; 75:8; Isa. 51:17, 22; Jer. 25:15–17; 49:12; Lam. 4:21; Ezek. 23:31–33; Hab. 2:16; Zech. 12:2). Here it also refers to the agony, guilt, and wrath associated with God's judgment of Jesus on the cross. Some have imagined that the Lord's plea, **"if You are willing, remove this cup from Me,"** was a sign of weakness on His part. But it was not weakness that prompted this request, rather the opposite. His absolute holiness demanded that He recoil at the thought of bearing sin, guilt, judgment, and wrath. No other response was possible for the eternally sinless Son of God.

Jesus accepted that the cross was God's plan. In John 12 He said, "Truly, truly, I say to you, unless a grain of wheat falls into the earth and dies, it remains alone; but if it dies, it bears much fruit" (v. 24); "Now My soul has become troubled; and what shall I say, 'Father, save Me from this hour'? But for this purpose I came to this hour" (v. 27); "And I, if I am lifted up from the earth, will draw all men to Myself" (v. 32). In Mark 8:31 "He began to teach [the disciples] that the Son of Man must suffer many things and be rejected by the elders and the chief priests and the scribes, and be killed, and after three days rise again" (cf. 9:31; Luke 9:22, 44). On the final journey to Jerusalem Jesus

> took the twelve aside and began to tell them what was going to happen to Him, saying, "Behold, we are going up to Jerusalem, and the Son of Man will be delivered to the chief priests and the scribes; and they will condemn Him to death and will hand Him over to the Gentiles. They will mock Him and spit on Him, and scourge Him and kill Him, and three days later He will rise again." (Mark 10:32–34)

In spite of experiencing satanic assaults beyond the capacity of the human mind to experience or conceive and agonizing over the prospect of bearing sin, Jesus fully submitted to the Father's will for Him to be the sin offering (2 Cor. 5:21) so that redemption of God's elect would be accomplished. Therefore He prayed, **"Yet not My will, but Yours be done."** Jesus soon demonstrated the reality of that submission when He said to Peter, "Put the sword into the sheath; the cup which the Father has given Me, shall I not drink it?" (John 18:11).

## RESTORATION

**Now an angel from heaven appeared to Him, strengthening Him. And being in agony He was praying very fervently; and His sweat became like drops of blood, falling down upon the ground. When He rose from prayer, He came to the disciples and found them sleeping from sorrow, and said to them, "Why are you sleeping? Get up and pray that you may not enter into temptation."** (22:43–46)

That **an angel from heaven appeared to** Jesus was unusual. Between His birth and His resurrection angels appeared only twice in Christ's life, at His temptation in the wilderness (Matt. 4:11) and His temptation in the garden. This one was sent to Jesus as an affirmation of the Father's care for Him, to strengthen His confidence that the Father would not ultimately forsake Him, but would restore Him (cf. John 17:5). The One who is above the angels, better than the angels, had a more excellent name than the angels, was worshiped by the holy angels, though for a while made lower than them (Heb. 1:4–2:18), was strengthened by an angel. In the midst of His prayer there was divine restoration.

Angels also minister, though not visibly as was the case with Christ, to those who prayerfully submit to God's will. "Are they not all ministering spirits," asked the writer of Hebrews rhetorically, "sent out to render service for the sake of those who will inherit salvation?" (Heb. 1:14; cf. Matt. 18:10).

The severity of Christ's struggle prompted the angel's **strengthening** of **Him. Agony** translates the Greek noun *agōnia*, which describes a state of extreme mental and emotional anguish and sorrow. The verb form of the noun refers to intense struggle, whether in athletic contests or combat. The Greek word translated **fervently** is related to a verb that means "to stretch." Here it describes the severe strain the Lord was under—so much so that there was an unusual physical reaction. Only Luke the physician (Col. 4:14) records that **His sweat became like drops of blood, falling down upon the ground.** This suggests a rare condition known as hematidrosis, which is characterized by blood oozing from the skin. It is most frequently caused by extreme mental and emotional strain, causing subcutaneous capillaries to dilate and burst, releasing blood to mingle with sweat. That was a graphic confirmation of the Lord's statement, "My soul is deeply grieved, to the point of death" (Matt. 26:38; Mark 14:34; cf. Heb. 12:3–4).

**When** Christ **rose from prayer** in triumph, He **came to the disciples and found them sleeping.** They were not sleeping because they were tired, or because it was late at night, or because it had been a busy week, or they had recently eaten a meal, or taken a long walk, or because it was dark. They were sleeping because they were overwhelmed with **sorrow,** fatalism, and despair. The disciples had been told that they were going to abandon the Lord, that Peter would deny Him, and that He would be arrested and go to the cross. From their perspective, their world had collapsed. Fatalism crept in, and there seemed to be nothing left to pray for. Luke condensed Christ's repeated warnings to watch and pray into one. **"Why are you sleeping?"** Jesus asked them. **"Get up and pray that you may not enter into temptation."** After the third and final time He came and found the disciples asleep He said to them, "Are you still sleeping and resting? It is enough; the hour has come; behold, the Son of Man is being betrayed into the hands of sinners" (Mark 14:41). There was no more time to pray or prepare; the enemy was at hand. But while Christ went to face the enemy victorious over temptation through prayer, the apostles would face the enemy and be defeated.

When the Lord Jesus Christ arose from the ground bloody, but unbowed, the battle was over; the devil defeated; the final temptation successfully overcome. He would triumph over His human enemies: Judas, the Jewish leaders, and the Romans. On the cross, He would defeat Satan (Gen. 3:15; 1 John 3:8) and be made sin for believers that they "might become the righteousness of God in Him" (2 Cor. 5:21). He would triumph over death by rising from the dead, and be exalted to the right hand of the Father (Acts 2:33; 5:31; 7:55–56; Rom. 8:34; Col. 3:1; Heb. 10:12; 12:2; 1 Peter 3:22) as King of kings and Lord of lords (Rev. 17:14; 19:16) forever (Rev. 11:15).

The cup was in Christ's hand and He was about to drink it. And His hand was steady. No wonder Philip P. Bliss wrote,

> "Man of Sorrows!" what a name
> For the Son of God, who came
> Ruined sinners to reclaim!
> Hallelujah, what a Savior!

# A Traitorous Kiss for the Triumphant Savior (Luke 22:47–53)

**28**

**While He was still speaking, behold, a crowd came, and the one called Judas, one of the twelve, was preceding them; and he approached Jesus to kiss Him. But Jesus said to him, "Judas, are you betraying the Son of Man with a kiss?" When those who were around Him saw what was going to happen, they said, "Lord, shall we strike with the sword?" And one of them struck the slave of the high priest and cut off his right ear. But Jesus answered and said, "Stop! No more of this." And He touched his ear and healed him. Then Jesus said to the chief priests and officers of the temple and elders who had come against Him, "Have you come out with swords and clubs as you would against a robber? While I was with you daily in the temple, you did not lay hands on Me; but this hour and the power of darkness are yours."** (22:47–53)

The previous section of Luke's gospel described the Lord Jesus Christ's agonizing experience of temptation in the garden of Gethsemane (see the exposition of 22:39–46 in chapter 27 of this volume). In this scene the Man of Sorrows faced another deeply painful experience, being betrayed into the hands of His enemies by one of His disciples. The narrative of this event is so dramatic, tragic, and in the end triumphant that it appears in all four Gospels.

The previous Saturday, six days before this scene in Gethsemane, Jesus had arrived in Bethany, a little village just east of Jerusalem. He stayed overnight there, most likely at the house of His friends Mary, Martha, and Lazarus, and on Sunday taught the many people who came there to meet Him. Monday saw His triumphal entry into Jerusalem when He was hailed as the Messiah by the fickle crowd, who would on Friday scream for His blood.

On Tuesday Jesus returned to Jerusalem from the Mount of Olives, where He spent each night (22:39) with the apostles in seclusion and safety. Then He attacked the heart of the apostate Judaism of His day by assaulting the corruption in the temple for the second time in His ministry (cf. John 2:13–16), again infuriating the religious leaders. Jesus then spent the rest of the day teaching the people who were in Jerusalem for Passover.

After spending the night on the Mount of Olives, He came back into the city on Wednesday for one final day of teaching as well as confronting and condemning the religious leaders. At the end of the day He returned again to the Mount of Olives with the disciples, where He instructed them on elements of the lengthy interval between His first and second comings.

Thursday was a private day spent with the disciples, and culminating in the final official celebration of Passover and the inaugural celebration of the Lord's Supper. Jesus also taught the disciples for the last time before His death (John chapters 13–16) and prayed a prayer reflecting His role as believers' high priest (chapter 17). Having exposed Judas, now fully under Satan's control (Luke 22:3), as the betrayer, the Lord dismissed him. Judas then left to make the final preparations with the religious leaders to arrest Jesus.

Late Thursday night or shortly after midnight on Friday morning, Jesus and the eleven remaining disciples left the upper room and went to the garden of Gethsemane. The Lord left eight of the disciples at the entrance and took Peter, James, and John a little further in. He then separated a short distance from them and prayed by Himself. Agonizing in prayer, Christ triumphed over the devil, whose effort to tempt Him to avoid the cross failed. Returning to the disciples, Jesus found them not praying, as He had repeatedly admonished them to do, but sleeping. As He rebuked them one final time, the crowd arrived to arrest Him.

The best way to examine the ensuing scene is to examine the characters involved. We witness first the arrival of the crowd, then the kiss of the traitor, the rebuke of the disciples, and finally the triumph of the Savior.

## The Arrival of the Crowd

**While He was still speaking, behold, a crowd came, and the one called Judas, one of the twelve, was preceding them;** (22:47*a*)

**While** Jesus **was still speaking** to the disciples and rebuking them for sleeping when they should have been praying (v. 46), the **crowd** arrived, with Judas **preceding them** as their guide. All three of the Synoptic Gospels record the abrupt transition from Christ's solitary time in prayer to His confrontation with a large group of people (Matt. 26:47; Mark 14:43).

At the head of the crowd was **the one called Judas.** He was further identified as **one of the twelve** (cf. 22:3; Matt. 26:14, 47; Mark 14:10, 43) apostles who had been with Jesus for all three years of His ministry. Daily Judas had heard His teaching and witnessed His miracles. He had the same privilege, honor, and inestimable opportunity to walk with the incarnate Son of God that the other apostles did. Judas was not an outsider; he was an insider.

If there is a more ugly and repulsive word than "traitor," it is the proper name synonym—Judas. As heinous and repulsive as Judas's act of betraying Jesus was, the gospel writers are restrained in their references to him. There is nothing of the vituperation and scorn that the writers of later non-biblical, apocryphal works heaped on him. For instance,

The apocryphal writing *The Story of Joseph of Arimathea* taught that Judas was the son of the brother of the high priest Caiaphas and that he was sent by Caiaphas to infiltrate the disciples and discover a way to destroy Jesus.

According to another apocryphal writing, *The Acts of Pilate*, Judas went home after the betrayal and found his wife roasting a chicken. When he told her he was planning to kill himself because he was afraid Jesus would rise from the dead and take vengeance on him, she replied that Jesus would no more rise from the dead than the chicken she was cooking would jump out of the fire and crow—at which instant the chicken was said to have done just that.

An ancient manuscript called *Coptic Narratives of the Ministry and Passion* maintained that Judas's wife was exceedingly greedy and that he was nothing more than the pawn of a manipulative wife. In the ancient Near East, to accuse a man of being subjugated to a dominating wife was considered highly slanderous.

A twelfth-century writing called *The Legendary Aura* claimed that Judas's parents threw him into the sea when he was an infant, because even at that early age they supposedly sensed he was diabolical and deserved to be destroyed. Somehow he managed to survive and grow to adulthood, and, according to the legend, soon after marrying a beautiful older woman, he discovered she was his mother.

Such bizarre accounts are common in extrabiblical literature. They are concocted to demonstrate the vileness of Judas and to reveal the contempt with which he was viewed. The gospel writers, by contrast, simply call him one of the twelve. Rather than minimizing the heinousness of Judas's treachery, this heightens the insidiousness of his crime more than any list of epithets could do. (John MacArthur, *Matthew 24–28*, The MacArthur New Testament Commentary [Chicago: Moody, 1989], 182–83)

After being exposed (Matt. 26:25) and dismissed (John 13:30) by Jesus as the betrayer, Judas went directly to the Jewish religious leaders. He had already made his deal with them (Matt. 26:3–16), and was now ready to consummate it. He knew that when Jesus and the remaining eleven disciples left the upper room, they would go to Gethsemane. Judas was eager to take advantage of the darkness and Jesus' isolation from the crowds to have Him arrested there.

Judas felt a sense of urgency because there were details that had to be attended to before they could seize Jesus. He had to find some of the religious leaders in the middle of the night, who could gather the rest. Then it was necessary to convince the commander of the Roman garrison at Fort Antonia that Jesus was an insurrectionist who posed a threat to Rome. Since Pilate was in Jerusalem at the time, the commander no doubt sought permission from him to provide the troops the Jewish leaders requested. Finally, they all had to enter Gethsemane, identify Jesus, and capture Him before He could escape.

The **crowd** consisted of several groups, including those listed in verse 52: the chief priests (who ran the temple enterprises), the officers of the temple (the temple's police force), elders (members of the Sanhedrin), scribes (Mark 14:43), and a detachment of Roman troops from the cohort stationed in Jerusalem. It is unlikely that the entire cohort (600-1000 men) would have been dispatched, since that would have left Jerusalem unguarded during Passover, when nationalistic feelings ran high. Yet enough troops (possible a maniple, consisting of about 200 men) were sent to warrant their commanding officer accompanying them (John 18:12). Always sensitive to the threat of insurrection (especially, as noted above, at Passover), the Romans came in overwhelming strength, armed (v. 52) and ready for trouble. John 18:3 notes that they carried lanterns and torches. The lights were not necessary to guide them to Gethsemane, since there was a full moon at Passover. They no doubt anticipated that Jesus would attempt to flee, and that they would have to search for Him in the darkness. The crowd came prepared to arrest Jesus as if He were a dangerous insurrectionist, like Barabbas (Mark 15:7).

The arrest of Jesus reveals several features about the crowd. First, it was unjust. Christ had committed no crime, either against God, Judaism, or Caesar. They were unjust, unfair, evil murderers, just like their father, the devil (John 8:44).

The crowd was also mindless. The majority had no legitimate reason for hating Jesus. He had healed the sick, fed the poor, cast out demons, raised the dead, taught the truth of God's kingdom, and upheld His glory, law, and word. But the majority of the crowd was seduced by the hatred of the leaders.

Third, the crowd was cowardly. They came fully armed to seize a humble Galilean, who was unarmed and undefended. A guilty conscience makes a coward; wickedness fears it may get what it deserves.

Finally, the crowd was profane. They had no reverence for the sacred Son, but sought to lay murderous hands on the holy Lord of glory.

The evil world still treats Jesus just as unjustly, mindlessly, cowardly, and profanely as the crowd did that night in Gethsemane.

### THE KISS OF THE TRAITOR

**and he approached Jesus to kiss Him. But Jesus said to him, "Judas, are you betraying the Son of Man with a kiss?"** (22:47b–48)

Although as noted earlier there was a full moon, the dense grove of olive trees in Gethsemane would have obscured much of the moonlight. Further, Jesus was surrounded by eleven men, and Judas may have feared that one of them would pretend to be Jesus while the rest hustled Him away to safety. Therefore he "had given them a signal, saying, 'Whomever I kiss, He is the one; seize Him and lead Him away under guard'" (Mark 14:44). After arriving at Gethsemane, **he approached Jesus to kiss Him.** So brazenly confident was Judas in his hypocrisy that he imagined that no one would suspect him of treachery.

Out of the various ways he could have done so (e.g., on the feet, the back of the hand, the palm, the hem of the garment), Judas chose the embrace and **kiss** on the cheek normally reserved for those with whom one had a close friendship. There could not have been a more despicable way for him to have pointed out the Lord than by treacherously and hypocritically pretending to be a devoted, loyal companion of His by expressing the most intimate sign of affection.

Of course, Jesus knew his evil heart and every detail of his wicked plan. After his cynical greeting, "Hail, Rabbi" (Matt. 26:49), but before he could kiss Him, **Jesus said to him, "Judas, are you betraying the Son of Man with a kiss?"** Undeterred, Judas fervently and affectionately embraced and kissed Him, thus fulfilling his signal. Jesus accepted the kiss and submitted to the shame of Judas's betrayal, telling him, "'Friend ("fellow"; "man"), do what you have come for.' Then they came and laid hands on Jesus and seized Him" (Matt. 26:50).

## The Rebuke of the Disciples

**When those who were around Him saw what was going to happen, they said, "Lord, shall we strike with the sword?" And one of them struck the slave of the high priest and cut off his right ear. But Jesus answered and said, "Stop! No more of this." And He touched his ear and healed him.** (22:49–51)

At last the situation became clear to **those who were around** Jesus (i.e., the eleven apostles). They saw the large crowd, many of them armed, with Judas in the lead, and realized **what was going to happen.** The apostles, no doubt remembering Christ's statement in Luke 22:36, "Whoever has no sword is to sell his coat and buy one," **said, "Lord, shall we strike with the sword?"** They had also just witnessed another incredible display of Christ's divine power, recorded in John 18. When the crowd arrived, Jesus calmly went to meet them (v. 4). He asked them who they were seeking (i.e., who they had orders to arrest), and they replied, "Jesus the Nazarene." The Lord replied by using the divine name, "I am" (v. 5; cf. John 8:24, 28, 58), which caused the entire crowd to fall to the ground (v. 6).

After they picked themselves up, Jesus again asked them, "Whom do you seek?" making them affirm again that they only had authority to arrest Him. He then demanded that they let the apostles go, "to fulfill the word which He spoke, 'Of those whom You have given Me I lost not one'" (v. 9). The Lord knew that being arrested would prove too much for their faith, and protected them (cf. 1 Cor. 10:13).

Emboldened by that display of Christ's power, the disciples eagerly asked Him, **"Lord, shall we strike with the sword?"** Impetuous as ever, Peter did not wait for the Lord to reply, but instead launched a one-man assault on the detachment (John 18:10). He **struck the slave of the high priest** (Malchus), who was no doubt standing in the front rank next to his master. Peter unsuccessfully aimed for his head, but only managed to **cut off his right ear.**

But Christ's kingdom was not a worldly one, and hence His followers did not need to fight to protect Him (John 18:36). The Lord immediately halted Peter's heroics with the stern rebuke, **"Stop! No more of**

**this,"** and then graciously **touched** Malchus's **ear and healed him.** He then gave three reasons for stopping the battle and rebuking Peter:

First, because "all those who take up the sword shall perish by the sword" (Matt. 26:52). Armed resistance could prove fatal, since murder is a capital offense. Jesus upheld the biblical principal of capital punishment, and affirmed that the government has the right to take the lives of those who commit murder (Gen. 9:6; Rom. 13:4).

Armed resistance was also foolish. "Do you think that I cannot appeal to My Father," the Lord told them, "and He will at once put at My disposal more than twelve legions of angels?" (Matt. 26:53). Since one angel killed 185,000 Assyrians (2 Kings 19:35), the power of the tens of thousands of angels Christ could have called upon is inconceivable. He did not need any help from the apostles and their two small swords.

Finally, armed intervention by the apostles disregarded the necessity that the Old Testament prophecies regarding Christ's death (e.g., Ps. 22; Isa. 53) be fulfilled (Matt. 26:54; cf. v. 24; Luke 24:25–26, 44–46).

After the Lord's rebuke, in fulfillment of another Old Testament prophecy concerning His death, "all the disciples left Him and fled" (Matt. 26:56; cf. Zech. 13:7). On the human level, their failure to watch and pray (Luke 22:46) had left them unable to cope with the trial that was at hand.

THE TRIUMPH OF THE SAVIOR

**Then Jesus said to the chief priests and officers of the temple and elders who had come against Him, "Have you come out with swords and clubs as you would against a robber? While I was with you daily in the temple, you did not lay hands on Me; but this hour and the power of darkness are yours."** (22:52–53)

After the disciples fled, Jesus confronted **the chief priests and officers of the temple and elders who had come against Him** and asked them, **"Have you come out with swords and clubs as you would against a robber? While I was with you daily in the temple, you did not lay hands on Me."** If He was the dangerous threat and rival to Caesar that they accused Him of being, why did they fail to arrest Him earlier in the week? The answer is that they feared the people's response (Luke 22:2). Only in the dark, isolated location of Gethsemane with an overwhelming force accompanying them, did they dare to arrest Him.

Jesus then gave the reason that they were unable to seize Him until this moment: it was **this hour** that God had sovereignly ordained to be theirs in association with **the power of darkness** (cf. Acts 2:22–23).

Throughout history there have always been people who, like the crowd, reject Jesus. There have also been false disciples, like Judas, who outwardly profess affection and loyalty to the Lord, but inwardly hate Him. Still others, like the eleven apostles, genuinely love Him, but are weak and vacillating. But towering over them all is the triumphant Savior, who surrendered Himself into the hands of sinners and willingly drank the cup of suffering, guilt, and bearing of sin that the Father gave Him so that sinners can be redeemed.

# The Danger of Spiritual Overconfidence
## (Luke 22:54–62)

**29**

Having arrested Him, they led Him away and brought Him to the house of the high priest; but Peter was following at a distance. After they had kindled a fire in the middle of the courtyard and had sat down together, Peter was sitting among them. And a servant-girl, seeing him as he sat in the firelight and looking intently at him, said, "This man was with Him too." But he denied it, saying, "Woman, I do not know Him." A little later, another saw him and said, "You are one of them too!" But Peter said, "Man, I am not!" After about an hour had passed, another man began to insist, saying, "Certainly this man also was with Him, for he is a Galilean too." But Peter said, "Man, I do not know what you are talking about." Immediately, while he was still speaking, a rooster crowed. The Lord turned and looked at Peter. And Peter remembered the word of the Lord, how He had told him, "Before a rooster crows today, you will deny Me three times." And he went out and wept bitterly. (22:54–62)

Throughout their time with Jesus, the disciples experienced high and low moments. When He called them, "they left everything and followed Him" (Luke 5:11; cf. Mark 1:16–20; Matt. 9:9–13; 19:27). Even when many other "disciples" deserted Him (John 6:66), they remained, since as their spokesman Peter said to Him, "Lord, to whom shall we go? You have words of eternal life" (v. 68).

On the other hand, they could be frustratingly obtuse. When they failed to understand the parable of the soils, Jesus chiding them said, "Do you not understand this parable? How will you understand all the parables?" (Mark 4:13). After they failed to grasp the meaning of another parable the Lord again rebuked them, asking, "Are you so lacking in understanding also?" (Mark 7:18). Their misinterpretation of Jesus' warning, "Watch out and beware of the leaven of the Pharisees and Sadducees" (Matt. 16:6), as a rebuke for forgetting to bring literal bread prompted the Lord's rebuke,

> You men of little faith, why do you discuss among yourselves that you have no bread? Do you not yet understand or remember the five loaves of the five thousand, and how many baskets full you picked up? Or the seven loaves of the four thousand, and how many large baskets full you picked up? How is it that you do not understand that I did not speak to you concerning bread? But beware of the leaven of the Pharisees and Sadducees. (vv. 8–11)

Caught in a powerful storm on the Sea of Galilee, the terrified disciples woke Jesus and cried out, "Save us, Lord; we are perishing!" (Matt. 8:25). Jesus again reprimand them: " 'Why are you afraid, you men of little faith?' Then He got up and rebuked the winds and the sea, and it became perfectly calm" (v. 26).

Sometimes the disciples' high and low moments came in the same incident. After miraculously feeding the thousands on the eastern side of the Sea of Galilee, Jesus sent the Twelve back to the other side while He dismissed the multitude (Mark 6:45), which was bent on forcing Him to become their king (John 6:15). After the crowd dispersed, the Lord went up the slope of a nearby mountain alone to pray (Matt. 14:23). Aware of the disciples' boat being far from the shore (Mark 6:47) and being battered by strong winds (John 6:18) and large waves (Matt. 14:24), Jesus left the mountain and "came to them, walking on the sea"

(v. 25). Imagining that they were seeing a ghost, the disciples "cried out in fear" (v. 26). But Jesus said to them, "It is I; do not be afraid" (v. 27).

Still not convinced, "Peter said to Him, 'Lord, if it is You, command me to come to You on the water'" (v. 28). After Jesus told him to come, Peter courageously climbed out of the boat in the midst of the raging storm and began walking on the water toward Him (v. 29). But his remarkable demonstration of faith was short-lived. "Seeing the wind, he became frightened, and beginning to sink, he cried out, 'Lord, save me!'" (v. 30). After rescuing Peter, Jesus rebuked him for his lack of faith (v. 31).

Peter was also the central figure in another incident that went from triumph to tragedy. One day when they were in the region of Caesarea Philippi, the Lord asked the disciples, "Who do people say that the Son of Man is?" (Matt. 16:13). They replied that the people were giving various answers to that question: "Some say John the Baptist; and others, Elijah; but still others, Jeremiah, or one of the prophets" (v. 14). Then He asked them directly, "But who do you say that I am?" (v. 15). Peter replied, "You are the Christ, the Son of the living God" (v. 16; cf. John 6:66–69). The Lord pronounced him blessed because the Father had revealed to him who He really was (v. 17).

Peter, however, descended fast from the height of privilege and commendation into the depths of folly and condemnation. After warning the disciples not to tell anyone that He was the Christ (v. 20; cf. Matt. 8:4; 12:16), Jesus told them that He had to "go to Jerusalem, and suffer many things from the elders and chief priests and scribes, and be killed, and be raised up on the third day" (v. 21).

Peter was shocked since, like his fellow Israelites, he expected the Messiah to drive out the Roman oppressors and usher in the earthly kingdom promised to Israel. There was no place in his theology for a dying Messiah. Peter brashly "took [Jesus] aside and began to rebuke Him, saying, 'God forbid it, Lord! This shall never happen to You'" (v. 22). Having just spoken revelation from the Father affirming Jesus' true identity, Peter now became the mouthpiece of Satan, through whom the devil tried to dissuade Jesus from going to the cross. Christ's response was immediate and crushing. The one whom He had just pronounced blessed by God (v. 17) He now shockingly addressed as Satan (v. 23).

But no incident more clearly reveals Peter's impulsive and

unpredictable nature than the one recorded in this section of Luke's gospel. No other story of Jesus' dealings with the disciples is both as low and high, dark and light, tragic and hopeful, or distressing and encouraging as this one. It was the worst failure followed by the most profound recovery. Peter's denial of his Master was his worst failure; Christ's restoration of him was His greatest demonstration of His triumphant love for Peter.

Edward Reynolds wrote concerning Peter's mixture of devotion to the Lord and fleshly overconfidence,

> Self-dependance [sic], pride, or any other carnal affection which is more deeply rooted in the particular nature of any man, do often intermix themselves in his most holy actions. It was faith that made Peter go down upon the water, but it was flesh that made him begin to sink: faith made him zealous in Christ's cause, but flesh drew his sword at Malchus's ear: faith made him follow Christ, but flesh made him follow afar off: faith made him accompany Christ to the garden, but flesh made him sleep, when he should have sorrowed: faith made him promise perseverance, but flesh made him peremptory in that promise: in a word, faith made him resolute to confess, but flesh to contradict his Master. ("Meditations on the Fall and Rising of Peter," in *The Whole Works of the Right Rev. Edward Reynolds, D.D.* [London: B. Holdsworth, 1826], 10–11)

The lesson to learn here is the danger of spiritual overconfidence. As the apostle Paul cautioned, "Therefore let him who thinks he stands take heed that he does not fall" (1 Cor. 10:12; cf. Prov. 16:18).

Peter's fall and restoration may be viewed under two obvious headings: the way down, and the way up.

## THE WAY DOWN

**Having arrested Him, they led Him away and brought Him to the house of the high priest; but Peter was following at a distance. After they had kindled a fire in the middle of the courtyard and had sat down together, Peter was sitting among them. And a servant-girl, seeing him as he sat in the firelight and looking intently at him, said, "This man was with Him too." But he denied it, say-**

ing, **"Woman, I do not know Him." A little later, another saw him
and said, "You are one of them too!" But Peter said, "Man, I am
not!" After about an hour had passed, another man began to
insist, saying, "Certainly this man also was with Him, for he is a
Galilean too." But Peter said, "Man, I do not know what you are
talking about." Immediately, while he was still speaking, a rooster crowed. The Lord turned and looked at Peter. And Peter
remembered the word of the Lord, how He had told him, "Before
a rooster crows today, you will deny Me three times." And he
went out and wept bitterly.** (22:54–62)

Luke condensed Peter's denials, but a comparison with the other
gospel accounts indicates they were stretched out over a period of several hours. They all took place in the courtyard shared by the quarters of
both Annas, the former high priest and still the power behind the scenes,
and Caiaphas, Annas's son-in-law and the current high priest. **Having
arrested** Jesus in Gethsemane, **they led Him away and brought Him
to the house of the high priest.** The trial that ensued before the Jewish
authorities took place in three phases. The first two phases, before Annas,
and then Caiaphas, occurred deep into the night. Since according to Jewish law a trial had to be held in the daylight, there was a third phase after
dawn, to formally legitimize the verdict they had already illegally arrived
at. Interwoven with the trials before Annas and Caiaphas were Peter's
denials.

Five stages in Peter's downfall can be noted, which can also be
viewed as five aspects of his unwarranted self-confidence. First, Peter's
pride was impudent. Back in the upper room Jesus had warned him,
"Simon, Simon, behold, Satan has demanded permission to sift you like
wheat; but I have prayed for you, that your faith may not fail; and you,
when once you have turned again, strengthen your brothers" (Luke
22:31–32). Peter's reaction to Christ's prediction of his fall and ultimate
restoration reveals his audacious brashness. He indignantly protested,
"Lord, with You I am ready to go both to prison and to death!" (v. 33).

Peter's confidence was not only impudent, but also insistent. A
short time later on the Mount of Olives, Jesus predicted that the disciples
would all forsake Him that evening (Matt. 26:30–31). Once again "Peter

said to Him, 'Even though all may fall away because of You, I will never fall away'" (v. 33). Jesus replied, "Truly I say to you that this very night, before a rooster crows, you will deny Me three times" (v. 34), prompting Peter's insistent, repeated (Mark 14:31) reply, "Even if I have to die with You, I will not deny You" (v. 35).

Third, Peter's confidence was indolent. Drastically overestimating his ability to cope with the situation in his own strength, Peter (along with James and John) ignored the Lord's instruction, "Pray that you may not enter into temptation" (Luke 22:40). Instead, he slept when he should have been watching and praying—even after the Lord repeatedly rebuked him for doing so (Matt. 26:40–45).

Fourth, Peter's confidence was impulsive. He wanted to show Jesus that his repeated declaration that he would remain loyal to Him to the end was no idle boast. Therefore when the crowd came to arrest Jesus, Peter impetuously grabbed a sword and attacked, cutting off the ear of the high priest's slave before Jesus stopped him (see the exposition of 22:49–51 in chapter 28 of this volume).

In the end, Peter's confidence imploded. When the crisis came he was not up to the task. His faith wavered and finally gave way, and he denied Jesus three times—just as the Lord had predicted.

As noted above, Jesus' Jewish trial consisted of three phases: a hearing before Annas, and another before Caiaphas and the Sanhedrin, both during the night, and a third after daybreak. The purpose of those hearings was not to fairly, impartially examine any alleged evidence against Jesus. They were instead nothing but attempts to manufacture charges against Him that could be used to convince the Romans to execute Him. In violation of every standard of fairness and justice, Annas interrogated Jesus (John 18:19), even though He had not been charged with any crime, clearly fishing for something he could use against Him. He was acting more like a corrupt prosecutor with no case than the fair, impartial judge he should have been.

When his efforts failed to trap the Lord into incriminating Himself, Annas sent Him to Caiaphas for a hearing with the Sanhedrin. That illegal hearing also failed to produce any legitimate evidence of guilt on Jesus' part. In desperation, the Sanhedrin resorted to using the perjured testimony of false witnesses to accuse Jesus of blasphemy. Like Annas, the Sanhedrin violated every legitimate ethical standard. As judges, they were supposed to fairly, impartially weigh the evidence presented to them. Instead they, like Annas, acted like prosecutors, soliciting testimony against Christ with none in defense. But the testimony of those witnesses contradicted each other (Mark 14:56). Even the testimony of the two witnesses who claimed to have heard Him say that He would destroy the temple was inconsistent (v. 59). Without any credible witnesses against Him, the case against Jesus should have disintegrated into nothing.

They would, however, not let the truth prevail. In desperation, Caiaphas placed Jesus under oath and demanded, "I adjure You by the living God, that You tell us whether You are the Christ, the Son of God" (Matt. 26:63). When He replied, "You have said it yourself; nevertheless I tell you, hereafter you will see the Son of Man sitting at the right hand of power, and coming on the clouds of heaven" (Matt. 26:63–64), Caiaphas had the answer he had hoped for. Jesus had incriminated Himself. In a hypocritical display of supposed devotion to God's glory the high priest "tore his robes [ironically, in violation of the law (Lev. 21:10)] and said, 'He has blasphemed! What further need do we have of witnesses? Behold, you have now heard the blasphemy; what do you think?' They answered, 'He deserves death!'" (vv. 65–66). Once Caiaphas had the "evidence" he so desperately sought and the Sanhedrin had heard Jesus' alleged blasphemy, there was no further need to rely on the testimony of the perjured witnesses. The Sanhedrin was finally able to render the verdict they had already decided on before they heard anything. This disgraceful farce of a trial was over.

> No one was permitted to speak in His defense. No voice of caution was raised at any point in the trial. No plea for mercy was entertained. None of the evidence that supported His claims was ever considered. Jesus was simply railroaded by the high priest's kangaroo court into a guilty verdict that had been arranged and agreed upon long before He ever came to trial. (John MacArthur, *The Murder of Jesus* [Nashville: Word, 2000], 117)

Meanwhile **Peter,** who had fled with the rest of the disciples, turned back and **was following at a distance,** along with another disciple (John 18:15), presumably John. Since John was known to the high priest, he was able to get Peter into the courtyard of the compound shared by Annas's and Caiaphas's residences (v. 16). Peter, standing with some of the high priest's slaves and officers of the temple guard who were warming themselves near a fire (v. 18), was trying to blend in and be undiscovered. His effort to remain anonymous was futile, however, because **a servant-girl** (the female servant stationed at the gate; John 18:17) **seeing him as he sat in the firelight and looking intently at him, said, "This man was with Him too."** Caught off guard and in a panic, Peter blurted out his first denial saying, **"Woman, I do not know Him."** The other gospel writers add that Peter also said, "I am not" (John 18:17); "I do not know what you are talking about" (Matt. 26:70); and "I neither know nor understand what you are talking about" (Mark 14:68). Peter was on his own; Jesus was not there to bail him out. So much for proud confidence. Left to his own resources, he was no match even for a lowly servant girl. R.C.H. Lenski writes,

> It took only a menial maid to fell the chief of the Twelve. Gone were all his high and heroic protestations to Jesus, gone all the spurious courage from his heart and from the hand that had snatched out the sword in Gethsemane. Here stands the arrant coward who is unable to confess his heavenly Lord and cringes in lying denial. (*The Interpretation of St. Luke's Gospel* [Minneapolis: Augsburg, 1961], 1087)

Immediately after this first denial Peter "went out onto the porch" (the corridor leading to the gate) (Mark 14:68) and the first rooster crowed. Unnerved, Peter headed for the exit. But before he could escape he was confronted again; another **man began to insist, saying, "Certainly this man also was with Him, for he is a Galilean too."** Matthew adds that another servant girl (the word translated "another" in Matt. 26:71 is in the feminine form) also identified Peter as having been with Christ, while Mark refers to "the servant-girl" (14:69); presumably the one from the gate who had already accused him repeated her accusation. Bombarded with accusations from all sides, Peter again denied any knowledge of Jesus, this time taking an oath to attest that what he was saying was true (Matt. 26:72).

Whether because his escape was blocked, or because his attachment to Jesus still would not allow him to leave, Peter stayed in the courtyard darkness. After **about an hour had passed,** he was confronted for the third time, when **another man began to insist, saying, "Certainly**

**this man also was with Him, for he is a Galilean too."** This man, a slave of the high priest and a relative of Malchus, whose ear Peter had cut off in Gethsemane, said to him, "Did I not see you in the garden with Him?" (John 18:26). Now thoroughly alarmed, Peter's denial was even more heated and emphatic. In response to this man and the rest of the bystanders who were also accusing him, Peter vehemently denied any knowledge of Jesus and "began to curse and swear" (Matt. 26:74). In addition to reaffirming his false oath that he did not know Jesus, Peter now pronounced God's curses on himself, calling for divine judgment to fall on him if he were lying. What had begun as a single lie to a single girl had escalated into a fury of lying denials to many of the bystanders in the courtyard, accompanied with cursing and swearing.

Dramatically and suddenly two things occurred: **a rooster crowed** for the second time (Mark 14:72) and **the Lord,** at that moment being escorted across the courtyard after leaving His hearing before Caiaphas and the Sanhedrin, **turned and looked at Peter. And Peter remembered the word of the Lord, how He had told him, "Before a rooster crows today, you will deny Me three times."**

The devastating reality of what he had done hit Peter with full force. All that Jesus had predicted he had done. His brash overconfidence had not given him the strength to meet this temptation. He had boasted too much, prayed too little, acted too fast, and followed too far. Overwhelmed with shame, guilt, and grief over what he had done, Peter **went out and wept bitterly.** Face-to-face with the truth of Jesus' prediction and the weakness of his sinful nature, Peter cried out for pardon and forgiveness.

## THE WAY UP

Peter had failed to believe the Lord's warning promise, rejected reproof, slept instead of watching and praying, and ended up boldly setting himself in the middle of the enemies of the Lord. Such audaciousness had led to a shocking, demoralizing defeat.

Still, in God's grace, mercy, compassion, and love, that was not to be the end of the story. After the resurrection, Jesus restored Peter. He granted him three opportunities, corresponding to his three denials, to reaffirm his love for Him (John 21:15–17). Peter's faith had not totally failed, as Jesus had said it would not (Luke 22:32), and he was restored to usefulness, as the early chapters of Acts record. As Jesus had also predicted, Peter later used his experience of failure and restoration to strengthen other Christians. He was able to share the glorious truth that although it may be severely tested, saving faith will never permanently fail (1 Peter 1:6–7; 2 Peter 1:1). Peter also exhorted believers to avoid overconfidence by being on guard, and continuing to grow in grace (2 Peter 3:17–18).

# The Sinless Savior Before the Sinister Sanhedrin (Luke 22:63–71)

# 30

**Now the men who were holding Jesus in custody were mocking Him and beating Him, and they blindfolded Him and were asking Him, saying, "Prophesy, who is the one who hit You?" And they were saying many other things against Him, blaspheming. When it was day, the Council of elders of the people assembled, both chief priests and scribes, and they led Him away to their council chamber, saying, "If You are the Christ, tell us." But He said to them, "If I tell you, you will not believe; and if I ask a question, you will not answer. But from now on the Son of Man will be seated at the right hand of the power of God." And they all said, "Are You the Son of God, then?" And He said to them, "Yes, I am." Then they said, "What further need do we have of testimony? For we have heard it ourselves from His own mouth." (22:63–71)**

The Jewish people of Jesus' day were justly proud of their system of jurisprudence, which was the most carefully constructed one in existence. It was in many respects even superior to our current justice system. Since God is a God of truth, truth was central to Israel's system of justice.

From the very outset God stressed to Israel how essential it was that all judges be focused on the pursuit of truth. When they were about to enter the Promised Land and be established as a nation, God commanded them,

> You shall appoint for yourself judges and officers in all your towns which the Lord your God is giving you, according to your tribes, and they shall judge the people with righteous judgment. You shall not distort justice; you shall not be partial, and you shall not take a bribe, for a bribe blinds the eyes of the wise and perverts the words of the righteous. Justice, and only justice, you shall pursue, that you may live and possess the land which the Lord your God is giving you. (Deut. 16:18–20)

By the time of Christ, Israel's judicial system had become well established. Every town with at least 120 men who were heads of households had a local court known as a Sanhedrin. This council, made up of twenty-three men (seven or three in smaller towns), acted as judge and jury in all legal matters. The Great Sanhedrin in Jerusalem was the final judicial authority in Israel, comparable to the Supreme Court of the United States. It consisted of seventy men from three categories (Mark 14:53): chief priests (mostly Sadducees), elders (religious and secular aristocrats), and scribes (mostly Pharisees).

The law mandated three requirements in a criminal proceeding: a public trial, a defense for the accused, and a confirmation of guilt by two or three witnesses (Deut. 17:6; 19:15; cf. Heb. 10:28). Because the last point was crucial to a just verdict, the law prescribed a severe penalty for false witnesses—the punishment that the accused would have received if he had been guilty was to be inflicted on the liars:

> If a malicious witness rises up against a man to accuse him of wrong-doing, then both the men who have the dispute shall stand before the Lord, before the priests and the judges who will be in office in those days. The judges shall investigate thoroughly, and if the witness is a false witness and he has accused his brother falsely, then you shall do to him just as he had intended to do to his brother. Thus you shall purge the evil from among you. (Deut. 19:16–19)

The rules were particularly strict in capital cases:

> On the day of the trial, the executive officers of justice caused the accused person to make his appearance. At the feet of the Elders were placed men who, under the name of *auditors*, or *candidates*, followed regularly the sittings of the Council. The papers in the case were read; and the witnesses were called in succession. The president addressed this exhortation to each of them: "It is not conjectures, or whatever public rumour has brought to thee, that we ask of thee; consider that a great responsibility rests upon thee: that we are not occupied by an affair, like a case of pecuniary interest, in which the injury may be repaired. If thou causest the condemnation of a person unjustly accused, his blood, and the blood of all the posterity of him, of whom thou wilt have deprived the earth, will fall upon thee; God will demand of thee an account, as he demanded of Cain an account of the blood of Abel. Speak."

> A woman could not be a witness, because she would not have the courage to give the first blow to the condemned person; nor could a child, that is irresponsible, nor a slave, nor a man of bad character, nor one whose infirmities prevent the full enjoyment of his physical and moral faculties. *The simple confession of an individual against himself*, or the declaration of a prophet, however renowned, would not decide a condemnation. The Doctors say—"We hold it as fundamental, that *no one shall prejudice himself*. If a man accuses himself before a tribunal, we must not believe him, unless the fact is attested by two other witnesses; and it is proper to remark, that the punishment of death inflicted upon Achan, in the time of Joshua was an exception, occasioned by the nature of the circumstances; for our law does not condemn upon the simple confession of the accused, nor upon the declaration of one prophet alone."

> The witnesses were to attest to the identity of the party, and to depose to the month, day, hour, and circumstances of the crime. After an examination of the proofs, those judges who believed the party innocent stated their reasons; those who believed him guilty spoke afterwards, and *with the greatest moderation*. If one of the *auditors*, or *candidates*, was entrusted by the accused with his defence, or if he wished in his own name to present any elucidations in favour of innocence, he was admitted to the seat, from which he addressed the judges and the people. But this liberty was not granted to him, if his opinion was in favour of condemning. Lastly; when the accused person himself wished to speak, they gave the most profound attention. When the discussion was finished, one of the judges recapitulated the case; they removed all the spectators; two scribes took down the votes of the judges; one of them noted those which were in favour of the accused, and the other, those

which condemned him. Eleven votes, out of twenty-three, were sufficient to acquit; but it required thirteen to convict. If any of the judges stated that they were not sufficiently informed, there were added two more Elders, and then two others in succession, till they formed a council of sixty-two, which was the number of the Grand Council. If a majority of votes acquitted, the accused was discharged *instantly*; if he was to be punished, the judges postponed pronouncing sentence till the third day; during the intermediate day they could not be occupied with anything but the cause, and they abstained from eating freely, and from wine, liquors, and everything which might render their minds less capable of reflection.

On the morning of the third day they returned to the judgment seat. Each judge, who had not changed his opinion, said, *I continue of the same opinion and condemn*; any one, who at first condemned, might at this sitting acquit; but he who had once acquitted was not allowed to condemn. If a majority condemned, two *magistrates* immediately accompanied the condemned person to the place of punishment. The Elders did not descend from their seats; they placed at the entrance of the judgment hall an officer of justice with a small flag in his hand; a second officer, on horseback, followed the prisoner, and constantly kept looking back to the place of departure. During this interval, if any person came to announce to the Elders any new evidence favourable to the prisoner, the first officer waved his flag, and the second one, as soon as he perceived it, brought back the prisoner. If the prisoner declared to the *magistrates*, that he recollected some reasons which had escaped him, they brought him before the *judges* no less than five times. If no incident occurred, the procession advanced slowly, preceded by a herald who, in a loud voice, addressed the people thus:"This man (stating his name and surname) is led to punishment for such a crime; the witnesses who have sworn against him are such and such persons; if any one has evidence to give in his favour, let him come forth quickly." . . .

At some distance from the place of punishment, they urged the prisoner to confess his crime, and they made him drink a stupefying beverage, in order to render the approach of death less terrible. (M. Dupin, "The Trial of Jesus Before Caiaphas and Pilate," in Simon Greenleaf, *An Examination of the Testimony of the Four Evangelists by the Rules of Evidence Administered in Courts of Justice* [London: A. Maxwell & Son, 1847], 887–90. Italics in original)

But in their murderous zeal to convict and execute Jesus, the Jerusalem Sanhedrin violated the lofty principles of fairness and meticulous concern for justice that marked the Jewish legal tradition. Those violations included,

a. The proceedings took place at the high priest's home and not in the temple (*m. Sanh.* 11.2).
b. Jesus was tried without a defense (*m. Sanh. 4.1* says that both sides of a case must be heard).
c. Jesus was accused of blasphemy without actually blaspheming in the technical sense of the term by pronouncing the divine name (*m. Sanh.* 7.5).
d. The verdict came in the space of one day, when two days were required for a capital trial (*m. Sanh.* 4.1).
e. Jesus was tried on a feast day....
f. Contradictory testimony nullifies evidence (*m. Sanh.* 5.2).
g. A pronouncement of guilt by the high priest is contrary to the normal order, which should start with the least senior members (*m. Sanh.* 4.2). (Darrell L. Bock, *Luke 9:51–24:53* [Grand Rapids: Baker, 1996], 1792)

Jesus' trials unfolded in six phases; three religious trials before the Jewish leaders, and three civil trials before the Gentile rulers Pilate and Herod. The three Jewish tribunals began shortly after midnight, when Jesus was brought before Annas, and lasted until after dawn, when the Sanhedrin formally condemned Him.

Christ's three illegal and unjust trials before the Jewish authorities may be discussed under five headings: the illegal, unjust questioning, the illegal, unjust convening, the illegal, unjust conspiracy, the illegal, unjust condemnation, and the illegal, unjust conduct. To offer the complete picture, material from Matthew and Mark will be used to supplement Luke's account.

## THE ILLEGAL, UNJUST QUESTIONING

After His arrest in Gethsemane, Jesus was taken first to Annas (John 18:12–13), who had been high priest from A.D. 6 to A.D. 15, when Pilate's predecessor as Roman governor removed him from office. Although no longer the high priest, he remained the real power behind the scenes (five of his sons and one of his grandsons had succeeded him in the position and Caiaphas, the current high priest, was his son-in-law).

Annas was notorious for his greed and immense wealth, which had largely come from the businesses in the temple that he and his sons controlled. For example, moneychangers changed foreign currency into Jewish money (at exorbitant rates), which alone could be used to pay the temple tax. Another racket Annas profited from was the sale of animals for sacrifice. People who brought their own animals to the temple would have them rejected by the priests; commonly only those sold there (at exorbitant prices) would be deemed acceptable. Annas and his cohorts would take their cut of the profits from both the moneychangers and the sellers of animals (cf. John 2:14). Annas hated Jesus, because His two assaults on the temple operations affected his economic operations. The scribes and Pharisees, on the other hand, hated and opposed Christ because He exposed their hypocrisy and attacked their self-righteous religious system. Their opposition was theological.

Annas's questioning of Jesus (John 18:19) flagrantly violated established jurisprudence. Since he was no longer the high priest and served in no official capacity, he had no legal authority to conduct what in modern terms would be considered an arraignment or preliminary hearing. Further, his questioning was an attempt to lead Jesus to incriminate Himself, an effort forbidden by Jewish law, just as the Fifth Amendment to the United States Constitution does today.

Christ's reply (vv. 20–21) challenged Annas to investigate the matter legitimately by questioning those who heard His teaching. Seeking to gain favor with the powerful priest, one of the officers struck Jesus and rebuked Him for His alleged disrespect for Annas. This was the first physical maltreatment Christ received. Striking a prisoner, particularly one not accused of a crime, was also illegal, as Jesus pointed out (v. 23; cf. Acts 23:2–3). But this was not an impartial hearing to determine whether there was enough evidence to bring Jesus to trial. The decision had already been made to put Him to death (John 11:53), and Annas was fishing for some legal grounds to justify that action.

## THE ILLEGAL, UNJUST CONVENING

Unable to come up with any evidence to use against Jesus, "Annas sent Him bound to Caiaphas the high priest" (John 18:24). While Annas had been questioning the Lord, Caiaphas had been hurriedly gathering the members of the Sanhedrin. When they were all (Mark 14:53) assembled, the second phase of the Lord's religious trial before the Jewish authorities began.

Like His hearing before Annas, this was also an illegal, clandestine trial; the judges were the lawbreakers. No trial was permitted at night, in private, in a house, or on a feast day (the members of the Sanhedrin celebrated Passover from sundown Thursday to sundown Friday [John MacArthur, *John 12–21*; The MacArthur New Testament Commentary (Chicago: Moody, 2008), 62–63]); there was no indictment and no witnesses; the Sanhedrin was not allowed to originate charges, but adjudicated only those brought before it; they had bribed the traitor, Judas, to lead them to Jesus so they could arrest Him. But the outcome of this trial, like Christ's hearing before Annas, was predetermined. The entire Sanhedrin would now attempt to do what Annas could not, and come up with a justification for the execution verdict.

## THE ILLEGAL, UNJUST CONSPIRACY

Desperately, "the chief priests and the whole Council kept trying to obtain false testimony against Jesus, so that they might put Him to death" (Matt. 26:59). For the highest court in Israel to manufacture a crime and then try to use the testimony of false witnesses to condemn an innocent man (Luke 23:4, 14–15) is shocking and unthinkable. They were unable to find any credible witnesses (Matt. 26:60); those they did secure contradicted each other (Mark 14:56). Finally two witnesses accused Jesus of claiming He would destroy the temple (Mark 14:58), by misinterpreting His words in John 2:19 as a reference to the Jerusalem temple instead of His body. Their testimony, however, was not consistent (Mark 14:59). Additionally, under Jewish law no one could be prosecuted for something he said. Adding to the illegality of this trial was the Sanhedrin's failure to call

any witnesses in defense of Christ, despite His challenge to Annas to interview potential witnesses (John 18:21).

The travesty continued. Like Annas, the entire Sanhedrin (Matt.
26:59) had failed to produce a single valid charge against Jesus, so that
after two hearings, they still had no case against Him.

## THE ILLEGAL, UNJUST CONDEMNATION

Frustrated by Jesus' calm refusal to participate in this mockery of
justice, Caiaphas demanded to know why He refused to answer. He "stood
up and said to Him, 'Do You not answer? What is it that these men are testi-
fying against You?'" (Matt. 26:62). But the Lord still remained silent (v. 63), refusing to give any credence to the testimony of false witnesses, and thereby
indicting the Sanhedrin that had called them. He would also remain
silent before Pilate (Matt. 27:13–14; John 19:9) and Herod (Luke 23:8–9).

Finally, desperate because the Sanhedrin was unable to identify
and manufacture evidence for a real crime, Caiaphas had to go back to
something Jesus had said. He focused on Jesus' claim to be the Messiah
and Son of God. Putting Him under oath, he said to Him, "I adjure You by
the living God, that You tell us whether You are the Christ, the Son of God"
(Matt. 26:63). Jesus replied, "I am; and you shall see the Son of Man sitting
at the right hand of power, and coming with the clouds of heaven" (Mark
14:62). The last vision the world has of Christ will not be of Him on the
cross; He will return in glory to judge the wicked and establish His earthly
kingdom.

Caiaphas was undoubtedly aware that Jesus had claimed to be
the Messiah. Early in His teaching He had applied the messianic text of
Isaiah 61:1–2 to Himself (Luke 4:21). When a Samaritan woman said to
Him, "I know that Messiah is coming (He who is called Christ); when that
One comes, He will declare all things to us" (John 4:25), Jesus said to her,
"I who speak to you am He" (v. 26). On Monday of Passion Week He had
accepted the massive messianic praise of the frenzied crowds. In
response to Caiaphas's charge, Jesus swore by the living God that He was
the Messiah promised in the Old Testament, the anointed king, and the
Son of God (Matt. 26:63–64).

Christ's affirmation of His deity was all Caiaphas needed to hear. In a mock display of horror and grief over God being so dishonored, "the high priest tore his robes and said, 'He has blasphemed! What further need do we have of witnesses? Behold, you have now heard the blasphemy'" (Matt. 26:65). The high priest, hypocritically acting as though Jesus had blasphemed, was the real blasphemer. Since the penalty for blasphemy was death (Lev. 24:16; John 19:7), the Sanhedrin no longer needed to search for false witnesses to testify against Christ, but rendered their verdict. There is no record of a proper vote, which would have begun, in the traditional manner, with the junior members and progressed to the most senior ones. Unilaterally, the high priest pronounced Jesus guilty, and in what was more the act of a lynch mob than the formal judgment of the highest court in the land, the rest of the Sanhedrin cried out, "He deserves death!" (v. 66). Here is yet another illegality in the trials of Christ: in Jewish law, a unanimous vote by the Sanhedrin negated a guilty verdict, since it was considered evidence of a lack of mercy, or even worse, a conspiracy —like this verdict.

## THE ILLEGAL, UNJUST CONDUCT

**Now the men who were holding Jesus in custody were mocking Him and beating Him, and they blindfolded Him and were asking Him, saying, "Prophesy, who is the one who hit You?" And they were saying many other things against Him, blaspheming. When it was day, the Council of elders of the people assembled, both chief priests and scribes, and they led Him away to their council chamber, saying, "If You are the Christ, tell us." But He said to them, "If I tell you, you will not believe; and if I ask a question, you will not answer. But from now on the Son of Man will be seated at the right hand of the power of God." And they all said, "Are You the Son of God, then?" And He said to them, "Yes, I am." Then they said, "What further need do we have of testimony? For we have heard it ourselves from His own mouth." (22:63–71)**

Shockingly, after condemning Jesus the Sanhedrin degenerated into little more than a rabble. Heedless of their dignified position as aristocrats and judges on the supreme court in the land, they completely abandoned self-control and spewed their vitriolic hatred at the Lord Jesus Christ. "They spat in His face" (Matt. 26:7) as Jesus predicted they would (Luke 18:32)—because to spit on someone was the ultimate sign of contempt (Num. 12:14; Deut. 25:9). They also "beat Him with their fists; and others slapped Him" (Matt. 26:67). They **were mocking Him and beating Him, and they blindfolded Him and were asking Him, saying, "Prophesy, who is the one who hit You?" And they were saying many other things against Him, blaspheming.** When the members of the Sanhedrin had had their fill of abusing Jesus, they turned Him over to the officers of the temple police, who continued the abuse (Mark 14:65).

This vile, ugly treatment came as no surprise to the omniscient Lord. In Luke 18:31 "He took the twelve aside and said to them, 'Behold, we are going up to Jerusalem, and all things which are written through the prophets about the Son of Man will be accomplished.'" The Jewish people's treatment of Him was in keeping with their past mistreatment of the prophets (cf. 4:24; 6:22–23; 11:47–50; 13:34–35; 20:9–16; John 4:44; Acts 7:52; Rom. 11:3; 1 Thess. 2:15; Heb. 11:37–38; James 5:10).

After they finished abusing Christ, **when it was day, the Council of elders of the people assembled, both chief priests and scribes, and they led Him away to their council chamber.** As noted earlier, the previous hearings before Annas and Caiaphas were blatantly illegal. But they were careful to observe the correct legal protocol in this theatrical show trial, which was designed to put a veneer over their corruption of truth and justice.

Going through the motions as if this were a fair, impartial trial they asked Jesus, **"If You are the Christ, tell us."** Before giving His answer, He replied, **"If I tell you, you will not believe; and if I ask a question, you will not answer."** Jesus made it clear that the Sanhedrin was not concerned about the evidence, fairness, truth, or justice. But His claim to be the Son of God was the truth, so He reaffirmed His identity by declaring: **"From now on the Son of Man will be seated at the right hand of the power of God." Son of Man** was the designation for Messiah in Daniel 7:13–14:

I kept looking in the night visions, and behold, with the clouds of heaven one like a Son of Man was coming, and He came up to the Ancient of Days and was presented before Him. And to Him was given dominion, glory and a kingdom, that all the peoples, nations and men of every language might serve Him. His dominion is an everlasting dominion which will not pass away; and His kingdom is one which will not be destroyed.

The Son of Man was to be given "dominion, glory and a kingdom" and be served by all the world. That is consistent with being given the most exalted place, the seat **at the right hand of the power of God,** a promise made directly by the Father to the Son in Psalm 110:1: "The Lord says to my Lord: 'Sit at My right hand until I make Your enemies a footstool for Your feet'" (cf. Matt. 22:41–45; Acts 2:33–35; Rom. 8:34; Col. 3:1; Heb. 10:12–13). Making sure for the record what Jesus was saying, **they all said, "Are You the Son of God, then?"** to which the Lord replied, **"Yes, I am."** Reprising their roles from the earlier illegal hearing at Caiaphas's house, **they said, "What further need do we have of testimony? For we have heard it ourselves from His own mouth."**

By condemning the Lord of glory (1 Cor. 2:8), the members of the Sanhedrin condemned themselves; all those who wrongly judge Jesus Christ will be rightly judged by Him. They ignored His miracles, which gave evidence that He was who He claimed to be (John 10:25, 38; 14:11), and His unparalleled teaching (Matt. 7:28–29; John 7:46). As a result, they condemned themselves to hell, as do all who fail to make the right judgment concerning Christ.

# Christ's Civil Trials—Part 1: Preliminary Hearings Before Pilate and Herod (Luke 23:1–12)

**31**

Then the whole body of them got up and brought Him before Pilate. And they began to accuse Him, saying, "We found this man misleading our nation and forbidding to pay taxes to Caesar, and saying that He Himself is Christ, a King." So Pilate asked Him, saying, "Are You the King of the Jews?" And He answered him and said, "It is as you say." Then Pilate said to the chief priests and the crowds, "I find no guilt in this man." But they kept on insisting, saying, "He stirs up the people, teaching all over Judea, starting from Galilee even as far as this place." When Pilate heard it, he asked whether the man was a Galilean. And when he learned that He belonged to Herod's jurisdiction, he sent Him to Herod, who himself also was in Jerusalem at that time. Now Herod was very glad when he saw Jesus; for he had wanted to see Him for a long time, because he had been hearing about Him and was hoping to see some sign performed by Him. And he questioned Him at some length; but He answered him nothing. And the chief priests and the scribes were standing there, accusing Him vehemently. And

**Herod with his soldiers, after treating Him with contempt and mocking Him, dressed Him in a gorgeous robe and sent Him back to Pilate. Now Herod and Pilate became friends with one another that very day; for before they had been enemies with each other.** (23:1–12)

This passage introduces two more figures of the rogue's gallery of characters in the unfolding drama of Christ's death: Pilate, the Roman governor of Judea, and Herod Antipas, the tetrarch of Galilee (Luke 3:1). Those two Gentile rulers would conduct the three phases of the Lord's civil trial.

Both Pilate and Herod were confident in their authority, but in reality neither had power over Jesus except what was granted to them by God. Pilate's question to the crowds, "What shall I do with Jesus who is called Christ?" (Matt. 27:22), presumed that he had authority to sit in judgment on Him. But when Pilate said to Him, "Do You not know that I have authority to release You, and I have authority to crucify You?" (John 19:10), Jesus answered, "You would have no authority over Me, unless it had been given you from above" (v. 11). Neither Pilate nor Herod was in charge of determining Christ's destiny. That had been predetermined by God in eternity past (Acts 2:23; 4:27–28). And in fact, Jesus will sit in judgment on them to determine their eternal destinies (John 5:22–30; Acts 10:42; Rom. 2:16; 2 Tim. 4:1,8).

The Sanhedrin had plotted to kill Jesus (John 11:47–53), and had confirmed that sentence in illegal trials after His initial hearing before Annas. Even so, they did not have the authority to execute Him (John 18:31), and thus were forced to bring Him before Pilate for the death sentence. From their perspective, the Sanhedrin did not want Jesus killed in an act of mob violence, like the stoning of Stephen, but wanted to maintain the veneer of justice. From God's perspective, Christ had to be executed by the Romans to fulfill prophecy. The language of Psalm 22 makes it clear that Jesus would be crucified. In Matthew 20:18–19 Jesus predicted that "the Son of Man will be delivered to the chief priests and scribes, and they will condemn Him to death, and will hand Him over to the Gentiles to mock and scourge and crucify Him, and on the third day He will be raised up" (cf. John 12:32). That He would be lifted up suits the Roman practice of crucifixion. The Jews preferred to execute people by throwing them down off a parapet before stoning them.

In a display of heinous unanimity **the whole body of** the Sanhedrin **got up and brought** Jesus **before Pilate.** They sought by such solidarity to demonstrate the justice of their cause; surely Pilate would not believe that the entire Sanhedrin could be wrong. In truth, that unanimity, as noted in the previous chapter of this volume, was considered evidence of a lack of mercy and rendered their verdict illegal.

Before looking at Christ's first hearing with Pilate, there is one matter that needs to be concluded: the tragic end of Judas Iscariot. When he left Gethsemane after betraying Christ, Judas evidently made his way to Annas's house and followed the Lord's two trials. What he had done was so incalculably wicked and the guilt so unbearable he should have fled, but was drawn to observe the unfolding of his deed, as torturous as it may have been.

Matthew records that when Judas saw that Jesus had been condemned and was being led away to Pilate for trial, "he felt remorse and returned the thirty pieces of silver to the chief priests and elders" (Matt. 27:3). His remorse was not true repentance, but mere worldly sorrow. In the volume on 2 Corinthians in this series I wrote the following, contrasting genuine biblical repentance with worldly sorrow:

> True biblical repentance is not psychological, emotional human remorse, seeking merely to relieve stress and improve one's circumstances. Though it inevitably produces the fruit of a changed life (cf. Matt. 3:8; Luke 3:8; Acts 26:20), it is not behavioral, but spiritual. The sorrow of the world—remorse, wounded pride, self-pity, unfulfilled hopes—has no healing power, no transforming, saving, or redeeming capability. It produces guilt, shame, resentment, anguish, despair, depression, hopelessness, even, as in the case of Judas (Matt. 27:3–5), death. (John MacArthur, *2 Corinthians*, The MacArthur New Testament Commentary [Chicago: Moody, 2003], 266)

In desperation, Judas sought to relieve the intense agony his guilt produced by attempting to undo what he had done. He "returned the thirty pieces of silver to the chief priests and elders, saying, 'I have sinned by betraying innocent blood'" (Matt. 27:3–4). Since Judas had been complicit in the plot to kill Jesus, he was in effect a false witness. He approached the Sanhedrin and declared that he had been wrong, and offered new testimony of Jesus' innocence. By law such testimonies were the court's duty to consider. Here also was a man suffering the torment of a slaughtered conscience, and as the spiritual leaders of Israel, they should have had compassion on him.

But Judas had served his purpose in their plans, and they had no further use for or interest in him. They callously dismissed him, saying, "What is that to us? See to that yourself!" (Matt. 27:4). Their harsh, uncaring treatment of Judas confirmed Jesus' characterization of them as those who "tie up heavy burdens and lay them on men's shoulders, but they themselves are unwilling to move them with so much as a finger" (Matt. 23:4).

After they dismissed him, Judas "threw the pieces of silver into the temple sanctuary and departed" (Matt. 27:5). "Sanctuary" translates the Greek word *naos*, which refers to the Holy Place, into which only the priests were allowed to enter. Judas forced the priests to take the money back (they used it to buy a field as a burial place; Matt. 27:6–10), but that did nothing to relieve his tormented conscience. Tortured by guilt so intense that death seemed a welcome relief, Judas "went away and hanged himself" (Matt. 27:5).

Meanwhile, Christ's trial before the Gentile rulers Pilate and Herod, like His Jewish trial before Annas, Caiaphas, and the Sanhedrin, unfolded in three phases. This passage relates the first two of those phases: His preliminary hearings before Pilate and Herod. The elements unfold in six stages: the accusation, the interrogation, the exoneration, the intimidation, the disposition, and the confirmation.


## THE ACCUSATION


**And they began to accuse Him, saying, "We found this man misleading our nation and forbidding to pay taxes to Caesar, and saying that He Himself is Christ, a King." (23:2)**

After formally condemning Jesus in a hearing shortly after dawn, the Sanhedrin brought Him before Pilate at his temporary headquarters (probably either at Fort Antonia or Herod's palace; Pilate's permanent location was at Caesarea). Since they had ceremonially cleansed themselves to eat the Passover meal later that day and did not want to become defiled by entering a Gentile dwelling, they refused to go into Pilate's headquarters (John 18:28).

In deference to their scruples Pilate, in the first lawful behavior so far in any of Christ's trials, "went out to them and said, 'What accusation do you bring against this Man?'" (v. 29). Feigning offense, they haughtily "answered and said to him, 'If this Man were not an evildoer, we would not have delivered Him to you'" (v. 30). Annoyed by their flippant, arrogant, disrespectful response to his formal request for the charges against Jesus, Pilate fired back at them, "Take Him yourselves, and judge Him according to your law" (v. 31).

Pilate was aware of the events of the week. He knew of the triumphal entry, the cleansing of the temple, and the large crowds who listened to Jesus' teaching, all of which caused the Jewish leaders to hate and envy Him (Matt. 27:18). But those were all Jewish issues, and no concern of his. He had not yet seen any evidence that Jesus had committed any crime against Rome. Pilate saw that the Sanhedrin wanted him to execute Jesus, but the failure to bring any legitimate charge against Him strongly suggested His innocence.

The Sanhedrin, forced to acknowledge that they had no authority to put anyone to death (John 18:31), and realizing that Pilate would not execute Jesus for blasphemy, a crime under Jewish law, invented false charges of insurrection. They said Jesus was **misleading** the **nation** into rebellion, **forbidding** them **to pay taxes to Caesar, and saying that He Himself is Christ, a King.** Those were serious crimes which, if true, would have compelled Pilate to take action to protect Rome's interests. All of them, however, were false. Jesus had never advocated rebellion against Rome. Nor did He teach the people not to pay taxes to Rome; in fact, He taught just the opposite (Luke 20:21–25). While Jesus is **a King,** His kingdom at His first advent was not an earthly one in opposition to Rome, as He would soon make clear to Pilate. Nor did the Sanhedrin offer any evidence to support those lies; they gave no specific instances of the Lord's alleged misconduct, called no witnesses, and instead impugned Pilate for questioning the legitimacy of their intent.

## THE INTERROGATION

**So Pilate asked Him, saying, "Are You the King of the Jews?" And He answered him and said, "It is as you say."** (23:3)

Pilate was familiar with the vehement protests of innocent men. But to his amazement, while Jesus "was being accused by the chief priests and elders, He did not answer" (Matt. 27:12). Even when "Pilate said to Him, 'Do You not hear how many things they testify against You?' " (v. 13), the Lord "did not answer him with regard to even a single charge" (v. 14). Leaving the Sanhedrin waiting outside, Pilate went back inside his headquarters and summoned Jesus for a private interrogation (John 18:33).

Incredulous that this man before him could be a king who posed a threat to Rome, **Pilate asked . . . "Are You the King of the Jews?"** Before answering that question the Lord proposed a counter question, "Are you saying this on your own initiative, or did others tell you about Me?" (John 18:34), intended to clarify the matter. If the question was Pilate's, he would be asking whether Jesus was a king in a political, earthly sense. In that case, He could be a potential threat to Rome. Jesus' answer would then be no; He was not a political or military leader. But Pilate was merely repeating the Sanhedrin's charge, as his reply, "I am not a Jew, am I? Your own nation and the chief priests delivered You to me" (v. 35), indicates.

However, Pilate was still no nearer to understanding the Jewish leaders' violent animosity toward Jesus and what, if any, crime He had committed to bring their animosity to this level. Perplexed, he tried once again to grasp the nature of the issue. "What have You done?" he asked Him (v. 35). Since it was obvious that Pilate was repeating the charge of the Jewish leaders, Jesus answered his question accordingly. He was Israel's true king, but not an earthly one who might threaten Rome's rule. "My kingdom is not of this world. . . . My kingdom is not of this realm," He replied (v. 36). To make certain that he finally understood the issue, "Pilate said to Him, 'So You are a king?' Jesus answered, 'You say correctly that I am a king. For this I have been born, and for this I have come into the world, to testify to the truth. Everyone who is of the truth hears My voice'"

(v. 37). Pilate's cynical response, "What is truth?" (v. 38) reflects the skeptical and cynical attitude of all who despair of finding the truth. He was, however, satisfied that Christ was not guilty of any crime against Rome.

### THE EXONERATION

**Then Pilate said to the chief priests and the crowds, "I find no guilt in this man."** (23:4)

Satisfied that Jesus was innocent, **Pilate said to the chief priests and the crowds** that had gathered, **"I find no guilt in this man"** (cf. vv. 14–15; Matt. 27:19, 24; Mark 15:14; John 18:38; 19:4, 6). His official ruling was that the Lord Jesus was not guilty of the crime against Rome the Sanhedrin had leveled against Him (see the discussion of v. 2 above).

### THE INTIMIDATION

**But they kept on insisting, saying, "He stirs up the people, teaching all over Judea, starting from Galilee even as far as this place."** (23:5)

The Jewish leaders vehemently disagreed with Pilate's verdict. Driven by vicious hatred of Jesus, they **kept on insisting, saying, "He stirs up the people, teaching all over Judea, starting from Galilee even as far as this place."** As far as they were concerned, Pilate's exoneration of Christ was not the end of the story. They had no interest in justice, but only wanted Pilate to accommodate their hatred. They had no case; there was no valid evidence, and no witnesses. All that was left for them was to try to intimidate Pilate into pronouncing Jesus guilty and executing Him.

Pilate was trapped. He knew Jesus was innocent. He was also afraid of Him because of His supernatural powers (John 19:7–9). But Pilate was clearly intimidated by the possibility that the Jewish leaders would cause him trouble with Caesar—which they would soon threaten to do (John 19:12).

## THE DISPOSITION

**When Pilate heard it, he asked whether the man was a Galilean. And when he learned that He belonged to Herod's jurisdiction, he sent Him to Herod, who himself also was in Jerusalem at that time.** (23:6–7)

The Jews' reference to Galilee suggested to Pilate a possible way out of his dilemma. Since they had mentioned Galilee, Pilate **asked** them **whether** Jesus was a **Galilean.** When he **learned** from them that He was and thus **belonged to Herod's jurisdiction, he sent Him to Herod, who himself also was in Jerusalem at that time.** It was not unusual for one ruler to transfer a prisoner to be tried before another; Festus, one of Pilate's successors as Roman governor of Judea, brought Paul's case before another member of the Herod family, Herod Agrippa II (Acts 25:23–27).

## THE CONFIRMATION

**Now Herod was very glad when he saw Jesus; for he had wanted to see Him for a long time, because he had been hearing about Him and was hoping to see some sign performed by Him. And he questioned Him at some length; but He answered him nothing. And the chief priests and the scribes were standing there, accusing Him vehemently. And Herod with his soldiers, after treating Him with contempt and mocking Him, dressed Him in a gorgeous robe and sent Him back to Pilate. Now Herod and Pilate became friends with one another that very day; for before they had been enemies with each other.** (23:8–12)

The account of the Lord's hearing before Herod appears only in Luke's gospel. Herod Antipas was one of the sons of Herod the Great, who died after a long rule in 4 B.C. When he died, his kingdom was divided among his sons. Herod Antipas was given Galilee and Peraea, over which he ruled from 4 B.C. to A.D. 39. With the exception of the accounts of Christ's birth, Antipas is the Herod who appears in the Gospels' record of Jesus' life and ministry.

Since Rome was in control of Israel, even though he was appointed ruler by his father, Antipas had to go to Rome to have his appointment confirmed. When he was young, his father, Herod the Great, had sent Antipas to Rome to be educated. Because of his connections in Rome, Antipas was able to secure his appointment.

When he returned to Palestine to begin his rule, the region was in turmoil. Earlier in that same year during the feast of Pentecost, a rebellion broke out, which devastated the area. When Antipas came back, he faced a massive rebuilding project. He built the city of Sepphoris, not far from Nazareth. Completed about A.D. 10, it became one of the chief cities of Galilee. Since Nazareth was only about four miles away, it is possible that Joseph, the husband of Mary the mother of Jesus, may have helped build Sepphoris. Antipas also built the city of Tiberius, in honor of Tiberius Caesar. Eventually the lake became known as the Lake of Tiberius.

Antipas married the daughter of Aretas IV, who ruled over the neighboring realm of Nabatea (the region Paul referred to in Gal. 1:17). This marriage was designed by Rome to unify the area. But while visiting his half-brother Herod Philip I in Rome, Antipas became infatuated with Philip's wife Herodias and had an affair with her. She was not only Herod Philip's wife, but was also Antipas's niece, making their affair not only adulterous, but also incestuous. She agreed to leave her husband and marry Antipas, provided that he divorce Aretas's daughter. It was for this illicit divorce and marriage to his brother's wife that John rebuked Antipas, provoking the wrath of Herodias, who eventually had John the Baptist beheaded (Matt. 14:3–11).

Antipas related to Jesus on three occasions. The first came shortly after the death of John the Baptist:

> Now Herod the tetrarch heard of all that was happening; and he was greatly perplexed, because it was said by some that John had risen from the dead, and by some that Elijah had appeared, and by others that one of the prophets of old had risen again. Herod said, "I myself

had John beheaded; but who is this man about whom I hear such things?" And he kept trying to see Him. (Luke 9:7–9)

Antipas is also mentioned in connection with Jesus in Luke 13:31–33:

Just at that time some Pharisees approached, saying to Him, "Go away, leave here, for Herod wants to kill You." And He said to them, "Go and tell that fox, 'Behold, I cast out demons and perform cures today and tomorrow, and the third day I reach My goal.' Nevertheless I must journey on today and tomorrow and the next day; for it cannot be that a prophet would perish outside of Jerusalem."

The third time Antipas actually met Jesus in the event recorded here. As noted above Pilate, seeking a way out of his dilemma, sent Jesus to Antipas, since he was the ruler over Galilee. Antipas **was very glad when he saw Jesus; for he had wanted to see Him for a long time** (cf. Luke 9:9), **because he had been hearing about Him and was hoping to see some** miraculous **sign performed by Him.**

But although **he questioned Him at some length,** Jesus **answered him nothing.** As He had before Pilate, the Lord also ignored the assaults of **the chief priests and the scribes,** who **were standing there, accusing Him vehemently.** This was shocking behavior on the part of someone accused of serious crimes. As noted earlier, such people invariably either loudly protested their innocence, or desperately pled for mercy. It was also an affront to the ruler to pointedly ignore him. But though Jesus "was oppressed and He was afflicted, yet He did not open His mouth; like a lamb that is led to slaughter, and like a sheep that is silent before its shearers, so He did not open His mouth" (Isa. 53:7).

Having been beaten and abused by the Sanhedrin and their officers (Mark 14:65), Jesus did not look like the man Herod had expected. He certainly did not appear to be a revolutionary; He had no army, no weapons, and no defenders. Finding the accusation unfounded and ridiculous (Luke 23:14–15) Antipas, **with his soldiers, after treating Him with contempt and mocking Him, dressed Him in a gorgeous** (lit., "brilliant," "shining," "radiant") **robe and sent Him back to Pilate.**

Luke adds as a footnote that **Herod and Pilate became friends with one another that very day; for before they had been**

**enemies with each other.** They had clashed on at least two occasions. Not only had Pilate slaughtered some of Antipas's Galilean subjects (Luke 13:1), but Herod had also gone over Pilate's head to Caesar to force Pilate to remove some Roman shields from his palace. At this point, however, the two men formed a friendship built around their mistreatment of Jesus and around a common hatred for the intimidating Jewish leaders that they had to deal with.

Herod's life ended in disgrace:

> Herodias would ultimately prove to be Herod's downfall. After Emperor Caligula granted Herodias's brother Agrippa I (Acts 12:1) the title of king, she demanded that Herod go to Rome and obtain the same title. (The gospel references to him as king [Matt. 14:9; Mark 6:14, 22] reflect informal popular usage of the term.) But before Herod and Herodias reached Rome, a messenger from Agrippa accused Herod of wrongdoing. As a result, Caligula deposed Herod who, accompanied by Herodias, was banished permanently to a city in what is now France.

> Antipas and Herodias are reminiscent of another ill-fated couple, Ahab and Jezebel. "Like Ahab," writes D. A. Carson, "Antipas was wicked but weak; and Herodias, like Jezebel, wicked and ruthless" (*Matthew*, in Frank E. Gaebelein, ed. The Expositor's Bible Commentary [Grand Rapids: Zondervan, 1984], 8:338). Antipas's weakness coupled with Herodias's ruthlessness ensured that eventually their sins could only bring disastrous consequences. (John MacArthur, *Luke 1–5*, The MacArthur New Testament Commentary [Chicago: Moody, 2009], 230–31)

The story of the Lord's hearing before Herod serves three important purposes. First, it confirms Pilate's verdict that Jesus was not guilty of any crime. Second, Herod and Pilate are two witnesses that confirm Jesus' innocence (cf. Deut. 19:15). Neither of them was biased in His favor; Pilate was indifferent to Him, and Herod had sought to kill Him (Luke 13:31). Finally, it confirms prophecy (Ps. 2:2; cf. Acts 4:25–27).

# Christ's Civil Trials—Part 2: The Final Verdict from the Fickle Judge (Luke 23:13–25)

## 32

Pilate summoned the chief priests and the rulers and the people, and said to them, "You brought this man to me as one who incites the people to rebellion, and behold, having examined Him before you, I have found no guilt in this man regarding the charges which you make against Him. No, nor has Herod, for he sent Him back to us; and behold, nothing deserving death has been done by Him. Therefore I will punish Him and release Him." [Now he was obliged to release to them at the feast one prisoner.] But they cried out all together, saying, "Away with this man, and release for us Barabbas!" (He was one who had been thrown into prison for an insurrection made in the city, and for murder.) Pilate, wanting to release Jesus, addressed them again, but they kept on calling out, saying, "Crucify, crucify Him!" And he said to them the third time, "Why, what evil has this man done? I have found in Him no guilt demanding death; therefore I will punish Him and release Him." But they were insistent, with loud voices asking that He be crucified. And their voices began to

**prevail. And Pilate pronounced sentence that their demand be granted. And he released the man they were asking for who had been thrown into prison for insurrection and murder, but he delivered Jesus to their will.** (23:13–25)

This passage relates the sixth and final phase of the illegal and unjust trials of the Lord Jesus Christ. Recapping, the first three phases comprised Christ's religious trial before the Jewish leaders, Annas, Caiaphas, and the Sanhedrin; the last three His civil trial before the Gentile rulers Pilate and Herod. Shortly after dawn on Friday of Passion Week, the Sanhedrin had conducted a brief tribunal. The purpose of that trial was to give the illusion of legitimacy to the false verdict of blasphemy they had already arrived at in their previous hearing. They waited until daybreak because Jewish law forbade any trial to be held at night.

Having decided to murder the Lord, the Sanhedrin brought Him to Pilate, since the Romans withheld from them the right of capital punishment. Knowing Pilate would not execute Jesus for blasphemy, a Jewish offense irrelevant to Rome, the Sanhedrin falsely accused Him of fomenting rebellion against Caesar. But Pilate, unable to find any evidence to support such a charge, sent Jesus to Herod who, unable to find evidence of guilt, returned Him to Pilate. Despite being repeatedly declared innocent by Pilate, Herod, and even Pilate's wife, Jesus was sentenced to death as if He were guilty.

The entire series of trials was filled with irony. The one whom men judged is the judge of all men; the one whom men condemned will eternally condemn them. The perfectly righteous, sinless, and innocent one was condemned as a blasphemer and criminal. The one who always pleased holy God did not please sinful men. Men sought to kill the very one who gave them life. The Lord Jesus Christ was declared a blasphemer for claiming to be who He truly is, making His accusers blasphemers. All of the wicked participants in Christ's trials who judged and condemned Him did nothing but what God had predetermined must happen. Their decisions did not determine His fate, but rather their own. They wasted the most monumental, unparalleled opportunity that anyone could ever have—a personal encounter with the Son of the living God, the Creator of the universe and the Redeemer of sinners.

What is striking about this passage is the majestic silence of Jesus. The one who is "Immanuel ... God with us" (Matt. 1:23); the "Holy and Righteous One" (Acts 3:14; cf. John 6:69); the one whom to know is to know God (John 8:19), to hate is to hate God (John 15:23), to believe is to believe God (John 12:44), to see is to see God (John 14:9), to honor is to honor God (John 5:23), and to receive is to receive God (Mark 9:37); the creator of everything that exists (John 1:3; Col. 1:16) and judge of everyone (John 5:22), the only savior of sinners (John 14:6); the glorious Lord before whom every knee will bow (Phil. 2:10) is virtually anonymous; almost an afterthought. Both Pilate (vv. 14, 22) and the Jewish leaders (v. 18) refer to Him simply as "this man." Only Luke identifies Him as "Jesus" (vv. 20, 25). The scene is shocking, as corrupt men hold mock trials and condemn the Lord of life to death.

Pilate's handling of this final phase of Christ's trials may be discussed under five headings: his adjudication, his accommodation, his alternative, his assertion, and his acquiescence.

## His Adjudication

**Pilate summoned the chief priests and the rulers and the people, and said to them, "You brought this man to me as one who incites the people to rebellion, and behold, having examined Him before you, I have found no guilt in this man regarding the charges which you make against Him. No, nor has Herod, for he sent Him back to us; and behold, nothing deserving death has been done by Him. (23:13–15)**

Pontius **Pilate** had been appointed the fifth governor of Judea by Emperor Tiberius in A.D. 26 and held that position for about ten years. He was proud, arrogant, brutal, and cynical (cf. John 18:38), but could also be weak and vacillating. Nothing is known of Pilate's career before he became governor, but he must have served in a series of lesser posts before being appointed to represent Rome in Judea. His duties would have required him to have knowledge of and experience in military, administrative, and judicial matters. That he really existed is attested to by

Tacitus, Philo, and Josephus, and by the Pilate Stone, discovered in Caesarea in 1961 and dating from Pilate's lifetime. The names of Tiberius Caesar and Pilate are inscribed on it.

Subsequent to their nighttime trials of Jesus, probably just after 5 A.M., the Sanhedrin had rushed Him to Pilate. The governor, after a brief preliminary hearing, sent Him to Herod, who questioned Him (and got no answers from Him), abused Him, and returned Him to Pilate, who then rendered his final verdict at about 6 A.M. (John 19:14). Obviously, three trials of such magnitude could not possibly have been completed in approximately one hour without an extensive abuse of the due process of law—as was the case in the three phases of the Jewish trial.

Word of Jesus' triumphal entry, assault on the temple operations, verbal confrontations with the Jewish leaders, and teaching had spread all through Jerusalem. But the governor knew that Jesus posed no threat to Rome. He also knew that the Jewish leaders were envious of Him (Matt. 27:18). Resentful of being pressured by the Jews to execute an innocent man, Pilate initially stood his ground against them. After receiving Jesus back from Herod, Pilate **summoned the chief priests and the rulers and the people,** mentioned here for the first time, **and said to them, "You brought this man to me as one who incites the people to rebellion, and behold, having examined Him before you, I have found no guilt in this man regarding the charges which you make against Him."**

But Pilate's attempt to take a stand on legal ground and thwart the Jewish leaders' murderous intent to kill Jesus was doomed to failure. And pressure would mount because they had Pilate at a severe disadvantage due to some previous blunders that he had made.

The first of those came shortly after he took office. Previous governors had wisely chosen not to bring emblems bearing Caesar's image into Jerusalem. They knew that doing so would provoke the Jews, who viewed them as idolatrous. Pilate, however, sent his soldiers into Jerusalem one night bearing standards with the image of Caesar. The next morning when they saw the standards, the Jews were furious. Protesters went to Pilate's permanent headquarters in Caesarea and demanded that he remove the offending standards. Pilate stubbornly refused to do so, or even to discuss the matter with them.

Finally, in exasperation, he agreed to see them. But instead of dialoguing, Pilate ordered his soldiers to surround them, and then threatened to execute them if they did not stop pestering him. When it became apparent that they might be prepared to die, Pilate was forced to withdraw his impetuous threat. There was no way he could have carried out such a massacre without severe repercussions from the Jews and Rome. Pilate's superiors were not pleased with his handling of this incident. He was charged with keeping the peace, yet his stubborn, hot-tempered folly had almost provoked a riot.

Pilate also enflamed the Jewish people by using money from the temple treasury to build an aqueduct to bring more water to Jerusalem. When the Jews predictably were outraged and protested, Pilate sent soldiers dressed in civilian clothes into the crowd. On his signal, they attacked and dispersed the protesters, killing many in the process.

Again conflict arose when Pilate had shields made in honor of Tiberius Caesar and hung them on a wall (a common way of honoring people in that day) in Herod's palace in Jerusalem. But the inscription on them referred to Tiberius as divine, and the Jews were severely offended. When Pilate rejected their pleas to remove the shields, the Jewish leaders protested to Emperor Tiberius, who angrily ordered Pilate to move the shields to the pagan temple of Augustus in Caesarea.

Further, Pilate's brutal slaughter of some Galileans in the temple (Luke 13:1) also did not endear him to his Jewish subjects.

The governor, then, had been on thin ice. One more riot, disturbance, or complaint reported to Rome could cost him his position. Eventually, an incident would force Pilate out, but ironically, as will be seen later in this chapter, it would involve not the Jews but their despised enemies, the Samaritans.

Pilate's appeal to the Sanhedrin's expected sense of justice as members of the highest court in Israel was doomed to fail. The Jewish leaders did not care that **Herod** found no guilt in Jesus, since he had **sent Him back to** them, nor were they swayed by Pilate's official judgment that **nothing deserving death** had **been done by Him.** Pilate was trapped in a situation rapidly escalating out of control. He would have to find a way to extricate himself.

## His Accommodation

**Therefore I will punish Him and release Him."** (23:16)

Hoping the Jews might be satisfied if Jesus was tortured and then set free, he declared, **"I will punish Him and release Him." Punish** is not the specific word for scourging, but is a form of the verb *paidueō*, which refers to the intent of such affliction—correction. The Romans sometimes punished people who had not been convicted of a crime, but may have been heading in that direction. Pilate was hoping that scourging Jesus (Matt. 27:26) would placate the Jews.

## His Alternative

**[Now he was obliged to release to them at the feast one prisoner.] But they cried out all together, saying, "Away with this man, and release for us Barabbas!" (He was one who had been thrown into prison for an insurrection made in the city, and for murder.)** (23:17–19)

Before he carried out his plan to punish and release Jesus, another thought occurred to Pilate. Verse 17 does not appear in the oldest Greek manuscripts of Luke, but Matthew 27:15 and Mark 15:6 indicate that Pilate **was obliged to release to them at the feast one prisoner.** Granting amnesty to a prisoner generated goodwill among Rome's subjects, and Pilate did so once a year at Passover.

Offering to release Jesus under this amnesty program seemed to be a reasonable alternative for Pilate. After all, he knew that Jesus was enormously popular with the people, as the events so far in Passion Week seemed to demonstrate. It made sense to bypass the leaders and appeal to His popularity among the people, who hopefully would then pressure their leaders into accepting Jesus' release.

Pilate offered to release either Barabbas, a notorious criminal **who had been thrown into prison for an insurrection made in the city, and for murder,** or Jesus. Barabbas was headed for crucifixion; in fact, the two robbers crucified along with Jesus may have participated with Barabbas in the insurrection. His name means "son of a father"; in a strange irony, Pilate was offering them the choice between Barabbas, the son of a human father, and Jesus, the Son of the heavenly Father.

At that critical point, the proceedings were interrupted: "While [Pilate] was sitting on the judgment seat, his wife sent him a message, saying, 'Have nothing to do with that righteous Man; for last night I suffered greatly in a dream because of Him'" (Matt. 27:19). She believed Jesus was a good and righteous man, not a criminal. She was afraid of her husband executing an innocent man, particularly this man—so afraid that her fears entered her dreams.

But while Pilate was listening to the message and mulling over its significance, the leaders of Israel seized the opportunity to manipulate the crowd against Jesus. Instead of asking for Pilate to release Him as the governor had assumed they would, **they cried out all together, saying, "Away with this man, and release for us Barabbas!"** The passionate adulation with which the people had greeted Jesus as Israel's Messiah on Monday had been twisted into contempt and lust for His death.

Pilate was trapped. He knew Jesus was not a revolutionary and he had assumed the crowd would ask for His release. Now he was in the unenviable position of not only having to execute a man he had officially declared innocent, a breach of justice, but also being forced to release a known and dangerous revolutionary, a breach of duty.

## His Assertion

**Pilate, wanting to release Jesus, addressed them again, but they kept on calling out, saying, "Crucify, crucify Him!" And he said to them the third time, "Why, what evil has this man done? I have found in Him no guilt demanding death; therefore I will punish Him and release Him." But they were insistent, with loud voices asking that He be crucified. And their voices began to prevail.** (23:20–23)

Trying to keep control of the rapidly disintegrating situation **Pilate,** still **wanting to release Jesus, addressed** the crowd **again.**

359

Surprised by their unexpected rejection of Jesus in favor of Barabbas, "Pilate said to them, 'Then what shall I do with Jesus who is called Christ?'" (Matt. 27:22), adding cynically, mockingly, "whom you call the King of the Jews?" (Mark 15:12). They replied in unison, **"Crucify, crucify Him!"**

After **he said to them the third time** that he had **found in** Jesus **no guilt demanding death,** Pilate revisited his earlier alternative (see the discussion of v. 16 above) and announced to the crowd, **"I will punish Him and release Him."** But it was too late for that, as the crowd had become **insistent, with loud voices asking that He be crucified. And their voices began to prevail. Insistent** translates a form of the verb *epikeimai*, which is used in Luke 5:1 of the crowd pressing in on Jesus on the shore of the Sea of Galilee, and in Acts 27:20 of the raging storm that hit the ship taking Paul to Rome. The word vividly describes the mob's intensity; roaring at Pilate like the howling wind of a violent storm, demanding that he crucify Jesus. **And their voices began to prevail.**

The pressure on Pilate had become irresistible. The frenzied crowd, urged on by its apostate Jewish leaders, was starting to riot (Matt. 27:24). Pilate knew that one more major incident would be the end of his career. He was forced to choose between protecting himself and protecting Jesus; he could not do both. In a symbolic and feeble gesture to indicate he was innocent of responsibility for Christ's death, Pilate "took water and washed his hands in front of the crowd, saying, 'I am innocent of this Man's blood; see to that yourselves'" (Matt. 27:24). Pilate used a Jewish (Deut. 21:1–9) custom to visually divest himself of any guilt in this unjust crime they had pressured him into allowing.

Their reaction was chilling: "And all the people said, 'His blood shall be on us and on our children!'" (Matt. 27:25). They assumed full responsibility for Christ's death—a responsibility that the Sanhedrin would later try to deny when they accused Peter and the apostles of "intend[ing] to bring this man's [Christ's] blood upon us" (Acts 5:28). But by their own words they claimed guilt for the death of the Son of God (Acts 2:22–23).

## His Acquiescence

**And Pilate pronounced sentence that their demand be granted. And he released the man they were asking for who had been thrown into prison for insurrection and murder, but he delivered Jesus to their will.** (23:24–25)

With no other choice, **Pilate pronounced sentence that** the people's **demand be granted.** Then, after **he released the man they were asking for who had been thrown into prison for insurrection and murder** (Barabbas), **he delivered Jesus to their will.** Both Matthew (27:26) and Mark (15:15) note that Pilate had Jesus scourged before delivering Him to be crucified.

The apostle John, however, reveals more details about what happened between Pilate's sentencing of the Lord and his delivering of Him to be crucified. After Pilate's soldiers finished scourging Jesus (John 19:1)—a punishment so brutal that many prisoners died from it—they placed a crown made of thorns on His head and dressed Him in a purple robe (probably one of the soldiers' cloaks) in mocking imitation of a king's royal robe (v. 2). Matthew 27:29 adds they put a reed in Christ's hand as if it were a royal scepter. The soldiers then began playing a cruel game with Jesus, mockingly treating Him as if He were really an earthly king (John 19:3). They also slapped Him in the face (v. 3) and beat Him on the head with the reed (Mark 15:19).

While they were enjoying their mocking game, "Pilate came out again and said to [the crowd], 'Behold, I am bringing Him out to you so that you may know that I find no guilt in Him'" (v. 4), thus declaring Christ's innocence yet again. When Jesus, beaten, bloodied, and wearing the crown of thorns, was led out, Pilate said dramatically, "Behold, the Man!" (v. 5). But if he hoped the sight of the Lord in that condition would elicit sympathy from the crowd, he was mistaken. Like sharks sensing blood in the water, "when the chief priests and the officers saw Him, they cried out saying, 'Crucify, crucify!'" (v. 6).

That was enough for Pilate. Wanting simply to be done with the whole sorry affair, "Pilate said to them, 'Take Him yourselves and crucify Him, for I find no guilt in Him'" (v. 6). Whether Pilate was actually giving them the right to execute Jesus or only mocking them again is not clear. But that he would even mention granting them the jealously guarded prerogative of capital punishment is further evidence that he was losing control.

They replied, "We have a law, and by that law He ought to die because He made Himself out to be the Son of God" (v. 7). As governor, Pilate was expected to uphold local laws insofar as they did not conflict with Rome's interests. The Jewish leaders demanded that Pilate honor their legal rights and order Jesus to be executed.

Now even more alarmed, Pilate took Jesus back inside. "Where are You from?" he demanded. Jesus, however, remained silent (v. 9). Though Pilate may have been cynical (cf. 18:38), he also, like many Romans, was superstitious. If Jesus had divine powers, or perhaps was a god or son of a god in human form (cf. Acts 14:11), he had just scourged and beaten someone who had supernatural power to take vengeance on him.

Exasperated by Jesus' continued silence and apparent lack of respect for his dignity and authority, Pilate boasted, "Do You not know that I have authority to release You, and I have authority to crucify You?" (v. 10) His boast was a hollow one, because while Pilate may have had the right to do both, he did not have the courage to do either.

Breaking His silence at last, Jesus replied, "You would have no authority over Me, unless it had been given you from above" (i.e., from God) (v. 11). Like everyone else involved in the death of the Lord Jesus Christ, Pilate did not have control over what was happening. God was in absolute, sovereign control.

In desperation Pilate repeated his effort to release Jesus, with no success. Playing their trump card, the "Jews cried out saying, 'If you release this Man, you are no friend of Caesar; everyone who makes himself out to be a king opposes Caesar'" (v. 12). That brought an end to Pilate's delaying. If the Jews reported their lie to Caesar that he had released a revolutionary, especially one who made himself out to be a king in opposition to Caesar, it would be the end of Pilate's career— maybe even his life. He had to pronounce immediately the sentence they demanded.

The governor therefore brought Jesus out, sat down on his official judgment seat, and with one final sarcastic taunt said to the Jews, "Behold, your King!" (v. 14), suggesting that this beaten, bloodied, helpless man was all the king they deserved. Furious, "they cried out, 'Away with Him, away with Him, crucify Him!'" (v. 15). Perhaps in one final act of cynicism and scorn, Pilate asked them, "Shall I crucify your King?" In a startling expression of blatant hypocrisy the chief priests replied, "We have no king but Caesar." In yet one more bitter irony, those who had falsely accused Jesus of blasphemy themselves blasphemed, since God alone was Israel's true King (cf. Judg. 8:23; 1 Sam. 8:7; Ps. 149:2; Isa. 33:22). Israel's apostasy had reached its nadir. But although they thought they were through with Jesus, they were not. One day they will face Him as their eternal judge (John 5:22–29). With all aspects of the trial done, Pilate handed Jesus over to be crucified by his own soldiers and escaped his own demotion for a while.

The incident that finally led to Pilate's removal from his position of power involved not the Jews, but the Samaritans. A group of them planned to climb Mt. Gerizim looking for valuable objects allegedly hidden on its summit by Moses. Assuming the Samaritans were about to revolt, Pilate ordered his troops to attack, and many of the Samaritans were killed. Outraged at Pilate's murderous violence against them, the Samaritans complained to his immediate superior, the governor of Syria. He removed Pilate from office and ordered him to Rome to be judged by Emperor Tiberius. But Tiberius died while Pilate was en route to Rome. Nothing is known for certain about Pilate after he reached Rome. Some accounts claim he was banished; others that he was executed; still others that he committed suicide. His cowardly injustice in sentencing the innocent Lord Jesus Christ to death to save his career ultimately failed. Later, as recorded in Acts 4, the disciples, looking back, saw all the elements of the trial and death of the Lord Jesus as fulfilled prophecy and the precise purposes of God taking place:

> And when they heard this, they lifted their voices to God with one accord and said, "O Lord, it is You who made the heaven and the earth and the sea, and all that is in them, who by the Holy Spirit, through the mouth of our father David Your servant, said, 'Why did the Gentiles rage, and the peoples devise futile things? The kings of the earth took their stand, and the rulers were gathered together against the Lord and

against His Christ.' For truly in this city there were gathered together against Your holy servant Jesus, whom You anointed, both Herod and Pontius Pilate, along with the Gentiles and the peoples of Israel, to do whatever Your hand and Your purpose predestined to occur. (Acts 4:24–28)

# Characters on the Road to the Cross (Luke 23:26–32)

# 33

**When they led Him away, they seized a man, Simon of Cyrene, coming in from the country, and placed on him the cross to carry behind Jesus. And following Him was a large crowd of the people, and of women who were mourning and lamenting Him. But Jesus turning to them said, "Daughters of Jerusalem, stop weeping for Me, but weep for yourselves and for your children. For behold, the days are coming when they will say, 'Blessed are the barren, and the wombs that never bore, and the breasts that never nursed.' Then they will begin to say to the mountains, 'Fall on us,' and to the hills, 'Cover us.' For if they do these things when the tree is green, what will happen when it is dry?" Two others also, who were criminals, were being led away to be put to death with Him.** (23:26–32)

The crucifixion of the Lord Jesus Christ is the most heinous act of apostasy and rebellion against God ever. The Jewish people had waited for centuries for the coming of the promised Savior and Messiah. But when He finally came, in spite of His unparalleled teaching, revelation of divine truth, offer of eternal life, and divine power over the demonic realm, the natural world, disease, and death, they rejected Him. "He came to His own," John wrote, "and those who were His own did not receive Him" (John 1:11).

Jesus' earthly journey to the cross began thirty-three years before His death in the small village of Bethlehem, near Jerusalem. He was born in the humblest of surroundings—a stable, with a manger for a crib. Soon after His birth, His journey took Him, along with Mary and Joseph, south into Egypt for protection from Herod, who sought to murder Him. After that danger had passed, His parents took Him north from Egypt into Galilee to their nondescript home hamlet of Nazareth. And there His life seemingly paused for thirty years.

When the Son of God reached thirty, His journey took Him to the Jordan River, where He was baptized by John the Baptist, and launched into public ministry. After three years of ministry Jesus came to Jerusalem for the last week of His life. As this section opens, it is Friday morning of that final week. Jesus would be crucified later that afternoon, and dead and buried before sundown. Here Luke records the final steps of Jesus' journey to Skull Hill (Luke 23:13).

The exact location of the site where the Lord was crucified is unknown. It may have been the traditional site, now obscured by a Roman Catholic church, the more recent one known as Gordon's Calvary, or a different site altogether. The location of His execution is not important; the redemption accomplished through His death is eternally unequalled in importance.

Temporally, Christ's journey to Skull Hill lasted thirty-three years. But that was simply the final step of a journey that began in heaven, the dwelling place of the eternal Trinity. Every step of the way was preordained, which is why the Bible describes Jesus as the Lamb slain from [before] the foundation of the world (Rev. 13:8 KJV); who had come to "save His people from their sin" (Matt. 1:21); and "did not come to be served, but to serve, and to give His life a ransom for many" (Mark 10:45). Contrary to the false teaching of some, Jesus' death came as no surprise to Him. In fact, He had repeatedly predicted it, in all its gruesome details (Luke 9:22, 31; 12:50; 13:32–33; 17:25; 18:31–33; 20:9–15; 22:22, 37).

Obviously, Jesus draws the primary attention on these final steps to the cross. He is the only one who speaks and that only once, and only on one topic—judgment. But along the way other characters appear in lesser roles. We meet the mixed murderers, the supporting stranger, the curious crowd, the weeping women, and the companion criminals.

## THE MIXED MURDERERS

**When they led Him away,** (23:26*a*)

The pronoun **they** refers to those listed in verse 13, "the chief priests and the rulers and the people." The chief priests included the Sadducees, who ran the temple operations, and the high priest and the former high priests, who were all related to one another. The rulers were the members of the ruling Sanhedrin, made up predominantly of scribes and Pharisees, along with some Sadducees. The growing crowd that gathered early that Friday morning was orchestrated and manipulated by the religious rulers into demanding the crucifixion of Jesus. Although they are not mentioned, some members of a third Jewish sect, the Herodians (Jews who supported the Idumean dynasty), no doubt also were present. Of course the Roman soldiers who made up the execution squad that performed the actual crucifixion were also present.

*Apagō* (**led away**) is sometimes used as a legal term to refer to leading someone to trial, punishment, prison, or execution (Matt. 26:57; 27:2; Mark 14:44; Acts 12:19).

Driven by their self-righteousness and hatred, these murderers orchestrated Jesus' execution by means of lies, manipulation, intimidation, and threats—thus bringing about the greatest miscarriage of justice the world has ever seen. The mixed multitude that pressed for His death represents all those who reject Jesus Christ in every generation (cf. Heb. 6:4–6).

## The Supporting Stranger

**they seized a man, Simon of Cyrene, coming in from the country, and placed on him the cross to carry behind Jesus.** (23:26*b*)

On the way to the place of execution the Roman soldiers in charge of Christ's crucifixion **seized a man** and pressed him into service (which they had absolute authority to do; cf. Matt. 5:41). Unlike the Roman soldiers and the centurion, who later believed in Christ (23:47; cf. Matt. 27:54; Mark 15:39), this man's name is given, **Simon,** as is the town he was from, **Cyrene. Simon** was a common Jewish name (there are nine men in the Bible named Simon, including two of the apostles). **Cyrene** was a city in North Africa, in modern-day Libya. It had a significant Jewish population, according to the first-century Jewish historian Josephus. Visitors from Cyrene were in Jerusalem on the Day of Pentecost and heard the apostles preaching in their language (Acts 2:10). There were enough men in Jerusalem from Cyrene that they, along with men from Alexandria (another major North African city), formed their own synagogue (Acts 6:9).

Simon was seemingly chosen at random while **coming in from the country** to Jerusalem to celebrate Passover. Unless he had been in the city earlier in the week, he would not necessarily have known anything about Jesus. The soldiers **placed on him the cross to carry behind Jesus.** This was not the usual procedure, since the condemned were required to carry their cross to the execution site. Perhaps in His weakened condition from scourging the Lord could no longer carry the cross by Himself and needed help. Or it may be that He was not moving fast enough to suit the soldiers.

Simon was in fact not chosen at random; God was sovereignly reaching down to draw him (cf. John 6:44). Mark 15:21 further describes him as "the father of Alexander and Rufus." That note obviously meant something to his readers, or Mark would not have included it. According to the traditional view, Mark addressed his gospel to a Gentile audience, initially the church at Rome—of which Simon's son Rufus was a prominent member (Rom. 16:13). Paul also refers to Rufus's mother, Simon's wife, as having been like a mother to him.

Here was a stranger, seemingly plucked spontaneously from the crowd to help carry Jesus' cross. Having gone all the way to Skull Hill with the cross, Simon would undoubtedly have stayed and experienced the full reality of the crucifixion. At some point he embraced the gospel of the Lord whose cross he had carried. His wife and sons also became believers and were known to the church at Rome. One of them, Rufus, was singled out by Paul as a choice servant of the Lord, and Simon's wife ministered to the apostle (Rom. 16:13). The church at Cyrene, in which Simon undoubtedly played a significant role, developed and grew strong, eventually sending out missionaries to preach the gospel to the Gentiles at Antioch (Acts 11:20). One of its members, Lucius, even served as one of the pastors at the Antioch church when Paul and Barnabas were sent out as missionaries (Acts 13:1).

## The Curious Crowd

**And following Him was a large crowd of the people,** (23:27*a*)

Many in the **large crowd of the people** that was **following** Christ had enthusiastically greeted Him on Monday at the triumphal entry. But He did not fulfill their expectations; He showed no sign of being the military and political deliverer they longed for, the one who would free them from the yoke of Roman tyranny. Instead of attacking the Romans, He attacked the temple operations (Luke 19:45–46), the heart of Israel's religion, and the leaders themselves (Matt. 23:1–36). The Lord's talk of His own imminent death further perplexed them, since there was no place in their theology for a dying Messiah (cf. Matt. 16:21–22).

The vacillating crowd did not know whether to praise Jesus or reject Him. Eventually, they reached such a state of confusion that the leaders of Israel were able to persuade them to demand His crucifixion. They were aware of His divine power, and hoped that He might be their Messiah. But they ultimately turned against Him, persuaded by their leaders' blasphemous lies that His power was from Satan, not God. They were also disappointed. After Christ's death, "all the crowds who came together for this spectacle, when they observed what had happened, began to return, beating their breasts" (Luke 23:48) in a universal sign of grief. They wanted Him to be their Messiah; probably until the very last, some of them were wishing that Christ would be the one who would fulfill their desires. Perhaps, at the last moment, He would come down from the cross, as His enemies mockingly challenged Him to do (Mark 15:32), and lead an assault against the Romans.

As throughout His ministry, the crowd had an interest in Jesus, but few made a true commitment to Him. Their minds were dark. They were ignorant; they were not responsive to the truth He taught. Their feelings toward Him were ambiguously selfish. They were not His enemies, but neither would they confess Him as Lord. Ultimately they were manipulated to cry for His death.

## THE WEEPING WOMEN

**and of women who were mourning and lamenting Him. But Jesus turning to them said, "Daughters of Jerusalem, stop weeping for Me, but weep for yourselves and for your children. For behold, the days are coming when they will say, 'Blessed are the barren, and the wombs that never bore, and the breasts that never nursed.' Then they will begin to say to the mountains, 'Fall on us,' and to the hills, 'Cover us.' For if they do these things when the tree is green, what will happen when it is dry?"** (23:27b–31)

The **women who were mourning and lamenting** Jesus were not His mother, Mary Magdalene, or any of the other women who accompanied Him and the disciples (Luke 8:2–3); they were professional mourners. It was traditional for women to mourn at the death of someone (cf. Luke 8:51–52), particularly someone prominent like Jesus, who many had hoped would be the Messiah. But though they were official mourners who were doing their duty, surely it was not without a measure of sincerity and sympathy. Nowhere in the Gospels is there a record of a woman who was hostile to Jesus, rebuked Him, or spoke evil of Him. These women were likely no exception.

**Mourning** translates a form of the verb *koptō*, which literally refers to pounding one's chest in a strong expression of grief. It symbolizes the agony of death. **Lamenting** refers to crying and wailing, or singing a dirge (the same verb used here is translated "sang a dirge" in Luke 7:32).

This mourning was not the fulfillment of Zechariah 12:10–14, which refers to Israel's yet future mourning when they "will look on [the one] whom they have pierced; and they will mourn for Him, as one mourns for an only son, and they will weep bitterly over Him like the bitter weeping over a firstborn" (v. 10). The time will come when the people will pound their chests and wail and lament, mourning over the tragic reality that they killed their own Messiah, but this was not that time.

These women represent those who were sympathetic toward Jesus, who were attracted to Him, finding in Him truth, tenderness, and compassion. They were not like the curious crowd, who were fickle, vacillating, and indifferent, nor were they like the mixed murderers, who hated and resented Jesus. But neither were they His true followers, those who had believed savingly in Him. Christianity is filled with people who are in some measure sympathetic to Jesus yet are not truly His disciples (Matt. 7:21–23; John 6:60, 66).

Jesus, however, did not seek that kind of sympathy. Instead of thanking the women, He rebuked them. **Turning to them** the Lord **said, "Daughters of Jerusalem, stop weeping for Me."** The phrase **Daughters of Jerusalem** is used in the Old Testament to refer metaphorically to Israel as a whole (Mic. 4:8; Zeph. 3:14; Zech. 9:9). Instead of weeping for Him, Jesus told them to **weep** tears of sorrow, remorse, and repentance **for** themselves **and for** their **children** in light of the judgment that was coming (cf. Luke 13:34–35; 19:41–44; and the exposition of 21:20–24 in chapter 20 of this volume). They, not Jesus, were the real victims.

The judgment that would fall on them in A.D. 66–70, when the Romans devastated Israel and destroyed Jerusalem, would be so severe that Jesus solemnly warned, **"For behold, the days are coming when they will say, 'Blessed are the barren, and the wombs that never bore, and the breasts that never nursed.'"** That was a shocking statement. Barrenness ran counter to the hope of every Jewish woman and was the worst stigma imaginable, as the stories of Hannah (1 Sam. 1:2–11) and Elizabeth (Luke 1:7, 24–25) illustrate. But speaking earlier of that time of terrible judgment Jesus had said, "Woe to those who are pregnant and to those who are nursing babies in those days; for there will be great distress upon the land and wrath to this people" (Luke 21:23). Such women would endure greater suffering than those without children.

Christ's prediction, **"Then they will begin to say to the mountains, 'Fall on us,' and to the hills, 'Cover us,'"** further indicates the severity of the imminent judgment. The Lord was quoting Hosea's warning to the apostate northern kingdom of Israel regarding the destruction of its capital city of Samaria by the Assyrians (Hos. 10:8). When the sixth seal judgment hits during the tribulation, the unbelieving world will "[say] to the mountains and to the rocks, 'Fall on us and hide us from the presence of Him who sits on the throne, and from the wrath of the Lamb; for the great day of their wrath has come, and who is able to stand?'" (Rev. 6:16–17). Israel's judgment in A.D. 66–70 was thus a preview of the future judgment of the world.

Jesus did not offer a final invitation to the people who were accompanying Him on the way to the cross, but rather pronounced a final doom on them. Their perspective was totally skewed. They needed to shed tears not for Him, but for themselves in light of their impending judgment.

The Lord concluded His warning with the proverbial saying, **"For if they do these things when the tree is green, what will happen when it is dry?"** He is the green tree, full of life and fruitfulness. If this is what the Romans did to Him, what will they do to the dry, dead, barren nation of Israel in A.D. 70?

THE COMPANION CRIMINALS

**Two others also, who were criminals, were being led away to be put to death with Him.** (23:32)

The final two characters on the road to the cross **were criminals,** who **were being led away to be put to death with** Jesus. As noted in the discussion of Luke 23:19 in the previous chapter of this volume, they may have participated with Barabbas in the insurrection and like him been sentenced to be crucified.

These two men illustrate the two options that face every person. Those who, like the one who repented (23:40–43), "confess with [their] mouth Jesus as Lord, and believe in [their] heart that God raised Him from the dead ... will be saved" (Rom. 10:9). On the other hand, those who, like the unrepentant man, reject Jesus will face eternal judgment (John 3:18). For more information on these two men, see the exposition of Luke 23:39–43 in chapter 34 of this volume.

# The King Crucified: The Comedy at Calvary (Luke 23:33–49)

**34**

When they came to the place called The Skull, there they crucified Him and the criminals, one on the right and the other on the left. But Jesus was saying, "Father, forgive them; for they do not know what they are doing." And they cast lots, dividing up His garments among themselves. And the people stood by, looking on. And even the rulers were sneering at Him, saying, "He saved others; let Him save Himself if this is the Christ of God, His Chosen One." The soldiers also mocked Him, coming up to Him, offering Him sour wine, and saying, "If You are the King of the Jews, save Yourself!" Now there was also an inscription above Him, "This is the king of the Jews." One of the criminals who were hanged there was hurling abuse at Him, saying, "Are You not the Christ? Save Yourself and us!" But the other answered, and rebuking him said, "Do you not even fear God, since you are under the same sentence of condemnation? And we indeed are suffering justly, for we are receiving what we deserve for our deeds; but this man has done nothing wrong." And he was saying, "Jesus, remember me when

**You come in Your kingdom!" And He said to him, "Truly I say to you, today you shall be with Me in Paradise." It was now about the sixth hour, and darkness fell over the whole land until the ninth hour, because the sun was obscured; and the veil of the temple was torn in two. And Jesus, crying out with a loud voice, said, "Father, into Your hands I commit My spirit." Having said this, He breathed His last. Now when the centurion saw what had happened, he began praising God, saying, "Certainly this man was innocent." And all the crowds who came together for this spectacle, when they observed what had happened, began to return, beating their breasts. And all His acquaintances and the women who accompanied Him from Galilee were standing at a distance, seeing these things.** (23:33–49)

The cross, with its injustice, cruelty, and suffering, was anything but a comedy. But the people who participated in the events of that day at Calvary turned it into one. To them it was a ludicrous, farcical event, a joke, the butt of which was Jesus. They found the idea that He was the king of the Jews to be laughable; and **were sneering at Him, mocked Him,** and were **hurling abuse at** Him. Jesus had already been stripped of His freedom when He was arrested, stripped of His rights when He was unjustly condemned, stripped of His friends when they all forsook Him, stripped of His ministry, and even stripped of His clothing, down to a loin cloth. All of that, however, was not enough to satisfy His enemies; they were about to strip Him of His life. In doing so, they wanted to make sure that they stripped Him of His honor, His dignity, and any respect that He might still command.

To that end they designed and staged the execution of Jesus to be a comical satire. They enthroned Him on a cross like a king enthroned above the people. On His head they placed a crown—not a gold crown, but a crown of thorns, sending blood streaming down His face. In their diabolical comedy, they crucified one thief on the right of Jesus and one on the left in a parody of a king's two most respected courtiers, the second and the third most honorable people in his court. Then they mockingly offered Him wine, as if doing their duty to serve the monarch's needs. Earlier in Pilate's judgment hall, they had put a rough soldier's cloak on Him as if it were a royal robe, with a reed as a royal scepter in His hand, and mockingly hailed Him as a king.Then they took the reed and beat Him in the head with it and spat on Him to show their utter disdain for the notion that He was royalty.

To the Jewish people, the idea of a crucified Messiah was absurd, ridiculous, and incomprehensible. They expected the messiah to be a conquering king, who would defeat Israel's enemies and establish his kingdom.They were looking for a coronation, not a crucifixion; for a messiah who killed his enemies, not one who was killed by his own people. The cross was foolishness to them (1 Cor. 1:18); a massive stumbling block that they could not get past (v.23).

But instead of proving that Jesus was not the Messiah, the cross proved that He was. The crucifixion fulfilled Old Testament prophecy. Psalm 22 gives a vivid description of crucifixion, features unknown in David's day. Isaiah, also writing at a time when crucifixion was unknown in Israel, wrote that Jesus "was pierced through for our transgressions, He was crushed for our iniquities; the chastening for our well-being fell upon Him, and by His scourging we are healed" (Isa. 53:5). Christ's crucifixion is also in view in Zechariah 12:10, where the prophet wrote,

> I will pour out on the house of David and on the inhabitants of Jerusalem, the Spirit of grace and of supplication, so that they will look on Me whom they have pierced; and they will mourn for Him, as one mourns for an only son, and they will weep bitterly over Him like the bitter weeping over a firstborn.

From God's viewpoint, however, what Christ's enemies thought was comical was deadly serious. In verses 28 and 29 of this chapter, Jesus said to the professional mourners following Him on the road to Calvary, "Daughters of Jerusalem, stop weeping for Me, but weep for yourselves and for your children. For behold, the days are coming when they will say, 'Blessed are the barren, and the wombs that never bore, and the breasts that never nursed'" (see the exposition of those verses in the previous chapter of this volume). This was not a time for laughing, but for weeping.

Execution by crucifixion dates back to the sixth century B.C. when it was apparently invented by the Persians.The earliest reference to the practice is the crucifixion of three thousand Babylonians by the Persian king Darius. Alexander the Great crucified two thousand citizens of Tyre in revenge for their treatment of him. The first-century B.C. Hasmonean king of Judea, Alexander Jannaeus, crucified eight hundred rebels. The Romans used crucifixion extensively, and perfected it as a brutal means of torture. After the capture of Jerusalem in A.D. 70, for instance, the Romans crucified so many Jews that they ran short of lumber.

The biblical account of the crucifixion of the Lord Jesus is remarkably restrained; it is not the physical sufferings of Jesus that are unique, but rather what they accomplished. Each of the gospel accounts use merely three Greek words (four words in English) to describe the actual crucifixion. For example, there are no details given about the hammering of the nails, the raising of the cross, or the elements that produce death. No such explanation was necessary for the Gospels' initial readers, since crucifixion was all too familiar to them. The Romans always crucified their victims in public places along highways so that everyone could see the horrible results of rebellion against Rome's authority.

In keeping with the Gospels' understated description of the crucifixion, the location of the **place called The Skull** (Aramaic "Golgotha"; Latin "Calvaria") is unknown. As noted in the previous chapter of this volume, it may have been the traditional site, now obscured by a Roman Catholic church, the more recently proposed site known as Gordon's Calvary, or a different site altogether. The New Testament does not describe the site as a hill, but it was customary for the Romans to crucify people in an elevated place to give the passersby a clear view. The place was perhaps called The Skull because it resembled a skull. Others believe that it was so named because the skulls of the people who were crucified were left lying around, though it is unlikely that the Jews would have permitted that. In either case, the name is associated with the gruesome reality of death.

Through the years there has been a lot of study done on the physical aspects of crucifixion. Perhaps the most concise and helpful treatment appeared in the March 21, 1986, issue of the *Journal of the American Medical Association* (vol. 255, no. 11) in an article entitled, "On the Physical Death of Jesus Christ" (William D. Edwards, MD; Wesley J. Gabel, MDiv; Floyd E. Hosmer, MS, AMI). According to that study everyone who was crucified was first beaten. The victim's arms were lifted up and tied to a pole, leaving him in a slumped position. Braided leather thongs with bits of metal and bone embedded in them were used to lash the victim from the bottom of the neck down to the back of the knees. Two lictors (attendants of Roman magistrates) hit him with alternating blows. There are no indications as to how many lashes the victims customarily received; that was at the discretion of the lictors. The bone and the metal would rip into the flesh, causing deep contusions and lacerations into the subcutaneous tissues, and then into the fabric of the muscles. The resulting pain and blood loss would lead to circulatory shock.

All three men crucified that day were scourged. But the soldiers, in their mockery of Jesus, put a robe on Him made of wool that would have irritated His open wounds. They also placed a crown of thorns on His head, beat Him in the head with a stick, and spat on Him. At some point, they tore the robe off Him, which would have ripped open the wounds. Further, the hematidrosis (bloody sweat) He experienced (Luke 22:44) made His skin hypersensitive. The Lord also suffered from lack of sleep, lack of food, and lack of water.

Crucifixion was a slow death, intended to inflict maximum agony and suffering. The victims carried their crosses, or at least the crosspiece, across the back of their necks and shoulders with their arms tied to it. Jesus received help from Simon of Cyrene in carrying His cross, either because in His weakened condition He could no longer carry it, or perhaps because He was not moving fast enough to suit the soldiers.

Arriving at the place of crucifixion, the prisoners would be offered sedation (which Jesus refused; Matt. 27:34) and then be thrown to the ground on their backs. The crosspiece would then be pulled under their shoulders and their arms nailed to it using tapered iron spikes five to seven inches long, and about a half inch square. They were driven through the wrists rather than the palms of the hands so they could carry the full weight of the slumping body.

The impaled victim was then lifted up, and the crosspiece was attached to the upright post, often called the stipes. The feet were then nailed with one nail, the knees bent up so that the victims could push up on the wounds in their feet as well as pull up on the wounds in their wrists in order to breathe. The sagging position of the body with the knees bent made it impossible to breathe steadily; the soldiers could cause death in minutes by breaking the victims' legs (cf. John 19:31–32). Needless to say, no one survived crucifixion.

The agonizing pain those crucified endured is almost incomprehensible. The most extreme word in English language to describe pain is the word "excruciating," which comes from the Latin word *excruciatus*, meaning "out of the cross." In order to breathe, a person had to pull and push himself up, causing the wounds on his back from the scourging to rub painfully on the rough wood of the cross. The nails in the wrists would crush or sever the long sensory radial motor median nerve, causing relentless bolts of pain. The nails in the feet would likely pierce the deep perineal and plantar nerves, causing the same results.

The weight of the body on the nail wounds as the victim struggled to push and pull himself upright to catch a breath caused pain so intense that he could not survive long. "It is likely that this form of respiration would not suffice and that hypercarbia [the presence of an abnormally high level of carbon dioxide in the blood] would soon result. The onset of muscle cramps or tetanic contractions, due to fatigue and hypercarbia, would hinder respiration even further" ("On the Physical Death of Jesus Christ," 1461).

When death finally, mercifully came hours or days later, the Roman soldiers confirmed it by piercing the victim's chest with a spear. The resulting flow of blood and water (serous pleural and pericardial fluid; John 19:34) would indicate death.

The mockery of the Lord Jesus Christ at the crucifixion was the ultimate act of sin and blasphemy. Here was sin at its apex; blasphemy at its pinnacle, as sinners mocked the Divine Son, sneered at the incarnate God, and with glib satisfaction piled sarcastic scorn on the Creator and Redeemer, the true King and Savior. Should not the true and holy God incarnate, who had revealed Himself as such by giving convincing proofs of His deity, react to such blasphemy in holy anger and swift judgment? To do so would have been consistent with the teaching of the Old Testament, where God declares, "The one who blasphemes the name of the Lord shall surely be put to death" (Lev. 24:16). Ironically the Jewish leaders, not content merely to blaspheme the Lord Jesus Christ, perversely accused Him of being a blasphemer (Matt. 9:3; 26:65; John 10:33).

Crucifying the Son of God deserved heaven's most immediate and severe judgment.Yet God mercifully delayed His punishment of the nation until A.D. 70. Such a delay in judgment is consistent with God's merciful nature.For example,despite Israel's sin (Isa.1:1–16),God repeatedly promised salvation, instead of immediate judgment, to those who repented and believed (Isa. 40:1–2; 41:14; 42:6–7; 43:1–7; 52:7–10; 53; 55:1–9). God was patient in the days of Noah, waiting 120 years before history's most extensive judgment. But God's patience has an end; His judgment will fall on the nation that abused and mocked His Son, and the comedy at Calvary would lead to sorrow of eternal proportions. But that was still future when the comedy plays out in this passage in four acts: the contrast,the conversion,the consummation,and the responses.

## THE CONTRAST

**But Jesus was saying, "Father, forgive them; for they do not know what they are doing." And they cast lots, dividing up His garments among themselves. And the people stood by, looking on. And even the rulers were sneering at Him, saying, "He saved others; let Him save Himself if this is the Christ of God, His Chosen One." The soldiers also mocked Him, coming up to Him, offering Him sour wine, and saying, "If You are the King of the Jews, save Yourself!" Now there was also an inscription above Him, "This is the king of the Jews." One of the criminals who were hanged there was hurling abuse at Him, saying, "Are You not the Christ? Save Yourself and us!"** (23:34–39)

The contrast in this passage between the merciless insults of the crowd and the merciful intercession of Christ on their behalf is striking.

### THE MERCILESS INSULTS OF THE CROWD

**And they cast lots, dividing up His garments among themselves. And the people stood by, looking on. And even the rulers were**

**sneering at Him, saying, "He saved others; let Him save Himself if this is the Christ of God, His Chosen One." The soldiers also mocked Him, coming up to Him, offering Him sour wine, and saying, "If You are the King of the Jews, save Yourself!" Now there was also an inscription above Him, "This is the king of the Jews." One of the criminals who were hanged there was hurling abuse at Him, saying, "Are You not the Christ? Save Yourself and us!"** (23:34b–39)

The crowd at Calvary consisted of four distinct groups. First were the common **people,** who **stood by looking on** as the comedy staged by their leaders and the Romans played out. They might have been expected to be more sympathetic to Christ than the religious leaders, soldiers, and two thieves crucified with Him. After all, just a few days earlier they had hailed Jesus as the Messiah at the triumphal entry. They had also enthusiastically received His teaching in earlier days (Luke 19:47–48).

But during Christ's trial before Pilate, the leaders had managed to turn the people against Him and persuade them to call for His crucifixion (Matt. 27:20–23). Now they had joined in the farcical game and were mercilessly hurling abuse and venomous sarcasm at Him (Matt. 27:39–40).

The **rulers** were insulting, taunting, and **sneering at** Christ to mock His claim to be the Messiah. The Greek verb translated **sneering** literally means to turn up one's nose in derision. Disdaining even to speak to Him, they said to the crowd, **"He saved others; let Him save Himself if this is the Christ of God, His Chosen One."** This sarcastic disdain was predicted in Psalm 22:7–8: "All who see me sneer at me; they separate with the lip, they wag the head, saying, 'Commit yourself to the Lord; let Him deliver him; let Him rescue him, because He delights in him.'" As Paul would later write, a crucified Messiah was a stumbling block to the Jews (1 Cor. 1:23).

The rulers viewed anyone hanging on a tree or a cross as cursed by God (Deut. 21:23), which was true of Jesus (Isa. 53:4, 10; Gal. 3:10–13). But what they did not recognize was that He became a curse for sinners to redeem them from the curse of the law (Gal. 3:13).

The third group in the crowd was **the soldiers,** who **also mocked Him, coming up to Him, offering Him sour wine, and saying, "If**

**You are the King of the Jews, save Yourself!"** They, of course, knew nothing about Jewish religion or theology; they were merely continuing the game they had begun at His trial (Matt. 27:27–30). Unlike the other two times they offered Jesus something to drink (Matt. 27:34,48), this was a mock act of obeisance and service to Him; they pretended that the **sour wine** was actually royal wine and offered it to Him as if He were a king.

Verse 38 notes that as was customary for crucified criminals, **there was also an inscription** nailed to the cross **above** Jesus. But instead of listing the crime for which He was being executed, this inscription read, **"This is the king of the Jews."** Combining all the gospel accounts reveals that the full text of the inscription was "This is Jesus of Nazareth, the King of the Jews." The inscription was the work of Pilate (John 19:19); it was his revenge on the Jewish leaders, who had forced him to execute a man he had declared innocent. They vociferously objected to the wording and insisted that he reword it to read that Jesus merely claimed to be Israel's king. However Pilate resolutely refused to change it, declaring, "What I have written I have written" (v. 22).

In keeping with the usual practice the soldiers had **cast lots, dividing up** Christ's **garments among themselves,** leaving Him naked except for a loin cloth. John 19:23 adds that they divided His clothing into four parts. Unwilling to ruin the seamless tunic, however, they cast lots for it (Psalm 22:18).

When Adam and Eve fell into sin, they immediately became conscious that they were naked. Nakedness has been associated ever since with moral guilt, symbolic of shame before God. After they unsuccessfully tried to make coverings for themselves, God killed an animal to make coverings for them to hide their shame and nakedness (Gen. 3:21).

At Calvary, Jesus was made naked in the place of believers, manifesting the symbol of moral guilt and moral shame before God. He was not covered by God as were Adam and Eve; He was judged by God, who poured out the full fury of His wrath on Him. And in a divine irony Jesus, the One made naked for believers, became the One who covers them with His righteousness (Rom. 13:14; Gal. 3:27; cf. Isa. 61:10).

The final component of the crowd was the two thieves crucified with Jesus. Luke records that **one of the criminals who were hanged**

**there was hurling abuse at Him, saying, "Are You not the Christ? Save Yourself and us!"**; Matthew (27:44) and Mark (15:32) note that both thieves were initially **hurling abuse at** Jesus.

THE MERCIFUL INTERCESSION OF CHRIST

**But Jesus was saying, "Father, forgive them; for they do not know what they are doing."** (23:34*a*)

This is the first of the Lord's seven sayings from the cross. One might expect that He would have pronounced judgment on those mocking Him, who were committing the ultimate act of blasphemy. Instead, in an act of mercy, He asked the **Father** to **forgive** those most wretched of sinners for their ignorant blasphemy, because, He said, **"they do not know what they are doing"**; that is, they were not aware of the full scope of their wickedness. "If they had understood it they would not have crucified the Lord of glory" (1 Cor. 2:8).

Instead of seeking vengeance on His enemies, "while being reviled, He did not revile in return; while suffering, He uttered no threats, but kept entrusting Himself to Him who judges righteously" (1 Peter 2:23). Justice would eventually be served; judgment would fall on the rejecting, unbelieving nation. But in God's grace and mercy, it would be delayed for forty years. Christ's intercession on behalf of His tormenters is yet another fulfillment of Old Testament prophecy (Isa. 53:12).

Christ's petition was in one sense a general prayer, revealing that there is no sin against the Son of God so severe that it cannot be forgiven those who repent (cf. Matt. 12:31–32). If forgiveness is available for those who crucified Him, it is available for anyone. But it is also a specific prayer that God would forgive those among the crowd whom He had chosen for salvation before the foundation of the world (Eph. 1:4). On the Day of Pentecost, three thousand Jews in Jerusalem were converted to Christ and baptized and the church was born. Within a few weeks, another five thousand or more people in Jerusalem embraced the faith of Jesus Christ. Surely many of those who came to Christ in those weeks after the resurrection were there in the crowd that day at Calvary. The church was in large measure born out of those who stood there and mocked the Son of God in answer to this prayer. The centurion and the soldiers under his command also came to faith in Christ (Matt. 27:54), as did many of the priests (Acts 6:7), possibly even some of the rulers. Even one of the hardened criminals crucified alongside Jesus was saved, and it is to the story of that conversion that Luke now turns.

## THE CONVERSION

**But the other answered, and rebuking him said, "Do you not even fear God, since you are under the same sentence of condemnation? And we indeed are suffering justly, for we are receiving what we deserve for our deeds; but this man has done nothing wrong." And he was saying, "Jesus, remember me when You come in Your kingdom!" And He said to him, "Truly I say to you, today you shall be with Me in Paradise."** (23:40–43)

The story of the penitent thief, found only in Luke's account of the crucifixion, is one of the many ironies at Calvary. Jesus was being mocked because He could not save Himself, yet He saved others, including the thief, by not saving Himself. He was accused by the rulers of Israel of claiming to be a king, and hence a threat to the power and authority of Rome. They warned Pilate that He needed to be executed before He could lead a revolt. And yet the same people who claimed to be protecting Rome from Jesus mocked, scorned, and ridiculed Him as impotent and helpless. He was treated like a king in a sarcastically cruel, comedic jest, yet He is God's true King. He was accused of blasphemy against God by those who blasphemed Him, the true God. Jesus, the innocent, righteous one, was executed by the guilty, turning justice on its head. He was cursed by His enemies, who hated Him, but cursed in an infinitely greater way by His Father, who loves Him. The One who gives life and is life, died that those who are dead might receive life.

One such spiritually dead sinner was hanging on a cross next to Him. He had initially joined the others in reviling and blaspheming Christ (see the discussion of v. 39 above). But then God opened his heart to the truth and miraculously, powerfully, sovereignly, instantly granted him faith and eternal life. The people, the rulers, the Romans, even his fellow thief did not understand what was truly happening at Calvary, but this man suddenly perceived the truth clearly. Through the power of the Holy Spirit, he was rescued from spiritual darkness and death and given light and life. Like Paul on the road to Damascus, he perceived the truth through a divine miracle in his soul.

Luke's account of the conversion of this Jewish criminal presents three evidences that his heart was savingly transformed. They are true of all those in whom God does His work of salvation.

First, he came to fear God and His judgment. In an instant this most wretched of men went from blaspheming and reviling Jesus, like the rest of those gathered around the cross, to rebuking his fellow thief for doing so. As noted above, both of the criminals crucified alongside Jesus initially reviled and blasphemed Him. But this man suddenly grew silent. While his body was enduring the trauma, agony, and unparalleled suffering of crucifixion, his mind became crystal clear. His perception of how Jesus should be treated was completely changed. He was appalled and horrified at how the Lord was being abused, as his words indicate.

Sharply **rebuking** the other thief he **said** to him, **"Do you not even fear God, since you are under the same sentence of condemnation?"** His sudden outburst must have startled and surprised the other criminal. But what the two of them had been saying about Jesus he now found repulsive and frightening. He confronted the tragic condition that only moments before had been his own. In a moment, he went from being part of it to being unable to comprehend it. He was convicted by the Holy Spirit that he was a violator of God's law. By his own admission, his sentence from a human judge was fair and just, and he realized that the torment he was enduring for breaking the law was insignificant compared to what he could expect for his sin from the divine Judge. He was afraid, not of those who were destroying his body, but of God, who would destroy both his body and his soul in hell (Luke 12:4–5).

It is characteristic for the unregenerate to have no fear of God (Rom. 3:18). But the conviction wrought by the power of the Spirit of God produces a holy fear of divine judgment. Convicted sinners cry out like the repentant tax collector in Luke 18:13, "God, be merciful to me, the sinner!" True salvation is not from material poverty or poor self-esteem, but from God's wrath, justice, and judgment.

Closely connected to fear of God's judgment is the second evidence of a changed heart, a sense of sinfulness. The repentant thief's further rebuke of the other malefactor reflects his acknowledgment of his own sinfulness. **"We indeed are suffering justly,"** he reminded him, **"for we are receiving what we deserve for our deeds."** Like the prodigal son in Christ's parable (Luke 15:17–19), this man came to his senses and admitted that he was a sinner. He understood that justice operates in the world of men, but perfectly in God's realm.

Here is an example of the true convert who confesses his guilt and absolute spiritual bankruptcy. He recognizes that he has nothing to offer God, nothing to commend himself to Him. He knows that he needs mercy and grace to escape judgment and be forgiven, because he is an unworthy sinner, a crouching, cringing, cowering beggar mourning over his transgressions (Matt. 5:3–4). Martin Luther understood that truth. After his death, his friends found a scrap of paper in his pocket on which the great reformer had written in Latin and German, "Hoc est verum. Wir sind alle Bettler." ("This is true. We are all beggars.")

The final evidence of the repentant thief's divinely transformed heart was his belief in Jesus Christ. The story of his transformation moves from an assessment of his sinful condition to an assessment of the Savior's character. When he said of Him, **"This man has done nothing wrong,"** he was confessing not merely the Lord's innocence of any crime, but also His sinlessness.

He then addressed Jesus directly as the Savior and humbly asked Him, **"Jesus, remember me when You come in Your kingdom!"** This was nothing less than a plea for the forgiveness apart from which no one will enter God's kingdom. He based his request on Christ's prayer that God would forgive those who crucified Him, which gave him hope that he too might receive forgiveness. He expressed belief that Jesus is the Savior, since he would not have asked for entrance to the kingdom unless he believed Jesus was willing and able to provide it. His was the plea of a broken, penitent, unworthy sinner for grace, mercy, and forgiveness.

Finally, he believed that Jesus was Israel's Messiah. He acknowledged that the Lord would one day establish His kingdom, which was promised in the covenants God made with Abraham and David, and reiterated repeatedly to the prophets. Since no one survived crucifixion, he understood that Jesus would have to rise from the dead to do that. He probably knew that Jesus had power over death, since the news of His raising of Lazarus had spread throughout Jerusalem. He no doubt was aware that Daniel 12:2 promised that the saints would be raised and given a place of glory in the kingdom. His request was that Jesus would raise him and grant him entrance to that kingdom.

The Lord's reply was astonishing. He prefaced it with the word **truly,** because what He was about to say was hard to believe. That a cursed criminal, whom the Jews would view as unredeemable, would be promised entrance to God's kingdom was an outrageous affront to their sensibilities.

The promise that this redeemed sinner would be with Jesus in heaven that very day invalidates the Roman Catholic teaching regarding purgatory. It also eliminates any system of works-righteousness, since the penitent thief had neither the time nor the opportunity to perform enough good deeds to merit salvation.

The wonderful promise that he would be with Jesus in **Paradise** (heaven; 2 Cor. 12:2; cf. Rev. 2:7 with 22:2, 14) speaks of his full reconciliation to God. He would not merely see Jesus from afar, he would be **with** Him. His restoration would be full and complete.

THE CONSUMMATION

**It was now about the sixth hour, and darkness fell over the whole land until the ninth hour, because the sun was obscured; and the veil of the temple was torn in two. And Jesus, crying out with a loud voice, said, "Father, into Your hands I commit My spirit." Having said this, He breathed His last.** (23:44–46)

The comedy staged by sinful men ended abruptly and dramatically at **about the sixth hour.** It turned instead into a tragedy, as God took center stage for Christ's final three hours on the cross. His presence at Calvary is often overlooked, but it is only when God arrived that

Calvary became the saving event that it was. God's wrath, poured out on His Son as He bore sin, is in fact the major reality of Calvary. That happened in the hours of darkness.

Five dramatic events mark those final three hours. First was the **darkness** itself that began at **the sixth hour** (noon) and **fell over the whole land until the ninth hour** (3:00 P.M.). Suddenly, at noon when the sun was at its apex, complete darkness enveloped the scene. The geographical extent of the darkness is not known. It was not caused by an eclipse, as some argue, since there is always a full moon at Passover, and there cannot be a solar eclipse when there is a full moon. Three hours is also far longer than a solar eclipse could have lasted.

Others suggest that the darkness was the result of Satan bringing the power of darkness to bear on Jesus. But Satan has no such power over the natural world. Besides, this was God's hour, not his.

The truth is that God brought the darkness, which is what would have immediately come into the minds of the Jewish people there. They knew that in the Old Testament God frequently associated Himself with darkness. When He appeared to Abraham, "terror and great darkness fell upon him" (Gen. 15:12). One of the plagues God brought on Egypt was a darkness so thick that it could be felt (Ex. 10:21–22), and He appeared to Israel on Mount Sinai in a thick cloud (Ex. 19:16). The Jewish people understood that supernatural darkness was associated with divine judgment (cf. Joel 2:1–2, 10, 30–31; Amos 5:20; 8:9; Zeph. 1:14–15), which is why after the darkness lifted, "when they observed what had happened, [they] began to return, beating their breasts" (Luke 23:48).

God arrived in the blackness at Calvary that day to unleash judgment, not in an eschatological sense against the ungodly, but in a soteriological sense against His Son. God brought the outer darkness of hell to Jerusalem that day (cf. Matt. 8:12; 22:13; 25:30) as He unleashed on Jesus Christ the full extent of His wrath against the sins of all who would ever be saved.

The darkness was not caused by the absence of God, but rather by His presence in full judgment, vengeance, and fury. Infinite wrath moved by infinite righteousness released infinite punishment on the Son. Because He is infinite, in just three hours He was able to absorb all the punishment of eternal hell for all who will ever believe. He bore in

His own body our sins (1 Peter 2:24), though He who knew no sin was made sin for us (2 Cor. 5:21), was wounded for our transgressions and crushed for our iniquities (Isa. 53:5), and was made a curse for us (Gal. 3:13). This was the cup that He pleaded with the Father in Gethsemane to remove, if possible.

The Lord's cry at the ninth hour, "'Eloi, eloi, lama sabachthani?' which is translated, 'My God, My God, why have You forsaken Me?'" (Mark 15:34), reveals that the Father did not immediately comfort Him when the darkness lifted. This is the only time in the New Testament that Jesus referred to God as anything but "Father." The doubled phrase "My God, My God" is an expression of affection mingled with disappointment (cf. Luke 10:41; 13:34; 22:31). God was there in the fury of judgment; why was He absent in comfort?

While hell involves the full fury of God's personal presence to punish, He will never be there to comfort, show sympathy, or bring relief. If Jesus was to endure the full suffering of hell, it had to involve both the punishment of God and the absence of His comfort.

The second event in those final three hours took place when **the veil of the temple was torn in two.** This happened immediately after the lifting of the darkness. Just as the priests resumed the slaughter of the Passover lambs, they were startled to hear a loud tearing noise coming from inside the Holy Place. God was ripping the curtain separating it from the Holy of Holies from top to bottom (Matt. 27:51). The atonement was complete; access to God was opened, and the New Covenant was ratified, rendering everything connected with the temple worship obsolete (Heb. 9:11–14; 10:19). Jesus had predicted the temple's physical destruction (Luke 21:5–6); God's tearing of the veil symbolized its spiritual destruction.

The third event was a powerful earthquake (Matt. 27:51). Like darkness, earthquakes are frequently associated with God's presence in the Old Testament (cf. Ex. 19:18; Pss. 18:7; 68:8; Nah. 1:5).

One result of the earthquake was the fourth event during those final three hours: "The tombs were opened, and many bodies of the saints who had fallen asleep were raised; and coming out of the tombs after His resurrection they entered the holy city and appeared to many" (Matt. 27:52–53). They did not appear until after Christ's resurrection, since He is "the first fruits of those who are asleep" (1 Cor. 15:20). Their resurrection demonstrates that life after death is the result of Christ's death (cf. 1 Cor. 15:26; 2 Tim. 1:10; Heb. 2:14).

The final feature was Christ's words from the cross. "After this, Jesus, knowing that all things had already been accomplished, to fulfill the Scripture, said, 'I am thirsty' " (John 19:28). He wouldn't drink anything all the way through His ordeal on the cross, so that He would fully experience God's wrath, but now in the calm aftermath, after His work of sin-bearing was over, He said simply "I am thirsty." His loud cry—too loud for one dying a natural death from crucifixion, indicating Jesus voluntarily gave up His life (cf. John 10:17–18)—**"Father, into Your hands I commit My spirit,"** signifies that communion with the Father had been restored. Since the work of redemption was now finished (John 19:30), **having said this,** Jesus **breathed His last.**

## The Responses

**Now when the centurion saw what had happened, he began praising God, saying, "Certainly this man was innocent." And all the crowds who came together for this spectacle, when they observed what had happened, began to return, beating their breasts. And all His acquaintances and the women who accompanied Him from Galilee were standing at a distance, seeing these things.** (23:47–49)

Taken together, the three responses to Christ's death picture the full response that is required of all believers.

The **centurion** (and the soldiers; Matt. 27:54) represent the convinced. What they had observed during Christ's trial and crucifixion had left them utterly amazed. No prisoner they had crucified had conducted himself in such a resolute, dignified manner.

They heard Jesus pray for the forgiveness of His killers. They saw the noble way He suffered. They heard Him cry out to His Father. They heard Him promise paradise to a repentant thief who had been cursing Him. Then they experienced the three hours of pitch blackness and an earthquake that split rocks.They heard Jesus just before He died cry with a loud voice,"Father, into Your hands I commit My spirit" (23:46).This was not behavior they had ever seen from a crucifixion victim. People who died in this torturous fashion suffered from oxygen deprivation to their brains and were incoherent long before they actually succumbed.They could barely breathe, let alone shout at the top of their voice. But this man took death by His own will and made it His servant.

They could not ignore reality.When the centurion **saw what had happened,** he **began praising God, saying, "Certainly this man was innocent."** This was more than merely the seventh affirmation of Jesus' innocence; it was an affirmation of His divine righteousness as the Son of God.These Roman soldiers became the first converts to Christ at His crucifixion, just moments after He died.

The fickle **crowds who came together for this spectacle** represent the convicted.They had run the gamut of emotions that fateful week, ranging from delirious joy on Monday during the triumphal entry at the prospect that Jesus was the Messiah they so eagerly longed for, to the opposite extreme of anger, hatred, and animosity at His trial before Pilate.There they asked for the murdering insurrectionist Barabbas to be released instead of Jesus, shouted loudly for Jesus to be crucified, and even willingly assumed responsibility for His death, crying out,"His blood shall be on us and on our children!" (Matt. 27:25).

After the dramatic events of the crucifixion, especially the darkness and the earthquake, the crowds had one last manifestation of emotion. **When they observed what had happened, they began to return** to Jerusalem, **beating their breasts** in a sign of grief, guilt, and fear (cf. 18:13).The event was not so funny anymore as they became terrified at the signs of God's wrath and judgment they had experienced.

Fear of God's person and judgment because of guilt and rejection of Jesus Christ is a necessary response. The crowd's reaction no doubt prepared the hearts of many who were later converted on the Day of Pentecost and in the events of the early chapters of Acts.

One final response was exhibited by those confounded by Jesus' death—**all His acquaintances,** including John (John 19:26) **and the women who accompanied Him from Galilee.** Unable to bear what was happening to the One whom they loved so profoundly, they had moved from a position near the cross (John 19:25–27) and now **were standing at a distance, seeing these things.** They were shocked, overcome with grief, unable to comprehend what had happened to Jesus. This was not the way His story was supposed to end. They were devastated —until Sunday morning, when the resurrection of the Lord Jesus Christ would forever change their lives.

# The Supernatural Burial of Jesus Christ (Luke 23:50–56)

**35**

**And a man named Joseph, who was a member of the Council, a good and righteous man (he had not consented to their plan and action), a man from Arimathea, a city of the Jews, who was waiting for the kingdom of God; this man went to Pilate and asked for the body of Jesus. And he took it down and wrapped it in a linen cloth, and laid Him in a tomb cut into the rock, where no one had ever lain. It was the preparation day, and the Sabbath was about to begin. Now the women who had come with Him out of Galilee followed, and saw the tomb and how His body was laid. Then they returned and prepared spices and perfumes. And on the Sabbath they rested according to the commandment.** (23:50–56)

The death of Jesus Christ was accompanied with supernatural signs: the darkness during His final three hours on the cross, the tearing of the veil separating the Holy of Holies from the Holy Place, the rock-splitting earthquake, and the resurrection of the dead saints. His resurrection came three days later. While Jesus' burial is often overlooked, it was as supernatural and divinely wrought as anything else that happened during His incarnation. So important is His burial that all four gospel writers provide details about. The moment Jesus yielded up His spirit and died, He entered alive into the presence of God in heaven, from which He controlled every detail of His own burial.

The divinely preplanned and prophesied features of Christ's burial provide strong evidence for some essential realities. They demonstrate that there is a divine purpose for history, God's sovereignty in all things, the authenticity of Scripture, and the veracity of the claims of Christ.

God moves directly in history in two ways. The first is by means of miracles, where He accomplishes His purposes by interrupting or suspending natural laws and processes. Miracles are relatively rare events, especially those performed by humans. Some of the more notable Old Testament miracles are the creation (Gen. 1–2), Enoch's translation to heaven (Gen. 5:24), the flood (Gen. 6–9), the destruction of Sodom and Gomorrah (Gen. 19:24–25), the burning bush (Ex. 3:2–3), the plagues in Egypt (Ex. 7–12), Israel's crossing of the Red Sea (Ex. 14:21–29) and the Jordan River (Josh. 3:14–17), the provision of manna (Ex. 16:13–15), Balaam's donkey speaking (Num. 22:28–30; 2 Peter 2:15–16), the destruction of Jericho's walls (Josh. 6:20), the stopping of the sun and moon (Josh. 10:12–14), Gideon's fleece (Judg. 6:37–40), Elijah's raising of the widow's son (1 Kings 17:17–24), Elijah's translation to heaven (2 Kings 2:11), Elisha's raising of the Shunammite woman's son (2 Kings 4:18–37), the healing of Naaman's leprosy (2 Kings 5:9–14), the killing of 185,000 Assyrian soldiers by an angel (2 Kings 19:35), the preservation of Daniel's three friends alive in the fiery furnace (Dan. 3:19–27) and Daniel in the lions' den (Dan. 6:16–23), and God's use of a large fish to save Jonah (Jonah 1:15–17; 2:10; Matt. 12:40).

The most significant outpouring of divine miracles took place during the Lord Jesus Christ's earthly ministry. The New Testament records more than three dozen miracles that He performed to verify His claim to be God incarnate (John 10:25; for a list of Christ's miracles, see the chart in *The MacArthur Study Bible* in the notes to Mark chapter 1). These are only examples of countless miracles not recorded by the gospel writers (John 21:25).

The church's birth was attended by the miracle of Pentecost, when the visitors to Jerusalem heard the apostles miraculously preach the gospel in their own languages (Acts 2:3–4). The ministry of Peter included the healing of a lame man at the temple gate (Acts 3:1–8), of those touched by his shadow (Acts 5:14–16), of Aeneas in the city of Lydda (Acts 9:32–34), and the raising of Tabitha (Dorcas) from the dead (Acts 9:40–41).

Paul also performed a number of miracles, including blinding Elymas the magician (Acts 13:8–11), healing a crippled man at Lystra (Acts 14:8–10), casting a demon out of a slave girl in Philippi (Acts 16:16–18), healing and casting out demons from those at Ephesus who touched his handkerchiefs and aprons (Acts 19:11–12), raising Eutychus from the dead at Troas (Acts 20:9–10), and surviving the bite of a venomous snake (Acts 28:3) and healing Publius's father and others (Acts 28:8–9) on Malta. In addition, the book of Acts refers to miracles performed by Stephen (6:8) and Philip (8:6–7,13).

The second way God operates in history is by means of providence, by which He constantly works in the world without interrupting natural law or suspending natural processes. Providence involves God accomplishing His purposes by taking all the infinite number of attitudes, choices, and acts of free human and spiritual beings and weaving them perfectly into His own purpose. That is a far greater display of divine wisdom and power than the momentary interruption of natural law by a miracle.

God's providence is evident throughout Scripture. Hannah spoke of it in her prayer recorded in 1 Samuel 2:6–9:

> The Lord kills and makes alive; He brings down to Sheol and raises up. The Lord makes poor and rich; He brings low, He also exalts. He raises the poor from the dust, He lifts the needy from the ash heap to make them sit with nobles, and inherit a seat of honor; for the pillars of the earth are the Lord's, and He set the world on them. He keeps the feet of His godly ones, but the wicked ones are silenced in darkness; for not by might shall a man prevail.

Eliphaz reminded Job that God "frustrates the plotting of the shrewd, so that their hands cannot attain success" (Job 5:12). In Psalm 33:10 the psalmist wrote, "The Lord nullifies the counsel of the nations; He frustrates the plans of the peoples," while Psalm 76:10 notes that God causes even the wrath of man to work to His praise. The book of Proverbs has much to say about God's providential control of the affairs of this world:"The mind of man plans his way, but the Lord directs his steps" (16:9);"The lot is cast into the lap, but its every decision is from the Lord" (16:33; cf. Acts 1:26); "Many plans are in a man's heart, but the counsel of the Lord will stand" (19:21);"Man's steps are ordained by the Lord, how then can man understand his way?" (20:24);"The king's heart is like channels of water in the hand of the Lord; He turns it wherever He wishes" (21:1). Isaiah wrote,"Be broken, O peoples, and be shattered; and give ear, all remote places of the earth. Gird yourselves, yet be shattered; gird yourselves, yet be shattered. Devise a plan, but it will be thwarted; state a proposal, but it will not stand, for God is with us" (Isa. 8:9–10).

God's providence is seen in His preservation and exaltation of Joseph (Gen. 39:2–3, 23; 45:7–8; 50:20); His hardening of the hearts of Pharaoh (Ex. 14:4), Sihon (Deut. 2:30), and the Canaanite kings (Josh. 11:18–20); His causing of David's rebellious son Absalom to reject Ahithophel's counsel in favor of Hushai's (2 Sam. 17:14); His stirring the heart of the King of Assyria to bring about the exile of the northern kingdom of Israel (1 Chron. 5:26); His influencing the decision of Rehoboam, which led to the division of Israel (1 Kings 12:15); His moving of Cyrus to allow the Jewish exiles to return to Jerusalem (Ezra 1:1; cf. Isa. 44:28–45:5); His placing Esther into a position where she could save her people (Est. 4:14); His moving Caesar Augustus to take a census, ensuring that Jesus would be born in Bethlehem (Luke 2:1–4); His using Paul's imprisonment for the progress of the gospel (Phil. 1:12); and His using Onesimus's fleeing from his master to bring about his salvation (Philem. 15–16). Even the killing of the Lord Jesus Christ, the most heinous act of wickedness in history, carried out God's plan (Acts 2:23; cf. 3:17–18; 4:27–28).

Nowhere in Scripture is God's providence seen more clearly than in the burial of Jesus, in which the Trinity was active behind the scenes controlling the actions of three groups of people: the neutral soldiers, the loving saints, and the hateful enemies.

## THE NEUTRAL SOLDIERS

God's providence in Christ's burial is seen first in the actions of the soldiers, which John records in chapter 19 of his gospel. Verse 30 reveals that Jesus "gave up His spirit"—after only six hours on the cross, sooner than a crucified person would normally die. The two thieves were still alive. Therefore "the Jews [the religious leaders of Israel], because it was the day of preparation, so that the bodies would not remain on the cross on the Sabbath (for that Sabbath was a high day), asked Pilate that their legs might be broken, and that they might be taken away." In keeping with Deuteronomy 21:22–23, they wanted the bodies of the three men taken down and disposed of before the start of the Sabbath (a "high day" because it was the Sabbath of Passover week) at sundown, lest they defile the celebration. (Ironically, these men may have defiled themselves if they went inside Pilate's residence or headquarters to speak with him; cf. John 18:28.) Here was hypocrisy at its most pernicious extreme. They were scrupulously careful to avoid any ceremonial defilement, while thinking nothing of murdering the Son of God.

Pilate, who by now was completely intimidated by the religious leaders, gave them permission, "so the soldiers came, and broke the legs of the first man and of the other who was crucified with [Jesus]" (v. 32). This procedure, known as *crurifragium*, hastened the death of the victim by smashing his legs with an iron mallet. No longer able to use his legs to help raise himself up to breathe, he would die of asphyxiation as soon as the strength in his arms gave out.

Significantly, "when [the soldiers] saw that [Jesus] was already dead, they did not break His legs" (v. 33). They were experts at determining death, since it was part of their job as executioners. As noted in the previous chapter of this volume, one of the soldiers thrust a spear into His side (v. 34), resulting in a flow of blood and water (serous pleural and pericardial fluid), which verified that He was dead. Their testimony, and that of the centurion (Mark 15:44–45), provide irrefutable evidence that Jesus was in fact dead. They also corroborate the apostle John's eyewitness testimony (v. 35). (For a refutation of false theories of the resurrection, see John MacArthur, *John 12–21*, The MacArthur New Testament Commentary [Chicago: Moody, 2008], 373–77.)

The soldiers' decision not to break Jesus' legs and the piercing of His side were not merely a part of the routine of crucifixion; they were fulfillments of Old Testament prophecy (vv. 36–37; Ps. 34:20; Ex. 12:46; Zech. 12:10).

The actions of the Romans were under divine control. They authenticated the promises of Scripture and validated the claims of Jesus Christ to be the fulfillment of those promises. They also confirmed His death, which in turn affirmed the reality of His resurrection, since He could not rise from the dead unless He had died. The Jewish leaders, Pilate, and the soldiers did what they chose to do, but in the end, the will of God was being done.

## THE LOVING SAINTS

**And a man named Joseph, who was a member of the Council, a good and righteous man (he had not consented to their plan and action), a man from Arimathea, a city of the Jews, who was waiting for the kingdom of God; this man went to Pilate and asked for the body of Jesus. And he took it down and wrapped it in a linen cloth, and laid Him in a tomb cut into the rock, where no one had ever lain. It was the preparation day, and the Sabbath was about to begin. Now the women who had come with Him out of Galilee followed, and saw the tomb and how His body was laid. Then they returned and prepared spices and perfumes. And on the Sabbath they rested according to the commandment.** (23:50–56)

With Jesus confirmed dead, the next step in the divine plan was for the removal of His body from the cross and its burial. For that task the Lord chose **a man named Joseph, who was a member of the Council, a good and righteous man (he had not consented to their plan and action), a man from Arimathea, a city of the Jews, who was waiting for the kingdom of God; this man went to Pilate and asked for the body of Jesus. Joseph** certainly risked much by doing what he did, since he **was a member of the Council** (the Sanhedrin)— the very group that hated Jesus, convicted Him in a sham trial, bullied

Pilate into sentencing Him to death, and mocked and taunted Him while He was on the cross. Although he appears in Scripture only in this incident, Joseph is important enough to be mentioned in all four Gospels.

The brief story of Joseph is the story of salvation. It is an unexpected, somewhat shocking testimony of faith in Christ set against the rejection of the nation and the hostility of the rest of the Sanhedrin. He was the lone dissenter, and **had not consented to their plan and action** to condemn and execute Jesus. Joseph was **a man from Arimathea,** the location of which is unknown. Some identify it with Ramathaim-zophim, the home of Samuel (1 Sam. 1:1); others with a town near Lydda, a city located on the road between Joppa and Jerusalem. Luke describes it merely as **a city of the Jews.**

That Joseph is characterized as **a good and righteous man** who was "waiting for the kingdom of God" (Mark 15:43) confirms the genuineness of his salvation (the word translated **righteous** is used of Christ in Luke 23:47; He was righteous by nature, Joseph was righteous by grace). He joins the list of righteous people whom Luke mentions, including Zacharias and Elizabeth, the parents of John the Baptist (1:5), Simeon (2:25), and Anna (2:36–37). According to John 19:38 Joseph was a disciple of Jesus Christ, albeit a secret one, who was afraid to make his faith in Christ known. But while many secret disciples were false disciples, and not true believers (John 12:42–43), he was a true disciple, as his actions demonstrate.

From his perspective Joseph, having gone **to Pilate and asked for the body of Jesus,** was finally ready to publicly affirm his faith. Perhaps he feared that if he failed to declare his faith in Christ in this hour of crisis he might not be accepted into the kingdom. The noblest thing he could think of to do to express that faith was to spare Jesus from the ultimate indignity of having His body thrown into the pit with the other crucified victims.

His act required courage, because other members of the Sanhedrin had, as noted above, gone to Pilate asking that the legs of the crucified victims be broken. Joseph must have arrived soon afterward, since the governor had not yet heard whether Jesus was dead, and had to ask the centurion to verify it. It may be that Joseph passed the others on their way out as he was going in to see Pilate. That would naturally raise the question of what he wanted to see the governor about. Perhaps Joseph was confident Pilate would release the Lord's body to him to ease his own guilty conscience for having executed a man whose innocence he had repeatedly declared.

But the real reason Joseph asked Pilate for Jesus' body was that he was moved to do so by God to fulfill prophecy. Isaiah prophesied of Jesus that although "His grave was assigned with wicked men, yet He was with a rich man in His death" (53:9). Joseph was rich (Matt. 27:57), and had a tomb available in which to bury Jesus (Matt. 27:60). His act also fulfilled Christ's own prediction that "just as Jonah was three days and three nights in the belly of the sea monster, so will the Son of Man be three days and three nights in the heart of the earth" (Matt. 12:40). For that prophecy to come to pass, the body of Jesus needed to be buried in a tomb in the earth, not thrown into a pit as crucified victims commonly were. And He had to be in that tomb some part of three days.

After receiving confirmation from the centurion that Jesus was dead, Pilate released His body to Joseph (Mark 15:44–45), who **took it down and wrapped it in a linen cloth.** At this point another follower of Jesus arrived on the scene to help Joseph prepare the body for burial. This was not one of the disciples, but Nicodemus (John 19:39), the prominent Jewish teacher who had had a nighttime interview with Jesus early in His ministry (John 3:1–21). Nicodemus brought a large amount of the spices the Jews customarily used to prepare a body for burial, since unlike the Egyptians, they did not embalm. Together, the two men "took the body of Jesus and bound it in linen wrappings with the spices, as is the burial custom of the Jews" (John 19:40), **and laid Him in** Joseph's new **tomb cut into the rock, where no one had ever lain. It was** late afternoon on Friday, **the preparation day, and the Sabbath was about to begin** at sunset. So He was buried on Friday and raised on Sunday.

But Joseph and Nicodemus were not the only loving saints there. **The women who had come with** Jesus **out of Galilee** and had been observers at the cross (Matt. 27:55–56) **followed** Joseph, **and saw the tomb and how His body was laid.** That the women saw Joseph and Nicodemus place Jesus' body in the tomb gives the lie to a second skeptical reason for denying the resurrection: that they went to the wrong tomb on Sunday morning (though even if they had, Joseph, Nicodemus, the Roman guard detachment, and the Jewish leaders did know which was the right one). Having seen where Jesus was buried, **they returned** to their homes **and prepared spices and perfumes** to finish preparing the Lord's body for burial. **And on the Sabbath they rested according to the commandment** (Ex. 20:10), intending to return to the tomb on Sunday morning after the Sabbath was over.

## The Hateful Enemies

Concerned that the disciples would fake a resurrection by stealing the Lord's body,

> on the next day, the day after the preparation, the chief priests and the Pharisees gathered together with Pilate and said, "Sir, we remember that when He was still alive that deceiver said, 'After three days I am to rise again.' Therefore, give orders for the grave to be made secure until the third day, otherwise His disciples may come and steal Him away and say to the people, 'He has risen from the dead,' and the last deception will be worse than the first." (Matt. 27:62–64)

The disciples, of course, had no such plans. They would hardly have stolen Jesus' body, pretended that He rose from the dead, and then given their lives as martyrs for that lie. Further, they did not expect Him to rise from the dead, and were in hiding because they were afraid that the Jews would come for them next (John 20:19).

Pilate granted their request, and told them, "You have a guard; go, make it as secure as you know how." And they went and made the grave secure, and along with the guard they set a seal on the stone" (Matt. 27:65–66). By that act, they falsified yet another skeptical denial of the resurrection, one that they themselves would put forth, that the disciples stole Jesus' body and faked the resurrection. The cowardly disciples, who had fled in panic when Jesus was arrested (Mark 14:50) and were terrified that the Jews would arrest them, would not have been able to wrest the body of the Lord away from a detachment of Roman soldiers. The Jewish leaders' claim that they did (Matt. 28:11–15) is ludicrous, and actually verifies that the resurrection took place, as William Lane Craig notes:

The point is that the Jews did not respond to the preaching of the resurrection by pointing to the tomb of Jesus or exhibiting his corpse, but
entangled themselves in a hopeless series of absurdities trying to
explain away his empty tomb. The fact that the enemies of Christianity
felt obliged to explain away the empty tomb by the theft hypothesis
shows not only that the tomb was known (confirmation of the burial
story), but that it was empty. ... The fact that the Jewish polemic never
denied that Jesus' tomb was empty, but only tried to explain it away is
compelling evidence that the tomb was in fact empty. ("The Historicity
of the Empty Tomb of Jesus," http://www.leaderu.com/offices/billcraig/
docs/tomb2.html; accessed 21 January 2014.)

God providentially works in every situation to accomplish His
purpose, and the burial of His Son was no exception. Like the gospel
accounts of His life, death, and resurrection, the account of Christ's burial
was "written so that you may believe that Jesus is the Christ, the Son of
God; and that believing you may have life in His name" (John 20:31).

# The Resurrection of Jesus Christ (Luke 24:1–12)

# 36

But on the first day of the week, at early dawn, they came to the tomb bringing the spices which they had prepared. And they found the stone rolled away from the tomb, but when they entered, they did not find the body of the Lord Jesus. While they were perplexed about this, behold, two men suddenly stood near them in dazzling clothing; and as the women were terrified and bowed their faces to the ground, the men said to them, "Why do you seek the living One among the dead? He is not here, but He has risen. Remember how He spoke to you while He was still in Galilee, saying that the Son of Man must be delivered into the hands of sinful men, and be crucified, and the third day rise again." And they remembered His words, and returned from the tomb and reported all these things to the eleven and to all the rest. Now they were Mary Magdalene and Joanna and Mary the mother of James; also the other women with them were telling these things to the apostles. But these words appeared to them as nonsense, and they would not believe them. But Peter got up and

**ran to the tomb; stooping and looking in, he saw the linen wrap-
pings only; and he went away to his home, marveling at what had
happened.** (24:1–12)

The resurrection of the Lord Jesus Christ is the most significant
event in history. Central to God's redemptive plan and the foundation of
the gospel, the resurrection is the essential truth apart from which there
is no Christianity. Paul put it bluntly in 1 Corinthians 15:17: "If Christ has
not been raised, your faith is worthless; you are still in your sins." The resurrection is not the epilogue to the story of Christ's life; it is its triumphant
goal, objective, and purpose.

The church has always understood the importance of the resurrection. Throughout its history it has met on Sunday, commemorating
Jesus rising. The church does not meet on Friday, because Easter is the
interpretation and validation of Good Friday. The resurrection is the
divine vindication of the work that Jesus did on the cross. Apart from the
resurrection the cross means nothing. When God raised Jesus from the
dead, He affirmed that He had indeed borne our sins in His own body on
the cross (1 Peter 2:24), and thereby propitiated or satisfied the justice of
God (Rom. 4:25).

The resurrection vindicates the hope of the gospel. The good news
of salvation is not just that believers might experience forgiveness of sin,
but rather that having been forgiven, they will live forever in the bliss of
heaven in glorified, physical, resurrected bodies. The message of the gospel
is not that people can be delivered from their troubles in this life. Nor does
it promise that they will live on in the sense of their continuing influence,
or that Christ merely lives on in His continuing influence, or in some nebu-
lous spiritual form. The Christian message is that Jesus Christ rose from the
grave in a glorified, physical body, and that believers one day will rise with
a body like His glorified body (1 John 3:2).

The truth is that despite the claims of false religions and philo-
sophical systems, death does not end human existence. Death is merely
the doorway into eternity, through which all must pass. Everyone will live
forever, fully conscious in spirit and body, either in everlasting joy, or everlasting suffering. There will be a resurrection to life, and a resurrection to
judgment (John 5:28–29).

The resurrection to life that comes through the resurrection of Christ (John 14:19; Rom. 4:25; 1 Cor. 15:20–23; 1 Peter 1:3; 3:21) has been the hope of God's people throughout redemptive history (Job 14:14; 19:25–26; Dan. 12:2; Acts 24:15), and the theme of apostolic preaching and teaching. On the Day of Pentecost, in the first Christian sermon, Peter said of Jesus, "God raised Him up again, putting an end to the agony of death, since it was impossible for Him to be held in its power" (Acts 2:24). When the Sanhedrin, "being greatly disturbed because [Peter and John] were teaching the people and proclaiming in Jesus the resurrection from the dead" (Acts 4:2), arrested Peter and John, Peter boldly proclaimed to them, "Let it be known to all of you and to all the people of Israel, that by the name of Jesus Christ the Nazarene, whom you crucified, whom God raised from the dead—by this name this man stands here before you in good health" (v. 10). Later he told Cornelius and those gathered in his house,

> You know of Jesus of Nazareth, how God anointed Him with the Holy Spirit and with power, and how He went about doing good and healing all who were oppressed by the devil, for God was with Him. We are witnesses of all the things He did both in the land of the Jews and in Jerusalem. They also put Him to death by hanging Him on a cross. God raised Him up on the third day. (Acts 10:38–40)

In the synagogue in Pisidian Antioch Paul proclaimed,

> For those who live in Jerusalem, and their rulers, recognizing neither Him nor the utterances of the prophets which are read every Sabbath, fulfilled these by condemning Him. And though they found no ground for putting Him to death, they asked Pilate that He be executed. When they had carried out all that was written concerning Him, they took Him down from the cross and laid Him in a tomb. But God raised Him from the dead. (Acts 13:27–30)

Paul declared to the pagan philosophers on Mars Hill in Athens that God "has fixed a day in which He will judge the world in righteousness through a Man whom He has appointed, having furnished proof to all men by raising Him from the dead" (Acts 17:31). He wrote to the Romans, "Therefore we have been buried with Him through baptism into death, so that as Christ was raised from the dead through the glory of the Father, so we too might walk in newness of life" (Rom. 6:4); to the Corinthians, "He who raised the Lord Jesus will raise us also with Jesus" (2 Cor. 4:14); and to the Ephesians, "[God] raised [Christ] from the dead and seated Him at His right hand in the heavenly places" (Eph. 1:20). Peter opened his first epistle by saying, "Blessed be the God and Father of our Lord Jesus Christ, who according to His great mercy has caused us to be born again to a living hope through the resurrection of Jesus Christ from the dead" (1 Peter 1:3).

It comes as no surprise, then, that all four Gospels contain an account of the events surrounding the resurrection, though none of them describe the actual event. Each of the gospel writers was inspired by the Holy Spirit to write a unique account, consistent with his own theme and intention. There is no evidence that the writers were, as some critics maintain, copying from a common source. The accounts are personal, unaffected, and uncontrived, which belies any kind of concerted effort on their parts to blend everything together. Thus Luke's account does not give all the details concerning the resurrection. It does not repeat some of the things that are recorded by Matthew, Mark, and John. But it also includes some details that are not in the other accounts. And because the Holy Spirit inspired all four, they harmonize perfectly (cf. John MacArthur, *One Perfect Life* [Nashville: Thomas Nelson, 2012]).

There are some core truths concerning the resurrection that all four gospel writers present. First, Jesus was truly dead. Second, on Sunday morning, the third day after He was placed in the tomb, the tomb was found empty. Third, angels appeared and explained what had happened. Fourth, the first eyewitnesses of the risen Christ were the women who had been His followers. Fifth, the apostles and the rest of the male disciples refused to believe the testimony of the women.

The previous two chapters in this volume presented evidence that Jesus had died on the cross; this chapter will present the other four key truths: the empty tomb, the angelic messengers, the witness of the women, and the unbelieving disciples.

## THE EMPTY TOMB

**But on the first day of the week, at early dawn, they came to the tomb bringing the spices which they had prepared. And they found the stone rolled away from the tomb, but when they entered, they did not find the body of the Lord Jesus.** (24:1–3)

The resurrection took place **on the first day of the week** in fulfillment of Jesus' prediction that He would be "three days and three nights in the heart of the earth" (Matt. 12:40; cf. 27:63; Mark 8:31; 9:31; 10:33–34). The Jewish people had no names for the days of the week, but numbered them in relation to the Sabbath, the seventh day of the week. The **first day,** therefore, was Sunday, the day after the Sabbath. The Saturday that Jesus' body was in the tomb was the last official Sabbath (Col. 2:16–17); the church, as noted earlier, meets on Sunday, in honor and remembrance of the Lord's resurrection (Acts 20:7; 1 Cor. 16:2; Rev. 1:10).

The women **came to the tomb bringing the spices which they had prepared** on Friday after watching Joseph and Nicodemus prepare Jesus' body and then place it in the tomb (Luke 23:55–56). They intended to return after the Sabbath to finish preparing the Lord's body for burial. Luke notes that they arrived **at early dawn;** Matthew "as it began to dawn" (Matt. 28:1); and Mark "when the sun had risen" (Mark 16:2). The varying terminology reflects the different ways the writers described the same time of day; early dawn was the time when it began to dawn because the sun had just risen. John notes that Mary Magdalene arrived earlier "while it was still dark" (John 20:1). Evidently all the women set out just before dawn while it was still dark, but Mary got to the tomb ahead of the others. Seeing that the stone had been removed, she assumed the worst—that grave robbers had broken into the tomb and stolen Jesus' body. She immediately left to report the shocking news to Peter and John (v. 2), who ran to the tomb to investigate (vv. 3–8). Overcome with grief, Mary returned to the tomb, but by the time she got there, the two disciples and the other women had come and gone. Since she did not cross paths with either group, she did not know about the angels (Luke 24:4–7).

Meanwhile the other women arrived at the tomb, where to their amazement, they unexpectedly **found the stone rolled away from the tomb.** The stone was far too heavy for them to maneuver, and the women had discussed the problem of how to move it while on their way to the tomb (Mark 16:3). They did not know of the guard detachment, which also would have prevented them from entering the tomb. It had been posted on Saturday (Matt. 27:62–66), when they were home observing the Sabbath. The guards, terrified by the earthquake and the appearance of the angels, had been rendered unconscious (Matt. 28:4). When they came to their senses they fled, and some reported what had happened to the Jewish leaders (v. 11), who initiated a cover-up (vv. 12–15).

With no stone or soldiers to hinder them, the women went inside the tomb, **but when they entered, they did not find the body of the Lord Jesus** (cf. Acts 2:36). The soldiers knew the tomb was empty, or they would still have been there guarding it. The Jewish leaders knew that the tomb was empty, or they would not have invented a false story to explain why it was empty. Mary knew the tomb was empty, or she would not have reported to Peter and John that it was. Peter and John also knew firsthand that the body of Jesus was not in the tomb. There is no explanation for the empty tomb other than that it was empty because Jesus had risen from the dead.

## THE ANGELIC MESSENGERS

**While they were perplexed about this, behold, two men suddenly stood near them in dazzling clothing; and as the women were terrified and bowed their faces to the ground, the men said to them, "Why do you seek the living One among the dead? He is not here, but He has risen. Remember how He spoke to you while He was still in Galilee, saying that the Son of Man must be delivered into the hands of sinful men, and be crucified, and the third day rise again."** (24:4–7)

The women were standing in or just outside the tomb, shocked and **perplexed** because the body of Jesus was gone. Suddenly, they went from being puzzled to being terrified. As they stood there in the light of dawn trying to figure out what could have happened to the corpse, **two men suddenly stood near them in dazzling clothing.** Matthew (28:2) and John (20:12) identify them as angels, appearing in human form (cf. Gen. 18:2; 19:1–5; Dan. 10:16).Although there were two of them (perhaps as witnesses; cf. Deut. 19:15), only one spoke. Similarly, although there were two demon-possessed men at Gerasa (Matt. 8:28), only one spoke (Mark 5:2, 7; Luke 8:27–28), and while there were two blind men healed on the road near Jericho (Matt. 20:30), Mark (10:46) and Luke (18:35) mention only the one who spoke. **Their dazzling clothing** (cf. Matt. 17:2; Acts 1:10; Rev. 19:14) identified them as divine messengers. Understandably, **the women were terrified and bowed their faces to the ground** (cf. Luke 1:12; 2:9; Dan. 8:15–18; 10:9; Matt. 28:2–4; Acts 10:3–4; Rev. 22:8).

In a mild rebuke **the men said to them, "Why do you seek the living One,** the one who is the resurrection and the life (John 11:25), the one over whom death no longer is master (Rom. 6:9), the one who was dead, but now is alive forevermore (Rev. 1:18) **among the dead?"** This angelic question is the first announcement that Jesus was alive. The angels went on to say, **"He is not here, but He has risen"** (lit.,"been raised"; the Greek verb is in the passive voice [cf. Acts 2:24, 32; 3:15, 26; 4:10; 5:30; 10:40; 13:30, 33, 34, 37; Rom. 4:24–25; 6:4, 9; 7:4; 8:11, 34; 10:9; 1 Cor. 6:14; 15:4, 12–20; 2 Cor. 4:14; Gal. 1:1; Eph. 1:20; Col. 2:12; 1 Thess. 1:10; 1 Peter 1:21]). **"Remember how He spoke to you while He was still in Galilee, saying that the Son of Man must be delivered into the hands of sinful men, and be crucified, and the third day rise again"** (Matt. 16:21; 17:22–23; 20:17–19; 26:2; 27:63). Since Jesus had predicted His resurrection, they should have been expecting it. But they obviously did not, since they brought spices with which to anoint His dead body.

### THE WITNESS OF THE WOMEN

**And they remembered His words, and returned from the tomb and reported all these things to the eleven and to all the rest. Now they were Mary Magdalene and Joanna and Mary the mother of James; also the other women with them were telling these things to the apostles.** (24:8–10)

After the angels' reminder, the women **remembered** the **words** Jesus spoke concerning His rising. As they left **the tomb** to report **all these things to the eleven and to all the rest,** the magnitude of what they had just experienced and heard dawned on them, and "they left the tomb quickly with fear and great joy and ran to report it to His disciples" (Matt. 28:8).

Meanwhile, Peter and John were en route to the tomb to investigate Mary Magdalene's report that Christ's body had been stolen by grave robbers (John 20:1–3). When the rest of the women returned, they confirmed Mary's report that the tomb was empty, and also filled in the details that she was unaware of. Mary did not look into the tomb, and did not see either the grave clothes or the angels. The other women reported the words of the angels to the nine apostles (Peter and John still had not returned) that the Lord had indeed risen, as He had said He would. They also related their encounter with the risen Lord, whom they had met on the way back from the tomb (Matt. 28:9–10).

That the resurrected Christ appeared first to women elevated women, who held an inferior position in Jewish society. It was a testimony to their love, devotion, and courage. They had witnessed His death at Calvary and His burial, and had seen the empty tomb. John is the only disciple recorded to have been at the cross, but he did not witness the burial; Joseph and Nicodemus buried the Lord's body, but they did not see the empty tomb. Now, with His appearance to the women, the evidence was complete, and only the women were eyewitnesses to the entire sequence of events. Luke may have specifically named three of them, **Mary Magdalene and Joanna and Mary the mother of James,** again in light of the law's requirement that "on the evidence of two or three witnesses a matter shall be confirmed" (Deut. 19:15).

At first glance **Mary Magdalene** seems out of place in the group of eyewitnesses. According to John 20:1–2, she had seen that the Lord's body was not in the tomb, jumped to the erroneous conclusion that grave robbers had taken it, and ran back to report her conclusion to Peter and John. Thus, she was not at the tomb with the other women.

But her story does not end there. At some point she decided to go back to the tomb. John 20:11 finds her "standing outside the tomb weeping and ... as she wept, she stooped and looked into the tomb." This time, as the other women had, she saw the two angels sitting inside (v. 12). They asked her, "Woman, why are you weeping?" and, still clinging to the belief that grave robbers had stolen Christ's body, "She said to them, 'Because they have taken away my Lord, and I do not know where they have laid Him'" (v. 13). At that point, whether because she sensed someone behind her or the angels gestured, "she turned around and saw Jesus standing there, and did not know that it was Jesus" (v. 14). He, too, asked her why she was weeping, and then whom she was seeking (v. 15). Leaping to another erroneous conclusion, "Supposing Him to be the gardener, she said to Him, 'Sir, if you have carried Him away, tell me where you have laid Him, and I will take Him away'" (v. 15). Then with a single word, Jesus revealed Himself to her: "Mary!" (v. 16). Instantly all of her confusion, doubt, and grief vanished, as she recognized the Lord. Overcome with joy and relief, Mary addressed Him as "Rabboni!" (a strengthened form of the word "Rabbi," used here to express supreme honor and reverence to her beloved Teacher) and clung to Him. He admonished her not to cling to Him, since He had not yet ascended to the Father, and sent her back to inform the disciples that He was to ascend to Him (v. 17).

With astonished joy, she raced back to the disciples, announced to them, "I have seen the Lord," and gave them His message (v. 18). Since she had the same experience as the other women of seeing the risen Christ, Luke rightly included her with them.

## The Unbelieving Disciples

**But these words appeared to them as nonsense, and they would not believe them. But Peter got up and ran to the tomb; stooping and looking in, he saw the linen wrappings only; and he went away to his home, marveling at what had happened.** (24:11–12)

Sadly, but predictably, the disciples dismissed the women's testimony as **nonsense,** mere idle talk and folly. No matter that the women's stories were identical, indicating that they all saw and experienced the same reality. No matter that their story had cohesion, was consistent, and provided details for which there was no other plausible explanation. The disciples thought the whole thing was absurd, and they would not believe them (cf.Luke 24:23–25).

Then Luke added as a side note Peter's visit to the tomb with John, which happened before the other women and Mary Magdalene returned.Along with John, **Peter got up and ran to the tomb** after Mary Magdalene's initial report. John outran him and got there first, but did not go inside.Peter arrived and,**stooping and looking in** (John 20:6 adds that he then entered the tomb), **he saw the linen wrappings only.** Puzzled and not yet sure what to make of it,**he went away to his home, marveling at what had happened.**

The disciples' unbelief offers further evidence that Jesus had risen. They would never have fabricated a resurrection, as the Jewish leaders falsely accused them of doing, since they were not expecting one. When the resurrection was reported to them by eyewitnesses, they scoffed at it and refused to believe. It was not until Jesus Himself appeared to them that they finally accepted that He had risen—and Thomas, who was not present when the Lord appeared to the other ten, refused to take their word for it. He would not believe until Jesus appeared a second time with him present.

But if the disciples did not take the body maybe,some argue,the Romans,Jews,or grave robbers did.

> But the Romans would have had no conceivable motive for taking Christ's body; Pilate would hardly have risked antagonizing the Jews by doing so. Nor would the Jews have taken the body; the last thing they wanted was to fuel speculation that Jesus had risen from the dead (cf. Matt. 27:62–66).But if either the Romans or the Jews had the body,why did they not produce it when the disciples boldly proclaimed the resurrection in the streets of Jerusalem a few weeks later? ...Grave robbers would not have unwrapped the body,left the valuable spices behind,or taken the time to neatly arrange the wrappings before they left. Nor would they have attempted to break into a tomb guarded by Roman soldiers. (John MacArthur,*John 12–21*,The MacArthur New Testament Commentary [Chicago: Moody,2008],376)

Nor is it plausible that the women mistakenly went to the wrong tomb,since they had seen where Joseph of Arimathea and Nicodemus buried the Lord's body. And if they had, the Jewish leaders and the Romans knew where the correct one was.Why did someone not simply go to the right tomb and retrieve the body? Similarly, if the body of Jesus was not buried, but thrown into a pit, why did someone not go and retrieve it? If Christ's body had been thrown into a pit it would mean that the story of Joseph of Arimathea and Nicodemus burying Him was false. In that case, those two would surely have debunked it.

The numerous appearances Jesus made after the resurrection provide the most convincing proof of His resurrection:

> Scripture records at least ten distinct appearances of Christ between the resurrection and the ascension: to Mary Magdalene (John 20:11–18), to other women who had been at the tomb (Matt. 28:8–10), to two disciples on the road to Emmaus (Luke 24:13–32), to Peter (Luke 24:34), to ten of the eleven remaining apostles, Thomas being absent (Luke 24:36–43; John 20:19–25), to all eleven apostles, with Thomas present (John 20:26–31), to seven of the apostles on the shore of the Sea of Galilee (John 21:1–25), to more than 500 disciples, probably on a mountain in Galilee (1 Cor. 15:7), to James (1 Cor. 15:7), and to the apostles when He ascended to heaven (Acts 1:3–11). In addition, the risen Christ later appeared to Saul of Tarsus on the road to Damascus (Acts 9:1–9), and several subsequent occasions (Acts 18:9; 22:17–18; 23:11). (*John 12–21*, 376)

As noted in the discussion of verse six above, the New Testament repeatedly affirms that God raised Jesus from the dead. To deny the resurrection, therefore, is not only to reject the compelling historical facts, but also to deny the testimony of the New Testament. But if the resurrection did take place as the overwhelming evidence indicates, then the Bible is true, Jesus is Lord, and every person is accountable to Him (cf. Phil. 2:10–11).

It is not enough merely to feel that Christianity is true, or even accept intellectually that it is. Feelings remove emotional barriers to experiencing the risen Christ; facts remove intellectual ones. But neither alone is sufficient to save. Only faith in the resurrection, "[confessing] with your mouth Jesus as Lord, and [believing] in your heart that God raised Him from the dead," will result in salvation, "for with the heart a person believes, resulting in righteousness, and with the mouth he confesses, resulting in salvation" (Rom. 10:9–10).

# Christit: The Living Expositor (Luke 24:13–32)

# Christ: The
# Living Expositor
# (Luke 24:13–32)

**37**

And behold, two of them were going that very day to a village named Emmaus, which was about seven miles from Jerusalem. And they were talking with each other about all these things which had taken place. While they were talking and discussing, Jesus Himself approached and began traveling with them. But their eyes were prevented from recognizing Him. And He said to them, "What are these words that you are exchanging with one another as you are walking?" And they stood still, looking sad. One of them, named Cleopas, answered and said to Him, "Are You the only one visiting Jerusalem and unaware of the things which have happened here in these days?" And He said to them, "What things?" And they said to Him, "The things about Jesus the Nazarene, who was a prophet mighty in deed and word in the sight of God and all the people, and how the chief priests and our rulers delivered Him to the sentence of death, and crucified Him. But we were hoping that it was He who was going to redeem Israel. Indeed, besides all this, it is the third day since these things happened. But also some women among us amazed us. When they were at the tomb early in the morning, and did not find His body, they came, saying that they had also seen a vision of angels who said that He was alive. Some of those who were with us went to the tomb and found it just exactly as the women also had said; but Him they did not see." And He said to them, "O foolish men and slow of heart to believe in all that the prophets have spoken! Was it not necessary for the Christ to suffer these things and to enter into His glory?" Then beginning with Moses and with all the prophets, He explained to them the things concerning Himself in all the Scriptures. And they approached the village where they were going, and He acted as though He were going farther. But they urged Him, saying, "Stay with us, for it is getting toward evening, and the day is now nearly over." So He went in to stay with them. When He had reclined at the table with them, He took the bread and blessed it, and breaking it, He began giving it to them. Then their eyes were opened and they recognized Him; and He vanished from their sight. They said to one another, "Were not our hearts burning within us while He was speaking to us on the road, while He was explaining the Scriptures to us?" (24:13–32)

The most important reality in the world is God's truth. The Word of God is the word of truth (Ps. 119:43, 160; John 17:17; 2 Cor. 6:7; Eph. 1:13; Col. 1:5; 2 Tim. 2:15; James 1:18), which is tried (Ps. 18:30), upright (Ps. 33:4), forever settled in heaven (Ps. 119:89), a lamp for the feet and a light to the path (Ps. 119:105), pure (Ps. 119:140), the source of reward (Prov. 13:13), good (Prov. 16:20), a blessing (Luke 11:28), sanctification (John 17:17), and the sword of the Spirit used in spiritual warfare (Eph. 6:17).

Only those who understand the Bible can know the truth about salvation from sin and eternal damnation in hell; only those who obey biblical truth can live fulfilled, obedient, blessed, effective, joyful lives. To understand Scripture is to understand everything from God's perspective, which is the only true view. All of God's purposes for humanity and all of His purposes in time and eternity can be known only to those who understand the Bible. Therefore the greatest service that can ever be rendered to anyone is to explain to them the meaning of Scripture.

Nowhere is that fact more powerfully illustrated than in this passage. In this His first post-resurrection appearance in Luke's gospel, Jesus confronted two of His followers who were ignorant, filled with doubt, and confused. It was not that they did not believe the Scripture, but that their understanding of it was deficient—and a deficient knowledge of Scripture is insufficient and dangerous. Therefore Jesus opened the Old Testament Scripture to them and dispelled their darkness and confusion about Him with the light of truth. The story of this encounter may be viewed from three perspectives: the need for understanding, the source of understanding, and the response to understanding.

## The Need for Understanding

**And behold, two of them were going that very day to a village named Emmaus, which was about seven miles from Jerusalem. And they were talking with each other about all these things which had taken place. While they were talking and discussing, Jesus Himself approached and began traveling with them. But their eyes were prevented from recognizing Him. And He said to them, "What are these words that you are exchanging with one another as you are walking?" And they stood still, looking sad. One of them, named Cleopas, answered and said to Him, "Are You the only one visiting Jerusalem and unaware of the things which have happened here in these days?" And He said to them, "What things?" And they said to Him, "The things about Jesus the Nazarene, who was a prophet mighty in deed and word in the sight of God and all the people, and how the chief priests and our rulers delivered Him to the sentence of death, and crucified Him. But we were hoping that it was He who was going to redeem Israel. Indeed, besides all this, it is the third day since these things happened. But also some women among us amazed us. When they were at the tomb early in the morning, and did not find His body, they came, saying that they had also seen a vision of angels who said that He was alive. Some of those who were**

**with us went to the tomb and found it just exactly as the women also had said; but Him they did not see."** (24:13–24)

As it does twenty-six times in Luke's gospel (and eight times in Acts), the phrase *kai idou* (**and behold**) introduces something new and unexpected. This encounter took place late in the day on Sunday, as evening was approaching (v. 29). **Two** disciples of Jesus, some of the rest of the followers of Jesus who were not apostles (24:9), **were going** home **that very day to a village named Emmaus.** Nothing is known for certain about Emmaus, which appears nowhere else in Scripture. Tradition identifies it with the village of Kubeibeh, seven miles northwest of Jerusalem.

As they trudged along the dusty road, the two men were heartsick, devastated, and utterly confused. All of their hopes and dreams concerning Jesus had been dashed. David Gooding summarizes their dilemma:

> Death and resurrection formed no part of their concept of Messiah's office and programme, which is why they had not really taken in what Jesus had said about his coming death. They were hoping for a Messiah who would break the imperialist domination of the Romans by force of arms. A Messiah who managed to allow himself to be caught by the Jewish authorities, handed over to the Romans and crucified before he had even begun to organize any guerrilla operations, popular uprising or open warfare—what use was he? If the Old Testament prophesied a liberator who should not die, but be triumphant, Jesus was already disqualified: he had died. After that, it was almost irrelevant to talk of resurrection. (*According to Luke* [Grand Rapids: Eerdmans, 1987], 351)

Like the apostles and the rest of the disciples who had heard the women's testimony to the resurrection, they did not believe it and thought it was nonsense.

On their way back to Emmaus from Jerusalem **they were talking with each other about all these things which had taken place.** The phrase **all these things** encompasses everything that had happened that week in relation to Jesus. They would have remembered the triumphal entry on Monday, when the massive crowds hailed Him as the Messiah, the Son of David. On Tuesday He disrupted the religious leaders' lucrative, corrupt financial operations by again attacking the temple operations (cf. John 2:13–17). Wednesday and Thursday He taught the people, foiled the religious leaders' attempts to trap and discredit Him, and then turned the tables on them and humiliated them into silence. But then on Thursday night and Friday came the shock of His arrest, mock trials, crucifixion, death, and burial. It was unimaginable and devastating that the one in whom they and others had placed their hope had been executed by the leaders of Israel.

**While they were talking and discussing** these disastrous events, trying to make sense out of what had turned their world upside down, a stranger joined them. That was not uncommon; most people traveled from place to place on foot and the roads were traversed by many people. But unrecognized to them, it was **Jesus Himself** in resurrected, glorified form who **approached and began traveling with them.** His appearance was not dazzling like the angels (Luke 24:4), or like His had been at the transfiguration (Luke 9:29). The men were not startled by His appearance; He seemed to be just another person on the road. They did not know who He was, because **their eyes were prevented from recognizing Him** until He revealed Himself, as was the norm after His resurrection (Matt. 28:17; John 20:14–15; 21:4). They would not, of course, have been expecting it to be Jesus, since they did not believe He would rise. By not revealing Himself to them until after He explained the Scripture, Jesus modeled the principle that the power lies in the explanation of biblical truth, not in the person doing the explaining.

Good teachers ask provocative questions and Jesus, the greatest of all teachers, was no exception. As they walked together on the road He asked the two men, **"What are these words that you are exchanging with one another as you are walking?"** They stopped abruptly and **stood still, looking sad** with disappointment, dumbfounded by the stranger's question. Incredulously and perhaps agitated, **one of them, named Cleopas, answered and said to Him, "Are You the only one visiting Jerusalem and unaware of the things which have happened here in these days?"** That Luke mentioned **Cleopas** by name suggests that he may have been Luke's source for this incident. He asked Jesus in essence how He could possibly have been unaware of what was common knowledge throughout Jerusalem, things that even a pilgrim **visiting** the city for Passover could not have missed.

Christ's follow-up question, **"What things?"** was intended to elicit a further response from them. Cleopas's unnamed companion now joined the conversation, and **they** responded with a summary of the situation from their perspective. They had been discussing **the things about Jesus the Nazarene,** and they proceeded to give a description of Him. He **was** first **a prophet** (John 4:19; 9:13–17), a spokesman for God. More specifically, He was the prophet of whom Moses wrote (Deut. 18:18–22; cf. Acts 3:22), that is, the promised Messiah. Their description was accurate but cryptic; Jesus was a prophet, but more than a prophet. Unlike all other preachers, He was **mighty in deed and word;** the countless miracles He performed throughout His ministry demonstrated His power over the natural and supernatural realms, and He spoke like no man had ever spoken before (John 7:46; cf. Matt. 7:28–29). His person and deeds were also pleasing **in the sight of God.** At His baptism "a voice out of the heavens said, 'This is My beloved Son, in whom I am well-pleased'" (Matt. 3:17), while at His transfiguration God declared, "This is My beloved Son, with whom I am well-pleased" (Matt. 17:5; cf. Matt. 12:18). Jesus was also admired by **all the people,** who praised God for the miracles He performed (cf. Luke 18:40–43; John 7:12).

But in shocking contrast to those accolades **the chief priests and** the **rulers delivered Him to the sentence of death, and crucified Him.** Even though Jesus was sentenced to death by a Roman governor in a Roman court and crucified by Roman soldiers, the two men did not mention the Romans, since they were merely the executioners carrying out the Jewish leaders' will. And even though in the end the crowds cried for Pilate to crucify Jesus, they did so because the chief priests and rulers manipulated them (Matt. 27:20). The religious elite were the real killers (cf. Acts 4:10; 5:30).

The execution of the Lord Jesus had created an existential and theological crisis for the men, who had been **hoping that it was He who was going to redeem Israel.** As noted earlier, a dead Messiah had no place in their thinking; they expected someone who would liberate them from Roman oppression and establish the kingdom promised in the Old Testament. The verb translated **redeem** appears only here in Luke's gospel, although the noun form is used in 1:68 to speak of the redemption of Israel.

Everyone knew that to redeem something required the payment

of a price (cf. Lev. 27:13, 15, 19, 27, 31). That should have been fresh in their minds in light of the just-completed Passover celebration, when animals were sacrificed as the price for forgiveness. But though they understood that redemption required death, they were never taught it would require the death of the Messiah Himself. As a result, they were shocked and confused when He was executed.

That it was now late in **the third day since these things happened** and they had no evidence that Jesus had risen seemed to confirm that their faithless assessment of the situation was correct. They acknowledged to Jesus, **"Some women among us amazed us. When they were at the tomb early in the morning, and did not find His body, they came, saying that they had also seen a vision of angels who said that He was alive."** To arrive at the conclusion that Jesus had not risen, they had to reject the clear testimony of the women that He had. Even though Peter and John **went to the tomb and found it just exactly as the women also had said,** thus verifying that part of their testimony, they were not persuaded, presumably because the two apostles **did not see** the risen Lord. However, if the women were proven trustworthy in what the disciples were able to verify, they should have concluded that they were also trustworthy in what was not yet verified. That they did not shows how deeply ingrained was their inability to believe that Messiah could die and rise again.

THE SOURCE OF UNDERSTANDING

**And He said to them, "O foolish men and slow of heart to believe in all that the prophets have spoken! Was it not necessary for the Christ to suffer these things and to enter into His glory?" Then beginning with Moses and with all the prophets, He explained to them the things concerning Himself in all the Scriptures.** (24:25–27)

The two disciples' confusion and unbelief clearly defined their need to understand the reality of what had happened. They needed to know not only that Jesus rose from the dead, but also that His death and resurrection are essential features of His messiahship. They needed to understand that what had taken place was God's plan for the redemption of Israel and the world. The risen Lord's questions and their responses had put Him in position to provide them with the answers they needed. Good expositions of Scripture are set up with questions.

Before instructing the men, Jesus first rebuked them for being **foolish men and slow of heart** (i.e., "dull," or "stupid") **to believe in all that the prophets have spoken.** Their confusion stemmed from their failure to understand and believe all that the Old Testament taught regarding the Messiah. They were right to expect Him to reign and rule; to establish His kingdom over Israel and the world.

But that was only part of the truth, as Jesus' question, **"Was it not necessary for the Christ to suffer these things and to enter into His glory?"** indicates. They, like all the Jewish people, were looking for a Messiah who would vanquish their oppressors, not be killed by them, and missed the truth that He first had to suffer before establishing His kingdom. There was no excuse for their lack of understanding, since the Old Testament was clear and understandable. Jesus repeatedly challenged His opponents, "Have you not read?" (Matt. 12:3, 5; 19:4; 22:31; Mark 12:10), and said that their errant theology stemmed from a failure to understand the Scripture (Matt. 22:29).

There was no excuse for failing to recognize the necessity for Messiah to suffer death. They knew that sin must be paid for by the death of a substitute. After Adam and Eve sinned in the garden, God killed an animal to provide coverings for them, picturing the death of an innocent substitute to cover the sin of a guilty sinner (Gen. 3:21). He accepted Abel's sacrifice because it was a blood sacrifice, and rejected Cain's because it was not (Gen. 4:3–5). After the flood, Noah built an altar and offered sacrifices (Gen. 8:20). The sacrificial system laid out in the Pentateuch, including the Day of Atonement and Passover, involved the deaths of countless thousands of innocent animals. It was self-evident, however, that those sacrifices did not ultimately satisfy God's justice, otherwise they would not have been constantly repeated, as the writer of Hebrews explains:

> For the Law, since it has only a shadow of the good things to come and not the very form of things, can never, by the same sacrifices which they offer continually year by year, make perfect those who draw near. Otherwise, would they not have ceased to be offered, because the

worshipers, having once been cleansed, would no longer have had consciousness of sins? (Heb. 10:1–2)

Having rebuked them for failing to know the significance of the Old Testament's teaching regarding Messiah's suffering, Jesus—the one to whom that teaching pointed (John 5:39)—personally tutored them in a true understanding of it. **Beginning with Moses and with all the prophets, He explained to them the things concerning Himself in all the Scriptures.** That teaching would undoubtedly have included such things as the Protoevangelium (Gen. 3:15); Abel's and Noah's sacrifices; the ark, which pictures Him as the true ark into which sinners enter and sail safely through the waters of divine judgment; the ram offered as a substitute in place of Isaac (Gen. 22:13); the Passover lambs, which pictured Him as the final sacrifice (Ex. 12; cf. 1 Cor. 5:7); the manna (Ex. 16), which pictured Him as the true bread from heaven (John 6:32–35); the five main offerings in Leviticus (burnt, grain, peace, sin, and trespass), of which He is the fulfillment; the Day of Atonement, where He is pictured by both the sacrifice on the altar and the scapegoat that bore away sin; the rocks that provided water in the wilderness (Ex. 17; Num. 20), which pictured Him as the source of spiritual provision for His people (1 Cor. 10:4); the prophet of whom Moses wrote (Deut. 18:18–22; cf. Acts 3:22), who was the Messiah; the one hanged on a tree, cursed by God and taken down before sunset (Deut. 21:22–23), and hated without a cause (Ps. 69:4). He might have taken them to Psalm 40:7, which the writer of Hebrews applied to Him (Heb. 10:7). He would surely have pointed out the details of His crucifixion given in the Old Testament (Pss. 22; 41:9; 69:21; Isa. 50:6; Zech. 11:12–13; 12:10; and especially Isa. 53); and Daniel's prophecy of the seventy weeks (Dan. 9:24–26), which predicted the exact day of His triumphal entry. Jesus also would have explained the prediction of His resurrection given in Psalm 16:8–10 (cf. Acts 13:34–37).

### THE RESPONSE TO UNDERSTANDING

**And they approached the village where they were going, and He acted as though He were going farther. But they urged Him,**

**saying, "Stay with us, for it is getting toward evening, and the day is now nearly over." So He went in to stay with them. When He had reclined at the table with them, He took the bread and blessed it, and breaking it, He began giving it to them. Then their eyes were opened and they recognized Him; and He vanished from their sight. They said to one another, "Were not our hearts burning within us while He was speaking to us on the road, while He was explaining the Scriptures to us?"** (24:28–32)

Christ's unparalleled survey of the Old Testament's teaching regarding Himself, particularly His death, left Cleopas and his companion stunned and overwhelmed. Their hearts were ignited by the Scripture explained (v. 32), since Jesus still had not revealed Himself to them. Understanding the meaning of the Bible fulfills the true believer's deepest longing, because it anchors faith in reality, producing profound joy. To know the true interpretation of Scripture is to know God and realize how His plan is unfolding and His sovereign purpose is being accomplished.

As the three men **approached the village where** Cleopas and the other disciple **were going,** Jesus **acted as though He were going farther.** He did so for the same reason He had questioned them, to elicit a response that would demonstrate the effect of the Scriptures on their hearts. And it did. They wanted more instruction and did not want the thrilling teaching to end.

So as Jesus started to leave, **they** strongly **urged** (the Greek verb literally means "to use force") **Him, saying, "Stay with us, for it is getting toward evening, and the day is now nearly over."** Their invitation was not motivated by hospitality, since by acting as if He were going farther, the Lord gave the impression that He had a place to stay. What they wanted was more understanding of God's revelation. To their great joy Jesus obliged and **went in to stay with them.**

Then in the midst of the continuing conversation, Jesus did something unusual. **When He had reclined at the table with them, He took the bread and blessed it, and breaking it, He began giving it to them.** It was the host's place to break the bread and initiate the meal, not the guest's. Evidently the two men were so caught up in Christ's teaching that they forgot all about eating. As Jesus performed this act of kindness, **their eyes were** suddenly **opened and they recognized Him.** As noted earlier, no one recognized the resurrected Jesus unless He revealed Himself to them. Perhaps the familiar way He broke the bread and the familiar words He used to bless the meal were the means Jesus used to open their eyes. Having revealed Himself to them, **He vanished from their sight.**

Instead of marveling over Christ's remarkable disappearance, **they said to one another, "Were not our hearts burning within us while He was speaking to us on the road, while He was explaining the Scriptures to us?"** What set their hearts on fire was the understanding of Scripture they had received from Him. The burning joy that resulted was so overwhelming that they immediately went out into the pitch black night and headed back to Jerusalem to share with the others the knowledge that they alone possessed—that Jesus' suffering and resurrection were firmly grounded in the Old Testament. God's plan was being fulfilled!

When the truth of Scripture becomes clear, the heart is set on fire for joy and for testimony. It was that blazing joy that prompted Henry Martyn to exclaim, "Now let me burn out for God"; David Brainerd to write in his diary, "Oh that I could be a flame of fire in the service of my God!"; and John Wesley to say of his conversion, "I felt my heart strangely warmed."

# The Living Christ Dispels All Doubt (Luke 24:33–43)

**38**

And they got up that very hour and returned to Jerusalem, and found gathered together the eleven and those who were with them, saying, "The Lord has really risen and has appeared to Simon." They began to relate their experiences on the road and how He was recognized by them in the breaking of the bread. While they were telling these things, He Himself stood in their midst and said to them, "Peace be to you." But they were startled and frightened and thought that they were seeing a spirit. And He said to them, "Why are you troubled, and why do doubts arise in your hearts? See My hands and My feet, that it is I Myself; touch Me and see, for a spirit does not have flesh and bones as you see that I have." And when He had said this, He showed them His hands and His feet. While they still could not believe it because of their joy and amazement, He said to them, "Have you anything here to eat?" They gave Him a piece of a broiled fish; and He took it and ate it before them. (24:33–43)

Denying the resurrection of the Lord Jesus Christ has always been a major tactic employed by Satan and his emissaries in their assaults on God and Scripture. They understand that if He did not rise from the dead, neither His words nor the rest of Scripture can be believed. Jesus predicted His resurrection (Matt. 12:38–40; John 2:18–22), as did the Old Testament (Ps. 16), and the apostles proclaimed it. If Jesus did not rise from the dead, then the Old Testament, His own claims, and the apostolic gospel proclamation were false, and Christianity collapses. As Paul wrote to the church at Corinth, which was under assault from false teachers who denied the resurrection,

> If Christ has not been raised, then our preaching is vain, your faith also is vain.…For if the dead are not raised, not even Christ has been raised; and if Christ has not been raised, your faith is worthless; you are still in your sins. Then those also who have fallen asleep in Christ have perished. If we have hoped in Christ in this life only, we are of all men most to be pitied. (1 Cor. 15:14, 16–19)

To deny the resurrection is to declare God a liar, because He "declared [Jesus to be] the Son of God with power by the resurrection from the dead" (Rom. 1:4). Such a denial places a person outside the sphere of salvation, since it is only those who "confess with [their] mouth Jesus as Lord, and believe in [their] heart that God raised Him from the dead, [who] will be saved" (Rom. 10:9).

To reject the resurrection requires ignoring the overwhelming historical evidence. There are several undeniable facts that must be explained away to support any theory seeking to deny the resurrection. First, Jesus actually died on the cross, as the Roman executioners in charge of His crucifixion verified (Mark 15:44–45; John 19:33–34). Second, He was buried in a tomb by Joseph of Arimathea and Nicodemus (John 19:38–42), and that burial was observed by the women (Luke 23:55). His body was not cast into a common grave where criminals were buried. Third, the tomb was found empty on Sunday morning, by Mary Magdalene (John 20:1–2), the rest of the women (Luke 24:1–3), and Peter and John (John 20:3–8). Finally, Jesus appeared to numerous people after His resurrection: Mary Magdalene, the rest of the women, the two disciples on the road to Emmaus, Peter, the apostles with Thomas absent and again with him present, five hundred believers at once (presumably in Galilee), His half-brother James, then all the apostles, and finally to Paul (1 Cor. 15:3–8). The only plausible explanation for those facts is that Jesus rose from the dead.

Still throughout history there have been skeptics, purveyors of "doctrines of demons" (1 Tim. 4:1), who have concocted various theories in a futile attempt to deny the reality of the resurrection.

The "swoon theory," for example, argues that Jesus did not really die on the cross, but went into a semi-coma due to shock and loss of blood. He was mistakenly thought to be dead, and so was taken down from the cross and buried while still alive. The spices and the coolness of the tomb later revived Him, and He left the tomb. When He met the disciples, they mistakenly assumed He had risen from the dead.

This theory faces insurmountable difficulties. The Roman soldiers who crucified Jesus were experienced executioners, well qualified to determine whether the victim was dead. They were satisfied that Jesus had died, so they did not break His legs to hasten His death (John 19:33). The centurion in charge of the execution confirmed to Pilate that Jesus was dead (Mark 15:44–45). Obviously, he would have made certain of that before making his report to the governor. The spear thrust into Jesus' side that brought forth blood and water also showed clearly that He was dead (John 19:34).

The "swoon theory" also cannot explain how Jesus, weakened by the severe physical trauma of scourging and crucifixion, could have survived for three days without food, water, and medical care. Nor does it explain how in such a weakened condition He could have freed himself from the grave clothes in which his body was wrapped (which Lazarus was unable to do; John 11:44), moved the heavy stone that sealed the tomb, overpowered the Roman guard detachment, and then walked several miles to Emmaus on nail-pierced feet. Most significantly, this notion cannot explain how a man in His condition, desperately in need of food, water, and treatment of His injuries, could have persuaded the disciples that He was the risen Lord, the conqueror of death and the grave. This theory blasphemously turns Jesus into a deceiver and a fraud, rejecting the testimony of Scripture that He lived a sinless life (Luke 1:35; 3:22; John 8:46; 14:30; 15:10; 2 Cor. 5:21; Heb. 4:15; 7:26; 1 Peter 2:22).

Equally improbable is the "hallucination theory," whose proponents maintain that Jesus' followers, overwhelmed by grief and sorrow, had hallucinations of seeing Him alive. A hallucination is an individual experience, not a group phenomenon. Jesus, however, appeared to various individuals and groups on at least ten different occasions, including more than 500 people at once (1 Cor. 15:6). His followers were unlikely to have generated such a hallucination, since they did not expect Him to rise from the dead (John 20:9) and rejected the initial reports that He had (Luke 24:11). A further embarrassment for this theory is that on at least three occasions the people allegedly having hallucinations of Jesus failed to recognize Him (Luke 24:13–32; John 20:15; 21:4). Nor can it explain how a hallucination could eat a piece of fish (Luke 24:42–43), direct fishermen to a school of fish (John 21:6), or cook a meal (John 21:9–13). Although it tries unsuccessfully to explain Christ's resurrection appearances, the hallucination theory offers no explanation for the empty tomb and the missing body.

Others who deny the resurrection propose that the women mistakenly went to the wrong tomb (even though two of them had observed Jesus' burial; Mark 15:47). Finding it empty, they leaped to the erroneous conclusion that Jesus had risen from the dead. But then Peter and John would also have had to have gone to the wrong tomb. Surely Joseph of Arimathea and Nicodemus, who buried Jesus, knew in which tomb they had buried His body. Obviously the Jewish leaders also knew which tomb was the right one, as did the Roman guard detachment they placed there. This theory has no answer for the obvious question: Why did someone not simply go to the right tomb and produce Jesus' body? The theory that His body was never in the tomb, but was thrown into a common grave, has the same fatal weakness. Had the Jewish authorities produced the body of Jesus when the apostles began preaching the resurrection, Christianity would have been stillborn. The existence of the church is proof that Jesus Christ rose from the dead.

Consistent with the other gospel writers, Luke gives eyewitness accounts of people who saw the risen Christ. First, he related the encounter two disciples had with the risen Christ on the road from Jerusalem to Emmaus (see the exposition of Luke 24:13–32 in the previous chapter in this volume). In this section the story continues with the appearance of Jesus to the apostles and disciples in Jerusalem. The account contains three elements: consistent profession, confounding presence, and convincing proofs.

## CONSISTENT PROFESSION

**And they got up that very hour and returned to Jerusalem, and found gathered together the eleven and those who were with them, saying, "The Lord has really risen and has appeared to Simon." They began to relate their experiences on the road and how He was recognized by them in the breaking of the bread.** (24:33–35)

The evidence was mounting that Jesus was alive and had risen from the dead. Mary Magdalene (John 20:11–17), the other women (Matt. 28:8–10), and Cleopas and the unnamed disciple (Luke 24:13–32) had all seen Him, and Luke's narrative is about to refer to one more appearance and describe yet another.

The story picks up where the previous section, describing the risen Lord's appearance to Cleopas and the other disciple, left off. After Jesus broke the bread, initiating the meal, "their eyes were opened and they recognized Him; and He vanished from their sight" (v. 31). Without finishing their meal, **they got up that very hour and returned to Jerusalem.** It was late in the evening, perhaps nine or ten o'clock, but the news they had would not keep. They headed back to the disciples they knew and loved in order to bring them the exciting news that Jesus was alive. Their report would confirm the testimony of the women and bring an end to the sorrow, sadness, despair, and despondency that had prevailed among Christ's followers when He left them.

Arriving at the secret meeting place in Jerusalem, they **found** that **the eleven and those who were with them** were still **gathered together. The eleven** is a technical term for the apostles, just as "the twelve" had been before the defection and death of Judas Iscariot (Matt. 26:14; Mark 3:16; 4:10; 6:7; 9:35; 10:32; 11:11; 14:17, 20; Luke 8:1; 9:1, 12; 18:31; John 6:67, 70, 71; 20:24) and would again be after Matthias was added (Acts 6:2; 1 Cor. 15:5). The Greek verb translated **gathered together** is in the passive voice, perhaps indicating that those present had been gathered by the prompting of the Holy Spirit to witness the appearance of Jesus that would take place that night. When the door was unlocked for the two men, they entered only to find that the news of Jesus' resurrection had preceded their arrival. The participle *legontas* (**saying**) is in the accusative case, indicating that what follows was said to them by those already there. Before the two could share their incredible news, the rest of the believers excitedly reported to them, **"The Lord has really risen and has appeared to Simon."** The testimony by Mary Magdalene, the other women, and Peter, along with Cleopas and the unnamed disciple with him that Jesus had risen and was alive, was consistent. This is the only reference to Jesus' appearance to Simon Peter in the Gospels, though Paul referred to it in 1 Corinthians 15:5. It may be that the details of that appearance are not recorded because God chose to be gracious to Peter, since it likely included rebuke by the Lord, as well as restoration.

Having heard the wonderful news of Jesus' appearance to Peter, the two **began to relate their experiences on the road and how He was recognized by them in the breaking of the bread.** But once again they were upstaged, this time by the arrival of the risen Lord Jesus Christ.

CONFOUNDING PRESENCE

**While they were telling these things, He Himself stood in their midst and said to them, "Peace be to you." But they were startled and frightened and thought that they were seeing a spirit.** (24:36–37)

The two newcomers were **telling** the rest of the disciples about the **things** that happened during their encounter with the risen Lord, when suddenly **He Himself stood in their midst.** He immediately **said to them, "Peace be to you,"** not only because it was a common greeting, but also because they were **startled and frightened.**

It was not the appearance of Jesus' body that caused them to be startled into a state of fear. His resurrection body was not dazzlingly, brilliantly lit like the angels at the tomb, or His own appearance at the trans-figuration. Mary Magdalene mistook Him for the gardener (John 20:15), and the two disciples for just another fellow traveler on the road to Emmaus. What prompted the **thought that they were seeing a spirit** was not Christ's appearance, but His entrance. His supernatural appear-ance in the room was as startling as His abrupt disappearance from the dinner table in Emmaus had been. Since no human being could sudden-ly materialize out of nowhere into a locked room, they panicked and thought they were seeing a ghost (cf. Acts 12:9).

## CONVINCING PROOFS

**And He said to them, "Why are you troubled, and why do doubts arise in your hearts? See My hands and My feet, that it is I Myself; touch Me and see, for a spirit does not have flesh and bones as you see that I have." And when He had said this, He showed them His hands and His feet. While they still could not believe it because of their joy and amazement, He said to them, "Have you anything here to eat?" They gave Him a piece of a broiled fish; and He took it and ate it before them.** (24:38–43)

Jesus' rhetorical questions, **"Why are you troubled, and why do doubts arise in your hearts?"** served as a mild rebuke to the fright-ened disciples. There was no legitimate reason for them to panic. The Lord then challenged them to see that He was not a ghost or hallucination by using their senses. They could **see** His **hands and** His **feet,** and verify that it was Jesus Himself. He invited them to **touch** Him **and see, for a spirit does not have flesh and bones as** they could **see that** He had. This is the same challenge Jesus would later make to Thomas, who was not pres-ent on this occasion (John 20:24). Christ's resurrection body was capable of conforming to any reality, physical or spiritual. It was a real, physical body with **flesh and bones,** which could be seen, speak, be touched, and eat, yet it could also pass through walls. Jesus could one moment be absent and in the next present, at one moment standing on the Mount of Olives conversing with the disciples, and the next ascending into heaven.

Resurrected believers will have bodies like His resurrected body (Phil. 3:20–21; 1 John 3:2; 1 Cor. 15:35–44). Having **said this, He showed them His hands and His feet,** so they could see that He had a real body, with the marks of His crucifixion.

Despite the fact that Jesus was present, **they still could not believe it,** not because of fear, but **because of their joy and amazement.** It seemed too good to be real, and they were torn between hope and skepticism, just like those praying for Peter's release from prison would later be (Acts 12:12–16).

Seeing that they were not fully convinced, Jesus offered further proof, and **said to them, "Have you anything here to eat?" They gave Him a piece of a broiled fish; and He took it and ate it before them** (cf. Gen. 18:1–8). It should be noted that some skeptics argue that the reference to **broiled fish** is an error. They claim that fish were not available in Jerusalem—despite the fact that one of the city's gates was known as the Fish Gate (Neh. 3:3; 12:39; Zeph. 1:10), and Nehemiah refers to merchants from Tyre who imported fish and sold them in Jerusalem (Neh. 13:16).

From its inception on the Day of Pentecost, the church's triumphant message has been that Jesus Christ has risen from the dead and is alive forevermore (Acts 2:22–32; 3:14–15, 26; 4:10–12; 5:30; 10:40; 13:30, 33–37). Erich Sauer writes, "The message of the cross is at the same time a message of the resurrection (Acts 1:22; 2:32). In this lies its invincibility" (*The Triumph of the Crucified* [Grand Rapids: Eerdmans, 1951], 40).

The bodily resurrection of the Lord Jesus Christ was necessary for at least three reasons. First, it demonstrated Christ's complete victory over sin. Sin brought spiritual death and physical death. If He only conquered spiritual death, He did not fully conquer sin. If He had not risen bodily, those who are His would not rise either. There would never be a restoration of the earth in millennial glory.

Second, Christ's bodily resurrection is necessary to demonstrate the purpose of God in humanity. Men and women were created to give glory to God. Their bodily resurrection, which is dependent on Christ's, is necessary so that men and women in some bodily form may give glory to God as they were originally intended to do.

Finally, and most significantly, the physical resurrection of Jesus

Christ offers visible proof that God was satisfied with His sacrifice. Saving faith comes when one acknowledges Jesus as Lord, affirming that God raised Him from the dead, and thus demonstrated His approval of Christ's atoning work on the cross.

If the story of Jesus ended at the cross, the disciples' hopes would have been shattered. They needed to know not only that He died, but also that He rose from the dead. The only way they would know that is to see Him in His physical, visible resurrected body. If they had not seen Jesus alive from the dead, they would not have carried the message any further. They would never have proclaimed the message of a dead, disappointing teacher. No one would have believed the Lord Jesus was the Redeemer, Savior, Son of God, and Lord if He hadn't visibly risen from the dead, as the apostle Paul wrote:

> If there is no resurrection of the dead, not even Christ has been raised; and if Christ has not been raised, then our preaching is vain, your faith also is vain. Moreover we are even found to be false witnesses of God, because we testified against God that He raised Christ, whom He did not raise, if in fact the dead are not raised. For if the dead are not raised, not even Christ has been raised; and if Christ has not been raised, your faith is worthless; you are still in your sins. (1 Cor. 15:13–17)

# The Great Commission: Proclaiming Forgiveness (Luke 24:44–49)

# 39

**Now He said to them, "These are My words which I spoke to you while I was still with you, that all things which are written about Me in the Law of Moses and the Prophets and the Psalms must be fulfilled." Then He opened their minds to understand the Scriptures, and He said to them, "Thus it is written, that the Christ would suffer and rise again from the dead the third day, and that repentance for forgiveness of sins would be proclaimed in His name to all the nations, beginning from Jerusalem. You are witnesses of these things. And behold, I am sending forth the promise of My Father upon you; but you are to stay in the city until you are clothed with power from on high." (24:44–49)**

This section of Luke's gospel sweeps from the beginning of revelation in Genesis to the end of redemptive history, viewing the mural of salvation from start to finish. The primary emphasis of the Lord's words here is found in verse 47, where He declared that repentance and forgiveness of sins would be proclaimed in His name.

The passage is Luke's account of the Great Commission (cf. Matt. 28:19–20), the Lord's mandate for the church to proclaim the saving truth of the "glorious gospel of the blessed God" (1 Tim. 1:11). That mandate is for all believers throughout all history, not merely those who heard the Lord speak these words. The gospel of Luke ends by putting the reader in the same position as the apostles and the disciples; everyone who names the name of Jesus Christ is responsible to proclaim the truth. The baton has been passed down from generation to generation, and it is our responsibility to pass it on to the next generation.

To fulfill the Lord's command to spread the gospel around the world is the overarching, all-consuming purpose of the church. Everything else, including understanding and teaching sound doctrine, worship, fellowship, prayer, pursuing holiness, and engaging in Christian service, is important and beneficial. But to do all of those things and not proclaim the gospel is to reject the purpose for which those elements exist. They are not the goal, but rather the means to accomplishing the goal of proclaiming the gospel and undergirding that proclamation with lives of credibility and integrity.

But while believers are responsible for evangelizing the lost, God is the one who ultimately seeks them. From the garden, where God called to Adam after the fall (Gen. 3:9), to the final invitation in Revelation 22:17, God has sought sinners. The goal of human history is God's redeeming men and women to bring them to glory as a bride for His Son, whom they will serve, honor, and worship forever.

In its conclusion, Luke's gospel proves what it claimed in the beginning. The angel declared to Mary that the son she would bear would be the Son of God (1:35). Jesus' life, miracles, power over demons, teaching, and resurrection demonstrated that He was. Zacharias, the father of John the Baptist, gave a Spirit-inspired prophecy in which he declared that the Messiah would accomplish redemption for His people through the forgiveness of their sins (1:77). Jesus Christ came, suffered, died, rose again the third day, and provided that forgiveness for all who believe in Him.

This penultimate section of Luke's gospel, which launches the history of the proclamation of the gospel, presents seven elements of the gospel mandate given to the church. It is biblical as to its foundation, historical as to its accomplishment, transformational as to its provision, Christological as to its appropriation, global as to its extent, personal as to its agency, and supernatural as to its power.

### The Gospel Is Biblical as to Its Foundation

**Now He said to them, "These are My words which I spoke to you while I was still with you, that all things which are written about Me in the Law of Moses and the Prophets and the Psalms must be fulfilled." Then He opened their minds to understand the Scriptures,** (24:44–45)

As noted in previous chapters of this volume, the Jewish people expected the Messiah to be a triumphant conqueror, not one who would suffer and die. To preach the gospel to them, the disciples would have to convince them from the Old Testament both that Jesus was the Messiah and that the Messiah had to die.

But they were woefully unprepared for that task. They had demonstrated a lack of understanding of the Old Testament and had failed miserably to comprehend most of what Jesus said to them. That was true even when He said it to them in simple, clear straightforward terms. The disciples had been subject all their lives to an inadequate, if not downright false, interpretation of the Old Testament by their rabbis. As a result, they were in no position to rightly interpret the Old Testament and needed someone to instruct them rightly. They required a total correction of their theology and hermeneutics as well as a clear understanding that Christianity was not a repudiation of Old Testament Judaism, but the fulfillment of it.

Despite Christ's repeated teaching on the subject of His death and resurrection (cf. Luke 9:22, 44–45; 18:31, 34; 24:6–8), the disciples still did not grasp the truth. He therefore reminded them of His **words which** He **spoke to** them **while** He **was still with** them during His earthly ministry; **that all things which are written about** Him **in the Law of Moses and the Prophets and the Psalms** (the threefold division of the Old Testament) **must be fulfilled.** Those were the Old Testament truths about Messiah that the disciples would have to believe wholeheartedly if they were to convince the Jewish people that Jesus was the Messiah. The **Law of Moses** was the Pentateuch (Genesis through Deuteronomy); the **Prophets** included both the former prophets (the historical books beginning with Joshua) and the later prophets (the major prophets; Isaiah, Jeremiah, Ezekiel, Daniel, and Lamentations, and the minor prophets; Hosea, Joel, Amos, Obadiah, Jonah, Micah, Nahum, Habakkuk, Zephaniah, Haggai, Zechariah, and Malachi); the **Psalms** represented the wisdom literature (Job, Psalms, Proverbs, Ecclesiastes, Song of Solomon).

Their evangelism was to be biblically based, so they needed clear understanding of the Scriptures related to Christ. The Old Testament promised the Messiah would come through the line of Abraham (Gen. 12:1–3; cf. Gal. 3:16), the tribe of Judah (Gen. 49:10; cf. Rev. 5:5), and the line of David (2 Sam. 7). Isaiah 7:14 predicted that He would be born of a virgin; Micah 5:2 that He would be born in Bethlehem. He would be betrayed by a close, trusted friend (Ps. 41:9); He would be beaten, spit on, and have His beard pulled out (Isa. 50:6; Mic. 5:1); the soldiers would gamble for His clothing (Ps. 22:18); He would be crucified (Ps. 22) and pierced (Zech. 12:10); His death would be vicarious (Isa. 53), and He would rise from the dead (Isa. 53:10; Ps. 16:8–11). The Christ of gospel history did not invent Himself, nor is He the invention of some people in the first century. He is the unmistakable fulfillment of divine prophecy.

Jesus **opened their minds to understand** those **Scriptures** and many other prophecies that were fulfilled in His first coming. As He had earlier done for the two disciples on the road to Emmaus, He gave them a sweeping messianic interpretation of the Old Testament. The disciples for the first time understood the messianic meaning of the Old Testament prophecies and used them immediately in their own interpretation of events (Acts 1:15–20), as well as their preaching and evangelism. In his sermon on the Day of Pentecost, Peter cited Joel 2:28–32 and Psalm 16:8–11, among others (Acts 2:14–36; cf. 4:23–26). Addressing the Sanhedrin, Peter cited Psalm 118:22 (Acts 4:10–11). Both Stephen (Acts 7) and Philip (Acts 8:26–35) employed sweeping features of the Old Testament in their evangelism, as did the apostle Paul (Acts 13:16–41; 17:1–3; 28:25–27). The disciples undoubtedly experienced the same passionate stirring of their hearts as did the two at Emmaus (Luke 24:32) and were eager to proclaim the Scriptures and their fulfillment as He had taught them. But not yet. Jesus instructed them to wait in Jerusalem until the Holy Spirit came to empower them for that task (Luke 24:49; Acts 1:4–5,8).

## THE GOSPEL IS HISTORICAL AS TO ITS ACCOMPLISHMENT

**and He said to them, "Thus it is written, that the Christ would suffer and rise again from the dead the third day,** (24:46)

It was **written** in the Old Testament **that the Christ would suffer and rise again from the dead the third day,** and that is exactly what happened. The resurrection was not mythological, or legendary; it was not a mystical or spiritual idea, but an event that happened in real, space-time history (cf. 1 Cor. 15:3–8). In fact, there is no better attested fact or event in ancient history than the resurrection of Jesus Christ.

## THE GOSPEL IS TRANSFORMATIONAL AS TO ITS PROVISION

**and that repentance for forgiveness of sins would be proclaimed** (24:47a)

The gracious, eternal provision of the gospel is the forgiveness of sins purchased by Christ's sacrifice on the cross and confirmed by His resurrection (Rom. 4:25). Forgiveness is a constant theme in Luke's gospel. Zacharias prophesied that God would "give to His people the knowledge of salvation by the forgiveness of their sins" (Luke 1:77). John the Baptist's ministry involved "preaching a baptism of repentance for the forgiveness of sins" (3:3). Jesus said to a paralytic, "Friend, your sins are forgiven you" (5:20) and to a sinful woman, "Your sins have been forgiven" (7:48). He commanded believers to pray, "Forgive us our sins" (11:4), and while on the cross prayed, "Father, forgive them" (23:34).

The apostles understood the importance of forgiveness and proclaimed it. On the Day of Pentecost Peter said to the crowd, "Repent, and each of you be baptized in the name of Jesus Christ for the forgiveness of your sins" (Acts 2:38). Later he declared to the Sanhedrin, "The God of our fathers raised up Jesus, whom you had put to death by hanging Him on a cross. He is the one whom God exalted to His right hand as a Prince and a Savior, to grant repentance to Israel, and forgiveness of sins" (Acts 5:30). He said to those gathered in Cornelius's house, "Of [Jesus] all the prophets bear witness that through His name everyone who believes in Him receives forgiveness of sins" (Acts 10:43). Paul told those gathered in the synagogue at Pisidian Antioch, "Therefore let it be known to you, brethren, that through [Christ] forgiveness of sins is proclaimed to you" (13:38).

Forgiveness of sins is available only to those who repent. Repentance is the foundational biblical, spiritual act that moves the heart in the direction of salvation. It is turning from sin's presence, power, dominance, and consequences to righteousness. Repentance involves a desire to leave sin behind and pursue righteousness. It is not simply feeling bad about one's circumstances, or condition, or the consequences that resulted from one's sins, but mourning over the reality of sin. Repentance is prompted by the Holy Spirit (John 16:8), who came to convict the world of sin, righteousness, and judgment, and is granted by God (2 Tim. 2:25; cf. Acts 11:18).

The attitude of repentance is seen in the Beatitudes (Matt. 5:1–11). To be repentant is to be spiritually bankrupt, to know that one is poor, to hunger and thirst after righteousness, to mourn over one's wretchedness, and consequently be humbled by that condition. The promise to the believing penitent person is that God will grant forgiveness of sin, because Christ has provided the sacrifice that pays the penalty for sin.

## THE GOSPEL IS CHRISTOLOGICAL AS TO ITS APPROPRIATION

**in His name** (24:47*b*)

Forgiveness of sin is available only through Jesus Christ, since "there is salvation in no one else; for there is no other name under heaven that has been given among men by which we must be saved" (Acts 4:12). **His name** is a metonym for His person (cf. Luke 9:48) and represents all that He is. To proclaim in the name of Jesus that there is forgiveness of sin is to do so consistent with who He is in all His fullness.

The apostles did everything in the name of Christ, which is the only source of God's power. After healing the lame man at the temple (Acts 3:1–8) Peter said to the astonished crowd, "And on the basis of faith in His name, it is the name of Jesus which has strengthened this man whom you see and know; and the faith which comes through Him has given him this perfect health in the presence of you all" (v. 16; cf. 4:10). The early church also baptized in the name of Jesus (Acts 2:38; 8:16; 10:48; 19:5; 22:16), suffered for His name (Acts 5:41; 9:15–16; 21:13), and evangelized in His name (3 John 7). It is no wonder, then, that Christians were known as those who called on the name of Jesus (Acts 9:14, 21).

## THE GOSPEL IS GLOBAL AS TO ITS EXTENT

**to all the nations, beginning from Jerusalem.** (24:47c)

The Old Testament teaches not only that Messiah would suffer and die, rise from the dead, and have repentance proclaimed in His name, but also that the gospel message of forgiveness in His name would be proclaimed to all the nations.

During His earthly ministry, Jesus had sent the apostles not to the Samaritans or Gentiles (Matt. 10:5), but only to "the lost sheep of the house of Israel" (v. 6). The Lord said of His own ministry, "I was sent only to the lost sheep of the house of Israel" (Matt. 15:24). Consequently, the Jerusalem church initially was reluctant to evangelize the Gentiles or Samaritans. But when persecution forced the believers to flee Jerusalem, some went to Samaria (Acts 8:1–2), and "Philip went down to the city of Samaria and began proclaiming Christ to them" (v. 5). Gentile evangelism, however, did not take place until Peter's vision (Acts 10:9–16) caused him to realize that "God is not one to show partiality, but in every nation the man who fears Him and does what is right is welcome to Him" (vv. 34–35). After some initial misgivings (Acts 11:1–3), the Jerusalem church accepted Peter's preaching the gospel to Gentiles, and the Jerusalem council (Acts 15:1–21) formally decided that Gentiles could be saved without first becoming Jewish proselytes and following Jewish ritual. Paul, the apostle to the Gentiles (Rom. 11:13), wrote,

> Christ has become a servant to the circumcision on behalf of the truth of God to confirm the promises given to the fathers, and for the Gentiles to glorify God for His mercy; as it is written, "Therefore I will give praise to You among the Gentiles, and I will sing to Your name." (Rom. 15:8–9)

Because of their ultimate rejection of Him, Israel had been cut off (Rom. 11) and left desolate (Luke 13:35) and facing the destruction that would come in A.D. 70 (Matt. 24:1–2). The time had arrived in God's plan of redemption to bring the gospel to the Gentiles.

Gentile salvation was not a new reality, however. The Old Testament clearly declares that Gentiles would be saved. In Genesis 22:18 God said to Abraham, "In your seed all the nations of the earth shall be blessed." In his prayer at the dedication of the temple Solomon prayed,

> Also concerning the foreigner who is not of Your people Israel, when he comes from a far country for Your name's sake (for they will hear of Your great name and Your mighty hand, and of Your outstretched arm); when he comes and prays toward this house, hear in heaven Your dwelling place, and do according to all for which the foreigner calls to You, in order that all the peoples of the earth may know Your name, to fear You, as do Your people Israel, and that they may know that this house which I have built is called by Your name. (1 Kings 8:41–43)

Isaiah wrote,

> Now it will come about that in the last days the mountain of the house of the Lord will be established as the chief of the mountains, and will be raised above the hills; and all the nations will stream to it. And many peoples will come and say, "Come, let us go up to the mountain of the Lord, to the house of the God of Jacob; that He may teach us concerning His ways and that we may walk in His paths." For the law will go forth from Zion and the word of the Lord from Jerusalem. (2:2–3)

> Turn to Me and be saved, all the ends of the earth; for I am God, and there is no other. (45:22)

> It is too small a thing that You should be My Servant to raise up the tribes of Jacob and to restore the preserved ones of Israel; I will also

> make You a light of the nations so that My salvation may reach to the end of the earth. (49:6)

> Arise, shine; for your light has come, and the glory of the Lord has risen upon you. For behold, darkness will cover the earth and deep darkness the peoples; but the Lord will rise upon you and His glory will appear upon you. Nations will come to your light, and kings to the brightness of your rising. (60:1–3)

Joel added, "And it will come about that whoever calls on the name of the Lord will be delivered; for on Mount Zion and in Jerusalem there will be those who escape, as the Lord has said, even among the survivors whom the Lord calls" (2:32; cf. Rom. 10:13), and Micah wrote,

> And it will come about in the last days that the mountain of the house of the Lord will be established as the chief of the mountains. It will be raised above the hills, and the peoples will stream to it. Many nations will come and say, "Come and let us go up to the mountain of the Lord and to the house of the God of Jacob, that He may teach us about His ways and that we may walk in His paths." For from Zion will go forth the law, even the word of the Lord from Jerusalem. (4:1–2)

The global command to reach the entire world extends the responsibility for evangelism from the apostles and disciples to all believers.

## THE GOSPEL IS PERSONAL AS TO ITS AGENCY

**You are witnesses of these things.** (24:48)

God has chosen to use exclusively human witnesses as His means of proclaiming the gospel in the present age, unlike the "angel flying in midheaven, having an eternal gospel to preach to those who live on the earth, and to every nation and tribe and tongue and people" (Rev. 14:6), who will also proclaim the gospel during the tribulation. Those witnesses were first of all the apostles and the rest of the early church, as the book of Acts indicates (1:8; 2:32; 3:15; 5:32; 10:39; 13:31; 22:15; 26:16), and by extension all believers throughout church history, since the apostles did not travel to the "remotest part of the earth" (Acts 1:8).

### THE GOSPEL IS SUPERNATURAL AS TO ITS POWER

**And behold, I am sending forth the promise of My Father upon you; but you are to stay in the city until you are clothed with power from on high."** (24:49)

Though believers are gospel witnesses, the gospel does not advance by human power, creativity, ingenuity, or zeal. "The weapons of our warfare," Paul wrote, "are not of the flesh, but divinely powerful for the destruction of fortresses" (2 Cor. 10:4). Therefore the Lord told the disciples that He would be **sending forth the promise of** the **Father upon** them. In the meantime, they were **to stay in the city** of Jerusalem **until** they were **clothed with power from on high.** The promise of the Father that would grant them divine power to witness is the coming of the Holy Spirit on the Day of Pentecost. Both the Old Testament (Ezek. 36:27; 37:14; 39:29; Joel 2:28–29) and Jesus (John 14:16–17; 20:22) promised the coming of the Holy Spirit, through whose indwelling Jesus is also with believers (Matt. 28:20). Since all Christians are indwelt by the Spirit (Rom. 8:9), all are empowered for effective witness. The question is, how faithful will they be?

# The Significance of the Ascension (Luke 24:50–53)

**40**

**And He led them out as far as Bethany, and He lifted up His hands and blessed them. While He was blessing them, He parted from them and was carried up into heaven. And they, after worshiping Him, returned to Jerusalem with great joy, and were continually in the temple praising God.** (24:50–53)

Our culture celebrates the birthdays of important people, even though there was nothing significant about their birth itself. No one, when he is born, has yet accomplished anything, nor can anything be determined for certain about what he might accomplish in the future. It is only when lives have been lived that achievements can be fully realized and appreciated.

The only person whose accomplishments were known before He was born was Jesus Christ. It certainly is right to celebrate His birth in honor of all that He would accomplish, although those things were still future when He was born. The massive celebration of Christmas reflects such a perspective. Generating far less interest is another event that should be celebrated, because it marked the completion of His incarnate work on earth. Except in some liturgical churches, it is generally ignored, but it also makes sense to celebrate with effusive joy and praise His ascension. His ascent back to where He came from ended His earthly journey not by going down in death, like everyone else, but by rising up to heaven in full view of His followers. Celebrating that glorious event would focus attention on all that He did accomplish during His earthly life and heaven's affirmation that He had done perfectly everything the Father had sent Him to do.

Luke's gospel began with the story of the Lord Jesus Christ's arrival on earth, and ends with His departure from it. His life began with condescension and ended with ascension; it began with incarnation and ended with exaltation; it began with expectation and ended with consummation; it began with the Son of God being born of a virgin and descending to earth, and ended with the Son of God being born from the dead and ascending to heaven; it began with hope unrealized and ended with hope fully realized; it began with a promise and ended with a fulfillment and a new promise; it began with the praise of Mary, Zacharias, Simeon, Anna, and the angels in anticipation of Messiah's arrival, and ended with the worship and praise of those who witnessed Messiah's departure.

Only Luke was granted the privilege of recording the magnificent and monumental ascension, the culminating event of Christ's earthly ministry. He describes it twice; in the last chapter of his gospel, and in the first chapter of Acts. The ascension is both the culmination of one volume of redemptive history and the inauguration of another. Luke's gospel tells the story of Christ on earth; Acts tells the story of the coming of the Holy Spirit and the eventual fulfillment of the Great Commission through the establishment of the church. Those two overlapping, interlocking histories end and begin with the same event—the ascension, thus affirming its significance.

Luke's account of the Savior's ascent presents the ascension and the reaction, to which will be added the sweeping implications.

## THE ASCENSION

**And He led them out as far as Bethany, and He lifted up His hands and blessed them. While He was blessing them, He parted from them and was carried up into heaven.** (24:50–51)

In the usual understated manner common to the biblical writers, Luke described in simple language an event beyond human comprehension. The account does not provide the details that would satisfy curiosity as to how this staggering, stunning miracle could have taken place.

In the previous chapter of this volume (vv. 44–49), Luke recorded three components of the Lord's interaction with the disciples after His resurrection. First, He gave them instruction on the Old Testament prophecies related to the Messiah's suffering, death, and resurrection, His provision of forgiveness, and the need to declare that good news to all the nations. Second, He commissioned them to proclaim repentance for the forgiveness of sins to all the nations, beginning in Jerusalem. Finally, He instructed them to remain in Jerusalem until they were "clothed with power from on high" (Luke 24:49) through the coming of the Holy Spirit on the Day of Pentecost. Those three features are all that Luke records of the time between the resurrection and the ascension, although he described them in more detail in the book of Acts. The continued history in Acts also provided some new details about those events, including further convincing proofs of Christ's resurrection and His correction of the disciples' mistaken belief that the promised messianic kingdom was about to be inaugurated.

Luke does not say when or where the Lord's interaction with the disciples took place. In Matthew's account the Great Commission was given on a mountain in Galilee (Matt. 28:16), sometime during the forty days between the resurrection and the ascension. Luke may be describing that same event, or another occasion when Jesus gave that same commission in a slightly different form. In either case, all we know is that Luke's account occurred in the weeks between the resurrection and the ascension.

When the time came for Him to leave the disciples, Jesus **led them**

**out as far as** (or,"in the vicinity of") **Bethany. Bethany** is a small village about two miles (John 11:18) east of Jerusalem near the Mount of Olives (Acts 1:12). It was a very familiar place to the Lord, since it was the home of His close friends Mary, Martha, and Lazarus (John 11:1). Jesus spent the first few nights of Passion Week in Bethany (Matt. 21:17; Mark 11:11–12; cf. Luke 22:39; John 12:1). He was also very familiar with the nearby Mount of Olives, where He gave the Olivet Discourse (Matt. 24:3), and where He went with the disciples after the Last Supper (Matt. 26:30). It was there that He agonized in prayer, to the point of sweating great drops of blood (Luke 22:39–46), and was betrayed and arrested (vv. 47–54). When He returns, "His feet will stand on the Mount of Olives, which is in front of Jerusalem on the east; and the Mount of Olives will be split in its middle from east to west by a very large valley, so that half of the mountain will move toward the north and the other half toward the south" (Zech. 14:4).

In His last act before He ascended, Jesus **lifted up His hands** (a common gesture associated with blessing [cf. Lev. 9:22; Ps. 134:2] that pointed toward heaven, from where all blessing descends) **and blessed them.** This was not a mystical or symbolic act, but a pledge to them of the blessings they and all believers would receive. Paul described these as "every spiritual blessing in the heavenly places in Christ" (Eph. 1:3). In the words He spoke, the Lord may have repeated the blessings He promised them on the night before His death, such as heaven, the Holy Spirit, love, mercy, grace, power, and answered prayer (John 14–17). His blessing summarized everything that is pledged to them and to all who believe by the goodness and grace of God.

The disciples were able to appreciate those promised blessings, since their doubts had vanished, and their fears had dissipated. They understood fully who Christ is and why He had to die, because they, for the first time, had an accurate knowledge of the Old Testament. They knew that He was alive from the dead, the Scripture was fulfilled, redemptive history was on schedule, and He would return to establish the kingdom. Their final lessons on those matters had been given in the days after His resurrection. So in forty days, they went from the depths of fear and doubt during Passion Week to the most exhilarating confidence in the truth.

Then, dramatically, **while He was** in the process of **blessing them** with all the blessings that were theirs in Christ, **He parted from them and was carried up into heaven.** Never has so little been said about such a monumental event. Only Enoch (Gen. 5:24) and Elijah (2 Kings 2:11) had been taken to heaven in their physical bodies. Unlike what happened in Emmaus, where Jesus suddenly vanished, here He rose up into heaven in a physical, literal form as they watched. In the account of this scene in Acts 1:10–11, two angels asked the disciples, "Men of Galilee, why do you stand looking [longingly, as if they were losing someone] into the sky? This Jesus, who has been taken up from you into heaven, will come in just the same way as you have watched Him go into heaven"; in other words, in the same physical form. His bodily ascension and return shows that heaven is a place that accommodates humans in their glorified, resurrected bodies. It is also a preview of the bodily resurrection of believers. And although He left, the Lord would still be with them and all believers (Matt. 28:20) through the indwelling Holy Spirit.

The New Testament records that when Christ arrived in heaven, He went to the right hand of God, the highest and most exalted place (Acts 2:33; 5:31; 7:55–56; Rom. 8:34; Eph. 1:20; Col. 3:1; 1 Peter 3:22), signifying that His work was completed (Heb. 1:3; 10:12; 12:2). He was also given the name Lord, the name that is above every name (Phil. 2:9), and exalted "far above all rule and authority and power and dominion, and every name that is named, not only in this age but also in the one to come" (Eph. 1:21).

THE REACTION

**And they, after worshiping Him, returned to Jerusalem with great joy, and were continually in the temple praising God.** (24:52–53)

Now that the disciples understood fully the person and work of Christ, there was no other way they could have reacted, other than by **worshiping Him.** With all their doubts and fears gone, all their questions answered, fully convinced that Jesus was the Messiah, the Son of God, the Savior and Redeemer, the disciples were ready to preach the gospel—even if it cost them their lives.

After Jesus was gone, they **returned to Jerusalem** as He had commanded them (v. 49; Acts 1:4) **with great joy,** which caused them to be **continually in the temple praising God.** Their training was complete, and they were full of praise, ready to preach, and some of them even prepared to write portions of the New Testament.

## THE IMPLICATIONS

The amazing implications of the ascension of the Son of God to heaven can be broken down into the following truths.

First, the ascension marked the completion of the work of salvation. After the cross and the resurrection, there was nothing further to be done to provide any aspect of salvation. Jesus' words from the cross, "It is finished!" (John 19:30), signified that He had accomplished the work the Father had given Him to do.

Second, the ascension marked the end of Jesus' limitations. During His incarnation, He had "emptied Himself, taking the form of a bond-servant, and being made in the likeness of men. Being found in appearance as a man, He humbled Himself by becoming obedient to the point of death, even death on a cross" (Phil. 2:7–8). At the ascension, He returned to the glory He had had with the Father before the world was created (John 17:5). Jesus had left heaven as spirit, but returned as the God-Man, whom He will remain forever.

Third, as noted earlier, the ascension marked Christ's exaltation and coronation.

Fourth, the ascension signaled the sending of the Holy Spirit, who until then "was not yet given, because Jesus was not yet glorified" (John 7:39). "It is to your advantage that I go away," Jesus had told the disciples, "for if I do not go away, the Helper will not come to you; but if I go, I will send Him to you" (John 16:7).

Fifth, the ascension marked the start of Jesus' preparing believers' heavenly home (John 14:1–3).

Sixth, the ascension marked the passing of the work of evangelism to His followers. Christ's work is both finished and unfinished (Acts 1:1). His work of providing redemption is completed, and nothing can be added to it (John 17:4; 19:30; Heb. 9:12). But His work of proclamation is not finished. The rest of the New Testament describes the continuation of that work by the early church, and it will not be completed until He returns.

Seventh, the ascension signaled the Lord's sovereign headship over the church (Eph. 1:20–23; Col. 1:18).

Eighth, the ascension marked Christ's triumph over Satan. As the apostle John wrote, "The Son of God appeared for this purpose, to destroy the works of the devil" (1 John 3:8; cf. Gen. 3:15; Heb. 2:14).

Ninth, the ascension signaled the Lord's giving the work of the ministry to gifted men. When He ascended, Jesus sent the Spirit, who not only gave spiritual gifts to individual believers (1 Cor. 12:4–11), but also gifted men to the church (Eph. 4:11–13).

Tenth, the ascension marked the beginning of the merciful and faithful (Heb. 2:17) and sympathetic (Heb. 4:15) high priest's work of intercession for His people (Heb. 7:25).

Finally, the ascension guarantees and secures Christ's second coming (Acts 1:11).

All Christians should celebrate all that Jesus accomplished for them, which culminated in the ascension. "For you know the grace of our Lord Jesus Christ," wrote Paul, "that though He was rich, yet for your sake He became poor, so that you through His poverty might become rich" (2 Cor. 8:9).

# Bibliography

Bock, Darrell L. *Luke 1:1–9:50.* Baker Exegetical Commentary on the New Testament. Grand Rapids: Baker, 1994.

Bruce, Alexander B. "The Synoptic Gospels," in W. Robertson Nicoll, ed. *The Expositor's Greek Testament.* Vol. 1. Reprint. Peabody, Mass.: Hendrickson, 2002.

Carson, D.A., Douglas J. Moo, and Leon Morris. *An Introduction to the New Testament.* Grand Rapids: Zondervan, 1992.

Ellis, E. Earle. *The Gospel of Luke.* The New Century Bible Commentary. Grand Rapids: Eerdmans, 1974.

Gooding, David. *According to Luke.* Grand Rapids: Eerdmans, 1987.

Guthrie, Donald. *New Testament Introduction.* Revised edition. Downers Grove, Ill.: InterVarsity, 1990.

Hendriksen, William. *Exposition of the Gospel According to Luke.* New Testament Commentary. Grand Rapids: Baker, 1978.

Hiebert, D. Edmond. *An Introduction to the New Testament.* Vol. 1. *The Gospels and Acts.* Chicago: Moody, 1975.

Lenski, R. C. H. *The Interpretation of St. Luke's Gospel.* Minneapolis: Augsburg, 1961.

Liefeld, Walter L., and David W. Pao. "Luke," in Tremper Longman III and David E. Garland, eds. *The Expositor's Bible Commentary.* Vol. 10. Revised edition. Grand Rapids: Zondervan, 2007.

Marshall, I. Howard. *The Gospel of Luke.* The New International Greek Testament Commentary. Grand Rapids: Eerdmans, 1978.

Morris, Leon. *The Gospel According to St. Luke.* The Tyndale New Testament Commentaries. Grand Rapids: Eerdmans, 1975.

Plummer, Alfred. *The Gospel According to St. Luke.* The International Critical Commentary. Edinburgh: T. & T. Clark, 1969.

Stein, Robert H. *Luke.* The New American Commentary. Nashville: Broadman & Holman, 1992.

# Indexes

## Index of Greek and Latin Words and Phrases

*lepta,* 169
*limos,* 205
*loimos,* 205

*makros,* 9
*makrothumeō,* 9
*mēpote,* 255

*naos,* 105

*penichrōs,* 169
*plousios,* 169
*ptōochos,* 169

*sunochē,* 234

*thumos,* 9

## Index of Scripture

| Genesis | | | | | | |
|---|---|---|---|---|---|---|
| 1–2 | 396 | 49:10 | 189,442 | 11:7 | 226 |
| 3 | 49 | **Exodus** | | 11:45 | 12 |
| 3:8–9 | 68 | 3:2–3 | 396 | 16:29–31 | 18 |
| 3:9 | 440 | 3:6 | 147 | 17:11 | 284 |
| 3:15 | 307,425,455 | 3:15–16 | 147 | 18:22–29 | 224 |
| 3:17–19 | 286 | 4:5 | 147 | 21:10 | 325 |
| 3:21 | 383,424 | 10:21–22 | 389 | 24:16 | 155,337,380 |
| 5:24 | 453 | 12 | 425 | 27:13 | 423 |
| 6:3 | 117 | 12:1–13 | 50 | 27:27 | 423 |
| 6:5 | 20 | 12:2–6 | 93 | **Numbers** | |
| 8:20 | 424 | 12:6 | 273 | 5:6–7 | 74 |
| 8:21 | 27 | 12:21–23 | 50 | 9:12 | 274 |
| 9:6 | 316 | 12:23 | 265 | 12:14 | 338 |
| 9:21 | 256 | 12:46 | 282,400 | 15:38–40 | 164 |
| 12:3 | 269 | 14:4 | 398 | 20 | 425 |
| 15:6 | 13 | 16:13–15 | 396 | 22:28–30 | 396 |
| 15:12 | 389 | 19:16 | 389 | | |
| 17:7–8 | 246 | 19:18 | 390 | **Deuteronomy** | |
| 17:18 | 2 | 20:4 | 135 | 1:39 | 28 |
| 18:1–8 | 436 | 20:10 | 403 | 2:30 | 398 |
| 18:2 | 411 | 21:32 | 271 | 4:2 | 250 |
| 19:24–25 | 396 | 22:1 | 74 | 7:25 | 225 |
| 22 | 50 | 22:22 | 5,166 | 10:18 | 166 |
| 22:14 | 50 | 24:8 | 284 | 16:3 | 282 |
| 22:18 | 446 | 32:11–13 | 2 | 16:16 | 265 |
| 24:12 | 2 | 34:6 | 188 | 16:18–20 | 330 |
| 24:12–14 | 17 | 34:6–7 | 263 | 17:6 | 330 |
| 26:24 | 147 | | | 18:18–22 | 422,425 |
| 38:6–10 | 145 | **Leviticus** | | 19:15 | 330,351, |
| 39:2–3 | 398 | 9:22 | 452 | | 411,412 |

| | | | | | | | |
|---|---|---|---|---|---|---|---|
| 22:7–8 | 382 | 149:2 | 363 | 43:11 | 68 |
| 22:14–17 | 51 | | | 44:6–7 | 221 |
| 22:18 | 383 | **Proverbs** | | 44:28–45:5 | 398 |
| 27:4 | 107 | 11:1 | 224 | 45:20–21 | 222 |
| 28:2 | 17 | 12:22 | 224 | 45:22 | 446 |
| 32:1 | 13 | 13:13 | 418 | 45:23 | 157 |
| 33:4 | 418 | 15:8–9 | 224 | 46:5–10 | 222 |
| 33:10 | 397 | 15:25 | 6, 166 | 46:9–10 | 287 |
| 40:7 | 425 | 16:4 | 287 | 49:6 | 446–47 |
| 40:8 | 304 | 16:18 | 322 | 52:13–53:12 | 46–47 |
| 41:4 | 61 | 20:9 | 13 | 53 | 51, 92, 289, |
| 41:9 | 53, 271, | 22:6 | 31 | | 316, 425 |
| | 289, 442 | | | 53:1–11*a* | 96 |
| 49:15 | 142 | **Ecclesiastes** | | 53:3 | 53, 110, 299 |
| 51:1 | 61 | 2:17 | 286 | 53:4 | 382 |
| 51:5 | 27 | 2:22–23 | 286 | 53:5 | 283, 377, 390 |
| 55:12–14 | 271 | 3:11 | 140 | 53:5–12 | 174–75 |
| 58:3 | 27 | 7:20 | 13, 27 | 53:7 | 350 |
| 65:4 | 107 | | | 53:9 | 55 |
| 68:5 | 6 | **Isaiah** | | 53:10 | 269, 288 |
| 69:21 | 52 | 1:1–16 | 381 | 53:11 | 13 |
| 73:24 | 142 | 1:17 | 6 | 53:12 | 298, 384 |
| 80:8–16 | 123 | 2:2–3 | 446 | 55:1–9 | 381 |
| 89:3–4 | 153 | 5:7 | 123 | 55:3 | 127 |
| 89:35–37 | 153 | 6:1 | 260 | 55:6–7 | 239 |
| 103.8 | 8 | 6:3 | 157 | 56:7 | 17, 106 |
| 104:3 | 231 | 7:14 | 189, 442 | 60:1–3 | 447 |
| 106:21 | 68 | 8:9–10 | 398 | 61:1–2 | 336 |
| 110 | 154 | 8:14–15 | 128 | 61:10 | 383 |
| 110:1 | 339 | 9:6–7 | 190 | 62:11 | 94 |
| 113 | 280, 282 | 11:1–2 | 189 | 63:1–4 | 238 |
| 113–118 | 280 | 11:4 | 238 | 63:10 | 117 |
| 114 | 280 | 13:6–13 | 232 | 64:6 | 13, 146 |
| 115–118 | 280 | 13:8 | 234 | 65:16 | 188 |
| 115:3 | 287 | 13:9–10 | 207 | 65:20–23 | 249 |
| 118 | 127 | 19:1 | 231 | | |
| 118:22 | 442 | 24:1–6 | 232–33 | **Jeremiah** | |
| 118:26 | 95 | 24:18–23 | 233 | 2:21 | 123 |
| 119:43 | 418 | 26:19 | 142 | 5:31 | 160 |
| 119:140 | 418 | 33:22 | 363 | 7:6 | 5 |
| 134:2 | 452 | 34:8 | 223 | 7:11 | 108 |
| 139:8 | 142 | 40:1–2 | 381 | 11:7 | 117 |
| 143:2 | 13 | 40:8 | 250 | 11:11 | 117 |
| 143:10 | 304 | 41:21–23 | 221 | 13:23 | 13 |

| | | | |
|---|---|---|---|
| 7:49 | 18,132 | 12:27 | 47 | 18:15 | 325 |
| 7:52 | 125 | 12:31 | 195 | 18:17 | 326 |
| 8:19 | 355 | 12:32 | 342 | 18:19 | 324,334 |
| 8:24 | 151,315 | 12:42–43 | 401 | 18:21 | 336 |
| 8:37 | 120 | 12:44 | 355 | 18:24 | 335 |
| 8:40 | 120 | 12:47 | 174 | 18:26 | 327 |
| 8:44 | 29,132,313 | 13–16 | 310 | 18:28 | 345,399 |
| 8:58 | 156 | 13–17 | 292 | 18:31 | 52 |
| 9:6 | 62 | 13:1 | 292 | 18:34 | 346 |
| 9:8 | 60 | 13:2 | 270,289 | 18:35 | 346 |
| 9:24 | 54 | 13:3–5 | 280 | 18:36 | 315,346 |
| 9:28 | 54 | 13:3–17 | 293 | 18:38 | 347,355 |
| 9:38 | 157 | 13:22 | 234 | 19:1 | 361 |
| 10:9 | 283 | 13:24 | 290 | 19:3 | 361 |
| 10:11 | 51 | 13:27–30 | 290 | 19:4 | 361 |
| 10:17–18 | 91,266, | 13:28–29 | 291 | 19:6 | 361 |
| | 278,391 | 13:30 | 312 | 19:7 | 337,362 |
| 10:25 | 339,396 | 14 | 192 | 19:7–9 | 347 |
| 10:27–29 | 216 | 14–17 | 452 | 19:9 | 336,362 |
| 10:30 | 155 | 14:1–3 | 228,247,454 | 19:10 | 266,342 |
| 10:33 | 380 | 14:3 | 191 | 19:11 | 362 |
| 10:41 | 116 | 14:6 | 151 | 19:12 | 362 |
| 11:1 | 93,452 | 14:9 | 355 | 19:14 | 356,363 |
| 11:14–44 | 64 | 14:12–18 | 298 | 19:15 | 363 |
| 11:16 | 49 | 14:16–17 | 448 | 19:19 | 383 |
| 11:18 | 92 | 14:25 | 407 | 19:23 | 383 |
| 11:25 | 58,90 | 14:26 | 126 | 19:25–27 | 393 |
| 11:25–26 | 147 | 15:1 | 283 | 19:26 | 392 |
| 11:35 | 300 | 15:5 | 283 | 19:28 | 391 |
| 11:41 | 17 | 15:18 | 215 | 19:30 | 391,454 |
| 11:44 | 431 | 15:25 | 81 | 19:31–32 | 380 |
| 11:45 | 120 | 16:7 | 454 | 19:34 | 380,431 |
| 11:47 | 64 | 16:8 | 444 | 19:36 | 282 |
| 11:47–50 | 90,268 | 17:3 | 36 | 19:38–42 | 430 |
| 11:47–53 | 342 | 17:5 | 302,305 | 19:40 | 402 |
| 11:49–50 | 120 | 17:6–26 | 298 | 20:1 | 409 |
| 11:53 | 334 | 17:11 | 216 | 20:1–2 | 412 |
| 12:1 | 93 | 17:17 | 418 | 20:3–8 | 430 |
| 12:6 | 271 | 18:2 | 300,301 | 20:6 | 414 |
| 12:9 | 93 | 18:10 | 315 | 20:11 | 412 |
| 12:12 | 93 | 18:11 | 305 | 20:11–17 | 433 |
| 12:12–13 | 95 | 18:12 | 313 | 20:12 | 413 |
| 12:16 | 95 | 18:12–13 | 333 | 20:14 | 413 |
| 12:24 | 55,304 | 18:13–23 | 105 | 20:14–15 | 421 |

## Apocrypha, Pseudepigrapha, and Early Christian Writings

### Apocrypha

### Pseudepigrapha

### Ancient Texts

### Rabbinic Writings

## Index of Subjects